ALBEN BARKLEY

ALBEN BARKLEY

A LIFE IN POLITICS

JAMES K. LIBBEY

UNIVERSITY PRESS OF KENTUCKY

Scholarly publisher for the Commonwealth,
serving Bellarmine University, Berea College, Centre College of Kentucky, Eastern
Kentucky University, The Filson Historical Society, Georgetown College,
Kentucky Historical Society, Kentucky State University, Morehead State University,
Murray State University, Northern Kentucky University, Transylvania University,
University of Kentucky, University of Louisville, and Western Kentucky University.
All rights reserved.

Editorial and Sales Offices: The University Press of Kentucky
663 South Limestone Street, Lexington, Kentucky 40508-4008
www.kentuckypress.com

In modified form the first four chapters appeared originally as articles in the *Register of the Kentucky Historical Society.* The following are reprinted with permission from the journal editor, David Turpie: "Alben Barkley's Clinton Days," vol. 78, no. 4 (Autumn 1980), pp. 343–61; "Alben W. Barkley: The Farmer's Son," vol. 92, no. 1 (Winter 1994), pp. 24–43; "Alben W. Barkley: The Making of the 'Paducah Politician,'" vol. 96, no. 3 (Summer 1998), pp. 249–68; "Alben Barkley's Rise from Courthouse to Congress," vol. 98, no. 3 (Summer 2000), pp. 261–78.
Unless otherwise noted, photographs are courtesy of the University of Kentucky Special Collections.

Library of Congress Cataloging–in–Publication Data

Names: Libbey, James K.
Title: Alben Barkley : a life in politics / James K. Libbey.
Description: Lexington, Kentucky : The University Press of Kentucky, 2016. |
  Series: Topics in Kentucky history | Includes bibliographical references
  and index.
Identifiers: LCCN 2015044831| ISBN 9780813167138 (hardcover : alk. paper) |
  ISBN 9780813167152 (pdf) | ISBN 9780813167145 (epub)
Subjects: LCSH: Barkley, Alben William, 1877–1956. | Vice-Presidents—United
  States—Biography. | Legislators—United States—Biography. | United
  States. Congress—Biography. | United States—Politics and
  government—1901–1953.
Classification: LCC E748.B318 L49 2016 | DDC 352.23/9092—dc23
LC record available at http://lccn.loc.gov/2015044831

This book is printed on acid-free paper meeting the requirements of the American National Standard for Permanence in Paper for Printed Library Materials.

∞

Manufactured in the United States of America.

Member of the Association of
American University Presses

To Joyce's nieces,
Cindi Stasko,
Jean Lombardo,
and Vera Libbey

Contents

Prologue

There is a reason why Alben W. Barkley, whose public career spanned fifty years from 1906, continues to have a presence in the twenty-first century. Aside from hundreds of national laws still in effect that he helped write and/ or approve, his name adorns a regional airport, a river dam, and a substantial lake. Paducah, the western Kentucky city where his political life began, exhibits a monument and a museum dedicated to his memory. The noted sculptor Walker Hancock cast a twelve-hundred-pound statue of him that resides in a hall of fame at the rotunda of Kentucky's state capitol building in Frankfort. (A copy of the likeness is located in the Margaret I. King Library of the University of Kentucky, the facility that houses tens of thousands of Barkley's personal papers.) Hancock was praised for capturing two enduring features of the man: his sense of humor and his rugged character. The latter attribute attracted the nickname "Iron Man," based on Barkley's strength and stamina on the political campaign trail. He overwhelmed opponents by his constant presence and forceful, witty speeches before the electorate. It is not gruesome but enlightening to introduce Barkley's biography by exploring the circumstances of his death.[1]

Late Monday morning, April 30, 1956, Alben and Jane Barkley drove from their motel to nearby Lexington, Virginia, with Jane at the wheel of their Lincoln. Barkley had to give up driving the car because of his deteriorating eyesight. Nevertheless, the senator had eagerly agreed to be the keynote speaker for a mock political convention conducted by students at Washington and Lee University. The couple arrived at the home of Francis P. Gaines in time to join the university president and his wife for lunch. After a leisurely meal filled with conversation about the afternoon's events, Alben went outside to sit in an open lead car for a parade with all the trappings of student-made floats. After the parade had wended its way through town and returned to the university, President Gaines invited the Barkleys to rest in the school's guesthouse. Alben took a short nap while his wife read a book. He was relaxed and well prepared for his keynote address. It would take about sixteen minutes to deliver—much shorter for the student event than many of his speeches for Congress, campaigns, and conventions. Naturally, he could not read from a typed text. He had outlined mentally the substance of his talk and, with only his wife for an audience, practiced his delivery several times. When Gaines came to the guesthouse to take the couple to the Deremus Gymnasium, Barkley at age seventy-eight appeared and felt fit. He looked forward with enthusiasm to the opportunity to address the basically young audience.[2]

By the time the motorcade had brought Barkley and his wife to the gym, some three thousand students, faculty, staff, and guests were already seated. At one side of the court, a temporary platform had been built. It was too small to hold all the dignitaries, both real and imagined. Special participants sat in front-row seats near the several steps leading up to the lectern. The mock convention began with opening remarks from youthful versions of older politicians. A real governor, Thomas B. Stanley of Virginia, introduced the keynoter. With a smile on his face, Barkley lightly walked up the steps and thoroughly enjoyed a cheering, foot-stomping ovation that he acknowledged with raised arms and hands above his head. It took a while to get his audience to quiet down, but he was able to begin the keynote address a little before five o'clock. After thanking Stanley for his kind introduction, Barkley again drew applause and laughter when he said: "I hope my remarks and my appearance . . . may receive the same approval after I finish that I have had before I start."[3]

He then mentioned that he had attended a law course at the University of Virginia, where he became enamored of its founder, Thomas Jefferson. Since Jefferson's election as president in 1800 the Democratic Party, Barkley stated, has been the "voice of the people." He added, however, that he "really studied democracy at the feet of Woodrow Wilson" when he first entered Congress. Barkley rattled off several laws from the Wilson era that were still extremely important. But, as the son of a farmer, he focused on the enactment of national laws to aid states in constructing roads that helped farmers market their products and enabled them to enjoy the cultural benefits of urban America. After a twelve-year interlude of Republican administrations, which he criticized, the Wilsonian Democrat acknowledged that he had aligned himself with the Franklin D. Roosevelt administration because it sought to help the American people during the Great Depression. "Therefore," Barkley continued, "I say without any equivocation that the Democratic Party has been the forward looking, progressive, constructive party in the history of our nation." Even though he often had friends among GOP opponents, he clearly held a very partisan view.[4]

Near the end of his remarks, Barkley told an anecdote. He acquired a national reputation for inserting some humor in most of his speeches. This particular tale centered on House speaker Thomas B. Reed, who tried but failed to secure the Republican Party presidential nomination against the more popular Ohio governor William McKinley in 1896. Barkley used the story to help explain why he would not be a presidential candidate in 1956. Like Reed in 1896, he knew that "present conditions" were simply not favorable. He concluded:

> But I have no longer any personal interest [in the nomination]. I have served my country and my people for half a century as a Democrat. I went to the House of Representatives in 1913 and served 14 years. I was a junior congressman, then I became a senior congressman, then I went to the Senate and became a junior senator, then I became a senior senator, and then a majority leader of the Senate, and then vice president of the United States, and now I am back again as a junior senator.
>
> And I am willing to be a junior. I'm glad to sit on the back row. For I would rather be a servant in the House of the Lord than to sit in the seats of the mighty.

At this point, Barkley took one step back, collapsed on the floor of the platform, and died almost immediately from a massive heart attack. The Iron Man was not indestructible after all, but he died at the very moment when he was doing what he loved most in life.[5]

1

Child of the Jackson Purchase

Throughout his chosen pursuit of politics, Alben W. Barkley would often reflect on the fact that he had been born in a log house. Sometimes half-jokingly, he would ponder this rustic birthright that had been a stepping stone into the White House for several of America's illustrious presidents. He would later, of course, come to know intimately the nation's first home, but always as a visitor, never as its occupant. His origins in humble surroundings and his aspirations for the highest office in the land, however, provide a convenient and even crucial introduction to that life force that drove him to experience one of the most extraordinary and extended careers ever witnessed in American politics. Three-quarters of a century after his birth in a Graves County log cabin near Wheel, Kentucky, Barkley remarked wryly that this single symbolic circumstance made it "inevitable that [he] should one day enter politics."[1]

Despite this confident statement, appearing more flippant in isolation than in context, there was no earthly reason for anyone to predict that the nearly primitive environment into which Barkley was born on November 24, 1877, would nurture anything more remarkable than the miracle of new life shared by a hundred other infants in Graves County that year. Far from being unique, numerous log cabins and simple homes dotted the undulating landscape of western Kentucky. What would be unusual would be that this son of a tenant farmer would overcome the impediments of poverty to achieve a national political stature equaled by few of his contemporaries.[2]

Poverty, not plenty, was the norm for many nineteenth-century inhabitants eking out a marginal existence in that portion of Kentucky sometimes referred to as the Jackson Purchase. In 1818, General Andrew Jackson had bought the land between the Tennessee and Mississippi Rivers from the Chickasaw Indians in a treaty signed under a sprawling oak on the banks of the Tombigbee River in Mississippi. For the princely sum of $20,000 per annum for fifteen years, the Chickasaw king Chinnuby and his nine chiefs surrendered all title to the land that would become not only eight Kentucky counties, including Graves, but also western Tennessee. The homogeneity of climate, soils, topographic characteristics such as good bottomland, and, later, inhabitants in the purchase area made that section a singular part of Kentucky and bolstered one historian's thesis that the commonwealth is indeed a land of contrast.[3]

What made the Jackson Purchase so peculiar were its ties to the state of Tennessee and the lower reaches of the Mississippi River. While the rest of Kentucky developed a schizoid relationship with North and South, western Kentucky, for good or ill, suffered no such crisis of identity. During the Civil War this western section acquired the reputation of being Kentucky's South Carolina, and one of its river towns, Paducah, became known as Kentucky's Charleston. In fact, Mayfield, the seat of government for Graves County, was the scene of a convention that strongly recommended the purchase's secession. Left to the wiles of its people and to different circumstances, that section of Kentucky and Tennessee might have formed a separate state. This geographic-cultural link in the history of the purchase area had a direct, twofold effect on the life of Alben Barkley.[4]

First, the Democratic Party, which gave succor to the South's peculiar and sometimes abhorrent way of life, dominated western Kentucky. Banished were the old Whigs. The later Republican Party found the area so inhospitable that for decades after the Civil War district Democrats secured majorities for most local, state, and national elections. The press, too, revealed this party allegiance by the inclusion of *Democrat* in the masthead of several town and county newspapers. Second, the prevalent unity of the section meant that after the initial influx of pioneers most migration occurred within the purchase and to such an extent as to blur the population and make a mockery of the border between the states of Kentucky and Tennessee. Thus it was that Alben's father, John Wilson Barkley, had been born across the line in Henry County, Tennessee, in 1854.[5]

John's father, Alben Graham Barkley, had been a native of North Carolina before the family migrated farther inland. The elder Barkley eventually moved his family into Tennessee and then, in 1866, to Wheel, Kentucky, and the two-story log house where his grandson and namesake would be born. Wheel was less a town than a community of small farmers not far from the village of Lowes. Like most of their neighbors in that northwest section of Graves County, Alben Graham and his wife, Amanda Louise Barkley, raised a large family on a small farm by growing dark tobacco.[6]

The staple had its advantages; otherwise it would be difficult to explain why so many employed themselves at such an arduous task. In fact, Graves County came close to producing more tobacco in 1880 than any other county in the state. The reason for all this activity lay, in part, with the soils of the area, which were suited to little else but tobacco cultivation. In good years a relatively small plot of tobacco could bring in sufficient cash to permit a farmer to pay part of his mortgage, buy some of the essentials he could not produce himself, and still have a little left over for taxes and the local preacher. However, like all crops—and perhaps even more than most—tobacco is subject to the whims of nature. In addition, the value of the cash crop depended on the vagaries of supply and demand in an international market and on the ever-present middlemen involved in warehousing, transporting, processing, and distributing this ancient, mildly narcotic weed in its final form. Dark tobacco, moreover, the sugary leaf used for chewing instead of smoking, was particularly and quite literally susceptible to the changing tastes and habits of tobacco users in America and Europe.[7]

Indeed, tastes changed, and the weather proved incorrigibly indifferent to the needs of plants and men. Regardless of these events, the Barkley family remained deeply rooted in and firmly fixed to the traditions of farmwork and tobacco cultivation. While the difficult life did not breed surrender to personal uselessness and pessimism, neither did it allow Alben and Amanda to invest their six children with a secure future. As the children reached adulthood and married, they each had to fend for themselves. The luxury exhibited by wealthier families in providing an inheritance of land and tools for the next generation was simply not possible for the Barkleys to duplicate. When John, for example, married Electa Eliza Smith at the age of twenty-two, he worked a tenant farm a scant quarter mile away from his parents' home.[8]

Electa, though not a beauty, had other attractions that made her an ideal tenant farmer's wife. Her thin lips and petite and angular features contrasted sharply with her husband's proclivity to roundness and with his oversized appearance, including the characteristically large Barkley ears, nose, and mouth. The latter he usually hid underneath an ill-kept, bushy beard. When John was forty, his incautious use of a taper to light a fireplace destroyed most of his facial hair. He did manage to salvage a mustache, and, in his maturity and dressed in his finest, he could exude an aura of near distinction. Electa, on the other hand, resembled nothing so much as a coiled spring—tight, strong, and resilient, stubbornly resuming her original form after a hard blow from the vicissitudes of life. She was only seventeen when she married, yet, as did other girls raised in the eddies of civilization, she achieved maturity at an early age. Born in Bowling Green, Kentucky, shortly before the Civil War, she lost her father, James Henry Smith, to the Confederate cause; he died a soldier's death as a captain with Morgan's Raiders. Her mother continued this pattern of fierce dedication to one's beliefs by raising Electa in a strict setting, teaching her through experience to be independent. This stamina and strong will, acquired early in life, served Electa well in the years to come when she and John raised eight children under impoverished circumstances.[9]

Even though they often found the skimpy fruits of their labor spotted to the core, the light of John and Electa's lives emanated from their children and especially from the first, Alben. This is hardly an idle statement based on hindsight. Contemporary and reflective observers alike note that, if John and Electa had any faults at all, they cherished their first child excessively. Later in his life, John would quote the Bible to those who noticed his doting behavior toward his son: "'Thou (shall) give honor and love to your first born child, for with that child the Lord blesseth thee.'"[10]

From Alben's birth they immersed the child in the sanctity of family designations by christening him not only with the name of John's father but also, for good measure, with the first name "Willie" to honor uncles on both sides of the family. But Willie Alben was called Alben, or "Ah-ben" as his father would say, particularly after Grandfather Alben passed away in 1880. "I kept the 'Willie' business as quiet as possible," Alben later confided, "and as soon as I was old enough to assert myself, I firmly let it be known that my official name henceforth was Alben William Barkley and no foolishness!" No record exists of the reaction of Alben's uncles to this change of name.[11]

What is amply recorded is the nearly primitive environment and subsistence existence surrounding the child's early years. And that was not all to surround him. Without benefit of modern impediments to nature's course, the life shared by John and Electa produced like clockwork a succession of siblings for Alben to play with: brothers Clarence, John, Harry, and George as well as sisters Ima, Bernice, and Ada. While children and their labor can be a blessing for a farm owner, the biennial appearance of a new mouth to feed spelled financial disaster for the tenant farmer. Almost frenetically, the Barkleys moved from one rented farm to another, at least five times between

1877 and 1886, in John's efforts to provide for his family. Whenever he could, he employed his spare time in labor he sold to wealthier neighbors for a dollar a day. Small wonder that he associated himself with others in the same plight to form the Wheelers—western Kentucky Democrats who sought to defend their interests in a movement anticipating the rural revolt known as the Populist crusade. John Barkley's commitment to agrarian democracy eventually extended to working as precinct captain for a candidate trying to win the clerk's office in Graves County.[12]

Electa bolstered her husband in his convictions and possessed no fear of speaking out. "She was an outstanding woman," recalled an acquaintance in 1951. "In her day women rarely took part in public affairs; but she was civic-minded and she'd have her say when things didn't go right." Although inhibited by legal restrictions and societal traditions from participating fully in John's political activities, Electa contributed vitally to family life in other ways. She converted their rented farms into warm, livable homes and transformed raw materials into usable household goods. While John worked their acres or those of their neighbors, she cooked meals, washed dishes, made soap, carded wool, spun yarn, knitted socks, dyed material, sewed clothes, and ironed the handmade garments she had washed over the black cookstove. By making or mending every conceivable domestic item, she preserved scarce money for the family's use. And all this work was interrupted only by the birth of each child with all the attendant burdens such "blessings" bring.[13]

As Electa hustled and bustled about in her first years of marriage, she had the occasional assistance of John's mother. Amanda had been midwife at Alben's birth, a service she gladly rendered in keeping with her reputation as the best midwife for miles around. In the case of Alben, however, she may have been midwife to more than just his birth. Whenever she spent time with him, she repeated to the growing youth the stories of her own childhood. She had shared a common ancestor with Adlai Stevenson and James McKenzie and played with cousins Adlai and Jim as a young girl. While she grew up to marry a farmer, Stevenson and McKenzie entered politics. The former would become Grover Cleveland's vice president and the scion of the Stevenson political dynasty, and the latter would represent Kentucky in Congress and later serve as the US ambassador to Peru. Between his father's community activities and his grandmother's stories, young Alben had his blood infused with political plasma at an early age.[14]

While Amanda may have sown the seed of politics in Alben's blood, the lad's sinews and muscles, stamina and responsibility came from rugged farm life. Once Alben could walk, Electa enlisted him to help with household chores and, slightly later, to care for his brothers and sisters. The child apparently came close to reaching the ideal of an obedient youth. "He never gave me a word of sass," Electa fondly told a *Louisville Courier-Journal* reporter in 1937. Thirteen years later Bernice, the youngest of the Barkley children, informed the author Bela Kornitzer: "I've been trying to recall, but I don't remember that papa ever scolded Alben for anything." However, in his memoirs, *That Reminds Me,* Barkley himself subverts this image of perfection, readily admitting his daily reluctance to perform one distasteful boyhood chore—maintaining the fireplace.[15]

Although the modern child learns to ride a bicycle or operate and play with a dizzying array of electronic gadgets and breakable toys, Alben gained an intimate knowledge of sturdy farm implements. "As soon as I was old enough to throw an axe over my shoulder or pull an end of a crosscut saw," he remembered "[my father] took me to the woods with him." Any winter that ten more acres of trees and brush were not cleared for spring planting John considered a total loss. Nothing went to waste. Brush could be burned, and logs could be hewed into planks for building material, chopped into wood for the fireplace, or split into rails for fences. And the warmer months, too, were filled to the brim with plowing, planting, and raising tobacco—sticky, sweaty work. When John and Alben finished their chores in the tobacco patch, they moved on to fields of corn, wheat, and fruit, the bounty of which the family consumed or sold on a small scale for additional spending money.[16]

All this work at an early age helped build a physical constitution that gave Alben enough durability to enjoy a long life in robust health. "He was always a husky fellow," Milton Jewell, Alben's childhood playmate, commented decades later, "and strong like his father." Indeed, Alben inherited from both parents in equal portions the family tendency for longevity and excellent health. John would not find it necessary to see a doctor until he reached the midpoint of his septuagenarian years, and, until shortly before her death at age eighty-nine, Electa puttered about in her own garden. Whatever fortuitous genetic code was responsible for Alben's endurance, it combined with ample doses of manual labor to produce an additional characteristic that he carried to the day he died: a voracious and insatiable appetite. "We'd have three pieces of meat in the morning at breakfast," Clarence used to say, "one for mom, one for pop, and one for Big Alben."[17]

Years later, after "Big Alben" set foot on the path of politics, he would never have to insult his hosts by turning down the assortment of foods presented to him at rallies, picnics, and dinners. But those years of travel, food, and entertainments associated with political office were still far off in the future. In the 1880s, the activities and experiences available to Alben and his family proved limited indeed. Only an occasional fair, a shopping trip, or a Sunday church gathering seriously disturbed the humdrum daily pattern of life. And young Alben's horizons remained quite confined except for accompanying his father on annual marketing trips to Mayfield or Paducah. Considering their neighbors' similar social conditions, Alben probably did not realize the near destitution of his family until a trip to Mayfield included a stop at one of the town's stores. "I observed with awe," Alben reflected later, "how clean the clerks looked—they dressed better on weekdays than we did on Sundays." In fact, at one point in his early life his ambition was to become a dry goods clerk in Paducah.[18]

Despite the poverty of money and experience endured by Alben and his family, their home life glowed with the warmth of harmony and mirth. "They were always a happy family, good natured and poking fun at each other, and always laughing," claimed a close friend. "Old John was the laughin'est man you ever saw." Alben could not help but acquire the infectious optimism, openness, and kindheartedness displayed by his father. John extended his sense of humor and generosity literally to all those about him, not just to his family. The Barkleys, for example, never locked their smokehouse door, and, if neighbors wanted to borrow tools, utensils, or food, they always received a welcome greeting. Part of this friendly spirit emanated naturally from the sense of cooperation engendered by the rustic, pioneer-like conditions of their lives. At least twice in their first years together the Barkleys, too, had had to draw deep from the wellspring of neighbors' good graces when their home was destroyed or damaged, first by fire, when Alben was nine, and then by tornado, when he was twelve. Spontaneously, friends gathered clothes and furniture and lent their labor to help the beleaguered family rebuild their home.[19]

Certainly, this general lesson in reciprocity, so fundamental to the covenant of humanity in rural America and so basic to human relations, was driven home to the eldest Barkley child. Just as importantly, young Alben observed his father's specific reactions to adverse events. John's childhood chum and lifelong friend Tom Biggs reminisced at age ninety-eight that John "hadn't a nasty bone in his body," but he did possess a quiet resolve and a strong willpower. Even though the family grew bigger and underwent the catastrophic rebuilding of two homes, John never abandoned his dream to have his own farm. In the summer of 1886, Electa and John scraped together enough money to hire a man, Boyd Watson, at fifty cents a day plus meals. Along with Alben, the older Barkleys and the hired hand worked feverishly in the tobacco field to raise and harvest a bumper crop. Their labor paid off. With over $600, they now had enough for a down payment on a fifty-two-acre farm near Lowes.[20]

The shift in residence closer to Lowes enabled John, already an elder in the local Presbyterian church, to assume the duties of Sunday school superintendent as well as sexton. He performed the latter task without compensation. Religion sustained the Job-like life of this farmer and his family. They reserved Sundays exclusively for the worship of God and things religious. Early in the morning Electa, with the help of Alben, would ready the children and fix a basket of food for their trip to church. John's prized possession, a two-horse wagon, carried the family to town. On their arrival, John would sweep the church and dust the pews, and in winter Alben helped his father kindle the fires. Sunday school preceded a lengthy service of hymns and sermons. During the service, Electa kept her restless youngsters complacent by occasionally dispensing morsels of food from the basket. The father would, as Mrs. Milton Jewell called to mind long after, "always sit there with Alben's hands in his": "John was a loud Amen-sayer. . . . He taught the children to do the same. You always knew when the Barkleys were in church. They'd shout and rejoice like anything."[21]

Not only did the Barkleys respond emotionally to the prayers, but John also especially enjoyed the hymns. He loved to sing, and at various times he participated in the choir or even directed its performance. He imparted this predilection for song to Alben, who in his later years as a politician never seemed embarrassed to break out in song whether or not an audience wanted to hear his warbling baritone voice. Music, then, was the only frivolity allowed in the Barkley home after church. At age seven or eight Alben learned to play the harmonica and later the guitar. He accompanied his father, who led the family in singing their favorite hymns, "Bringing in the Sheaves" and "Nearer My God to Thee." John banished all other forms of work or play on the Sabbath. While this meant that Alben was spared from chopping wood, he also missed his mother's cooking as she refused to light the cookstove on Sundays unless the minister joined them for supper.[22]

The strict observance of the Sabbath illustrated not a one-day aberration but a rigid pattern of life that extended throughout the week. Liquor and profanity never entered the home or passed the lips, and here John set the example. His only "vice" was an infrequent "chaw" of tobacco, and the strongest terms he used were "confound it" or "CONFOUND IT" when he wanted to emphasize a particularly exasperating moment. As with strong spirits and cross words, games of chance such as cards and dice never passed the threshold either. And, without radio, television, computers, and the other electronic gadgets that often promiscuously fill the modern mind, conversation absorbed the Barkleys' evening hours, and Alben became an apt student of the art. Even when the youth was only five or six, John boasted to his son's Sunday school teacher: "My Ah-ben's been blessed with a silver tongue. You listen to the sermon's he'll preach."[23]

The hope articulated by John that his son would enter the ministry helped explain his parents' insistence that he gain an education. To modern parents it must seem strange that education would have required any conscious thought at all, let alone conscious support. Yet public schools were not the norm in commonwealth communities until the latter half of the nineteenth century. Labeled by contemporaries, and sometimes contemptuously, as *common education,* public schools were not like today's schools, rigidly graded and elaborately built institutions for captive audiences. In fact, the casual observer would not be able to distinguish Breckenridge's School House, the two-story brick building that Alben attended, from the other houses located in and around Lowes. The young student's father had rented one of his farms from the well-to-do Breckenridge family that provided the building for the advancement of education.[24]

In addition, schools during Alben's youth were neither totally free nor absolutely mandatory. Even by 1900 only half of Kentucky's school-aged population regularly attended school. Farmers around Graves County would often find that the priorities of the homestead exceeded those of the school and would take their children out of class to put them to work. Also, public expenditures on education at the time totaled less than five dollars per pupil. For the school systems to stretch this miserly amount, parents had to purchase textbooks and supplies for their own youngsters. This proved a serious impediment to the access of all children to "free" education. Alben's school attendance, as a matter of fact, marked a genuine sacrifice on the part of John and Electa to secure precious funds for his books. Finally, the concept of yearly units or grades had limited meaning when it came to schoolrooms filled with children of all ages and backgrounds. School terms, rather than grades, fell snugly into abbreviated five-month sessions between fall harvest and spring planting seasons. Thus, it is quite impossible to compare Alben's first years of school with any modern concept of primary or secondary education.[25]

Even though one cannot specify with any certainty the quality and amount of education Alben acquired, he gratified munificently those special ambitions his parents imbued in him, and he rewarded their sacrifice generously with his success. "[His teacher, Miss Hunt,] came home with Ah-ben about the middle of the first term," stated John Barkley in a 1926 interview, "and told us never let up on Ah-ben's education, for there was something in him and we ought to do everything possible to help bring it out." Such personal attention and vocal praise were repeated in later school terms by two of Alben's other teachers, Elizabeth Lowe and Gertrude Backus. "Both of them," Alben claimed, "were kind enough to encourage me in my ambitions and even to predict, somewhat generously, that I might someday become President of the United States." Admittedly, the ravages of time may have prompted Barkley to engage in a bit of self-flagellation or admit a cruel reversal of a self-fulfilling prophesy: he made the comment reported above just a year after his one and only serious attempt to secure his party's nomination for the office of president, an effort that obviously ended in failure. Nevertheless, his speaking and writing abilities as an adult affirm his progress at school better than legions of specious quotations.[26]

Besides the formal and informal education that Alben received in values and experiences from home, church, and school, a fourth institution helped shape the preadolescent young man—Kentucky's ubiquitous country store. The village of Lowes actually enjoyed, not one, but two such establishments. John Lowe, a descendant of the town's founder, owned one; Rodam Peck owned the other. The Barkleys carried their trade with the former, not because Peck weighted his scales or short-armed his fabrics, but because Lowe strongly supported the dominant Democratic Party. In fact, any simpleminded visitor during the administration of President Grover Cleveland could have fathomed which store belonged to the active Democrat because there the town's post office would also be located. At intervals, however, history has a way of inundating politicians, of sweeping them down and under, of making matchwood of their plans and positions. The year 1888 proved to be such a time for the incumbent Cleveland, who lost the White House to the Republican Benjamin Harrison of Indiana. Alben then discovered one of the baser principles of politics when, shortly after Harrison assumed office, Lowe lost his supervision of the post office to the GOP activist Peck.[27]

Whether Lowe or Peck, the store owner did not so much hustle orders and hawk wares as he forgathered his customers in a place that functioned as the town's nerve center. Products passed across the counter in exchange for credit or cash as a matter of course. The soul and appeal of the country store, however, lay in the practice of women and especially men lingering there by the potbellied stove to tell tall tales, exchange local news, trade Barlow knives, or swap funny stories that used as a standard comedy device the discomfiture of the high and mighty. The aroma of candies and spices mixed uneasily with odors of tobacco and kerosene, providing a pungent greeting for young Alben whenever he stopped by the store. The lad never missed a chance to enter this microcosmic world and listen to the town's heart as expressed in the words and actions of those who paused there. The friends and neighbors he met at the store helped temper and forge a genuine talent he displayed for liking, talking to, and listening to people. Like many artists or writers, he unveiled his talents at an early age, though his particular prodigy involved being gregarious rather than being a virtuoso with the brush or the pen. John Lowe, furthermore, took pity on the impoverished youth and gave him an additional reason to visit the store more often. He would get first crack at cleaning up a barrel of sugar after Lowe had emptied and packaged most of its contents. Occasionally, too, Alben would be a paying customer for he sometimes worked for two bits a day at the livery stable. Like most boys, he would usually spend his funds on sweet, frivolous foods. Around the age of twelve, however, one of his more remarkable purchases was a bar of sweet-smelling soap.[28]

Alben's investment and his attention to personal hygiene and appearance did not, however, disclose an effeminate bent or a sissy attitude. Quite the contrary, in the rough and rugged rural world his husky physique and aptitude for "wrestling" were tested by his schoolmates on plenty of occasions. He did, however, also earn a reputation for gallantry. "We all remarked on that," George Goodman, a contemporary, stated. "The girls liked him. And he had an eye for feminine beauty." This early attraction Alben had for members of the opposite sex prompted him at times to use the scented, store-bought soap rather than his mother's thoroughly antiseptic but unexciting soap made of lye and hog fat. Indeed, adolescent stirrings and the feminine charms of Sadie Ward, the pastor's daughter, compelled Barkley to undertake the first major speech of his young life.[29]

Each year the Presbyterian church sponsored a Children's Day when youngsters conducted Sunday worship through recitations from the Bible and brief orations on religious themes. Fate conspired to propel Alben to the pulpit for his first and weakest attempt at making a speech. As the son of an elder who also waxed enthusiastic over all church activities, the young man had his father's expectations to fulfill. As a love-struck youth with a crush on the pastor's daughter, moreover, he readily jumped at the chance to perform for the object of his infatuation. He practiced and practiced his short speech until he had the confidence to laugh at his mischievous neighbor Joe Dunn, who told Alben the day before the event: "Boy, I'll bet you're going to forget your speech tomorrow." The next day, not the slightest smile crossed the nervous lad's face as his turn came to go to the front of the church. When he looked out over the congregation, Alben's glance fell on the twinkling eyes of Joe Dunn, whose captivating grin split his face from ear to ear. Alben stuttered and stammered and forgot then and thereafter every line of his speech. He beat a hasty retreat, leading to his father's temporary embarrassment and Alben's permanent estrangement from Miss Ward.[30]

If one is to believe the faint, amorphous recollections that constitute the sum of available knowledge about young Alben, this speech would be the only setback the youth suffered in his first thirteen years as a child of the Jackson Purchase. Such a conclusion, however, would ignore his birth in the bleakest of circumstances imaginable and his nurture in an impecunious household whose members bordered daily on achieving the unfortunate distinction of being called *indigent*. The fact of his hard life, not his ignoble first speech, should have and would have been his true setback had it not been for his father's singular optimism and hopeful devotion to the future of his first-born. No doubt, modern psychologists might view with apprehension the peculiarly doting behavior of this father for his son. Yet history is rife with examples of parents who scrimped and sacrificed for the sole purpose of elevating that special offspring rather than themselves. Ironically, it would be in John Wilson Barkley's failures as a farmer that the seeds of Alben's success would be planted.

2

Clinton and College

Through the apartment windows over stores facing the courthouse, a dozen or more pairs of eyes squinted into the driving rainstorm trying to pick out the cause for all the evening's commotions. As the initial cloudburst moved east, leaving a steady cold drizzle in its wake, the sheltered witnesses made out the outlines of three open wagons plus a number of bedraggled figures of all shapes, sizes, and ages. Piercing the darkness and the rain came the sounds of a distraught cow that lumbered heavily through puddles and mud as it wended its way in helter-skelter fashion around the courthouse square. Immediately behind the half-crazed beast ran a strapping youth of fourteen. He made quite a sight with his stringy hair matted down by rain, his sturdy frame splashing through the street, and his mouth open with shouts of frustration that only encouraged the cantankerous cow to greater exertions.[1]

For what seemed like an eternity, Alben W. Barkley had chased the cow around the center of Hickman County's seat of government, Clinton, Kentucky. As if by tacit agreement between boy and beast, the cow finally came to an abrupt, half-exhausted halt behind the third wagon. Within the bed of the horse-drawn relic lay a newborn calf that had been the invisible tie holding the cow near the back of the wagon for the twenty-five-mile trip south and west from Lowes to Clinton. The cloudburst temporarily disoriented the cow and provided the cause for the ruckus that provided the night's entertainment for the citizens in the central part of town. If nothing else, the cow's frightened and disorganized behavior stood as a symbol for the Barkley clan on this date of December 28, 1891.[2]

The Barkleys had fought and lost their battle against nature's elements and a farmers' market glutted by international competition and weakened by declining prices that anticipated the disastrous economic depression of 1893. By the fall of 1891, John Barkley, exasperated and frightened, finally decided to relinquish his farm, pay his debts, and move his family to Clinton. He and his wife had relatives in Hickman County and through these contacts had learned of the availability of tenant farms for raising wheat. One can only speculate on the trauma involved for the family in tearing up its roots from the soil of Lowes and tobacco cultivation and traveling to a different area, farm, and crop in order to earn a living. The normal joys and hopes of Christmas were compromised in the Barkley household by the necessity of packing their life's belongings in three wagons—two neighbors volunteered their vehicles and services—and preparing to leave on a two-day journey toward an uncertain future in vehicles open to December's inclement weather.[3]

The pathetic caravan's progress climaxed in the dreary rainstorm and embarrassing incident with the Jersey cow. One of the saving graces of the entire venture was that the Barkleys had been to Clinton before. In fact, the first clear recollection Alben possessed concerned an earlier trip to the town in 1883 when by chance he and his parents happened to view the ground-breaking ceremonies for the principal building that would later house Marvin College. Foggy memories and unwitting biographers later claimed that John Barkley uprooted his family for the sole purpose of enrolling his first-born in that school. Such a conclusion ignores the elder Barkley's apparent loyalty to the Presbyterian Church. Accepting the argument for the moment, John would have been more attracted to the Presbyterian-sponsored college in nearby Mayfield than the Methodist-connected Marvin in faraway Clinton. In addition, some earlier writers transposed the future into the past and assumed erroneously that, because Alben did indeed graduate from Marvin in 1897, he and his parents must have arrived in Hickman County in 1893. However, it is safe to conclude that, at the end of December 1891, simple survival, not higher education, formed the backdrop to John Barkley's actions.[4]

John rented from Bob and Burnett Johnson a fifty-acre farm just west of Clinton, beyond the hill from the cemetery for blacks that separated the farm from the Illinois Central Railroad line. The Barkleys' home, simple and crude, as fit for horses as humans, accentuated the family's abasement. Later, Bob Johnson told a reporter: "We rented [John Barkley] the place, and about all I remember of the first year was the extreme poverty of his family." Obviously, John salvaged little more than enough cash from the farm he sold in Lowes to pay his debts. But one other substance, perhaps more valuable than money, was kept by the Barkleys—hope.[5]

With the few remaining dollars, father and mother enrolled Alben in the small seminary school operated by James H. Shelton on Jackson Street, a half block west of the courthouse. From January to May, Alben hiked his way each day during the week to and from school. When weather permitted, he saved wear and tear on his shoes by carrying them over his shoulder and waiting to put them back on when he entered the school and the room of his teacher. Though no grade reports remain to tell of his performance, the fact that the school's principal shortly entered a more lucrative career in law may have been one of the more important lessons he learned from this experience. It impressed him sufficiently to remember Shelton in an article he wrote for the *Hickman County Gazette* sixty-one years later.[6]

Shelton would join four other lawyers interpreting the law for Clinton's seventeen hundred residents in the 1890s. The town must have appeared to be a veritable metropolis in Alben's eyes after his years in Lowes. Snuggled about the courthouse were dry goods, grocery, and furniture stores as well as a bank and a newspaper, the *Clinton Democrat,* published by E. B. Walker. It would be Walker who converted the paper to the *Hickman County Gazette* and current masthead. The town also boasted specialty shops for books, jewelry, baked goods, barbering, and tailoring. Although a decade would pass before electricity arrived, five years for running water, and four years for telephones, the shopkeepers had built elevated wooden sidewalks for the convenience of their customers, and the town had graveled the principal streets: Washington, running north and south, and Clay, crossing east and west on the north side of the central square. Four churches, including a Presbyterian one that the Barkleys attended, gave spiritual sustenance to the community whose sober citizens did not allow saloons or taverns or the sale of inebriating beverages. Yet the tendency toward conservative parochialism and self-sufficient smugness was balanced by the nearness of the Mississippi River, the presence of the railroad, and the existence of two small colleges, Marvin and the Baptist-affiliated Clinton College.[7]

These cultural and cosmopolitan elements would eventually help Alben understand and enter a larger world than the rural village he had known at Lowes. But, for his father, the relatively larger town of Clinton offered a different type of opportunity. As Alben returned from school and crossed the railroad tracks, he could look north to the white-frame city depot and to the less attractive, four-story Beshears and Jackson Wheat Mill, and, in between, he could watch the figure of his father, who worked for the Illinois Central in the railroad yard. Part-time employment became the norm for the head of the Barkley household. Even after John and Alben had harvested their first wheat crop, the scramble for jobs beyond the farm's boundaries continued unabated. And the search went on as well for that farm that would yield the bumper crop. Within the span of seven years, this quest led the family to pick up its belongings and traipse to Pete Jackson's farm south of Clinton, then to Joe Jackson's to the east. Finally, in 1896, the Barkleys settled just north of town and rented the Galbraith place from their original landlords, the Johnson brothers.[8]

These meanderings of the Barkley family paint a somber picture of failure. While John was apparently quite expert at growing tobacco, he never mastered completely the proper technique for raising wheat. In addition, when he did harvest an above-average crop, his minor triumph turned to gall and wormwood when he had to sell his wheat for a declining price in a depressed market. Finally, the methods employed on the Barkley farm harked back to such a primitive age that a resurrected visitor from ancient Egypt could have felt at home walking along the cultivated field with Alben and John as they scattered seeds of wheat from a bag over their shoulders in a rhythmic pattern as old as man's knowledge of agriculture. At harvesttime, Alben followed his father, who cut the wheat with a scythe, and tied the straws into bundles. Only the use of a mechanical thresher to separate grain from chaff distinguished the Barkleys from their preindustrial ancestors. Expensive pieces of machinery, the principal threshers around Clinton were owned by Polk Jackson, George Burton, and the Hilliard brothers, Calvin and Ernest.[9]

At one time or another, Alben and his father worked for all these men. The Barkleys joined threshing crews that traveled with the machine from farm to farm translating straw and husk into salable grain. Alben earned his dollar a day by performing, in the summer of 1892 and later, every task connected with the harvest process: pitching the wheat onto wagons, driving the teams of horses to the thresher, tying the sacks of grain, and riding a mule hitched to a pole that dragged and spread the displaced straw over the fields to replenish the soil. In an era when several miles meant an hour's journey, the threshing crew could not afford the time it took to return home. Thus, in the evening the men took out their blankets and gathered around the indispensable cook wagon. It was during these evenings out in the fields that young Alben gained among his neighbors (and employers) a countywide reputation for his voracious appetite. "He could eat," Ernest Hilliard related, "more Irish potatoes than any man I ever saw, and he used to amaze us all when he got to the cook-wagon."[10]

After supper the men, ranging from the adolescent to the wizened, relaxed around the fire to share a "chaw" or smoke of tobacco, reminisce about their lives, and amuse themselves with humorous tales. As was normal for a lad his age in rural Kentucky, Alben picked up the habit of smoking a corncob pipe and also the custom of telling stories. These rustic evening soirees out in the wheat fields provided him with enough material to store, savor, and use for a lifetime. Bathed in religion and New Testament parables, he became a specialist not simply in quips and one-liners but also in funny sketches and vignettes that illustrated a moral or gave an example of the human condition. As he repeated and mastered these stories, he would later be able to recall or embellish them on command and insert them expertly within extemporaneous remarks. He achieved the artistry of a word painter whose stories add the precise dash of color or shade to set off the subject and make the point.[11]

Since the men toiled from dawn to dusk with few breaks in between, they did not spin their yarns for very long into the evening hours before retiring. Generally, Alben and the others slept on the straw around the thresher, though occasionally a sudden storm drove them under wagons or into the farmer's barn. Thus, Alben spent a week or more at a time away from home, but he did come to know virtually every farm and farmer in Hickman County—a formidable asset on which he could draw twenty years later when he first ran for Congress. Not only did he win at least a nodding acquaintance with most of Hickman's rural residents; he gained more than a passing knowledge of the county's dirt roads. In fact, he helped maintain them.[12]

The ancient English custom of shire responsibility for highway construction had been passed through prerevolutionary Virginia to the state's Kentucky stepchild. Once each year, the county court appointed fifty or so overseers who, in turn, served work summonses on county men to create road repair crews. It is always a shock for the unenlightened to discover that the feudal corvée or labor tax existed in the commonwealth during the nineteenth century. Yet the custom flourished as Kentucky's major effort in building or repairing wagon paths and even turnpikes when the latter reverted from private to public ownership. Wealthy men, of course, could purchase a proxy or pay a tax and avoid the call, but the Barkleys never fell into that privileged category. Naturally, Alben and his road crew companions, especially the younger ones, tried to convert the peevish chore into a social event. As with his encounters on the harvest teams, he made new friends and swapped old stories. His father, however, like most of the mature adults, despised these road calls, which took him away from his fields. The work, reluctantly given and haphazardly accomplished, resulted in a less than satisfactory network of county roads that, nonetheless, were the farmers' lifeline. Alben would come to appreciate this fact, and road improvements would become a principal issue or objective in his years as a politician.[13]

The common experience that Alben shared with neighbors and friends on road repairs or in wheat fields also bestowed on him a more refreshing opinion of blacks than was normally found in town or city, North or South. Particularly in the 1890s, here and there in rural America the plain folk readily dispensed with or ignored the conventional racist views of society to acknowledge the similarity of problems associated with eking a living out of the soil. There were always blacks on crews repairing roads or threshing wheat. Thus, Alben labored side by side with the sons of former slaves. He counted this experience as a blessing that enabled him to hold the documented liberal stance on race relations that he revealed in his maturity. It would be wrong, however, to confuse modern liberal concepts with nineteenth-century tolerance. Alben could not avoid completely all the prejudices of his time and place. He could and did, however, accept the basic idea of equal opportunity for all. And the touching communal spirit with blacks that he portrayed in his autobiography bears some merit. The tenant farm up the road from the Barkleys' first home near Clinton was rented by a black family headed by Matt Vincent. Alben traded chores with him, and in general the families combined forces in their mutual struggle with the elements. In fact, sixty years later Barkley could still remember and even sing the song Matt Vincent had taught him when they worked together.[14]

While hard work characterized his life, Alben did have opportunities for play. And he took advantage of them. His friends found him to be so full of devilish fun and humor that they gave him "Monk," short for monkeyshines, as his nickname. Aside from high jinks and jokes, the teenager enjoyed playing Saturday afternoon baseball games in the vacant lot behind Hans Creasap's home in Clinton. The pickup game was never noted for its strict adherence to rules, and boys who came from farms around town showed more enthusiasm than finesse in the positions they played. Nevertheless, in the summer of 1892, on one of these outings to the baseball field, Alben talked in between innings to one of the adult bystanders, J. C. Speight, who happened to be along with J. C. Dean, copresident of Marvin College. The result of this conversation permanently changed the young man's life.[15]

Alben may have been sure of himself in telling jokes or playing baseball, but he approached with faltering step and stuttering tongue Marvin's copresident. Speight had recently given Alben's friend Charlie West a janitorial scholarship that waived the four-dollar-a-month tuition fee charged to Marvin's students. And Alben hoped that he might secure a similar scholarship. Unfortunately, he had to ask as well that he be permitted to miss some days in the fall and spring terms in order to continue to help his father and family on the farm. Despite the favor and the conditions Alben had to attach, Speight decided two weeks later to award the tenant farmer's son a janitorial scholarship. Out of gratitude Alben permanently and his parents temporarily switched allegiance to the Methodist Church.[16]

A Methodist bishop, Enoch M. Marvin, had given his name to the school, which first opened its doors to seventy-six students on August 31, 1885. Two years earlier, five-year-old Alben had witnessed the laying of the cornerstone of the single, $15,000 brick building that remained until 1900 the sum total of the college's facilities on the four-acre campus. The property, located just north of town on Washington Street, belonged to the Methodist Conference of the Methodist Episcopal Church (South), and the money raised for the building reflected a desire by the conference and Clinton's citizens to have a religious school that would prepare young adults for life. The key word is *prepare*. Today, there is no simple or proper equivalent one could use to compare and understand Marvin's mission, except perhaps the prep school concept.[17]

Although the school would expand and build a president's home (1900) and a men's dormitory (1910), in 1892 the single building housed intermediate, commercial, and collegiate divisions. Alben enrolled in the latter and the class of 1897. Given his past education, it would take him five years to earn a bachelor of arts degree. The collegiate division, with 20–30 of the 160 total students, was the smallest. Indeed, years later Barkley could count his 1897 classmates on one hand and remember their names: Lily Fostyr, Ernest Hilliard, Thomas Kennedy, and Charlie West. A decade after he graduated, the school ended its college division and reverted to a preparatory school only. In 1922, Marvin ceased to function as the advance of public education in western Kentucky made its role obsolete.[18]

Marvin may never have been a full-fledged college in the modern sense, but the course of study Alben followed broadened his outlook, challenged his intellect, and filled his mind with quantities of information from classical quotes to logical principles on which he could draw for the rest of his life. The flavor and rigor of his studies can be gleaned from a sample curriculum taken from his junior year: rhetoric, original essays, chemistry, trigonometry, surveying, moral philosophy, Latin, and Greek. All this was preceded daily by a religious exercise of song, prayer, scriptural readings, and biblical lessons.[19]

Alben, of course, found his day beginning well before the start of these religious services. He and Charlie West would walk up the wooden planks toward the college when the building was still a silhouette in the predawn light. As Alben gazed in front of him, he could see the vague outlines of shrubbery and trees neatly balanced on either side of the walkway running up the small hill and leading to the huge double wooden doors that gave entrance to the two-story brick building. The first time he took the journey he must have been slightly awed, not only by the studies that faced him, but also by the comparatively large size of the structure he would help clean so often for the next five years. Dormers on the roof and an octagonal cupola rising to the sky gave the attractive edifice an appearance of height and depth beyond its actual dimensions.[20]

No visual trick was necessary, however, to enlarge the huge, high-ceilinged recitation rooms found inside. On chilly mornings Alben knew his classmates and faculty counted on him to have the coal stoves glowing with warmth much in advance of the religious exercises that started each day's session. He and Charlie carried out ashes, brought in coal and water, and lit the fires in each of the four first-floor classrooms. Then they scurried up the central staircase to repeat their work in the two classrooms and the oversized study hall/library located on the second floor. After the rest of the students arrived and the day's lessons got under way, Alben had the additional responsibility of watching the clock and running outside to ring the college bell that signaled the end of each period. Finally, the cojanitors stayed in the building when classes had ended to dust the desks and sweep the floors.[21]

Five decades later, when little remained of the building except the foundation stones, a wooden sign was placed in front that proclaimed: "Barkley Swept Here." The inspiration for this jocular parody on commemorative plaques came from Will Clayton, undersecretary of state, when he and his wife, a former Marvin coed, visited Clinton shortly after the end of World War II. The couple stayed in the Jewel Hotel, the converted dormitory, which was all that survived of Marvin College. "Clayton," the hotel owner, L. A. Birk, commented to an interviewer, "had just returned from Europe, and as we were going over the grounds . . . [he] said that everywhere in Europe he'd seen plaques and markers commemorating the fact that some famous person slept here, or was born here, or fired the first bullet here. 'Why don't you put up a sign saying that Barkley Swept Here,' he suggested. Well we all laughed, but after they left I thought that was a good idea and had the sign made."[22]

The sign has since been replaced by a permanent marker of metal and concrete, but the thought expressed captures both the humor of the later politician and the humility associated with his earlier years. It also illuminates the serious business education had become for the eldest son of John Barkley, yet near the end of his life Alben painted in his memoirs an idyllic picture of his college days. By then he had been associated for decades with graduates of America's leading institutions, had visited hundreds of campuses, and had been awarded numerous honorary degrees. Thus, he merged these with his own experiences until fact and fancy, reality and ideal mixed together to form a synthesis in his autobiography. True, the older politician spoke of his work and classes at Marvin, but he matched symmetrically these mundane matters with comments on the lighter moments of college life: hayrides, square dances, swimming trips, social events, plus the courting of several coeds via his guitar. He even mentions the use of Clinton's first telephones to serenade and woo, but unsuccessfully, a young lass.[23]

No doubt, over the course of five years Alben was involved in all those extracurricular activities mentioned in his book, but from day to day, term to term, particularly at first, his social life fell somewhere between little and none. Because of his janitorial duties, his schooldays began so early and ended so late that the adolescent had few free moments to spare if he hoped to keep up with his studies at night. "Besides," his classmate Ernest Hilliard recalled, "Alben was so poor he did not have clothes to wear to the social functions we boys attended so he stayed home." One might question whether his contemporaries were so obviously better off than he, though it has been recorded that the tenant farmer's son stored his shoes at Marvin and wrapped his feet in burlap for the hike to and from the school. Regardless, Alben spent an enormous amount of time studying. His classmate and cojanitor Charles West took top honors in the class of 1897, but Alben by all accounts was a solid student.[24]

If poverty and work dimmed Alben's social life, and if his academic accomplishments prompt the adjective *solid* rather than *brilliant,* he never-theless did find one area of interest in which he acquired social acceptance and considerable glory. From the very first of his college days he partici-pated actively in the Periclean Debating Society. The society's functions, like Marvin's intramural sports program, remained informal. It met during the academic year each Friday night in the second-floor study hall/library. Informality aside, Presidents Speight and Dean personally supervised the students' progress and considered the society a vitally important and inte-gral part of the college experience. And Alben took the society just as seri-ously as his mentors. The young man would spend hours on the weekend wandering through the woods and brush around his family's farm and interrupt the peaceful sounds of nature booming out arguments and recita-tions that he would use during the society's weekly sessions.[25]

At first, flowery prose and excessive hyperbole marred Alben's logic and speeches. Clarence Heaslet, Barkley's contemporary, listened to the young man as the neophyte speaker delivered a talk entitled "Oh Ocean Our Slave and Master." It was, Heaslet admitted succinctly, "the awfulest thing I ever heard." But five years of experience permitted Alben to mature metaphori-cally as well as physically. By the time he had become a senior, he was so adept at writing speeches and preparing arguments that other members of the Periclean Debating Society sometimes paid him small sums for his help. Not only did he improve the texts of his speeches, but the years of practice also paid handsome dividends in his ability to memorize long pieces, to deliver them effectively and forcefully, and to think on his feet and extempo-rize whenever the occasion demanded. All these elements blended together in perfect fashion to make him a strong contender for the gold medal that would be awarded to the best speaker in the annual oratorical contest asso-ciated with the graduation exercises of 1897.[26]

The contest promised to draw such a crowd that Marvin College arranged to have it held in the principal room of the courthouse. Family, faculty, and friends joined school-aged children from around the county to pack the courthouse in what proved to be one of the highlights of the sea-son. Naturally, Alben's parents were very proud. They bought him a new pin-striped shirt with stylish snap-on cuffs. L. C. Moss, the owner of one of the local dry goods stores and a friend of the family, loaned the young man a black suit. And, when his turn came and Alben began his memorized speech entitled "American Statesmanship," everything seemed quite perfect. But he acquired a gesture—flailing his right arm through the air and crashing his fist into the open palm of his left hand—that he carried with him throughout his life.[27]

Unfortunately, midway through the speech, this gesture unhinged with a snap one of Alben's cuffs. His mind went blank. Unlike his experience six years earlier in Lowes, the nineteen-year-old had developed the stage presence of a veteran actor. Before the judges and members of the audience could turn to each other with raised eyebrows, he captured everyone's attention by calmly straightening his sleeve and putting his cuff back on. Meanwhile, he forced his mind back to his speech, and by the time he had adjusted his cuff he coolly resumed his talk. For such presence of mind as well as excellence of presentation the contest judges awarded him the gold declamation medal. His effort apparently was impressive. "Everyone," insisted a contemporary witness, Theresa Troutman, "said he'd be president some day."[28]

It would be difficult to deny or defend Mrs. Troutman's assertion, although it does appear to be an exaggeration. And, certainly, a latter-day objective observer who is far removed from the time and place of Alben's triumph would not dare ascribe presidential aspirations to the nineteen-year-old. What is very clear, however, is the driving ambition that Alben possessed to lift himself out of the environment of poverty in which he had been raised. By the exertions and sacrifices of his parents, and by the example of those educators whom he had come to admire at Marvin, he decided that education, specifically in the area of law, seemed the surest route to achieve a modicum of dignity and financial security. Thus, when he graduated from Marvin College with an A.B. degree in the spring of 1897, he resolved to continue his studies by attending Emory College in the fall.[29]

The jump from Clinton to Oxford, Georgia, looms abrupt and distant until one reflects on the fact that the Methodist Church also sponsored Emory College. Alone, however, that bit of information is meaningless, for the Methodists had been prolific organizers of small institutions of higher education that dotted like seedlings the American landscape. Like Marvin, many of these new starts struggled, withered, and died, but Emory matured, blossomed in size and prestige, and in 1919 moved to Atlanta. In 1897, however, the religious connection inspired Barkley's decision only indirectly. More importantly, Emory's influence permeated the school in Clinton. Several of Marvin's faculty and presidents, including Speight and Dean, graduated from Emory, and one of Alben's revered professors, E. F. Fincher, urged the young man to attend the southern college and study law. If all these subtle pressures did not pull Alben along the path leading to

Oxford, Georgia, his classmate and friend Thomas Kennedy certainly did since he planned to enroll in Emory himself.[30]

Barkley's decision to go on with his education and study law was easy. His benefactors and models, Speight and Dean, on whom Alben had patterned his life, had not only attended Emory but also left Marvin in 1896 for careers in law and politics. Still, he would find that decision difficult to implement. No janitorial scholarship awaited him at the new school. Furthermore, working two or three weeks at a dollar a day for one of the threshing crews would not begin to raise the $200 he would need for room, board, tuition, and travel to and from Emory for the 1897–1898 academic year. So the determined young man answered the advertisement of an Ohio firm to become a drummer for cooking crockery in the southern half of Graves County.[31]

In more recent times, door-to-door salesmen have all but disappeared. By contrast, nineteenth-century rural Americans, starved for news and new faces that represented the outside world, often welcomed the traveling salesman, if not for his wares, then for his company. So a resolve to raise money through sales was not such an impractical measure. From his small savings, and from his parents, Alben scraped together a few dollars and went to Water Valley, a small hamlet in southern Graves County, where he rented a room, hired a horse, and started on his adventure to sell crockery to the wives of farmers in the area. He carried his wares in a satchel, and, hair slicked back and dressed in his best, he gave every appearance of being a young doctor. And "Doc" Barkley did very well. Despite his ample ears, nose, and mouth, his slender but robust figure presented a handsome sight, and his mellow baritone voice, coupled with his experience at speech and debate, gave him every advantage in his sales pitch to his rural female customers.[32]

A single problem marred Alben's success. When his company's cooking crockery approached the heat of a stove, it cracked. Alben discovered this unhappy reality when he returned for a second canvass of his territory. Farmers and their wives were not so happy to see him then. His strong sense of morality from his strict religious upbringing led him to ride to each farm and exchange money for the defective crockery. These future constituents in Graves County never forgot his honesty, and they would shower him with their votes and confidence when years later he ran for Congress. But, morality and the blessings of the future aside, Alben had to leave for home near the end of the summer more broke than when he had arrived. In a last-minute act of desperation, the young man managed to convince seven or eight

Clinton businessmen to cosign a note for $200 at 10 percent interest that gave him the funds he required to spend a year at Emory.[33]

With this financial cloud over his head, Barkley left by train with Kennedy for Oxford, Georgia, in the fall. Both young men remained there under the supervision of President Warren Candler for only one academic year; Kennedy moved on to Vanderbilt University, and Barkley ran out of money. But the year Alben spent at Emory, despite the paucity of records and information, provides some special glimpses into his life. He enrolled, for example, as a sophomore, and, thus, for the first time in his career as a student one has a reasonably objective standard by which to measure his educational progress. In addition, he studied classics, joined a fraternity (Delta Tau Delta), and jousted oratorically as a member of Emory's Few Debating Society. The cumulative effect of these activities confirmed the road toward law that he had paved for himself.[34]

That road, however, would have to bypass Emory. Bereft of funds, Alben returned to Clinton and his family's rented farm, where he worked in the summer of 1898. To pacify his creditors, and as a stop-gap measure, he accepted a position to teach in the intermediate department at Marvin College for $25 per month. The teaching position reflected in part his abilities, but it also illustrated the difficulties Marvin and other small schools experienced in maintaining an adequate staff. Either way, the decision to accept the position was not the wisest choice Barkley would ever make. The college had a hard time paying its faculty. And Barkley found it difficult to control his classes, having shared too many dates or too many pranks with the young women and men who constituted his charges. Too often his classes degenerated to the level of a sailors' repartee. In the midst of this disastrous fall term, Alben's family moved to Paducah. John Barkley abandoned his exertions against the whims of nature and the market, and, at the end of the fall harvest, he took his wife and children to the Ohio River town, where he accepted employment and found security in a weekly paycheck from a cordage mill. Forced to rent a room and buy his meals, unsure about his pay from Marvin, and unable to keep ahead financially so as to reduce his debts, Alben decided in December to tender his resignation at Marvin and join his parents in Paducah.[35]

Seven years to the day after his ignominious entrance into Clinton, Alben Barkley left the town on December 28, 1898, for the city that became synonymous with his name. As time went by and memories grew clouded, his Clinton days moved further to the background and closer to obscurity. Yet Clinton, not Paducah, nurtured a farm boy, educated a youth, and watched a young man mature to adulthood. It gave him stories, work, experiences, a college education of sorts, and a forum to hone his talent for speech. In later years, the people of Clinton and Hickman County somehow found that his stories grew funnier, his appetite larger, his work heavier, and his ambition loftier. These exaggerations aside, Barkley took with him fond memories of Clinton, and he left behind many friends and numerous acquaintances. Neither he nor they forgot each other no matter how often in the future Barkley would be called the *Paducah politician*.

3

Barkley's Reconciliation with His Roots

Alben W. Barkley's remarkably meek and quiet entrance into Paducah contrasted sharply with all the commotion and fuss attending his first day in Clinton seven years before. The only note to herald the event was the sound of fifty cents change that jangled in his pockets and represented the entire fortune he would bring to the city that became synonymous with his name. With little more than an extra shirt and the clothes he wore, Alben had to join the rest of the Barkley clan in a small rented home nestled within the working district. His parents made a decision that Alben forgot to credit when he finally wrote his memoirs. John and Electa Barkley allowed the eldest to have free room and board while he pursued to the fullest his ambition to read law and enter the bar.[1]

A formal education and a law degree had not yet supplanted the tradition of a young man studying law with an established firm and then taking the bar exam. Since Barkley retained a substantial debt, his attendance at law school had become a dream he could no longer fulfill. Fortunately for him, Paducah had plenty of lawyers in need of clerks to ease the casework attending the voluminous litigation associated with the lively town that the native and humorist Irvin S. Cobb described laconically as a bit "untidy." The city had a reputation for warm, witty, and hospitable people who, nonetheless, exhibited a streak of boldness and independence.[2]

These latter characteristics combined with those of individuals who worked in Paducah's railroad, steamboat, tobacco, lumber, and whiskey industries to provide a colorful mixture of resilient characters who kept the local constabulary on its toes. The confluence in the space of fourteen miles of the Cumberland, Tennessee, and Ohio Rivers brought an additional element to the town. Rough-hewn Tennessee lumbermen would accompany their rafts of logs for sale to the mills in the fall. As at the end of a western cattle drive, loggers grabbed their pay and headed for town. The taverns around the wharf area on Market Street became unsafe for the city's more venerable citizens.[3]

Except for this annual invasion, some of the town's wildness had been tamed by the time Barkley had arrived. The steamboat era approached its end, and the country folk with their simpler values and fundamental religions pressed respectability on a town that catered to farmers by processing or shipping rural products and supplying farm implements. Nevertheless, legal row on South Fourth Street remained the scene of considerable activity as numerous people entered or left the offices near the heart of Paducah. Uniformly, visitors to law firms were greeted with the aromas of furniture leather and pipe tobacco. In addition, the truly established member of the bar had an office that, before the days of air-conditioning, exuded the musty odors of many books, from Blackstone to Kent, on the processes of law. It was the latter that drew Barkley to the establishment of the attorney Charles K. Wheeler at the start of 1899.[4]

The former drummer and Marvin teacher carried with him a letter of introduction from his friends in Clinton. It seemed to Barkley, at least at first, that to read law in Wheeler's office would be the type of personal coup that guaranteed a promising future. After all, since the election of 1896 Wheeler had upheld the purchase area's interests in the US Congress as the representative for Kentucky's First District. The contacts and insights he ostensibly could provide in law and politics must have dazzled Barkley's eyes and reinforced his parents' intent to subsidize their eldest child while he drank deep from the cup of knowledge in Wheeler's hands. Nothing, however, tarnishes so quickly as the silver lining around a dream when it confronts the oxidizing element of reality.[5]

The congressman took Barkley in and hired him as a clerk, but his duties in the nation's capital often kept him away from his office. When he was present, the pair did not evince the father-son, mentor-pupil fraternity Barkley had enjoyed with Marvin College's copresidents. Perhaps the young man did not make a favorable impression. Long after the event he remembered the time Wheeler returned unexpectedly from Washington and caught him reading a novel rather than the law. The politician could not hold back a look of utter disdain for his clerk. Barkley explained that he had taken only a short break, and, indeed, the miscreant tome had been written by none other than the famous and highly regarded English author Charles Dickens. Neither the explanation nor the quality of the novel prevented Wheeler from leveling a critical blast at his sometime protégé. "Young man," he admonished, "you will never become a lawyer by reading that book."[6]

If Wheeler's brusque behavior and frequent absences built a wall between the two, then other differences added breastworks and stanchions to help assure that their association would never lift above the tie found in a perfunctory relationship. Succinctly put, Barkley did not agree with Wheeler's politics. The congressman had entered his post as a so-called free-silver Democrat who looked to William Jennings Bryan for the bases of his ideas. As a powerhouse orator from Nebraska, Bryan captured the hearts of agrarian rebels when he supported the 1896 Democratic platform, which called for the free and unlimited coinage of silver at the ratio of sixteen ounces of silver to one of gold. Had Bryan and his populist friends gained a toehold in the federal government and implemented a silver policy, the nation's gold standard would have been compromised, and the resulting inflation might have given relief to debtors in rural and urban America.[7]

Bryan came within 600,000 votes of accomplishing this goal. His electrifying "Cross of Gold" speech at the 1896 Democratic national convention earned him the party's nomination but at the expense of splitting Democrats between the so-called silver bugs and gold bugs. And the endorsement of Bryan by rural rebels in the dying Populist Party only accentuated the gulf and allowed the Republican William McKinley of Ohio to enter the White House. This national division extended to the state and local levels, particularly in Kentucky, where battles between silver and gold Democrats assumed such vicious dimensions that normally Democratic Kentucky gave its vote to McKinley and, the preceding year, had permitted the election of W. O. Bradley, the first Republican governor in the commonwealth's history. Even the Jackson Purchase of western Kentucky did not escape the strident debate over silver and gold. While the silverite Wheeler went to Congress, several gold Democrats from the purchase area went to Frankfort as representatives in the state legislature.[8]

One final division over the issue must be noted—the one within the Barkley household. John Barkley had been in debt for most of his life, and his earlier tie with the protopopulists led him to gravitate effortlessly toward the Bryan camp. When Henry Watterson, the editor of the Democratic *Louisville Courier-Journal*, endorsed McKinley, the elder Barkley stopped buying the statewide weekly edition, which he had purchased each Saturday since the time he and his family had resided near Lowes. Alben, on the other hand, supported the gold Democrats. Youth is a time for formulating values and testing beliefs, and, like other teenagers, the younger Barkley took occasional delight in asserting the independence of his views. But, more importantly, his revered benefactors at Marvin College, Speight and Dean, won elections as conservative Democrats. The former represented Hickman and Fulton Counties in the state legislature, and the latter served Hickman County as its judge.[9]

Shortly after Alben moved to Paducah, Speight and Dean left Clinton for Mayfield, entered a partnership, opened a law firm, and joined the Republican Party. Young Barkley never contemplated pushing his youthful ideas and sympathies for gold Democrats to the logical conclusion of siding with the Grand Old Party, but for years he held the strong belief that unthinking partisanship nibbled away at the democratic process. When he had attended Emory College, he had relished taking the affirmative in the debate: "Resolved, that independent action in politics is more beneficial to public institutions than loyalty to a political party." And in Paducah the accumulation of these experiences and concepts added a note of reserve that prevented him from working in concert with Wheeler.[10]

Finally, the congressman's tight-fisted attitude left Barkley no choice but to terminate his "employment" with the man at the earliest possible moment. The free-silver, inflation-loving Wheeler ironically reimbursed his law clerk by paying him nothing at all. He felt that access to his books paid Barkley for his services, and, in his simplified ledger, the net result was zero. The young man could not survive long on Wheeler's concept of generosity. Alben could be found on Saturdays clerking in Jim Rudy's shoe store and during weekday evenings studying shorthand with Wheeler's secretary, Lulu Flowers, who showed more compassion than her boss. Within two months he acquired sufficient knowledge of stenography to take depositions and earn a little cash. He probably considered money to be the most significant result of his new talent. Actually, this attribute, not money, altered Alben's future. His hard work and stenographic skills brought him to the attention of other lawyers on legal row, most notably Judge William S. Bishop and Colonel John K. Hendrick.[11]

In the summer of 1899 the barristers Bishop and Hendrick hired Barkley away from Wheeler by offering him $15 a month to clerk in their office. Small wonder Barkley had kind words for the new employers whenever he reminisced about these early days. Perhaps unfortunately, however, most of these fond memories crowded around Judge Bishop. And who could fault Barkley for remembering Bishop? The judge deserved his reputation for being the best lawyer and having the best law library in western Kentucky. Moreover, he embodied a large number of memorable opposites: his squeaky voice issued from a portly frame, his speech pattern shifted easily between country colloquialisms and elegant English depending on the audience, his fearless presence before a jury crumbled into a shaking mass when a thunderstorm appeared, and his rigorous mind for the law withered away into absentmindedness in his personal life. In short, he was an unforgettable character, so much so that the humorist Cobb used him for thirty years as the prototype for the fictional character Judge Priest in numerous books and stories.[12]

Despite Cobb's fictional renditions, Bishop was not a judge, at least not in 1899. Kentucky has had an inordinately large number of captains, majors, colonels, and judges, in part because commonwealth citizens enjoyed using and retaining former ranks and old labels, and in part because those who gained a certain standing within a community seemed to acquire such titles without ever fighting in a war or sitting on a bench. Years earlier, of course, Bishop had been a common pleas judge and then served a term as circuit judge for the First Judicial District. But, when Barkley moved into the office of his new preceptors, he had been retired as a judge, and shortly thereafter he would retire as a lawyer. Fortunately, it had been "Colonel" Hendrick who had wanted Barkley, and, thus, it was Hendrick who retained the impoverished law clerk when he joined forces with J. J. Miller to create a new law partnership.[13]

In Hendrick, Barkley found a man with whom he could identify completely. The colonel was a gold Democrat pure and simple. Moreover, he was not the exception to the rule that the hustings are as naturally the haunt of lawyers as the bar. He had been to Congress and in fact lost his seat to Wheeler in 1896. By employing Barkley, Hendrick accomplished a small act of spite that redounded to the young man's benefit. For the next year and a half, Alben studied furiously to master the law, in between taking depositions and doing background investigations on briefs for his employer. Hendrick seemed to be less the taskmaster than Wheeler and more the example of a Fourth Street lawyer. The colonel delighted in sharing the conviviality of his peers. On pleasant days he would go outside and put his expansive body on a split-bottomed chair and play checkers with his partner or with one of his rivals. And occasionally he would saunter north to Billy Gray's sample room or south to Jim Sherrill's—these little walks explain the colonel's reputation for perspiring profusely after the slightest exertion.[14]

Hendrick fit so neatly within the ambiance of Paducah's law culture that his alliances smoothed Barkley's path. In January 1901, the law clerk received an appointment from Hendrick's friend Judge L. D. Husbands to fill a vacancy as court reporter for the circuit court. And, not long after, he passed with ease his bar examination, in part because the panel of Paducah lawyers that reviewed his knowledge had been well acquainted with his guide in the law. Thus, in a relatively short period of time, Barkley achieved his dream and could open his own small office on Broadway, the city's main street. That he considered his law practice to be a part-time career can be seen by the fact that he kept the court reporter post and, indeed, clung to it for financial security for the next four years. Rather than his new profession, it was his stipend of $50 a month as an employee of the court that vaulted him out of extreme poverty and into the middle class.[15]

For the first time Alben could contribute substantially to his own maintenance within the Barkley household. Since he made no effort to leave his parents and establish his own home, he could finish paying off his debts in Clinton and still have money left for those pursuits normal for a young man his age. In this period he seemed to be trying to make up for all the hard, lean years he had endured on the farm, in the school at Marvin, and in the law offices where he had clerked. He joined the Broadway Methodist Episcopal Church and entered fully into its social as well as its religious life. In addition, he sampled nearly every legal pleasure available to a country boy in Paducah at the turn of the century: visiting circuses, river showboats, summer fireworks, community socials, and touring troupes such as the original Buffalo Bill Wild West Show.[16]

So seriously did Alben take his social life that he enrolled in Miss Effie's dancing classes, where he learned the two-step, the waltz, and the schottische and all the graces and etiquettes practiced on the ballroom floor. Mention a dance, and Barkley showed up. He radiated energy at such affairs, and the young ladies of Paducah found him to be very attractive. Physically, he was thin and muscular, and the way he carried himself exaggerated his height so that he looked to be six feet tall even though he would have to stand on his toes to surpass that mark. His brown wavy hair framed a pleasant face accented by a rounded mouth and a Roman nose that gave him a classical appearance irresistible to several of the belles of the river city. One in particular, Dorothy Brower, possessed the dark and sophisticated good looks to force Barkley to reciprocate with his attentions for the young lady who was five years his junior.[17]

Whether he dated Dorothy or other girls, it would be a mistake to consign Barkley to the category of a frivolous blade. He did not react to the social swirl of early adulthood in the manner of a child who finds a $20 bill on a sidewalk outside a well-stocked candy store. For one thing, he never accepted the hard-drinking, quick-fisted stereotype common to the less genteel young men of the city. In fact, his very sobriety and evident discretion added a dash of stability and appeal to his physical attributes. His almost frenetic entrance into Paducah's social milieu had a purpose beyond the gratification of pleasures he had missed throughout the first two decades of his life. Barkley, after all, had to overcome his background as an outsider and construct those ties and build those contacts that other lawyers, native to Paducah, acquired as an integral part of their birthright.[18]

Thus, Barkley attended dances and socials, and he sought membership in every local organization in sight: the Woodmen of the World, the Elks, the Odd Fellows, the Zenda Club, and the Improved Order of Red Men. Only his lack of adequate funds and decent suits stopped him from gaining membership in the exclusive Cotillion Club. He brought to these societies his youthful enthusiasm as well as his special talent nurtured from his college days. In essence, he became each club's speaker-in-residence. "I had," he remembered facetiously, "a natural inclination to stop whatever I was doing and start making a speech any time I saw as many as six persons assembled together." Witty and congenial, relaxed and unpretentious, and eager and willing, Barkley accepted every speaking engagement proffered to him. He spoke at clubs to which he belonged as well as those to which he did not. His rich baritone voice could be heard mellifluously preaching a lay sermon on Sunday behind a Methodist pulpit or gleefully telling an anecdote on Monday before a sportsman's group.[19]

Fifty years later, Barkley hinted broadly that all these speeches and social activities performed the function of a preliminary canvass among potential voters prior to his actually running for office. However, the passage of time condensed years into moments that flew through the mind of the older adult. All the evidence suggests that, rather than using himself as a stalking horse for his own political future, Barkley strove first to establish himself as a lawyer within the community. And, as an outsider who had never attended a school of law, he was particularly sensitive to his shortcomings. His desire to create a reputation and demonstrate an expertise as an attorney is the only logical explanation for the perfectly extraordinary step he took in the summer of 1902.[20]

Barkley closed his office, took leave of his position with the circuit court, and enrolled in a two-month law course at the University of Virginia in Charlottesville. It is the type of activity more reminiscent of a man entering his forties who uneasily traverses the dividing line into advanced middle age than a twenty-four-year-old who had ostensibly accomplished the principal goal of his life. Yet the concentrated period of study offered by the university in July and August allowed Barkley to fill in those gaps caused by the haphazard approach commonly used by those who read for the bar examination instead of studying law in an organized fashion at a recognized school. Under the supervision of experts such as Raleigh C. Minor, Barkley underwent systematic instruction through fifty lectures and absorbed those basic principles he had managed to miss when he surveyed law texts in the offices of Wheeler and Hendrick.[21]

While Barkley studied hard and gained confidence in his knowledge of the law, he also devoted these two months to the type of introspection he had never had the opportunity to engage in during his hectic younger years. The law lectures were interrupted by weekends that were free for the participants to use as they wished. Barkley employed his time leisurely touring the campus and reading about its original architect, Thomas Jefferson. As time passed, the Paducah lawyer took weekend jaunts to nearby Monticello. Jefferson's home was not yet a national shrine, spruced up and eagerly awaiting the buses of ticket-paying tourists who have their thirty-minute chance to see the home. Barkley, by contrast, spent hours at a time meandering about the structure Jefferson had designed and built. Even in its disheveled state Monticello could not subdue the brilliance of the mind that had created it.[22]

Jefferson's imprint left an indelible mark on Barkley. Then and thereafter he would measure men and politics by whether they resembled Jefferson or the Jeffersonian ideal. Unfortunately, to state that over the years he slowly cast his mind into the mold of Jefferson is not the tidy answer one might look for in terms of the question concerning Barkley's philosophy. It should not be forgotten that Jefferson remained an anomaly among his contemporaries. The most cosmopolitan of men, he upheld the virtues of rural life; the author of the Declaration of Independence and the passage "all men are created equal," he kept his slaves; the American president who eschewed the power of national government, he used that power to double the size of the United States. Yet in him there is a thread that weaves around and through these contradictions—a tie to the needs and interests of the common man.[23]

It would be the latter that also wove its way into the fabric of Barkley's philosophy. The man who has been burned can best describe the pain of fire, and the fire that Barkley had experienced was the life of the struggling farmer. In years to come he discovered that his most consistent political support and identity came from rural voters with whom he could sympathize completely. However, like Jefferson, he had an inconsistency, as seen in the fact that he had supported the gold Democrats. Self-made men tend to be conservative, especially in money matters. Thus, throughout Barkley's life there would be evidence of a dual streak—a desire to promote the welfare of the rural and the poor and a tendency toward fiscal restraint. Within Barkley were the seeds of Jefferson but also of Jefferson's protagonist Alexander Hamilton. Nevertheless, after he returned to Paducah in September, his ideas bore more resemblance to the agrarian doctrine of his father than they had for many years.[24]

When Barkley arrived back at his office and resumed his duties as court reporter, he found that this period of self-analysis and self-improvement produced more than an affinity for Thomas Jefferson and knowledge of the finer points of the law. The separation he experienced from Dorothy Brower strengthened his fascination for the charms of the young lady whom he had dated from time to time for the previous two years. Dorothy had graduated from high school in Paducah in 1900, but her parents, Charles and Laura Brower, were originally from Tiptonville, Tennessee. For years Charles Brower had used Paducah as a base of operations for his employment as an itinerant salesman. Eventually, he saved enough money to buy a hardware store in Tiptonville and moved his family there, including his eldest daughter, Dorothy. Barkley's occasional letters to the girl grew longer and arrived more regularly after his sojourn in Virginia. The distance that separated the pair made them feel more fondness for each other. Increasingly, Barkley wanted to see Dorothy, and over the winter of 1902–1903 he made frequent weekend train trips to Tiptonville in order to be with the woman he came to love.[25]

In this romantic interlude, Barkley illustrated a characteristic that he carried with him to his grave. Like all mortal beings, he had his impetuous moments, but on the whole he approached most problems with the meticulous care and durable energy of a farmer who begins to lay plans for preparing the soil for spring planting immediately after the fall harvest. He refused, for example, to propose to Dorothy until after he had saved $800, money sufficient for a down payment on a home. Aside from this characteristic, there was an additional reason why Barkley wanted to purchase a house before he took a bride. Apparently, his parents assumed that after twenty-five years their Alben would remain with them as their source of comfort for the rest of their lives. "I almost cried myself sick," Electa later confessed, "when he came home and told me he was going to get married." The eldest Barkley child knew instinctively that his and Dorothy's relationship would bear an unwholesome burden under the stifling custody of his parents' watchful eyes should the bridal couple move in with John and Electa.[26]

Thus, the $800 was used for a down payment. When Alben and Dorothy exchanged vows in Tiptonville on June 23, 1903, they could leave the altar, travel to Paducah, and enter their own home. The house was a castle only in the minds of the newlywed couple. In fact, the four-room structure resembled nothing so much as a summer cottage. The gas-lit, white-frame house was small, unpretentious, and rustic even by the standards of a border-state river town. Yet within the home love abounded and to the point where the birth of the couple's children—David Murrell (February 11, 1906), Marian Frances (September 14, 1909), and Laura Louise (October 28, 1911)—spurred the family to seek larger dwellings two times between 1906 and 1909. The latter move was to a two-story frame house on, appropriately, Jefferson Street.[27]

There is more than a casual relationship between changes in address and the birth of children and Barkley's career. For example, David Barkley, or "Bud" as he was called, arrived after a decent interval following Alben's first electoral victory. The spacing and timing of the children's appearance as well as the relatively few number of births indicate a design or pattern that defies the normal course of nature. In this apparent family-planning venture, the mark of Alben is clearly etched on the course of the couple's lives and highlights a quality of Dorothy's that was neither unusual for her contemporaries nor attractive to the prototypes of modern womanhood. Dorothy subsumed her personality and dedicated herself to the real or fanciful necessities of her husband's and children's lives.[28]

So quiet and unobtrusive was Dorothy that the researcher examining Barkley's voluminous correspondence must plow through years of letters before a single reference to her is found. She was not, however, an unthinking automaton. She possessed for her time a high level of education, and others have described her as cultured, if not erudite. While some modern women might be dismayed by her submissive role, she held in her high intelligence, whimsical smile, and penetrating eyes a formidable power over her husband and over the family's affairs. Finally, her dark hair clipped short, parted neatly, and combed back in republican austerity remained unchanged for the nearly forty-four years of her married life. Her personal and impeccable habits mirrored the steadying influence she exerted to enable Alben to keep his sanity in the decades that followed as he entered the chaotic and rugged life of a public figure. Dorothy shared with Alben a mutual interest in antique furniture and the various curios purchased during their later travels, but most of all she supported her husband in his political ambitions.[29]

Ambition alone explains Barkley's decision the very next year to enter the race for county attorney. It was the lowest rung on the political ladder and a post not designed to draw candidates who hoped to impart a political philosophy or an elaborate program. The person in office functioned as the county's watchdog pure and simple. Irvin S. Cobb would have been gentler in dealing with Barkley. It was perfectly normal, so Cobb claimed in an anecdote, for one in three of Paducah's lawyers to run for office every four years. Hence, Barkley did the expected, though there were better reasons for tossing his hat into the political arena. In defeat, his name and face would become more familiar to the citizens of Paducah and McCracken County—an asset that would help him in his profession regardless. In victory, his forensic skills as a trial lawyer would be sharpened by repeated use, and he could hope for higher office or, at worst, expect an augmented law practice at the end of his term. Add to these points the fact that the county attorney could earn a substantial salary, and there seemed no reason for him not to run for the office. He had absolutely nothing to lose and everything to gain.[30]

Even so, Barkley charged after the post as if it were the highest office in the land or, more correctly, as if the advance of his fortune depended on victory. The campaign he waged is interesting simply because he demonstrated a flair or style of operation that he maintained for all his campaigns right up to 1954. Since he lost only once in his lengthy period of public service, his approach to this first campaign is particularly instructive. At the outset, he announced his candidacy to the local press on December 19, 1904, well in advance of the March primary. As with most contests fought later, the primary rather than the general election was the key to winning office. Democrats in western Kentucky so outnumbered Republicans that the GOP often found it difficult to field enough candidates for all the available vacancies, let alone try to contest them in the general election.[31]

Another quality that arose with singular regularity during Barkley campaigns was the fact that the contests hinged on his performance and often on his resources. Thus, in 1904–1905, Barkley had to use his personal funds, some $250, and act as his own treasurer, campaign manager, public relations expert, advance man, and principal speaker. Naturally, in some of his later campaigns for more important offices, he could count on organized assistance. There is, however, some evidence to suggest that he never mastered completely the proper use of a political machine to win elections. In a large city, for example, he would have been the perfect ward captain, but he would not have survived long as the city boss. More often than not, the organization and leadership of his campaigns emerged solely at the time and place of his personal appearance before the public.[32]

And, for the humble post of county attorney, Barkley overwhelmed the electorate by his physical presence. The energy and drive he displayed on the hustings became his special hallmark. He went to a print shop and bought a set of campaign cards that asked, below his picture, for the recipient's "vote and influence" on the day of the Democratic primary. Unlike other candidates, who would ply their cards to shoppers along Broadway on Saturdays, Barkley pounded the pavement and knocked on doors in an effort to see each constituent. Once he had exhausted the possibilities in Paducah, he borrowed a mule from his uncle Andrew, swapped it along with $25 for a one-eyed horse named Dick, and rode out to the countryside. Over the hills and through the bottoms he wended his way around McCracken County to speak with every farmer in sight. "If there was a single house in the county I missed," Barkley mused in 1949, "it must have been a mighty dark night."[33]

Barkley slept where he stopped, prevailing on farmers to give him lodging in their homes or barns before he continued his canvass. He spoke with individuals and gave renewed meaning to the phrase *stumping for office* by talking before small groups of men while he stood quite literally on a tree stump. In between these rural speeches he posted his cards and handbills on fences and earned the respect and votes of farmers by helping them with their chores. So plucky and zealous was he that, when he stopped by the Rehkopf Tannery, he boldly sought to shake hands with the workers who were accessible from the road only by way of a narrow plank over open vats that contained the odiferous solution used to treat the animal hides. Unfortunately, he slipped off the plank and tumbled into a vat. The workers laughed uproariously and then pulled their soaked visitor out of the tub. Barkley's sense of humor allowed him to smile at his own predicament, and, because the workers appreciated his gamely sportsmanship, they reportedly remembered him well on the day of the primary.[34]

Barkley's fearless and energetic approach to his campaign and his gregarious and special affinity with rural residents fused with one other quality that he had longed possessed—a supreme ability to make speeches and engage individuals in debate. Our ancestors of the early twentieth century had not yet experienced the glossy, prepackaged video shows found on screens in homes and theaters; all entertainments of that bygone era were live. Moreover, the most popular amusement, especially in western Kentucky, was the traditional preelection debate among candidates running for office. Regretfully, the position of attorney fell so low on the totem pole of county offices that it drew little attention in the local press. What has been recorded, however, is the focus Barkley gave to his talks when his rivals, David Cross and Eugene Graves, joined him for a series of debates beginning March 6, 1905, at Florence Station. Cross and Barkley attacked the incumbent Graves for seeking a third term. The pair cried *sinecure* and *monopoly* often and effectively before audiences in Paducah and around the county, yet both men could also answer Graves's countercharge that they lacked experience. Barkley, of course, had been a court reporter for four years and knew the judicial system; Cross held appointment as a judge of the Paducah police court.[35]

When the results came in from the March 30 Democratic primary, Barkley's travels in the county proved decisive. He won the election with 1,525 votes, while Graves took 1,096, and Cross came in last with 602. Since Graves beat Barkley in Paducah, the margin of difference occurred in the country, where Barkley garnered nearly 60 percent of the vote. One did not have to be very imaginative or overly bright to note that Barkley's victory was due to the farmers. He had begun his years in Paducah striving to overcome the poverty of his childhood and youth. He seemed through his choice of profession, acquaintances, and activities to be trying to put as much distance as he could between himself and the tenant farms where he had grown up. Ironically, the values and experiences of his earliest years, rather than those he had nurtured in Paducah, had permitted him to gain victory at the polls. Thus, he emerged from this first battle in politics as a man reconciled with his roots. If nothing else, the reevaluation of his political philosophy that began in 1902 received the strongest reinforcement in the sense that he understood that his real strength and natural interest lay with those individuals who worked with their hands.[36]

4

From Courthouse to Congress

Twenty-eight-year-old Alben W. Barkley was sworn in as McCracken County's prosecuting attorney on the first Monday of 1906. The post ranked in the cellar of the political hierarchy, yet the caliber of the people's lawyer often determined the quality of government and the extent of justice in a county. The office had evolved in the nineteenth century and gained recognition and definition in the 1850 and 1891 constitutions. By the turn of the century, the responsibilities of the post included prosecuting people accused of breaching the peace, advising officers of the county courts, assisting the commonwealth's attorney in prosecuting felons in district court, hauling delinquent taxpayers before the court, making sure that lawyers did not withhold judgments collected for clients, and reviewing all claims brought before the fiscal court. Over the next four years, Barkley attended more than six hundred hearings and prosecuted approximately three hundred individuals, relatively normal numbers for a county of thirty-five thousand people. It was in the fiscal court where he earned a reputation that transcended the county line.[1]

In McCracken County, the fiscal court consisted of eight elected magistrates supervised by a county judge. It formed the heart of the system of government because it determined taxes, approved contracts, and paid claims for services rendered to the county. These were the prime elements connected with the basic functions of government, and counties dominated by one political party faced the possibility of mismanagement. When acting in concert, the county judge and the magistrates could favor their families, friends, and followers to the detriment of those who had failed to support them in the last election. Add the county attorney to such a courthouse clique, and the system of checks against the formidable powers of the fiscal court disintegrated since, by statute, the people's lawyer stood as the sentinel protecting county residents from corruption.[2]

Barkley's maverick candidacy and electoral victory gave him a degree of independence not normally found within the county. Years later, he would be noted for partisan politics and strident faith in the Democratic Party. In this period, however, he remained aloof from the coterie of courthouse politicians who endured and prospered despite the perennial charges of knavery raised by the Republican minority, whose only strength lay in Paducah. This point would be crucial for his future. In the immediate context, his relative autonomy explains his unorthodox approach to work before the fiscal court. Rather than swim with the tide, Barkley carefully reviewed and successfully challenged padded contracts and inflated claims against the county government and saved the taxpayers $35,000, a huge amount of money for the time. He also prosecuted two magistrates for their illegal interests in contracts approved by the court.[3]

These misdemeanor charges did not cause the type of scandal one might imagine. Magistrates received little compensation for their time, and the plan of county government established in the state constitution virtually encouraged such officeholders to pounce on whatever rewards they could ferret out of the system. Barkley was attempting the unexpected, however, and marked himself as apart from the petty and sordid deals common to most courthouse rings around the state. He appeared before the appellate court to argue against the fiscal court–approved 62 percent raise for Circuit Judge William M. Reed and successfully challenged County Clerk Hiram Smedley's attempt to have the fiscal court authorize funding to alphabetize a list of mortgages recorded in his office, supposedly a regular part of his job.[4]

This muckraking approach was rooted in Barkley's rural background as he knew that the price of corruption was higher taxes, which were a great burden on poorer farmers and workers like his father. He favored tax cuts, fought pay raises for county officials, and also recommended a $150,000 bond issue to pay for graveling county roads. By becoming the voice of McCracken County farmers, he inadvertently backed into the agrarian wing of the progressive movement. Kentucky was not in the front ranks of progressivism, but neither was Paducah isolated from it. Feature articles regularly appeared in the local press on nationally renowned progressive figures, and the city experimented in the reforms of the period by installing a commission form of government based on the Galveston, Texas, example.

Barkley had little to do with the politics and reforms of Paducah, but neither did he exist in a vacuum that isolated him from the trends of the times.[5]

However incidental this association may have been, the fact that Barkley's views and actions paralleled those of the well-publicized progressive movement soon earned him notice beyond his home area. In June 1907, Democratic State Central Committee chairman Henry B. Hines invited him to serve on the Speaker's Bureau. The next month, his growing reputation as an excellent orator and virtuous public servant gained him election as president of the State Association of County Attorneys. He used this pulpit to call for the abolition of state-salaried commonwealth's attorneys, claiming that they responded too zealously to the whims of the party that controlled Frankfort and that they accomplished little in the district courts without the aid of county attorneys. This suggestion was spoken much more for effect than anything else, but it earned Barkley notice in newspapers across the state.[6]

Barkley's duties with the Speaker's Bureau kept him before the local voters as he served as the official party spokesman in McCracken County for the 1907 gubernatorial and 1908 presidential elections. His own term was up in 1909, and his growing local fame led him to consider seeking higher office. True to his style of an early start, he announced in August 1908 that he would be a candidate for county judge the following year.[7]

Two months later, two other decisions appeared to justify completely the course Barkley had set for his career. The executive committee of the county's Democratic Club unanimously endorsed his candidacy, and the incumbent, Richard T. Lightfoot, discreetly settled on retirement. It looked as though the 1909 election would be vastly different from the 1905 affair when the sheriff challenged Lightfoot. The candidates descended to an unenlightened level of activity, literally playing tug-of-war with the auditor's books while attempting to prove each other guilty of malfeasance. Despite Lightfoot's victory, more than a few voters acquired the unshakable notion that the last part of Lightfoot's name ought to be changed to reflect a different appendage.[8]

While Lightfoot and local Democrats embraced his candidacy, Barkley soon discovered his good fortune to be a mixed blessing. On the one hand, he would not face opposition in the primary. On the other, being described as a "faithful" and "regular" party member meant being adopted by an organization that exuded a foul odor from its lengthy and unchallenged tenure in county affairs. The precariousness of Barkley's position did not become fully apparent until spring 1909, when the roof over the heads of the courthouse ring cracked. In May, the circuit court grand jury handed down a twenty-count indictment against County Clerk Smedley, who had been embezzling property tax monies. His folly was that he had actually provided receipts to property owners for funds he had kept. When the sheriff visited these supposedly delinquent taxpayers, they produced the receipts, ultimately leading the authorities back to Smedley.[9]

By the time of Smedley's arrest, his mind flitted along in a state of imperfect euphoria caused by what contemporaries called *toxic insanity,* a euphemism for *drug addiction.* Smedley had been stealing incautiously to support his habit but carefully enough that Barkley had uncovered losses of only $1,582.50, which the county had recovered from the bonding company that insured Smedley. To Barkley's horror, however, a full audit found a $6,000 shortage that could be traced to the felonious county clerk and $10,000 in additional pilfering by other Democratic officials.[10]

His conviction meant jail time for Smedley at the Eddyville State Penitentiary, but the developments surrounding it nearly meant death for Barkley's fledgling political career. No matter what disclaimers he might make, Barkley had been elected on the same ticket with a felon and endorsed by the same party that had failed to explain why it had not exposed the loss of vast sums of money in the county coffers it controlled. He ignored the predicament completely in his memoirs, writing only: "At the next election I was nominated and elected to the office of county judge."[11]

This single sentence illustrates the posthumous guerrilla war Barkley has waged against would-be biographers. This particular ambush has led at least two scholars and numerous commentators to declare that he ran unopposed in 1909. The Republicans, however, were neither so weak nor so witless as Barkley would have us believe. Paducah Republicans watched like gleeful vultures as the local press inflicted new wounds on the bloodied and weakened courthouse ring. For the first time since Union troops left the city following the Civil War, the Grand Old Party had a serious chance to capture the county government, and the Republicans knew it.[12]

City Republicans chose Thomas N. Hazelip to run against Barkley. In many ways, Hazelip's life mirrored that of his opponent. Born the same year as Barkley, Hazelip grew up in rural Kentucky, attended a small sectarian college in Bowling Green, read law, entered the bar, and set up practice in Paducah. Contemporaries perceived him as a forward-looking individual, and, indeed, he would later be a reform-minded mayor of

Paducah and chairman of the First District committee of the Progressive (Bull Moose) Party. Like Barkley, he had added his name to the rolls of numerous organizations, including some in which Barkley also held membership. What distinguished the Republican from the Democrat was the former's limited political experience, a point that was not necessarily negative in view of the county's political mismanagement. Significantly, Hazelip had been a federal tax agent since 1904 and understood the importance of a good audit.[13]

When they met for the first of a series of debates on October 2, 1909, Hazelip delivered a verbal thrashing that Barkley would long remember. The Republican lumped Barkley with the courthouse ring and called the Smedley affair only the tip of the iceberg. In fact, new allegations against Lightfoot had surfaced. Thrown on the defensive, Barkley offered only the feeble counter that he had nothing to do with the corruption and those who had perpetrated it. Hazelip responded that his opponent had been elected on a corrupt party ticket and urged that the entire courthouse clique be swept out of office.[14]

Realizing that he was in a fight, Barkley made sure he would not be handled so roughly again. He sharpened his oratorical skills and tried to ensure appreciative audiences for future debates by using the county clerk candidate Gus Singleton as a de facto cheerleader. He also decided to lean more heavily on his record. Humility aside, he had been recognized by Democrats and Republicans alike as the moral leader of the political community. Not only could he state that he had obeyed the law, but he also thundered home his genuine accomplishments in helping save the county money, lowering the levy, eliminating the road debt, and financing the sinking fund. He also turned the linkage tables on Hazelip, dredging up the decade-old Goebel affair, which had haunted Republicans across the state. Disassociation was Barkley's point, however, as he declared that Hazelip was no more responsible for William Goebel's assassination than he himself was for Smedley's nefarious activities. He opined that Hazelip's attempt to link him to Smedley's deeds was "enough to disgust decent people."[15]

This strategy proved wise. Republicans claimed five of the eight traditionally Democratic magistrate seats on the fiscal court, but Barkley effectively avoided the taint that fell on his fellow local party members and won by a comfortable margin, 3,184–2,662. He edged Hazelip in the Paducah precincts and handily swept the farm vote. It was a stunning victory in what was clearly a local Republican year and marked Barkley, who turned thirty-three in the weeks between the election and when he took office, as a rising political force.[16]

While Barkley mentioned nothing about the election in his autobiography, he gleefully recounted his first official duty. After he was sworn in on January 3, 1910, his campaign compatriot Singleton, the county clerk, ushered him into the courtroom, where his eyes widened on seeing every other courthouse employee and a dozen friends waiting for him. In the center of this mixed group stood a sheepish couple nervously fingering some sort of document. Before Barkley had a chance to understand his predicament, someone handed him the text for a civil marriage, and the man who had just taken an oath of office found himself stumbling through the vows. Traditionally, county judges ended such ceremonies with a sermonette. Considering the near state of shock in which Barkley found himself and the extraordinary number and mirthful demeanor of the "witnesses," it was all he could do to wheeze inaudibly one or two words of advice before shutting the text and shouting, "You're Married!"[17]

Barkley's half-humorous, half-disastrous initiation serves to illustrate the diversity of his new duties. County judges only occasionally exercised a strictly judicial function and then primarily for lesser offenders and juvenile delinquents. Since the judge administered estates, appointed workers, inspected the prison, and handled a dozen other tasks connected with the operation of government, a more accurate title would have been *judge-executive,* as the position later came to be known.[18]

Leading the fiscal court was chief among those new duties. The events of the previous year and the Republican majority among the magistrates dictated a new approach, and the newly minted judge's operating procedures differed significantly from the methods of his predecessor. Barkley established the tone for his administration at the first meeting on January 7, delivering what can be described only as a state-of-the-county address. Unlike many presidents in their State of the Union messages to Congress, Barkley made his agenda clear and easily understandable, recommending debt reduction, road improvements, appointment of a county purchasing agent, private contracts for roadwork, court review of all claims, and an annual audit of county books. All but one of these recommendations would receive favorable action during his time in office.[19]

Barkley's administration was the most vigorous and effective the county had witnessed and also included the appointment of a county inspector of weights and measures and the elevation of almshouse keeper to a salaried position. The latter stroke effectively removed the job from the onerous and pervasive system of fees, which accounted for the pay of many county workers, and essentially created an early form of the professional social worker. All these measures were passed in Barkley's first twelve months despite the Republican majority among the magistrates.[20]

Barkley counted the single strike against this otherwise excellent record as an asset. The administration neglected to reduce the debt in favor of pushing for road improvements. The push to widen and gravel each county road eclipsed the other elements of his program to become the distinguishing characteristic of his administration, if not its mania. In the campaign, he had pledged to farmers that road improvements would be made without the forced corvée. Road contracts gave farmers the opportunity to volunteer their labor for pay, and the county gained excellent roads from semiprofessional crews eager to do the work. The political double play that Barkley initiated put extra money in the pockets of those constituents most faithful to him and gave McCracken County's rural residents easy access to Paducah's markets, products, and cultural benefits.[21]

By championing good roads, Barkley repaid a debt to the farmers as well as to the memory of his youth, when he had worked on road crews in Hickman County, but the cost involved illustrated a less attractive side to his administration. By the end of the first year, the county was heavily in debt, a fiscal problem that defied solution during his reign. The lack of money meant that other programs had to be cut back or eliminated. For example, Barkley refused to provide textbook monies for the children of indigent families.[22]

Barkley also left himself open to charges of nepotism by naming his father as the juvenile court probation officer. "I hesitated to make the appointment," Barkley later explained, "because I didn't want to make the Judge's office a family matter, although I knew that my father was well qualified by character, ability, and experience." Evidence suggests that John Barkley, who could draw on the background of raising eight children, performed credibly in the position. Apparently, he also enjoyed the opportunity to be a part of the courthouse action as Alben's youngest brother noted: "Papa would have liked to be in politics more than he was."[23]

Just as John Barkley was settling into his new job, his eldest son decided to seek work elsewhere. Any biographer would be perplexed on which side of the ledger, debits or credits, to place Alben Barkley's decision. Obviously he had ambition, and perhaps he felt that he had exhausted the possibilities of the post of county judge. Ironically, he loved the title, and friends continued for years to address him as Judge Barkley. Yet one month short of his second anniversary in office, December 14, 1911, he told the press that he planned to enter the Democratic primary as a candidate for the First District seat in Congress.[24]

By engaging in the dangerous game of reading the future into the past, it is plausible to speculate that Barkley had made up his mind early in public life to make Congress a milestone, if not the capstone, of his political career. Within the context of this scenario, the incumbent, Ollie M. James, was merely a catalyst in precipitating Barkley's plans when the former publicly announced his intention to seek a Senate seat. Several other circumstances helped shape the decision, however. Congressional seats did not come open often as incumbents traditionally stayed in Washington for several terms. James had served four before deciding to declare for the Senate when Thomas H. Paynter chose not to seek reelection, so Barkley might have had to wait a decade or more for another opportunity if he did not seize this one. The thought of succeeding James also had to appeal to Barkley, who counted the "Marion Giant" (six feet, six inches tall and three hundred pounds) among his heroes. A "magnetic speaker," James would be chosen to give a central address at the 1912 Democratic national convention and had chaired the state delegations at the 1904 and 1908 conventions. Barkley had the growing regional prominence to be considered as a possible successor and, indeed, had been mentioned as such by the Paducah press as early as February 1911 after only a year as county judge.[25]

Barkley was seen as a strong contender for the seat, but a political miscalculation nearly cost him the race. Joseph E. Robbins, a Mayfield lawyer who had ably served Graves County at various times as its state representative and a county and circuit judge, also announced early, and he and Barkley seemed sufficiently formidable in voter appeal to ward off the challenge of even the most foolhardy office seeker. Robbins encountered health and financial problems, however, and in March 1912 decided to withdraw. He confided this news to Barkley and made the generous offer to allow his opponent to name the moment for the announcement. The sagacious move would have been to ask Robbins to hold the secret for as long as possible, at least until much closer to the August primary, in order to keep other challengers out of the field. On impulse, however, Barkley told Robbins that he could make the news public immediately, and, within thirty days of the March 23 announcement, three notable contenders had entered the field: Jacob Corbett, judge of Ballard County; John K. Hendrick, Barkley's former employer and mentor, who had preceded James in Congress; and Denny Smith, the commonwealth's attorney for Trigg County, who had the backing of the state Democratic machine in Frankfort.[26]

Barkley's early entry into the race turned out to be his saving grace. He had already committed to stand on the platform shaped during the 1908 presidential campaign by the national party and its nominee, William Jennings Bryan. So far and so quickly had he moved away from the gold bug–conservative wing toward the populist-progressive one between 1902 and 1908 that during the latter year he had spearheaded the formation of Bryan Clubs throughout the First District. Before his new challengers entered the race, he had already claimed two key issues dear to farmers' hearts: lowering the tariff and lowering the boom on railroads through stricter regulation by the Interstate Commerce Commission.[27]

It also helped that Barkley was the only progressive among the four. Corbett, Hendrick, and Smith echoed each other's conservative views, allowing Barkley to stand apart from the crowd. This distinction became more evident during June and July, when the four candidates decided to save expenses by campaigning together. In rented cars or buggies, they bounced around the countryside exchanging barbs when in front of audiences and swapping jokes while on the road. What made the chemistry interesting was the volatile relationship between Barkley and Hendrick. The Colonel seemed genuinely irked that his former office boy stood for everything that he himself adamantly opposed, including prohibition. "Why, if you elect him," the chubby and perspiring Hendrick exclaimed at one engagement, "next thing you know he'll be asking you to send him to the Senate." The charge of ambition rang true in the case of Barkley, but the wrong person had sounded the alarm. Barkley freely admitted his ambition, then quickly countered that Hendrick had run for a wide variety of posts himself. "The good colonel will run for anything not nailed down or locked up," crowed Barkley. "Why, when the Pope died some years ago, nobody would tell Hendrick, for fear he would declare for that office." The jibe was a political masterstroke as Barkley spun the taint of ambition back on his opponent and at the same time reminded listeners of Hendrick's flippant disregard for religion, a point on which newspapers were already criticizing him.[28]

The thirty-four-year-old Barkley preemptively defused the age issue, declaring early in the campaign that his relative youthfulness gave him the necessary zest to fulfill the arduous duties of Congress. Hendrick's castigation of Barkley because of his membership in Woodmen of the World also backfired. Hendrick claimed that Barkley's involvement with the organization was solely for the purpose of political advancement. Even if it was, Barkley took his obligations to the group seriously, and even during the campaign he made himself available to deliver funeral orations over the graves of deceased members of the order. These actions smacked of sanctimoniousness to Hendrick, but, while railing against Barkley, the Colonel slipped in an attack on the fraternal order, outraging the estimated five thousand First District voters who were fellow Woodmen.[29]

In short, Hendrick was as clumsy in public as Barkley was clever. Moreover, fate struck a blow for Barkley in the midst of the debates. While his opponents chided him for his liberal views and cast him as a socialist for his advocacy of federal support for road construction, Democrats convened in Baltimore at the end of June and, after bitter and lengthy debates and numerous ballots, selected the progressive T. Woodrow Wilson as their presidential nominee. The national platform reflected Barkley's positions and included a plank calling for federal monies for roads. Adroitly, Barkley converted the accusation of socialism into evidence of party regularity, which made his opponents appear to be unfaithful Democrats who existed in a netherworld beyond the party's limits.[30]

Rain and clouds dampened and darkened the primary, August 3, 1912. Political pundits speculated that the miserable weather proved a boon to Barkley. Presumably his rural friends, the farmers, had nothing better to do than go to the polls and vote for the farmer's son. Climatic conditions made little difference, however, as Barkley nearly matched the combined total of his three opponents, taking 48.2 percent of the vote. The three counties in which he had lived, Graves, Hickman, and McCracken, contributed 67 percent of their support. It was a spectacular victory and launched what would prove to be a spectacular four decades of national-level public service. There were still many more chapters to be written in Alben Barkley's career, but the six years that took him from courthouse to Congress were an important formative period, honing the skills, developing the instincts, and defining many of the issues that would serve him well in the years to come.[31]

5

Congressman Barkley and the New Freedom

Because Alben W. Barkley ran unopposed in November's general election, the August primary decided the victor for Kentucky's First District seat in the US House of Representatives. The winner, however, received a quick lesson on the high expectations for patronage from a number of constituents. He acquired, for example, a bumper crop of letter requests for postmaster appointments. One individual started a petition campaign as early as October. Barkley could only shake his head. The Democratic nominee for president, Woodrow Wilson, had to win the November 1912 election and be inaugurated in March 1913 before he could be in a position to consider a Barkley recommendation on a postal appointment. Moreover, to Barkley's deep regret, the nation's current leader, President William Howard Taft, had recently sliced a juicy piece out of the patronage plum. He placed all fourth-class postmasters, the ones most common in Kentucky's First District, under the Civil Service, thus guaranteeing that such postmasters would continue to be Republicans no matter which party captured the White House in 1913.[1]

Fortunately, the early supplications regarding and complications introduced by patronage were accompanied in equal measure by correspondence of a different nature. Barkley enjoyed reading congratulatory letters from friends and admirers who apparently sought only to express their good wishes without hinting at the hope for a government job. From the standpoint of the congressman-elect, the most valued message came from the Mayfield lawyer J. C. Dean. Marvin College's former copresident had played a major role in granting a tuition-free education to Barkley in return for his janitorial services. Additionally, Barkley received a nice note from the man he would replace in Congress, Ollie M. James. Kentucky's senator-elect not only applauded the Paducah politician's victory but also offered to show him around the nation's capital and reveal the inner political workings of Capitol Hill. Finally, House speaker Champ (J. Beauchamp) Clark sent a kind letter. In it he respectfully asked Barkley to consider supporting his reelection to the speakership.[2]

Barkley enthusiastically promised his vote to Speaker Clark. The Kentucky-born Missouri representative reciprocated by going out of his way to assist Barkley during his first sessions in Congress. Over time, however, the new congressman appreciated one of the many undercurrents that operated in the House of Representatives. Tension existed between the speaker and the occupant of the White House. Clark had competed for and lost his bid to be the party's presidential nominee at the June 1912 Democratic national convention. An old-time warhorse with a consistent progressive record, he had nearly twice as many delegates committed to his candidacy as did Woodrow Wilson when the Baltimore meeting first opened. In the midst of the forty-six ballots it took to select a nominee, William Jennings Bryan, the populist and three-time Democratic candidate for president, shifted his support to the governor of New Jersey. The defection left Clark bitterly disappointed as it subsequently prompted Wilson to nominate Bryan for the post of US secretary of state.[3]

There would be times in the awkward Wilson-Clark relations when the speaker would hold back his support from, and occasionally attack, the president's legislative recommendations. Such situations proved uncomfortable for Barkley. He valued Clark's friendship but admired Wilson. "I came to revere him," he admitted decades later, "as the greatest statesman and greatest president under whom I served." (Well, so much for Franklin D. Roosevelt and Harry S. Truman. The also-rans must have been the Republicans Warren G. Harding, J. Calvin Coolidge, and Herbert C. Hoover.) A Virginian by birth, Wilson graduated from Princeton University, studied law at the University of Virginia, and completed a Ph.D. at Johns Hopkins University. His doctoral dissertation, published as *Congressional Government,* thoughtfully and thoroughly analyzed the federal lawmaking process. It earned him prestigious teaching positions that brought him back to Princeton University as professor of jurisprudence and political economy. His outstanding reputation as a writer and lecturer won him the presidency of Princeton in 1902.[4]

Eight years later Wilson was nominated to run as a Democrat for the position of governor of New Jersey and won the election. He gained favorable national attention by his effective leadership in securing forward-looking legislation. As a knowledgeable but recent politician, however, he entered the Democratic gathering in Baltimore as the darkest of dark horses. His competition to be the party's standard-bearer in 1912 included not only Clark but other, more experienced men, especially Oscar W. Underwood of Alabama, who chaired the powerful House Ways and Means Committee. On the forty-sixth ballot, Bryan was joined by Underwood and his bloc, coupled with boss-controlled delegations, to nominate Wilson—one of the most extraordinary upsets in convention politics. The victor faced a badly split Republican Party. In June GOP regulars picked Taft for a second term; party rebels endorsed Theodore Roosevelt, the twenty-sixth president, to lead the Progressive (Bull Moose) Party in August. On the surface, with a divided Republican Party, it might seem that Wilson had been handed the keys to the White House before the November election.[5]

On the other hand, in early August, when Roosevelt won the third-party nomination, the future results of the upcoming election actually looked hazy at best. Roosevelt had been a popular president (1901–1909) who sang the song of New Nationalism in 1912. In his mind, the nation's chief executive should serve as the steward of public welfare. The federal government would encourage, though regulate, huge corporations as it protected workers. Taken to its logical extreme, New Nationalism would center economic power in Washington. By contrast, Wilson was essentially a states'-rights Jeffersonian who simply lacked his opponent's unified and labeled vision. Late in August, as his campaign sputtered, Wilson met the progressive Louis D. Brandeis, who opposed special privilege in the tradition of Thomas Jefferson. After consulting with the attorney, Wilson's ideas coalesced around the federal government dismantling monopolistic corporations while encouraging entrepreneurs and strengthening small businesses. Hence Wilson's New Freedom program touted economic democracy as a means of preserving and enhancing political democracy.[6]

With an approach that appealed to Democratic progressives and even to some Republicans, Wilson captured more votes than either of his opponents. The very nature of the three-way race handed him a landslide victory in the Electoral College when he won forty of forty-eight states. During his inaugural address on the Capitol steps on March 4, 1913, the twenty-eighth president suggested in general terms the direction his administration would take. He hoped to reform the tariff, address banking and currency issues, improve agriculture through efficiency, science, and business, and deal with those industries that restrict the liberty of labor and exploit, without renewing, natural resources. He noted forcefully: "There can be no equality or opportunity, the first essential in the body politic, if men, women and children be not shielded in their lives, their very vitality, from the consequences of great industrial and social processes which they can not alter, control, or singly cope with. Society must see to it that it does not itself crush or weaken or damage its own constituent parts."[7]

The same day Wilson delivered his inaugural address and took the presidential oath of office, Barkley was sworn in to Congress. To save money, Dorothy and the children remained in Paducah at their home on Jefferson Street. It was John Barkley who accompanied his son to Washington and witnessed the swearing-in ceremony. The pair stayed in the Congress Hotel. With Speaker Clark's help, Alben arranged to have his father appointed as the official doorkeeper of the US House of Representatives. The position kept John near his son and at the center of the country's political life. He could never have asked for anything more. Alben's sister Ima remembered: "When Papa and Alben were both in Washington, we were all so happy. . . . [John] enjoyed Washington. He was in love with all the buildings there, and especially the Capitol." The father was good company for the son, but Alben missed his wife and children. He was horrified to discover that his daughter Laura Louise, just a toddler, did not seem to recognize him when he returned to Paducah after the first congressional session.[8]

As a result, Alben and Dorothy felt that they had to make an adjustment in their living arrangements. Fortunately, Barkley earned a congressional salary of $7,500 a year. It was, for 1913, a handsome sum of money and gave the family the option of moving to Washington. They kept the home in Paducah and asked Clarence Sherrill, the president of the Sherrill-Russell Lumber Company of Paducah, to look after the house and yard in their absence. The family traveled home by train to the First District as often as possible to make certain that friends, neighbors, and constituents would keep Alben in mind every two years on election day. In Washington, the Barkleys resided briefly in the Congress Hotel and then the Burlington Hotel before moving to an apartment not far from Capitol Hill on Fourteenth Street. During the latter portion of Barkley's service in the House of Representatives, they moved to an apartment at 1760 Euclid Avenue near Rock Creek Park shortly after the family acquired its first automobile, a Dodge touring car, in 1917. No matter when congressional sessions started or ended, the family soon chose to remain in the capital city from September to June to give the children the educational stability of attending the same school for the full duration of each academic year.[9]

Meanwhile, in March 1913, Congress absorbed Barkley's life. His first task was to prepare a rank ordering of his preferences for committee assignments. Naturally, because Kentucky's First District was surrounded by or contained the Cumberland, Mississippi, Ohio, and Tennessee Rivers, his first choice went to the Rivers and Harbors Committee. After a pleasant discussion with and earnest encouragement by Georgia representative William C. Adamson, chair of the Interstate and Foreign Commerce (after 1981 the Energy and Commerce) Committee, Barkley indicated the latter as his second choice. It turned out that his second choice became his first and only assignment. Interstate and Foreign Commerce enjoyed the high status of one of twelve exclusive committees, the work of which was considered so important that members held no other post. Indeed, it served as the centerpiece for several key legislative measures during the two Wilson administrations. And Barkley enhanced his reputation in Congress by his devoted work and effective contributions. Three years later, Adamson conveyed to Barkley his admiration: "I cannot refrain from expressing to you my appreciation of your faithful and able assistance during your entire service on our Committee. . . . Too much cannot be said in your praise."[10]

One immediate, personal benefit to Barkley's membership on the exclusive committee was his association and then lifelong friendship with Sam T. Rayburn of Texas. Twenty-seven years later, the Tennessee-born Rayburn served as House speaker. In 1913, Barkley and Rayburn were 2 of 114 freshmen Democrats, many of whom credited the head of the ticket, Wilson, with contributing to their electoral triumphs. The large number of new faces helped confirm the party's dominance over Congress. In the House, there were 291 Democrats to 127 Republicans plus 17 third-party representatives; the Senate contained 51 Democrats and 44 Republicans plus 1 member of the Progressive Party. It must be understood, however, that congressmen of both parties traversed the political spectrum from Left to Right. Regardless, House majority leader Underwood held a commanding position as chair of both the Ways and Means Committee and the Committee on Committees. He exercised power over legislation through the Democratic caucus. A 1909 party rule stipulated that, when two-thirds of the Democratic congressmen approved a measure, it would bind the support of all caucus members on the House floor unless they recused themselves because of prior pledges made to constituents or earnestly believed the measure did not adhere to the US Constitution.[11]

The importance of party cannot be emphasized enough in the Wilson era. There were several times when the Democratic caucus approved legislation that was passed one day later by the House. On such occasions, no more than a dozen or so Democrats voted against the bill. In fact, it was not unknown for Democrats to exclude Republicans from the deliberations of standing and conference committees. While Wilson may have initially entertained thoughts of attracting support from selected GOP senators and representatives, he quickly saw the advantage of keeping in close touch with Democratic lawmakers. Indeed, in his 1908 *Constitutional Government in the United States,* he expressed his conviction that the president could and should play a dominant role in his party. He noted that, unlike state senators and district representatives, the president was a national figure who exercises leadership by implementing the national will through proposals to the lawmaking part of government. Collectively, these ideas explain why Barkley and his Democratic colleagues on Capitol Hill experienced Wilson's personal attention.[12]

Years later, Barkley's second wife, Jane, described her husband's first consultation with the president through the colorful image of a college freshman seeking the advice of a highly regarded professor. That word picture is charming but unrealistic. Both men, not just Barkley, were freshmen in terms of their elected offices, and both were modestly experienced politicians eager to succeed in their new positions. Wilson wanted Barkley's vote for his New Freedom program; Barkley wanted legislation favorable to his constituents as well as patronage that employed his more vocal supporters. In short, both hoped to be reelected. From Barkley's vantage point, the good news occurred when Wilson made it clear that he would always try to accept the congressman's recommendation for patronage appointments in Kentucky's First District. The bad news was that Wilson would not overturn President Taft's initiative to place fourth-class postmasters under the Civil Service.[13]

The Pendleton Civil Service Act of 1883 gave the president discretionary powers to expand the number of job categories that would be removed from patronage and placed under the US Civil Service Commission. Since the time of Chester A. Arthur, several presidents selectively exercised these powers to shield some appointees from political removal. Wilson doubted from a legal standpoint that such powers could reverse the process. Moreover, it would be bad form to try. Senator George H. Pendleton of Ohio had been a fellow Democrat. Importantly, Wilson and most knowledgeable Americans of both political parties recognized the Pendleton Civil Service Act as a significant, positive reform that anticipated the later progressive movement. The legislation was designed to improve government so that it could better serve the nation's citizens by hiring competent employees on the basis of merit and examination, not party membership. Wilson could only offer to make certain that future fourth-class postmaster candidates would take an exam. First District demographics alone would likely guarantee the future appointment of a Democrat. If in 1913 the president could not offer immediate patronage help to Barkley, he nonetheless saved him from a serious dilemma two years later.[14]

Early in 1915, the Mayfield, Kentucky, post office had an opening under the patronage system. It should have been a golden opportunity for Barkley to make one of his boosters very happy. Unfortunately, not one but ten prominent Barkley supporters sought and expected to receive the recommendation to President Wilson for the job. The congressman faced a serious predicament; he did not want to upset or lose the goodwill of those nine individuals who failed to receive his endorsement. Fortunately, in consultation with Wilson, Barkley discovered that the president favored the candidacy of W. Lindsay Hale, whose sister had married a Princeton University colleague. The congressman and the president worked out a deal. Wilson would appoint Hale but give Barkley a courteous and diplomatic letter that he could share with the nine office seekers who failed to get the position. All nine accepted with grace the president's decision. Barkley, who already knew Wilson to be a fellow Jeffersonian and used, as he did, Sir Isaac Pitman's stenography method, moved from admiring Wilson to considering him his hero.[15]

During the interim, Wilson had kept Barkley and his colleagues on Capitol Hill busy with pressure to pass legislation that implemented his New Freedom program. On the day of his inauguration, the president requested a joint session of Congress. He wanted to encourage the national legislature to approve tariff reform, which had been one of the more important campaign issues of the Democratic Party. In the process, on April 8, 1913, he became the first president since John Adams to deliver his message to Congress in person. Immediately, it has to be pointed out that Barkley had absolutely nothing to do with writing or developing the tariff measure called for by Wilson. It had, in fact, been prepared by the Sixty-Second Congress

(1911–1913) and massaged by the House Ways and Means Committee during the lame-duck session that had adjourned in March 1913. (The Twentieth Amendment to the US Constitution of 1933 not only advanced the presidential inauguration to January 20 but also ended the terms of senators and representatives on the third day of January.) Because the bill came out of Ways and Means, it was identified initially with the name of the committee's chair as the Underwood Tariff.[16]

While Barkley took no part in drafting the tariff bill, he joined several other new congressmen who had been asked by Oscar Underwood to speak in favor of the lower tariff legislation on the House floor on April 24. Ollie James made the event special when he slipped out of the Senate chamber to listen to the maiden speech of his First District replacement. Barkley chose not to dwell in his address on how a lower tariff might generate revenue for foreign countries that could, in turn, facilitate the purchase of US products such as dark tobacco from his district. Instead, his thirty-minute talk focused on the tariff as a tax. The tax raised revenue for the federal government as it raised prices on consumer goods. To be sure, tariffs originally protected America's infant industries against foreign competition. But Barkley noted that over time the tariff continued to increase long after infant industries had become giants. It enabled privileged classes that controlled industrial giants that had no competition to charge more for their products and thus expand their wealth to the "detriment of the unfavored masses."[17]

Barkley, the partisan Jeffersonian Democrat, could not resist identifying Republicans as belonging to the party of privilege. They were the ones responsible for raising beyond reason taxes on imported goods. Conveniently, he forgot to mention that the Republican Payne-Aldrich Tariff of 1909 did feature some reductions; however, it also deceitfully raised rates on hundreds of items. The trick used was the ad valorem tax. It avoided charging a duty on discrete items like hammers, shirts, or wines; instead, the amount of the tax on each product varied on the basis of its value. And Barkley absolutely turned the Payne-Aldrich free list into a clever joke: "When the people have asked for free lumber in order that they might build humble houses in which to abide, the Republicans have responded by placing acorns upon the free list. . . . When we have implored them to give us cheaper beef and pork, they have responded by placing hoofs and horns upon the free list. When we have asked for cheaper clothing so that we might protect ourselves from the winter's chill, they have cheerfully responded with free rags."[18]

Besides having fun at the expense of the opposition, Barkley acquired over time a reputation as one of the great storytellers of Congress. He had a funny tale in some of his formal and most of his informal talks whether in the House or on the hustings. His first speech followed that pattern. He told the one about a Kentuckian from Christian County who had married a young lady but ended up living with his wealthy in-laws. He borrowed money and a team of mules and went west with his bride to establish a farm and an independent life. Unfortunately, his efforts in Colorado and Kansas failed. Returning to Kentucky and the home of his in-laws, he wrote on the side of the wagon the reasons for returning:

> Colorado irrigation,
> Kansas winds and conflagration,
> High tariff and taxation,
> Bill Taft's administration,
> Roosevelt's vociferation,
> Hell-fire and damnation,
> Bring me back to my wife's relations.

Barkley repeated this story in his memoirs but forgot to tell the reader the punch line or why he included it in his maiden address before the House of Representatives, in favor of the Underwood-Simmons Tariff Act. "I trust," he concluded, "that I am not incorrect in assuming that something of the same feeling actuated the American people and caused them to return to the fold of the Democratic Party where 'equal rights to all and special privileges to none' shall be the motto. [Applause on the Democratic side.]"[19]

To be honest, although Barkley's speech was well received by Democrats, it was not crucial in any sense to the passage of the bill. It simply set the pattern for his future presentations. The lopsided control of the House by his party allowed the measure to be approved on May 8 by an equally lopsided vote of 281–139. In the Senate, where Democrats held only a small majority, things did not go so smoothly. Several Democratic senators balked at first at putting sugar and wool on the free list. They threatened to join Republicans in defeating the legislation. Once that issue was resolved, Republican senators leisurely debated and argued against the bill. Finally, under the leadership of Democratic senator Furnifold M. Simmons of North Carolina, chair of the Senate Finance Committee, the Senate approved the measure by a vote of 44–37 on September 9. The bill then went to conference committee to resolve differences between the House and the Senate versions. Since the final product of the two chambers reduced the tariff's overall rate from around 38 percent to 30 percent, it thereby reduced federal revenue. Hence, the Underwood-Simmons Tariff Act also authorized a graduated income tax of 1–6 percent on incomes above $3,000. The tax was based on the recently ratified Sixteenth Amendment to the US Constitution.[20]

At the White House a little after nine o'clock in the evening of October 3, 1913, President Wilson signed the tariff bill into law. Simultaneously, the US Treasury Department sent telegrams to customs collectors throughout the country that put the new tariff rates and the free list into operation. Surrounded by Democratic legislators, including Barkley, Wilson delivered an extemporaneous talk. He claimed that the new tariff accomplished a great service for the American people but that the next step must be banking and currency reform. Already he had introduced that topic in a second visit to Congress on June 23. Three days later, Democrats Carter Glass (VA) and Robert L. Owen (OK) introduced legislation in the House and the Senate, respectively, starting the president's second phase of reform. Signed into law by Wilson two days before Christmas 1913, the Glass-Owen Federal Reserve Act created twelve Federal Reserve banks. The Federal Reserve banks rediscounted loans of member banks via Federal Reserve notes that enabled those member banks to make additional loans. The act also expanded money supply and bank credit. Moreover, it allowed the governing Federal Reserve Board to control currency inflation by raising or lowering the rediscount rate.[21]

These two major pieces of legislation demonstrated for Barkley and many Americans the strong leadership exercised by the president, who clearly dominated the Democratic Party. The party's unity of purpose and, hence, success was a lesson learned by Barkley. As with the debate on the tariff, he participated in the debate on the House floor in support of the Federal Reserve System. In September, his second speech showed his keen ability to master the complex issues found in the bill. He applauded especially the fact that the proposed legislation placed the commercial paper of farmers on the same basis as that of merchants and manufacturers. It would allow some expansion of agricultural credit. Barkley argued that even more and direct credit should be opened to farmers in the future. Wilson had endorsed that idea in the spring when he appointed the Rural Credits Commission. Chair of that group, Democratic senator Duncan U. Fletcher of Florida, played a significant part in framing a bill. With the enthusiastic backing of Barkley and other rural legislators, the Federal Farm Loan Bank Act was eventually approved and then signed into law by Wilson on July 17, 1916.[22]

Meanwhile, the final leg of the three-legged New Freedom stool was also the centerpiece of the 1912 presidential campaign. Wilson promised to restore freedom and competition among businesses by destroying monopoly. In January 1914, he made yet another presentation to a joint session of Congress inviting its members to take action on antitrust legislation. A number of bills emerged over time, but only two actually crossed Wilson's desk in the White House. The first was the Federal Trade Commission Act of September 26, 1914. In this case, Barkley did more than simply stamp his seal of approval on someone else's work. The Interstate and Foreign Commerce Committee took a small part in preparing the measure. Barkley not only entered in the deliberations but also helped refine the final text of the bill. In reality, the Federal Trade Commission proved to be the cornerstone of Wilson's antitrust program. It replaced the earlier Bureau of Corporations and assumed new powers. It was endowed with the authority to define unfair trade practices and issue cease and desist orders against unfair competition.[23]

On the surface level of slogans and symbols, the Clayton Antitrust Act, drafted by Democratic representative Henry D. Clayton of Alabama, appeared to be decisive legislation for eliminating monopoly. The final product, however, seemed to disappoint most progressives. Even Wilson lost interest in the bill, though he did sign it into law on October 15, 1914. It prohibited price discrimination, interlocking directorates, corporate acquisition of stocks from competing corporations, and "tying agreements" preventing retailers from handling products of competing manufacturers. But Senate conservatives of both parties added phrases that watered down all the prohibitions. Small wonder Wilson considered the Federal Trade Commission to be the key in the antitrust endeavor. Barkley participated in the Clayton bill by joining colleagues who favored farmers and workers and amended the legislation. It would fulfill the 1912 Democratic platform by exempting farm and labor organizations from antitrust laws.[24]

Barkley felt that such farm and labor groups should not be lumped together with huge and powerful corporations that engaged in conspiracies in restraint of trade. The farmer's son plainly demonstrated the impact of heritage on his thinking when he endorsed the rider by stating in conclusion:

So that we may in truth say that this amendment exempting such organizations from the operation of the antitrust law give [sic] to labor and to agriculture what it asks and is entitled to. It recognizes the difference between the man whose only asset is his power to work and the man who seeks to use labor and the products of labor for monopolistic purposes. It recognizes the self-evident truth that all real wealth in the final analysis is produced by those who toil, and that therefore the man who toils and eats his bread in the sweat of his brow has a moral and legal right to cooperate with others of his fellow men in the same condition for the purpose of mutual help, protection, and improvement not only of the conditions of labor, but for the advancement of the compensation which he receives therefore.[25]

Barkley's speech was remarkable for another reason. It had three distinct parts. The first part summarized in clear language the essence of the Clayton bill. After heartfelt comments on the amendment in the second part, the third listed all the principal measures approved by Congress up to June 1. The tally included the recently enacted Smith-Lever Act, which established the agricultural extension system to aid farmers. To members of his congressional audience, two-thirds of Barkley's address might be viewed as downright silly except for the fact that 1914 was an election year. The speech, publicized as a news release in the First District, was in fact Barkley's campaign speech to his constituents, though delivered in print, not in person. The congressman did not visit the First District during primary season even though he had three Democratic opponents. Instead, he sent constituents a form letter. In it he explained in part why he would not be able to get home: "Since my election, Congress has been in almost continuous session, and I have been constantly at my post of duty trying faithfully to represent the interest of the people who have honored me with their votes."[26]

It would be a mistake to think that with an overwhelmingly Democratic district Barkley could afford to take a relaxed, cavalier attitude toward elections. He shrewdly understood the political process and never took votes for granted. He served as his own campaign manager and knew how to gain and keep the positive attention of voters. With secretarial help in Washington, cards for constituents' birthdays, births, and deaths regularly left his office in bundles. He supplied modest financial help to Democratic candidates for county offices in his district. Moreover, he wrote to each county chair of the Democratic Party and secured from each the names and addresses of precinct committeemen so that he could keep in touch with every party worker. He continued active memberships in a dozen charitable and social organizations. When home, he gave talks to various groups and awarded medals for oratorical contests at several schools. Finally, he wrote letters of recommendation for job seekers looking for a position with county or state government. Even when the candidate failed to get the sought-after position, Barkley obtained that person's vote for a lifetime of elections out of gratitude.[27]

Because Barkley spent so much time interacting and communicating with people who voted him into office, he did not always have to expend much effort campaigning across his district in the weeks before an election. The second session of the Sixty-Third Congress had lasted a record-setting 321 days when it ended in mid-October 1914. This is the reason Barkley failed to make a single appearance back home in the period leading up to the August primary. Despite the four-man race to see who would be the Democratic candidate, the incumbent garnered 76 percent of the vote and carried every county in the First District. Barkley did make a few speeches before the November general election, but there was never any doubt over whether he would retain his seat in Congress. As a result, he spent as much time campaigning in Maine for two colleagues as he did in the commonwealth. Adding to his growing reputation as a diligent legislator and good storyteller, Barkley also attracted the attention of congressional leaders for his unselfish support of the party and its candidates, including those outside Kentucky.[28]

The fall of 1914 witnessed not only Barkley's reelection victory but also the end to the New Freedom program. During the previous eighteen months, Congress had been busy and fruitful in one of the most productive sessions in history. Fifty-one resolutions and 354 laws had been approved and signed—though two-thirds of the latter focused on claims and pensions. Most importantly, the national legislature addressed, revised, and reformed the government's approach to tariff, monopoly, and banking and currency. In a letter shared publicly by the White House as a press release, President Wilson informed Secretary of the Treasury William G. McAdoo that the New Freedom program had been fulfilled. As a result the president could predict: "For the future is clear and bright with promise of the best things. While there was agitation and suspicion and distrust and bitter complaint of wrong, groups and classes were at war with one another, did not see that their interests were common, and suffered only when separated and brought into conflict. Fundamental wrongs once righted, as they may now easily and quickly be, all differences will clear away."[29]

The letter only revealed the level of the president's naïveté. Wilson sincerely presumed that the New Freedom legislation would result in cooperation, understanding, and common purpose in America's economic realm. In his view, the ills of the past had been overcome—let the healing begin! Even his highly regarded and generally favorable biographer Arthur S. Link had to shrug his shoulders and admit: "There is little evidence that Wilson had any deep comprehension of the far-reaching social and economic tensions [in the nation]." Many progressives such as Herbert Croly, chief editor of the *New Republic,* expressed puzzlement, if not outright disappointment, over the president's letter. Most progressives considered the New Freedom to be merely a nice beginning. How Barkley felt about the letter is unknown. Decades later, his memoir and interview comments pertaining to Wilson made no reference to the hiatus in the progressive program from November 1914 to January 1916. What he remembered were his pleasant meetings with Wilson and invitation to attend the president's marriage to Edith Bolling Galt on December 18, 1915. As a result, he compressed the fourteen-month period and failed to recognize Wilson's inconsistent support for reform.[30]

Regardless, it must be understood that Barkley played a minor role in the New Freedom agenda. All the legislation approved by Congress would have been signed into law anyway with or without Barkley's presence. But, on the personal level, the New Freedom and Barkley's experiences in Congress had a major impact on his life. Put bluntly, in Wilson he found a hero who strengthened the Kentuckian's partisanship by the very success of the Democratic Party in fulfilling the president's program. At the same time, Barkley gained attention as a hardworking legislator and excellent speaker who salted his presentations with funny stories. Before long, he would seek the chance to deliver talks for pay. During the interim, and on a daily basis, he did something to keep and promote the favorable notice of his constituents. He especially sought and supported bills that helped farmers, who, in turn, kept him in office with their votes. And, throughout it all, his wife and children served as the bedrock foundation on which he could construct a towering political career.[31]

6

The Reformer in Time of War

When Barkley won Kentucky's August 1 primary election, the die was already cast for what would be known as the Great War. The Serbian nationalist Gavrilo Princip assassinated Franz Ferdinand, heir to the throne of the Austro-Hungarian Empire, when the archduke visited Sarajevo on June 28, 1914. The capital of a province illegally absorbed by Austria and ardently desired by Serbia, Sarajevo came to symbolize the nationalism and rivalry that helped ignite the wider madness of horrific battle. The Austrian declaration of war on Serbia, July 28, set into motion the alliance system that pitted the Central Powers of Austria, Germany, and later Turkey against the Allied Powers of Great Britain, France, Russia, and later Italy. Over time, ten other nations joined the conflict, ranging from Japan in the East to the United States in the West. On August 4, after a lengthy cabinet meeting, President Wilson went to an upper room in the White House where his first wife lay dying. As he sat by her side, he wrote a draft proclamation of American neutrality that also offered his offices to European powers as a mediator with the hope of recapturing precious peace.[1]

On August 18, the president followed up his proclamation with an appeal to US citizens to be neutral in thought and deed. While most Americans strongly favored neutrality, few were impartial. One-third of the population, for example, had been born in countries now embroiled in conflict and often took sides. Even Wilson and his key advisers and some cabinet members tended to view the Allied Powers as less a threat to American interests and security than the Central Powers. The strange thing in all this is that the president had expected to center his administration on domestic reform, which he felt qualified to implement. But he soon had to focus much of his time and attention on foreign affairs. Amazingly, he chose to make matters worse when he personally delved into an impossible conundrum across the border in Mexico. He used every conceivable measure, including military force, not once but twice in the premature effort to convert Mexico into a democratic model for all Latin America. Instead, he caused more harm than good by alarming the people of that region with his strident interventionist behavior.[2]

It would be easy to say that Barkley followed Wilson's plea for strict neutrality, but such a comment would be misleading. The reality is something else. True, Barkley attended the 1921 Stockholm conference of the Inter-Parliamentary Union (IPU) and became a member. Founded in the late nineteenth century by the British and the French, the IPU promoted dialogue among legislators of member nations as it sought to employ arbitration to resolve conflicts. Eventually, Barkley served as head of the American delegation that attended annual or semiannual conferences in different capital cities of the world on a rotating basis. It would be a stretch to consider his views on foreign affairs as sophisticated. With experience, however, his knowledge of international relations would reach a high level of understanding. But none of this is true of the congressman in 1914. Barkley expressed few opinions on the eruption of war in Europe and US intervention in Mexico. Indeed, reviewing his life before the start of World War I, there is no period when he could or did devote serious time or travel to the study of foreign cultures.[3]

This does not mean Barkley remained clueless about the impact of the Great War on the United States and specifically on the Jackson Purchase area of Kentucky. Some of his constituents would make him sensitive to the importance of international events. The quick outburst of war disrupted an American economy already weakened by a recession. Stock prices fell, trade with Europe became uncertain, and European investors began liquidating their holdings in the United States. Moreover, the large and powerful British navy ruled the seas, at least on the surface, and used ships and minefields to blockade the Central Powers. Since Germany and Austria normally imported substantial amounts of American cotton, just the thought of a blockade caused the price of cotton to plummet so low it failed to cover the costs of producing the crop. As sales dropped, anguish grew among First District cotton growers as well as in their congressional representative. With other members of Congress from cotton regions, Barkley added his voice to those requesting relief from the Wilson administration in August 1914.[4]

Treasury secretary McAdoo tried to rescue the situation. Through cooperating banks, he created the Cotton Loan Fund. It initially garnered $135 million and used warehouse receipts for stored cotton as collateral for loans to farmers until cotton was sold. To be sure, one can credit the secretary for his efforts, but the loan-receipt system proved unsatisfactory because cotton prices remained depressed. Matters actually worsened on August 20, 1915, when the British government added cotton to its absolute contraband list. The latter prevented even neutral countries near or bordering on Germany (the Netherlands and the Scandinavian countries) from importing American cotton. For instance, it would be all too easy for a Danish merchant to resell US cotton to Germany, which could make the fiber into military uniforms for soldiers who then could kill British troops. Barkley and his cotton constituents were extremely upset. Fortunately, a solution arrived in the form of an Anglo-French commission on September 10. The group negotiated a $500 million loan with several US banks led by J. P. Morgan. A portion of the British funds bought American cotton at the prewar price of ten cents a pound. The distress of farmers and congressmen in cotton-growing states was soon relieved.[5]

In addition to cotton, Barkley expressed his concerns about whether the British or any of the belligerents viewed tobacco products as contraband. It will be remembered that he had helped grow dark tobacco as a youth and that the substance appealed primarily to Europeans. In November 1914, the Kentucky congressman requested an official comment from the State Department on the prospects of exporting the 1914 crop—a statement that he could share with First District tobacco farmers. Secretary of State William Jennings Bryan personally responded to Barkley's inquiry: "So far as the Department has been informed none of the belligerents have listed tobacco as either absolute or conditional contraband of war and apparently no difficulty should be experienced in the exportation of tobacco to any foreign country including the belligerents." Regrettably, the matter changed abruptly on March 11, 1915, when the British Order in Council imposed restrictions on the sale of tobacco (and other products) to neutral countries that resold American goods to Germany and Austria. Like cotton, the price of dark tobacco fell precipitously to a point below production costs.[6]

Barkley could not begin to understand why tobacco would be identified by the British as contraband in wartime. It did not feed, clothe, or arm German and Austrian soldiers. A German private would not be endowed with preternatural vision by chewing dark tobacco from Mayfield, Kentucky, and thus able to shoot accurately and kill quickly a British trooper in a distant trench across no-man's-land on a field in Flanders. The State Department felt the same way about numerous products and lodged a number of complaints. At last, in November 1915, the British government rescinded the embargo and allowed the Netherlands, Denmark, Norway, and Sweden to import US tobacco and even transship it to Britain's enemies. The British change of heart prompted First District dark tobacco farmers to plant and raise in 1916 a bumper crop. At the same time, however, the British began opening private international mail and blacklisting neutral merchants, including Americans, who seemed eager to sell goods to the Central Powers. These pieces of bad news accompanied the August 24, 1916, British decision to place American tobacco on the absolute contraband list once again. The timing was terrible; it occurred near the end of the tobacco-growing season.[7]

Ironically, in the midst of the slump in tobacco sales abroad, Barkley chose to quit smoking. The decision had nothing whatsoever to do with wartime commerce or British-American relations. While he had chewed tobacco only once and hated it, he did enjoy lighting up a pipe, though by the time he became a congressman he had turned to cigars. He observed that Bennett Clark, the House parliamentarian (1914–1917) and son of Speaker Champ Clark, had gained weight. A trim Barkley wanted to match Bennett's girth and discovered that the latter had gained the new, expanded waistline when he stopped smoking. So he followed suit and acquired the weight and rotund figure that characterized his profile to the day he died. Apparently, he viewed a large waist as a measure of success, experience, and/or wisdom. This seems ludicrous today when medical experts unanimously attest that neither smoking nor being overweight promotes good health. And no one now automatically equates a plump physique with accomplishment, maturity, and/or intelligence.[8]

Without any of the medical and legal baggage that tarnishes tobacco in the twenty-first century, in 1916 the smokeless farmer's son felt absolutely free to do everything possible to help voters who grew tons of dark tobacco in the First District. Barkley collaborated on this issue with his Kentucky colleague Senator Ollie M. James. The senator had become a major figure in the Democratic Party. He served as permanent chair of and one of two keynote speakers at the party's national convention held in St. Louis in June. Later, at the end of August, he succeeded in getting the Senate to approve two amendments that he had attached to a general revenue bill. Neither amendment mentioned Great Britain, but both responded to the British addition of tobacco to the absolute contraband list. The first amendment authorized the president to restrict imports from a belligerent that impeded trade in American products. Any US citizen who circumvented the president's decision faced fines of up to $50,000 and prison time of up to two years. The second amendment focused on ships that willingly complied with a belligerent's obstruction of American commerce. Such vessels could be detained by orders of the president. US citizens who assisted floating violators confronted the same financial and prison punishments listed in the first amendment.[9]

On September 6, 1916, Barkley delivered a speech on the House floor that targeted the injustice of the British embargo on tobacco, an embargo that also had the support of the Allies. This time he was all business and deadly serious. He failed to embellish or lighten his presentation with funny tales or cute stories. His sole purpose centered on soliciting House support for the two amendments—he called them *provisions*—that James had added to the Senate's version of the House-initiated revenue bill. Naturally, the two pieces of legislation would have to be reconciled in conference committee before undergoing a final vote by both chambers. Barkley did not want the provisions removed. He explained the unfortunate financial result of the Allied effort to deny tobacco to Germany and Austria by also withholding the product from any country that might transship the leaf to Britain's enemies. He argued that the embargo violated international law since tobacco could not be construed as war contraband. He then impressed House members with the need for adequate compensation for the grower by carefully detailing the numerous, time-consuming steps and hard handwork necessary to produce a successful, small field of marketable tobacco. He finished by stating:

> I hope that when the offending nations stop long enough in their present madness to recognize the justice of our claims they will be prompt to recognize them, so that it will not be necessary to bring into operation and make use of the weapon which we are seeking to place in the hands of the President by the adoption of these provisions. We know that we have justice and equity on our side. I believe that this House realizes that this is true, and I look confidently forward to the overwhelming adoption of these provisions in behalf of millions of American citizens, asking for nothing except the just and righteous privilege of pursuing their honest enterprises with success and freedom. [Applause on the Democratic side.][10]

In one sense, Barkley's speech was in vain, but its failure had nothing to do with the amended legislation. Germany took this exact moment to impose an embargo of its own. For the war's duration, members of the Central Powers smoked or chewed only Turkish tobacco from the Ottoman Empire. One could say farewell to tobacco as absolute contraband on the British list but also good-bye to the German and Austrian markets for American leaf. Nevertheless, it is interesting to note that for the first two years of the war Barkley understood that Great Britain posed the most problems for the export and sale of agricultural products from his Kentucky district. For this reason, he steadfastly endorsed President Wilson's suggestion for a ship purchase bill in the opening months of the conflict. At the time, the United States had only six merchant vessels, which meant that the large British transport fleet carried most of America's seaborne commerce. And, of course, such ships complied fully with London's restrictions on trade with neutrals and belligerents. Barkley and other members of the Interstate and Foreign Commerce Committee prepared the legislation, which the House overwhelmingly approved, 215–121, on February 16, 1915.[11]

The House initiative would have provided up to $30 million to purchase ships. While few individuals in the Wilson administration wanted to discuss the matter publicly, it was understood that the easiest, quickest, and cheapest way to secure a fleet of transports was to buy the half million tons or so of German vessels that remained stuck in US harbors owing to the British blockade. Republicans and some Democrats in the Senate killed the measure. They wanted neither the US government in the otherwise private shipping business nor a dispute with Great Britain. The British considered German ships prizes of war and threatened to seize any German transport purchased by the United States found outside coastal waters. On the other hand, by 1916 London's broad definition of war contraband, open interception of private mail, and expansive blacklist of American merchants prompted Congress to revisit, revise, and approve in 1916 the earlier bill. One day after Barkley's September 6 speech, President Wilson signed the Shipping Act into law. It created the US Merchant Marine and the US Shipping Board. The latter was empowered to acquire via $50 million non-German vessels through the Emergency Fleet Corporation.[12]

The prevalence of international markets for First District farm products makes it easy to appreciate Barkley's support for the Shipping Act as a partial counter to British meddling with America's trade. What may be surprising was his almost total neglect and limited criticism of German behavior on the high seas. Many historians mark a dramatic change in American attitudes with the sinking of the *Lusitania* by a German submarine on May 7, 1915. The deaths of 1,198 passengers and crew, including 128 US citizens, were viewed as a heinous crime. It placed Germans in the category of indefensible outlaws who ignored well-established international rules for naval warfare. Those codes did not include torpedoing without warning unarmed vessels and making no provision to save innocent lives. The British blockade and restrictions caused inconveniences; the German submarine destroyed lives and property. Americans continued to value neutrality, but except for some hyphenates most citizens now favored an Allied victory in the war. Barkley noted that Wilson sharply denounced illegal submarine assaults on unarmed ships in several messages to the German government. And he was pleased that the president enjoyed diplomatic success in securing a German promise not to attack passenger ships.[13]

After another submarine attack on a passenger ship followed the *Lusitania* tragedy, Wilson threatened to terminate diplomatic relations with Germany. Such a break would have been considered a step away from a declaration of war. The Germans answered, not happily, but nevertheless with a pledge to uphold international law for all merchant vessels even in their submarine war zone around the British Isles. Wilson gained a second diplomatic victory without embroiling the United States in war. During Barkley's speech of September 6, 1916, an opponent sought to deflect the discussion away from the British and toward the Germans by revisiting the *Lusitania* incident. Barkley responded: "I do not care to inject a discussion concerning the *Lusitania* case in my remarks upon the tobacco situation, but I will answer the gentleman by saying that the President has held Germany to strict account on account of the sinking of the *Lusitania,* and he obtained from Germany recognition of our rights under international law without mustering in a single soldier and without spilling a drop of blood. [Applause on the Democratic side.]"[14]

All things considered, it is not obvious that Barkley ever gave serious thought to which side started the war, which side was right or wrong, or which side might hinder or advance American interests and security by winning the war. In short, he played the perfect neutral sought by Wilson when he asked citizens not to think or act in a way to favor one set of belligerents over the other. Hence, he reacted to the cotton and tobacco embargoes not because he hoped the British would lose the war but only because they were interfering with the export to Europe of First District goods. In this sense, he mimicked the Wilson administration, which publicly berated British impediments to American commerce. Indeed, in 1916 it seemed possible for a disinterested observer to ponder whether, if the United States entered the war, it would fight the Allied or the Central Powers. This was especially true from November 1916 through January 1917, when, on top of British blacklists, mail violations, and trade restrictions, London proved unresponsive to the peace moves sponsored by both Washington and Berlin.[15]

While Barkley aligned himself perfectly with Wilson in terms of the war, he did not follow him in taking more than a year's vacation from reform. On December 22, 1914, a little over a month after Wilson's famous letter to Treasury secretary McAdoo announcing the completion of the administration's progressive program, Barkley spoke and voted in favor of the Hobson resolution. Offered by Representative Richmond P. Hobson of Alabama, the measure called for the addition to the US Constitution of an amendment prohibiting the manufacture, transportation, sale, and consumption of alcoholic beverages. Even though it received a majority vote, 197–190, the resolution failed to secure the necessary two-thirds majority. Thus, it died in the House. In retrospect, it is understandable why many Americans would question the progressive nature of the Barkley-supported legislation. The current attitude about the issue has been captured adroitly by Thomas R. Pegram in *Battling Demon Rum*. "Prohibition," he notes, "once the shining goal of reform aspirations, slipped into popular memory as a laughable and embarrassing episode in misdirected zeal."[16]

Indeed, the Prohibition era left a sorry history of a well-intentioned reform gone wrong. Between the Eighteenth Amendment of 1919 and its repeal by the Twenty-First Amendment of 1933, millions of Americans broke the law on a daily basis. What rumrunners failed to bring into the country illegally was distilled by hundreds of bootleggers. They often supplied speakeasies under the protection of police and local authorities corrupted by payoffs. Because groups dealing in illegal liquor often became territorial in operating and/or supplying "retail" outlets, gang-related violence erupted in larger cities, especially Chicago and New York, all too often turning streets into battlegrounds with brutality, gunplay, and assassination. Inevitably, later commentators, such as Richard Hofstadter in *The Age of Reform,* decided that prohibition was regressive, not progressive. "For Prohibition," Hofstadter claimed, "was a pseudo-reform, a pinched, parochial substitute for reform which had a widespread appeal to a certain type of crusading mind." He went on to point out: "It was linked not merely to an aversion to drunkenness and to the evils that accompanied it, but to the immigrant drinking masses, to the pleasures and amenities of city life, and to the well-to-do classes and cultivated men."[17]

Frankly, Barkley could have been Hofstadter's poster child for the "pseudo-reform" of prohibition. The Kentuckian grew up hundreds of miles west of the "cultivated men" of the Northeast. His "parochial" early life in rural America and religious upbringing gave him an "aversion to drunkenness." He really did oppose the "immigrant drinking masses." Also, his hyperbolic speeches in favor of prohibition bespoke of a "crusading mind." Finally, his lifelong conversion to the Methodist Church was symbolically significant because Methodists took leading roles in the Anti-Saloon League (ASL) and the Women's Christian Temperance Union. Both groups played a critical part in turning the tide in favor of establishing the Eighteenth Amendment. But, no matter to what extent one can fit Barkley into the mold for a typical prohibitionist, Hofstadter pushed his argument too far. The antiliquor crusade was an integral part of the Populist-Progressive era, which sought government solutions to address social needs related, for example, to child labor, unsafe foods, and medical misbranding as well as reforms concerned with elections, taxes, and labor. And prohibition gained the adherence of the top progressive politicians, including Senators William E. Borah, Robert La Follette, Charles L. McNary, George W. Norris, and Morris Sheppard.[18]

The male-directed ASL employed all the progressive political tools to achieve government solutions to social ills. Prohibitionists attacked or defended individual politicians in primaries and general elections; they also employed the initiative and the referendum on the local and state levels. Like other reformers, ASL members drew on the authority of experts and social research that pointed to the negative effects of excessive alcohol drinking on safety and efficiency in the workplace as well as on mortality rates. The American Medical Association (AMA) condemned alcohol as a beverage. Just when Barkley strongly endorsed the Hobson resolution in Congress, the AMA was in the process of dropping whiskey and brandy, once popular medicinal drinks, from its list of medically approved drugs. Experts published exhaustive tables of facts and figures demonstrating the relationship between drinking and poverty, child neglect, family abuse, crime, prostitution, and sexually transmitted disease. Social workers and individuals in the settlement house movement, such as Jane Addams, constantly struggled against saloons in order to improve conditions in those urban neighborhoods populated with recent immigrants.[19]

Despite Hofstadter's postmortem assault on prohibition as reform, contemporaries marked Barkley's strident advocacy of the crusade against alcohol as strong evidence of his progressivism. On the other hand, unlike some past and recent public officials, Barkley never collapsed his reform-minded efforts around one cause. In 1915, for example, he vocally argued and voted for legislation on child labor, federal health and education programs, women's suffrage, minimum wages, and additional sources of credit for farmers. Though he could not be linked to one issue, he clearly aligned himself with those who labored in field and factory. In large measure, the failure of these bills to be enacted into law must be assigned to President Wilson. Only as January 1916 arrived did he wake up to the fact that he had to recommit himself to the progressive movement. He and many congressional Democrats might not be reelected unless they attracted votes from members of Theodore Roosevelt's defunct Progressive Party. Even after Roosevelt returned to the GOP, the party remained badly fractured between conservatives and reformers. Thus, in the words of Arthur Link, Wilson "became a new political creature" when he announced on January 28 his nomination of Louis D. Brandeis to the US Supreme Court.[20]

Born in Louisville, Kentucky, the son of Jewish immigrants from the Austrian Empire, Brandeis received his LL.B. degree from Harvard College in 1877. A Boston lawyer, he served as special counsel in five different states preserving laws benefiting workers in terms of hours and wages. He later fought railroad monopolies in the Northeast and helped Wilson develop the New Freedom program. Clearly, most politicians, newspapers, and magazines recognized instantly that the president's recommendation was a clarion call for reform. Indeed, with the exception of the New Deal legislation of 1933, the Democratic Sixty-Fourth Congress of 1916 enacted the most impressive set of reform measures in a single year in the nation's history. And Barkley began the process. In January, along with Morris Sheppard (TX) in the Senate, he introduced a prohibition resolution for the District of Columbia. When finally passed and signed into law by Wilson, the Barkley-Sheppard Act made it unlawful to manufacture or sell intoxicating liquors in Washington. As one might well understand, the ASL appreciated and applauded Barkley's "dry" leadership position in Congress. In fact, the lobby group invited him to address one of its public meetings in the capital.[21]

Unfortunately, the House Rules Committee, to which Barkley's District of Columbia prohibition resolution was sent, sat on it until the Senate approved the similar Sheppard measure early the next year. Meanwhile, as a member of the Interstate and Foreign Commerce Committee, Barkley introduced on January 31, 1916, a misbranding bill. It expanded the Pure Food and Drug Act of 1906 by calling for all commercial articles crossing state and US borders to be labeled truthfully. The omnibus bill proved too sweeping and far ahead of its time to become law. Nevertheless, the debut of these reforms set the stage for the year's significant progressive legislation that did reach the status of national law. Two days after presenting the House with the misbranding bill, Barkley argued in favor of a child labor bill sponsored by Representative Edward Keating (CO) and Senator Robert L. Owen (OK). It excluded from interstate commerce all goods manufactured with labor by children under the age of fourteen.[22]

Opponents argued that the child labor proposal would violate states' rights. It was an awkward moment for Barkley, who otherwise appreciated those rights. Additionally, most of those who employed that argument were southern Democrats. These were the very individuals with whom he had collaborated in matters related to wartime foreign trade in American cotton and tobacco. So, when he spoke in favor of the Keating-Owen bill, he first stated: "I believe in States' rights." On the other hand, he could be flexible when "the benefit of humanity and the progress and enlightenment of our Nation" were at stake. He continued by trying to use a gentle bit of logic that suggested that in one sense states' rights was not an appropriate reason to oppose the current bill: "If Congress has the right to prevent the shipment of an article in interstate commerce because it may endanger some one's anatomy when it gets to its destination it has the same right to regulate and prevent interstate commerce of an article if it endangers some one in its manufacture and production." This reasoning helped the child labor measure breeze through the House later that same day in a lopsided vote of 337–46.[23]

Later, the US Supreme Court struck down the Keating-Owen Child Labor Act. Remarkably enough, and long after the fact, the Court's ruling destroyed the basic argument that Barkley had used to encourage his colleagues to vote in favor of the bill. The justices decided that the regulation of interstate commerce had absolutely nothing to do with the conditions of labor that produced articles of trade. Only later would the New Deal address the issue, first in labor codes adopted by the National Recovery Administration (1933), and then in the Fair Labor Standards Act (1938). Both prohibited child labor under the age of sixteen. Another but more lasting bill that drew firm support from Barkley and Wilson was the Federal Farm Loan Bank. The president and his administration had earlier opposed a similar measure and, instead, suggested that credit arrangements for farmers should be worked out locally or through cooperatives rather than via the national government. In 1916, however, Wilson needed the farm vote if he wanted to live in the White House another four years.[24]

From the moment he entered Congress, Barkley advocated rural credits for his farmer constituents; he also wanted to correct for current generations the unfortunate experience faced by his family when he was fourteen. The fifth farm on which the family lived near Lowes was owned, not rented, by his father. It was for John Barkley the highlight of his agricultural career. In 1891, however, a poor crop coupled with debts and limited credit facilities forced him to sell the farm, pay his debts, and move the family to Clinton. One can speculate that, had he had access to credit and kept his family in Lowes, the future minister of the local Presbyterian Church would have been Alben. Regardless, Barkley joined his voice with those, especially from congressional farming districts, who earnestly gave their approval to what became the Federal Farm Loan Bank Act. It created twelve federal land banks parallel to the Federal Reserve banks that offered farmers low-interest loans for up to forty years.[25]

There were several important pieces of progressive legislation signed into law by the president between July and September 1916 that Barkley endorsed mainly with his vote rather than with his rhetoric. First, the Warehouse Act allowed farmers to secure credit on the basis of their crops, not their land. It authorized licensed and bonded warehouses to issue receipts against certain agricultural commodities. Those receipts, in turn, could be used as collateral for loans. Second, almost as a cap to his own career as a county attorney and county judge who stressed creating good roads, Barkley gladly voted to approve the Rural Post Roads Act. It fulfilled the 1912 plank in the Democratic platform by transferring federal funds to states for the construction of roads over which the US mails could be carried. The dollar-matching contributions to the states occurred only after they established a highway department dedicated to building roads. Renewal legislation in 1921 initiated the start of a future systematic network of numbered US highways. Third, the Federal Workmen's Compensation Act, a groundbreaking measure, gave uniform sick and accident benefits to government employees as well as death benefits to dependents.[26]

A second piece of groundbreaking legislation garnered approval with

more than simply a vote from Barkley. In June, a potential crisis of catastrophic proportions flared up when railroad managers flatly turned down
the demands of four union brotherhoods (engineers, firemen, conductors,
trainmen) for an eight-hour day and time-and-a-half pay for overtime. Some
400,000 railroad workers voted almost unanimously to strike. At a time
when large trucks and national highways simply did not exist, all people and
goods traveled by train. Imagine, then, urban centers without any food for
residents and fuel for electricity to power homes, hospitals, shops, factories,
office buildings, and electrified transportation systems such as the ubiquitous trolley. America's economic life would collapse. Wilson met with both
union leaders and railroad executives. The unions accepted the president's
compromise: an eight-hour day but no overtime pay and creation of a commission to study railroad labor problems. When railroad managers rejected
the compromise, the brotherhoods set a strike for September 4, 1916. That
deadline caused frantic activity in Washington. Near the end of August,
Wilson urgently met with Democratic leaders in the Capitol Building. The
next day, August 29, he made a pleading presentation for a bill that would
prevent the strike from happening.[27]

In consultation with House majority leader Claude Kitchen (NC), the
chair of the Interstate and Foreign Commerce Committee, Adamson, took
on the task of preparing the bill that would carry his name. According to
Adamson, Barkley actually did a significant amount of the work of drafting the final piece of legislation. It was a hectic moment in the Kentuckian's
life because of a deadline measured in hours, not weeks or days. Finished on
August 31, the draft was reviewed by Wilson and congressional leaders and
accepted. On September 1, the House overwhelmingly voted in favor of the
bill; next day, after a lengthy and somewhat acrimonious debate, the Senate
followed suit. Wilson signed the Adamson Act while sitting appropriately
in a private railroad car in Washington's Union Station on September 3. He
then headed by rail to Hodgenville, Kentucky, for a campaign address at
Abraham Lincoln's birthplace.[28]

Even though the act did not go into effect until January 1, 1917, the
brotherhoods canceled the strike and for good reason. The legislation created an eight-hour day for railroad workers, time and a half for overtime pay,
and a commission to study and address future railroad problems. It fulfilled
everything labor and the president hoped to accomplish as it delivered a fig-
urative slap in the face to railroad executives who had turned down Wilson's
recommendation for a compromise. And, of course, it caught the attention

of workers across the nation who hoped the eight-hour day would become the future standard in the workplace, which it did. Is it any wonder the American Federation of Labor vowed to support the president's reelection? And, for those in the know, the Adamson Act added to Barkley's growing reputation. Subsequently, the capital's Economic Club invited the congressman to address its members at the New Ebbitt Hotel on the subject "Regulation or Control of the Railway Transportation of the United States."[29]

Shortly after Wilson signed the Adamson bill into law, the first session of Congress adjourned, heralding the start to the fall's election campaigns. In reality, Barkley had few concerns personally, not only because no Democrat had opposed him in the August primary, but also because, as we have seen, he never stopped campaigning. His Republican opponent in the general election was Thomas N. Hazelip, who had run against him unsuccessfully in the 1909 contest for county judge. Even though he was a former local leader of the Progressive (Bull Moose) Party, Hazelip posed no threat to the incumbent candidate. Hence, the hundred or so speeches Barkley delivered in the fall campaign focused on reelecting Wilson and Vice President Thomas R. Marshall. In the process, he appeared in Illinois, Missouri, Tennessee, Maine, other parts of Kentucky, and, of course, in the First District. He finished the campaign season with a rally in Paducah and on election day beat Hazelip by a record fourteen thousand votes.[30]

As his campaign strategy illustrates, Barkley zeroed in on reelecting Wilson, whom he judged to be the greatest president since Thomas Jefferson. The congressman had a reason to be worried. In the first instance, earlier in 1916 there seemed to be a good chance that Theodore Roosevelt might be drafted by the GOP as its nominee for another term in the White House. A sharp critic of Wilson's foreign policy and a leading progressive figure, Roosevelt neglected publicly to state his interest in returning to the presidency but privately encouraged the Roosevelt Nonpartisan League to promote his candidacy. The former president and Roughrider hero of the Spanish-American War spurred Barkley to join his Kentucky colleagues Senator James and Seventh District congressman J. Campbell Cantrill in an effort to delay the commonwealth's legislature from submitting to the electorate an amendment to the state's constitution giving women the right to vote. In his memoirs, Barkley argued that he always favored women's suffrage, but in 1916 he wanted to avoid any controversial issue sponsored by Democrats that might diminish votes for Wilson. Fortunately for Barkley, because of his past and future service as a champion of female voters, what happened in 1916 disappeared down a side road into an all-but-forgotten footnote to history. After the election, he helped approve the Nineteenth Amendment to the US Constitution allowing women nationwide to vote in 1920.[31]

Roosevelt failed to get the Republican nomination in June, and the remnant of his 1912 Progressive Party disbanded a short time later. None of this was good news to Barkley since Charles Evans Hughes won the GOP convention's endorsement. The New York lawyer gained statewide and even national notice for his vigorous investigation on behalf of the Albany legislature into financial irregularities by the Empire State's utilities and insurance companies. Progressive Republicans elected him governor before President Taft appointed him an associate justice of the US Supreme Court in 1910. Hughes seemed to reunite a fractious party of reform and regular Republicans and, thus, posed a serious threat to Wilson's reelection; even Roosevelt delivered an early campaign speech in his support. These events prompted Barkley to urge the president to conduct an active national campaign, one that included numerous personal appearances and many speeches. Wilson reluctantly and only partially followed the congressman's advice. It explains Barkley's multistate swing as a self-appointed surrogate for Wilson, who remained quiet and close to Washington or at his New Jersey summer home. He did suddenly erupt, however, into action with a hard-hitting speech at the end of September accompanied by a thorough canvass of middle America in October.[32]

To be honest, it was not Barkley but another Kentuckian who did the most to reelect Wilson. When the Democrats met in St. Louis on June 11, 1916, to pick the president as their nominee, Senator Ollie M. James served as the convention's permanent chairman and keynote speaker. It was James, a great orator, who electrified the delegates and handed Wilson the one issue that guaranteed his victory. During a rousing speech, he caused a riotous, twenty-minute demonstration when he captured the delegates' desire for the country to remain at peace in a world gone mad with war. Pandemonium broke out when he shouted: "Without orphaning a single American child, without widowing a single American mother, without firing a single gun or shedding a drop of blood, he [Wilson] wrung from the most militant spirit that ever brooded over a battlefield the concession of American demands and American rights." James made Wilson the peace candidate who "kept us out of war." That phrase handed Wilson victory in an otherwise close race. On the other hand, the fall election handed Barkley a foreboding sign. Republicans ended up with four more representatives than did the Democrats in the House. Champ Clark did retain his position as speaker but only because a number of independent representatives caucused with the now smaller of the two major parties. And, paradoxically, when the peace president opened the Sixty-Fifth Congress on April 2, 1917, he asked the joint session to approve a declaration of war. Obviously, a series of unhappy events marked the period between November 1916 and the following April.[33]

Right up to the declaration of war, Barkley seemed to have been the perfect neutral Wilson had called for in 1914. While he did not express a philosophical bent toward one side of the conflict or the other before 1917, he did react strongly to the war's impact on the foreign trade of his district's agricultural products. Thus, he participated actively in the House to provide the president with the legislative tools necessary to preserve US neutral rights via the authority to punish misbehaving belligerents and expand America's merchant fleet. Although he deeply appreciated Wilson's efforts to keep the United States out of the war, he did not join him in taking time off from reform. The Kentuckian advocated in 1915 bills against child labor and in favor of workers, farmers, national roads, and women's suffrage. Over time, all these proposals received the president's endorsement, but in 1916 or later. Finally, Barkley enhanced his reputation nationally by his leadership in the prohibition movement as well as within the Democratic Party by his loyal support of its programs and candidates.

7

The Congressman
in War and Peace

The peace president certainly tried to live up to his sobriquet. But, in December 1916, the Allies rejected both Germany's apparent willingness to negotiate peace terms and Wilson's call for the combative powers to state their war aims as a prelude to a peace conference. Wilson did not give up. He made, in the words of the historian Kendrick A. Clements, a "bold assertion that the horrors of modern war gave neutrals as well as belligerents moral justification to demand its end." On January 22, 1917, the president addressed the US Senate and called on the battling nations to seek a "peace without victory." Some senators gasped when he stated that he expected the United States to participate in the negotiations to end the conflict as well as in a "league of peace" to prevent future wars. And the projected, hoped-for negotiations must embrace, he said, the "practical convictions" of "the peoples of America." These convictions included such elements as liberty for small nations, a limit to armaments, freedom of religion and of the seas, and the right of peoples to govern themselves.[1]

The response of the Germans was unexpected, if not astonishing. On January 31, German ambassador Johann von Bernstorff handed the State Department in Washington a note that answered Wilson's earlier request for German war aims. They included territorial adjustments, additional colonies, a degree of German control over Belgium and Poland, and financial compensation for companies and individuals injured by the Allies during the war. American foreign affairs experts dismissed the aims as totally unrealistic. At the same time, Bernstorff delivered a second message that cynically answered Wilson's call for peace without victory. The message announced that the next day German submarines were free to sink without warning all belligerent and neutral ships in the waters around France, Great Britain, and Italy. A German embassy official claimed that unrestricted submarine warfare would end the conflict and hand Germany a victory within thirty days. This strategy, however, absolutely violated the pledge to America made by the German government to conform to the international law of the seas after a submarine torpedoed the *Sussex*.[2]

On February 3, Wilson once again delivered an address before a joint session of Congress. This time he reminded its members of the administration's earlier ultimatum to Germany that had threatened to end relations unless Berlin restricted submarine warfare. Since Germany now retracted its 1916 pledge, Wilson told the two chambers: "I have, therefore, directed the Secretary of State to announce to his excellency the German Ambassador that all diplomatic relations between the United States and the German empire are severed and that the American Ambassador at Berlin will be withdrawn: and, in accordance with this decision, to hand to his excellency [the Secretary of State] his passport." Later that month, the British intercepted and provided the United States with a copy of an infamous telegram sent to Mexico by German foreign secretary Arthur Zimmermann. Should war flare up between the United States and Germany, Zimmermann offered Mexico a military alliance that would reward the country's participation with the states of Texas, New Mexico, and Arizona.[3]

The telegram was published by newspapers across the United States on March 1 and caused a frenzy of bellicose comment and activity directed against Germany. For example, on that day Alben W. Barkley joined most of his colleagues in the House of Representatives in voting to approve an administration bill that would arm US merchant vessels to protect them against German submarines. To the disgust of many editorial writers, several noninterventionist senators killed the bill through an effective filibuster. Regardless, the merchant ships were armed as the president employed the authority vested in his office by a piracy statute Congress had approved nearly one hundred years earlier. Late in March, three US ships, the *City of Memphis,* the *Illinois,* and the *Vigilancia,* sank with loss of life from submarine attacks. These were clearly acts of war. After observing from a distance the bloody conflict in Europe for more than two years, Wilson agonized for several days before deciding to ask Congress for a declaration of war. The latter was made easier in March when the only Allied Power to have an autocratic government experienced a revolution. Russia and its new leaders had removed the Romanov tsar and promised a constitutional republic. As a result, Wilson's message to Congress on April 2 elevated the argument for war by declaring America's fight would be "for democracy, for the right of those who submit to authority to have a voice in their own Governments."[4]

Barkley spoke and voted in favor of the war declaration, which quickly cleared both chambers and went into effect on April 6. It should not be forgotten, however, that he originally had been a follower of William Jennings Bryan, a famous pacifist. The latter resigned as secretary of state in June 1915 to be replaced by Robert Lansing. Bryan quit the high-profile post because he thought that Wilson threatened to ensnare the United States into war with Germany over the deadly submarine attack on the *Lusitania*. Barkley too favored peace, but, unlike Bryan, he had the patience to see that Wilson's stiff rhetoric with Berlin eventually produced a German agreement to restrict submarine warfare. When the Germans abandoned the pledge, it disappointed Barkley. Like that of many other citizens, his disappointment turned to hostility when Germans sank American ships, killed American sailors, and attempted to enlist Mexico in war with the United States. Obviously, Barkley's views on war shifted dramatically. Moreover, he liked Wilson's call for war as a quest to promote freedom. In his remarks on the House floor on April 5, he embellished Wilson's focus on liberty. In support of the declaration of war, he ranged over American history to suggest that the nation's earlier conflicts had centered on the same value. Among other examples, he noted that the American Revolutionary War brought liberty to the people just as the Spanish-American War secured independence for Cuba (but, in reality, Cuba remained a US protectorate until 1934).[5]

A speech and a vote are strong indicators, but Barkley did much more to show his conversion from avowed neutralist to war advocate. Within thirteen months after the official declaration of war, he purchased three Liberty Loan bonds worth a total of $1,500 through the Paducah branch of the Metropolitan Life Insurance Company. The bonds provided funds for the war effort and represented a whopping 20 percent of his annual salary. They were held in safekeeping by Paducah's City National Bank. And see how the politician in Washington took care to keep his presence felt in Paducah. He could have bought and kept the bonds in the nation's capital. Besides a personal financial commitment, Barkley voted with the majority to pass a war revenue bill in Congress. Much of the money went to expand immensely the US Army; its authorized strength in 1917 stood at a little over 200,000 officers and men. Interestingly, the US Navy was much better prepared for war. Already a large military force, the navy received approval from Congress in

August 1916 for a construction program to add 157 warships to its inventory. At the time, the building program could be touted as a strategy to keep war away from US shores. Two oceans and a strong navy would prevent a potential enemy from even considering an attempt to transport a seaborne army for the purpose of attacking America. On the other hand, once the country did enter war with Germany, a strong US Navy sent 373 ships to Europe, including 85 destroyers. The latter successfully protected from submarine attack over two million American soldiers who were shipped safely across the Atlantic Ocean to the battle zone trenches in France.[6]

Such a large number of troops was possible only because Secretary of War Newton D. Baker shook things up by indicating that the army needed 500,000 men immediately and would soon need to double that figure. Some form of conscription was necessary because to rely on volunteers would not guarantee the quick acquisition of enough men. And, if the army did contain only volunteers, some observers, influenced by Social Darwinism, suggested that America's most energetic and patriotic young men might be lost in battle. It would leave too many unpatriotic slackers at home to propagate future generations of Americans. Regardless, Speaker Champ Clark left the rostrum to attack the selective service bill on the House floor. He and several other representatives believed that conscription violated democratic values, remembered draft riots from the Civil War, and worried about providing military training to African Americans. White southerners feared racial violence. Among other comments, Clark stated that he could not distinguish between a conscript and a convict. The quip riled Barkley, who took the floor to rebuke Clark and his like-minded congressional colleagues.[7]

Barkley criticized the bill's opponents for voting for the war declaration and then sitting on the sidelines while ignoring the tremendous need to expand the army that would soon enter battle. Pointedly, he remarked: "Every soldier must follow his commander in chief." His implication was, of course, that in wartime members of Congress should also obey the commander in chief of the US military. Other arguments, of course, focused on the practical nature of conscription in order quickly to create a huge army. Additionally, drafting physically fit men solely on the basis of age (initially twenty-one to thirty) was very democratic and without class distinction. It also would help Americanize the large immigrant population. Introduced in the House on April 19, the selective service bill was approved by an overwhelming vote of 395–24 on April 28. The Senate passed a similar measure 81–8 at midnight the same day. Because the House and the Senate versions differed, it took more time in conference for both chambers to review and vote on the final conference report. Wilson signed the bill into law on May 18, 1917. The delay caused few problems because, as Secretary Baker admitted, the lack of supplies meant that the new army would not be called to the colors before September.[8]

In the two weeks between the House vote on the declaration of war and the chamber's first consideration of the selective service bill, Barkley met with Wilson. He told the president that he wanted to join the army. In one sense, Barkley may have simply demonstrated his ardent support for Wilson and the country in the immediate aftermath of the decision to engage Germany in the conflict. Beyond that, one can only speculate as to the seriousness of his desire to join the military. He had no army experience. Seven months out from his fortieth birthday, he seemed a bit old to endure the rigors of boot camp as a private. Alternatively, since he was born not long after the Civil War, he may have learned that several militarily inexperienced politicians in that earlier conflict had received appointments directly to the officer corps during the struggle over union and slavery. Under those circumstances, he might have made a decent supply captain far from the field of battle, but not a good combat leader. It seems likely that Wilson told Barkley what he wanted to hear, namely, that he hoped he would stay in Congress and champion the administration's war legislation. But Wilson also urged him to seek the advice of Secretary Baker. When Barkley talked with the war secretary, Baker agreed with Wilson. He noted that, if all 531 members of Congress volunteered to join the army, it would represent a tiny, meaningless drop in a large bucket of water; however, the quick loss of all House and Senate members would be a disastrous disruption in the functioning of constitutional government.[9]

Barkley followed the advice of Wilson and Baker; he stayed in Congress and backed the president's wartime legislation. It must be observed, however, that April 6 marked the virtual end to progressive reform during the war. What did emerge was the enormous expansion of government power to mobilize the economy so as to supply a massive military. Newly created agencies included the Food Administration, the Fuel Administration, the National War Labor Board, and the War Industries Board. Also, the Railroad Control Act temporarily nationalized the country's transportation system. Some progressives hoped that these new government powers would be used to promote social justice at the end of the conflict. Their hope was misplaced. Business executives generally headed these new or nationalized organizations that furnished, transported, or labored over crucial war materiel. The process only enhanced the image of corporate executives who knew that such restrictive legislation as the Federal Trade Commission Act and the Clayton Antitrust Act ceased being enforced. True, women's suffrage came close to passage as the Susan B. Anthony resolution. The House approved it, but the Senate failed to reach the necessary two-thirds majority by two votes on September 26, 1918. Even Wilson's personal appearance and plea before the Senate on September 30 failed to nudge the upper chamber. Only after two antisuffrage senators lost their elections in the fall did that body pass the suffrage amendment resolution on June 4, 1919, nearly seven months after the war ended in an armistice signed on November 11, 1918.[10]

Thus, prohibition represented the only wartime success of a reform in the progressive tradition, and Barkley stood in the middle of those individuals responsible for the related legislation and constitutional amendment. The war helped the dry position taken by the Paducah politician and other members of Congress who, by 1916, favored some form of prohibition by a supermajority. Americans who had a beer or a glass of wine at mealtime or drank liquor occasionally would ordinarily oppose prohibition. Such "wets," however, could only agree that in wartime converting tubers, grains, and fruits into alcoholic beverages wasted nourishing foods needed by US soldiers or destitute Europeans such as Belgians who were victimized by war. Hence, there was widespread support for a June 1917 bill reported out of the House Agricultural Committee by its chair, Asbury F. Lever (D-SC). It granted the administration wartime control over foods; section 13 handed the president discretionary powers to prohibit the use of foods to make intoxicating libations. Because Wilson never supported absolute prohibition, several dry representatives offered awkward amendments not germane to section 13. Each was ruled out of order. Barkley saved the situation for the dry position by using political savvy. He successfully offered a substitute that kept section 13 almost intact—merely altering phrases to reduce presidential options. In essence, Barkley cleverly altered the legislation so that it constituted a temporary prohibition amendment. It passed the House on June 23 by a vote of 365–5.[11]

For a variety of reasons, the Senate balked over the sweeping measure approved by the House. To facilitate timely passage of the larger bill, Wilson addressed a major issue when he got the Anti-Saloon League (ASL) to agree that he should have discretionary power over beer and wine. It worked. The final conference bill passed by both chambers allowed the president an option over stopping the conversion of grains and fruits into beers and wines. Barkley voted in favor of the final Lever food and fuel bill for two reasons. First, despite conferees waffling over fermented drinks, the act signed by Wilson on August 10 ended the production of distilled spirits. Second, the dry members of Congress had decided to work up a resolution proposing to give the states the opportunity to ratify a prohibition amendment to the Constitution. The historian Gerald S. Grinde acknowledged that during the House debate Barkley's speech supporting the resolution seemed weak. He focused on how prohibition would aid the war effort. His comments became more interesting when he talked about the loss of federal tax dollars that would result from the complete end to liquor sales. He recognized that the liquor industry had served as the government's tax collector even though it gave Washington only a fraction of the cash taken from the millions who drank alcoholic beverages. He argued optimistically that prohibition would enhance the population's wealth and productivity and, hence, boost the source of federal revenue. Regardless, the House and the Senate passed the resolution, completing their work on December 18, 1917. That same day, Secretary of State Lansing forwarded the resolution to the forty-eight states, which then considered ratifying the Eighteenth Amendment to the Constitution. Prohibition went into effect on January 16, 1919, one year after three-fourths of the states had ratified the document.[12]

With the fate of the prohibition amendment left up to state legislatures, Barkley focused his attention on numerous other House activities related to the war. Over the winter and spring of 1917–1918, the sundry matters before Congress included, among others, the declaration of war against the Austro-Hungarian Empire (the United States ignored the other Central Powers—Bulgaria and the Ottoman Empire), the establishment of daylight savings time to conserve electricity and fuel for industrial use, and the creation of the War Finance Corporation, which funded banks to cover loans for the expansion of factories manufacturing military supplies. Thanks to Congress, Wilson and his administration gained enormous powers to put the country on a war footing, provide the army with men, and make available the money needed to clothe, feed, house, equip, train, and transport a huge army within America and to Europe. The speed of this process distressed the enemy. On June 14, 1917, Major General John J. Pershing and his small staff arrived in France to begin building the foundation for the

American Expeditionary Force (AEF). By July 4, 1918, he would be joined by one million US soldiers; that number would double before war's end.[13]

At the close of May 1918, the US First, Second, and Third Divisions had indeed begun battle with the Germans. At twenty-eight thousand men each, the units were three times the size of many European divisions. When over the winter of 1917–1918 the Germans realized how quickly the United States had responded in mobilizing for war, they husbanded their forces and transferred close to fifty divisions from the Eastern (Russian) Front to the Western. Revolution effectively resulted in Russia's unofficial withdrawal from the war during 1917 and its official withdrawal when the new Soviet government ratified the Brest-Litovsk Treaty in March 1918. That same month the Germans conducted what they expected to be their last and victorious offensive against the British and French before a large US Army could enter the fray. But the Americans helped guarantee that the last German offensive operation would not be victorious. The German military's initial advance in the early spring prompted General Pershing to abandon, but only briefly, his desire to establish an autonomous American army with its own sector, like the British and the French, on the Western Front. Instead, he agreed to split his battle-ready forces among Allied troops confronting the German onslaught. The Third Division at Château-Thierry held the bridgehead over the Marne River and aided the Allies in stopping the German offensive in that location not far from Paris. Farther north, the First Division initiated America's first offensive of the war by taking Cantigny. Shortly thereafter, the Second Division moved against the Germans in Belleau Wood and into the annals of Marine Corps history. Casualties among the three units amounted to 11,384. It gave friend and foe alike a bloody affirmation of US determination and combat capability.[14]

The early heroics of American forces, promise of an even larger role for the AEF in the near future, and recognition that the war was one of the towering moments in US history prompted Barkley's decision in July 1918 to travel to Europe and witness firsthand the most significant episode of his generation. Besides, his son David (Bud) seemed disappointed that his father had not joined the army. With all the talk about war at school among his teachers and fellow students, Bud hoped at minimum that his father would visit the scenes of battle and bring home lots of souvenirs from the front lines. Barkley was accompanied by five colleagues from Congress: James B. Aswell (LA), Marvin Jones (TX), James H. Mays (UT), Charles H. Randall (CA), and Milton H. Welling (UT). Interestingly, the group was neither an official, fact-finding committee nor sponsored in any way by the House or a government agency. Barkley and his companions paid their own expenses simply to see for themselves and experience an event that in many ways had changed the nation and the lives of their constituents.[15]

Barkley and his congressional cohorts boarded a troopship on August 9, 1918, and traveled to Europe, where they spent six weeks before returning to the United States at the beginning of October. As members of the US Congress, the legislative body of an associate member of the Allied Powers, the six-member group enjoyed special treatment. After all, they were partly responsible for war revenue bills that supplied billions of dollars to aid the Allies and build an American armed force that would assist in turning the tide against Germany. Indeed, Barkley and his companions received literally the royal treatment. They met and conversed, and in two cases dined with, four monarchs, the heads of state for Belgium, France, Great Britain, and Italy; they also talked with three heads of government: British prime minister David Lloyd George, French premier Georges Clemenceau, and Italian premier Vittorio Orlando. Barkley kept a running record of the group's activities, but a number of experiences made such a serious impression on him that he remembered them vividly several decades later.[16]

In Scotland, Barkley proudly spent time with a fellow Kentuckian, Rear Admiral (later Admiral) Hugh Rodman, who was born in the commonwealth's capital city of Frankfort. Rodman commanded the US Navy's Ninth Battleship Division, which had merged successfully, though temporarily, with the British Grand Fleet. Besides seeing royal and political leaders, Barkley took his first airplane ride in England and viewed London from the sky. Thirty years later, he gained fame as the first American politician running for national office to canvass the country via airplane. Meanwhile, he and his party spent the most time in France and headquartered at their expense at the well-appointed Crillon Hotel in Paris. From there the small group went north to Ypres, a Belgian town sadly blown to pieces during the course of three major battles. In a visit to the front lines, Barkley ended up only seventy-five feet from the German trenches. Using a bayoneted rifle, he held a helmet just above the British earthworks. In an instant, eleven enemy bullets struck the metal headpiece. The group returned to Paris before departing eastward to the French trenches where the Americans had fought alongside French troops before moving southeastward to the AEF's own sector along the Western Front.[17]

On this particular trip, Barkley took the opportunity to walk around the Château-Thierry battlefield, where American and French troops had stopped the German offensive. He collected various military equipment such as helmets and bayonets left on the field by fallen German soldiers. He later gave the collection to his twelve-year-old son David, who could then do a show-and-tell at school and brag to his classmates that his father had been to war. That was no lie. Barkley had been to war. The enemy on the ground and in the air had fired at him. He heard the thundering roar and felt the shaking earth from exploding artillery shells; he spent enough time in the grungy, vermin-infested trenches to appreciate the grim process of war from the perspective of the common soldier. And he endured the grievous shock and repugnance of visiting a field hospital in the midst of battle. As long as he lived he would never forget seeing the blood and wounds of young men so recently in combat; their only hope, unfulfilled in some cases, was that they would live to see another day. Understandably, Barkley remarked long afterwards: "You wonder if anyone ever wins a war."[18]

Near the end of their sojourn, Barkley and his companions traveled to Italy. They visited the northeast region of the front facing the forces of the Austro-Hungarian Empire, which then occupied portions of the Italian Alps. From the Allied side, the good news was that the Italian army had been rebuilt successfully after its punishing defeat at Caporetto eleven months earlier; also, the polyglot Austro-Hungarian Empire had entered the final days before its self-destruction. Its troops would flee haphazardly from Italy at the end of October, and the government would sign an armistice on November 3, 1918. (Bulgaria, on September 29, and the Ottoman Empire, on October 30, had already surrendered.) In the meantime, the congressmen went to Mount Grappa near the Piave River, where the Italians had established a major artillery installation to rain down explosive shells on Austrian soldiers in the river valley. Italian gunners invited Barkley to pull the lanyard on an artillery piece that fired a round of ordnance in the direction of the enemy. When Italy's King Victor Emmanuel at his nearby headquarters heard about the American congressional delegation, he invited the men to dinner. With Barkley sitting beside Victor Emmanuel, the king surprised him by his knowledge of Kentucky and the commonwealth's reputation for fast horses and fine tobacco. For the benefit of many of his constituents, Barkley repeated the episode in speeches at home and claimed how he had promoted postwar Kentucky tobacco sales with Italy's monarch.[19]

On the one hand, it is easy to understand why Barkley wanted to visit the western battlefields of Europe. Aside from the motivations already mentioned, he and his colleagues had spent a considerable amount of time researching, preparing, debating, and approving legislation pertaining to the war. In one sense, it was logical for the six men to want to see the effect and material results of their labors. On the other hand, even Barkley had to confess: "Looking back on it, I realize [the trip] was a foolhardy and perhaps unnecessary thing that we congressmen did." If nothing else, one or more of the men might have been wounded or killed as noncombatants during their several times on or near the front lines. But, in addition, the "fact-finding junket" did not lead to wartime legislation, a shorter conflict, or recommendations to strengthen the US military and Allied Powers. The excursion did, however, demonstrate two things to Barkley. It impressed on him the importance of foreign affairs to both his state and his country. Also, it showed him the benefit of his carefully maintained and politically astute position in the First District. He could be thousands of miles from Paducah and not worry a thing about either the primary or the general election of 1918.[20]

By contrast, President Wilson may have publicly expressed too much concern over the fall campaigns and the November elections. The historian Daniel M. Smith notes one of several flaws in Wilson's character; the president seemed to behave like a prime minister in a parliamentarian type of government who heads the majority party (or coalition of parties) that controls the government and administers the country. In the presidential, two-party system that emerged in the United States, things are more complicated and occasionally downright messy. The president may not belong to the majority party that organizes Congress. Sometimes, the majority in the House may be the minority in the Senate, and vice versa. As the war was winding down in the fall of 1918, Wilson felt that he had to be like a prime minister with a majority of his party in Congress so that he could exercise leadership in domestic and foreign affairs. Frankly, by 1918, he considered most Republicans in the nation's legislative body to be obstructionists. In short, he did not want to make concessions to or trade-offs with the GOP in order to gain a truncated, bastardized form of his program for postwar America and the peacemaking process in Europe.[21]

Thus, on October 25 the president released a plea to the American people that began:

My fellow countrymen: The congressional elections are at hand. They occur in the most critical period our country has ever faced

or is likely to face in our time. If you have approved of my leadership and wish me to continue to be your unembarrassed spokesman
in affairs at home and abroad, I earnestly beg that you will express
yourselves unmistakably to that effect by returning a Democratic
majority to both the Senate and the House of Representatives. . . .
The leaders of the minority in the present Congress have been . . .
anti-administration. At almost every turn since we entered the war
they have sought to take the choice of policy and the conduct of
the war out of my hands. . . . The return of a Republican majority to either House of the Congress would, moreover, be interpre-
tive [sic] on the other side of the [Atlantic Ocean] as a repudiation
of my leadership.[22]

Barkley and his Democratic colleagues in Congress received an advanced
copy of the president's plea. Some Democrats, especially the fifty or so who
had struggled to get elected or reelected in House districts in 1916, welcomed
the statement. A few congressmen such as Barkley actually counseled the
president against releasing such an appeal to the press. Barkley believed that
it would cause mischief by antagonizing Republicans and energizing GOP
members to vote. Whether caused by the president's statement or simply the
normal pattern for midterm elections, Republicans captured Congress with
a slight majority in both chambers. Regardless, they loudly proclaimed that
the American people had repudiated Wilson's leadership. He compounded
what Barkley considered a mistake by deciding to head the American peace
delegation to Paris after Germany signed the November 11 Armistice. Wilson would negotiate a war-ending treaty with shrewd European leaders who
knew that he had been weakened by the recent polls. In addition, the president simply did not acknowledge the new political landscape when he failed
to ask a single prominent Republican to join the delegation. He might have
considered, for example, former president William Howard Taft and/or
Elihu Root, a former US secretary of state and recipient of the 1912 Nobel
Peace Prize. Wilson, a scholarly expert on US government, almost brazenly
chose not to appoint a Republican member of the Senate Foreign Relations Committee. The latter could and would review the completed treaty,
hold hearings, and recommend alterations to the document before the
Republican-controlled Senate considered and voted on the measure.[23]

Barkley, of course, had nothing to do with the peace talks held in Paris.
There, Wilson took complete charge of the American delegation and par-

ticipated directly in the negotiations producing the Treaty of Versailles that formally ended the war with Germany. The diplomatic discussions required the president to hedge and compromise on important issues in order to assure that the treaty had embedded within it the creation of a League of Nations. Wilson expected the new peace organization to address any short-comings that had taken place in composing the treaty. By the same token, Barkley had no direct involvement in the debates about the treaty's fate in the United States, which duty fell constitutionally to the Senate. Henry Cabot Lodge (MA), who simply detested Wilson, chaired the Senate Foreign Relations Committee. At first, the committee delayed consideration of the treaty, and, when it finally reported it to the Senate, it recommended attaching amendments or reservations. Twice the Senate voted on the Treaty of Versailles (November 19, 1919, and March 19, 1920), and both times the treaty with fourteen and then fifteen reservations failed. Wilson, who made concessions in Paris but refused to do so in Washington, demanded loyal Democratic senators to vote it down. The measure never secured the necessary two-thirds majority.[24]

The pact's defeat in the Senate had two results. America did not join the League of Nations, and it technically remained at war with Germany. Like some other contemporaries who lived long enough, Barkley was inclined to believe that, because the United States chose not to become a member of the league, it somehow enabled expansionist powers to engage much of the world in a second war two decades after the first one. Such "if history" is interesting to contemplate but fruitless in reality because it is fiction. The fact is, officially and unofficially, the United States soon participated in league-sponsored activities related to such problems as disarmament, illicit drugs, and the slave trade. By 1932, an American sat on the league Council (the executive body) and deliberated with its members in an advisory capacity. Domestic problems and attitudes, not the issue of league membership, kept the United States from taking a stronger role to prevent Germany, Japan, Italy, and lesser powers from using force rather than diplomacy in foreign relations. Nevertheless, America's failure to join the league explained Barkley's actions since that body was so closely linked to his hero, Woodrow Wilson. The congressman supported and participated in the Inter-Parliamentary Union (IPU) as a form of compensation since the IPU's goal, similar to that of the league, was to preserve international peace. Additionally, he voted against the June 1921 resolution (signed July 2) ending America's war with Germany. He argued on the House floor that the only formal method to terminate the war was to ratify the Treaty of Versailles as presented in the US Senate by President Wilson on July 10, 1919.[25]

In several ways, things changed for Barkley as a result of events that coincided with the conclusion to the Great War. In the first instance, whether or not Wilson, war's end, or state politics caused it, Republican majorities in Congress affected his position on the Interstate and Foreign Commerce Committee. A couple of Democratic departures left him as one of the leaders of the minority party on the committee. The ranking Democrat was Thetus W. Sims (TN). Also, as was normal and expected in such circumstances, Republicans removed Barkley's father, John, from his position as doorkeeper of the House of Representatives. While he served in that capacity, John Barkley did not live with Alben and his son's family; aside from privacy issues, the apartment housed enough people already with two adults and three children. Presumably, the children's grandfather continued to stay in one of Washington's hotels during congressional sessions and at other times with his wife, Electa, in their Paducah home on 220 North Eighth Street. According to Barkley's children, John always ate Sunday dinner at the family's apartment during congressional sessions. The enhanced aspect to Barkley's family life stopped permanently on March 3, 1919, when the last session of the Sixty-Fifth Congress closed.[26]

Not only Barkley but Congress and the nation were affected at least indirectly by another postwar event. Between December 4, 1918, when President Wilson left New York for Europe on board the *George Washington,* and March 4, 1921, when Warren G. Harding was inaugurated president, the United States had neither a full-time nor a fully functional head of state. Except for interludes, Wilson spent much of his time in Europe negotiating and later attending the signing of the Treaty of Versailles. Two days after he returned home for good on July 8, 1919, he personally presented the treaty to the Senate. As already suggested, the Foreign Relations Committee did everything possible to delay reporting the pact to the upper chamber. The opposition party prompted Wilson to appeal over the heads of Republican senators by going directly to voters and giving protreaty speeches across the country. A stroke forced him to cancel his last five presentations; then, on October 2, he suffered a second, massive stroke. It left him paralyzed on the left side, partially blind, and suffering recurrent kidney failures and urinary blockages. From then until February 1920, he remained largely isolated in the White House under the care of physicians and his wife, Edith; he was too weak to consider issues or make policies. While he partially recovered and his intellect seemed almost normal at times, he had a great deal of difficulty reading or concentrating on anything. Moreover, his personality changed for the worse. His stubborn and self-righteous characteristics became grossly exaggerated and made it impossible for him to deal with ambiguous situations that required thoughtful negotiation or alternative thinking.[27]

The contrast between the power and effectiveness exercised by Wilson between 1913 and 1914 and between 1919 and 1920 is stunning. In his first years in the White House, he regularly appeared in the Capitol Building, where he demonstrated direct leadership and ownership of a consistent legislative agenda. In 1919–1920, the evidence of presidential power and program goals all but evaporated as a consequence of his weakened health and absolute fixation on securing Senate approval of the Treaty of Versailles without the attached reservations. Is it any wonder, then, that congressional sessions became shorter and produced fewer pieces of major legislation? For example, the first session of the Sixty-Sixth Congress opened on May 19, 1919, and, other than discussion of the treaty, focused much of its attention on the problem of implementing the Eighteenth Amendment to the Constitution. Prohibition had already been approved by more than the required number of states. The amendment, however, left to Congress and the states the duty of legislating specific measures for enforcement. Hence, one day after the session began, Barkley offered a bill to extend wartime prohibition as a quick means of continuing prohibition since the amendment would not actually go into effect until January 1920.[28]

Barkley's continued leadership in the drive to implement prohibition nationwide was acknowledged the following month. The ASL invited Barkley to address its national convention. For some time after 1919, he earned extra money giving talks to various groups concerning prohibition. He welcomed fees and honorariums because his personal finances always bordered on chaos owing to his loans and cosigned loans to family members and favored constituents. Meanwhile, his draft legislation went to Andrew J. Volstead (MN), who chaired the House Judiciary committee. The chair and his committee produced the national prohibition bill, which was popularly named after Chairman Volstead. Barkley, of course, supported the bill. Indeed, he wanted to toughen it with an amendment that allowed private homes to be searched if the owners sold liquor.[29]

The Volstead Act became law on October 28, 1919, but without Barkley's amendment. Nevertheless, the new law had its own surprises. The Eighteenth Amendment prohibited only the manufacture, transportation, and sale of "intoxicating liquor." Initially, many Americans who drank beer or wine could support the amendment because their favorite beverages were fermented and not distilled with a high alcoholic content like liquor. By contrast, the Volstead Act defined any beverage, including beer or wine, as intoxicating if it had an alcohol content of more than a half of 1 percent. Thus, national peacetime prohibition began literally with millions of Americans not only opposed to but eager to violate both the amendment and especially the hard-line legislation enacted by Congress. Obviously, this social experiment could not and would not last. To be sure, Barkley remained dry during the Prohibition era but not after 1933, when it ended.[30]

Meanwhile, Barkley had acquired such national attention from prohibitionists and such a strong reputation as a progressive that he proved to be the ideal keynote speaker at Kentucky's state Democratic convention held in Louisville on September 4, 1919. Invited by Governor James D. Black with the enthusiastic endorsement of the State Democratic Committee, he represented perfectly the party's two major factions at odds with each other. Progressives aligned themselves with Senator Augustus O. Stanley, who won the US Senate seat in 1918 shortly after Ollie M. James died. Prohibitionists followed Kentucky's other senator, John C. W. Beckham. The rift between factions occurred, in part, because Stanley's defense of Kentucky's famous bourbon whiskey industry may have cost him the 1914 US Senate race won by Beckham, who had clung to a platform composed of one issue—prohibition.[31]

What was interesting about Barkley's selection as keynote speaker is that Black (a dry) had been lieutenant governor under Stanley (a wet) and inherited the governor's post in 1919 when Stanley resigned after winning the 1918 election as Kentucky's other senator. At the time that Barkley spoke at the state convention, Black was running for governor in his own right in the 1919 general election. He hoped that the keynoter would help unite Democrats behind his campaign. By this time an experienced officeholder and orator, Barkley constructed his speech carefully to avoid all the pitfalls in the commonwealth's factional politics. He only stopped long enough to criticize Republicans in his otherwise effusive praise of the Wilson administration for its accomplishments in domestic and foreign affairs. At that moment in 1919, Wilson remained a popular figure among Kentucky Democrats. He (or Mrs. Wilson) had not yet vetoed the Volstead bill. So Barkley's speech was well received by both the Stanley and the Beckham sides of the Democratic coin.[32]

Barkley had only a couple of days to write his speech. His life was absorbed by problems connected with the railroads. In fact, except for the Volstead Act, his prime legislative concern and activity from July 1919 to February 1920 centered on what eventually emerged, after much debate and discussion, as the Esch-Cummins Transportation Act, which went into effect on February 28, 1920. The process had its origins in the spring of 1919 when Wilson indicated that he expected to return railroad lines to their private owners. Initially, he mentioned that this should happen before year's end but later set a March 1, 1920, deadline. Frankly, like a number of progressives, Barkley was happy with the wartime measure; railroads ran efficiently, needed repairs occurred, owners received guaranteed profits, and workers gained pay raises. Thus, he appreciated the idea expressed earlier by William G. McAdoo, then director-general of the US Railroad Administration, that the government continue to operate railways for at least five more years. At this point, it is important to keep in mind that the director-general had married Eleanor Wilson and was the president's son-in-law and, for some, the heir apparent to the man Barkley admired most. The affinity Barkley had for McAdoo was amplified by this family relationship and partly explains his behavior toward the transportation bill as well as presidential politics in 1920.[33]

Experiencing controversy over the Treaty of Versailles, and suffering from a serious health problem, the president neither demonstrated nor exercised much leadership over legislation transferring railroads from government to private hands. This is why congressional action took such a lengthy, tortured path to completion. Barkley worked overtime with Republicans to create a decent and fair law. In the House, John J. Esch (WI), who chaired the Interstate and Foreign Commerce Committee, introduced a rough draft of a transportation bill and then turned the proposed statute over to a special subcommittee that included Barkley for reworking. Barkley played an important part in revising the bill and then supporting it in the House debate. It passed the lower chamber on November 17, 1919. The messy and time-consuming part of the bill's travel through Congress developed from the fact that the Senate version, sponsored by Albert B. Cummins (IA), differed significantly from what the House approved. As a result, the two bills went to a conference committee on which Barkley also served.[34]

The resulting majority report from the House-Senate conference committee seemed to Barkley so flawed that, on February 19, 1920, he issued a minority report reflecting the views of those Democrats *and* Republicans on the committee who opposed the minority report that the measure should be rejected. The bill was clearly against the interests of workers, farmers, and progressives. From Barkley's perspective, the only good thing that he and others on the conference committee had accomplished was to weed out a section of the Senate bill that made railroad strikes illegal. By contrast, Barkley held key sections of the legislation to be totally unacceptable. First, the bill would establish a railway labor board to arbitrate labor disputes. It sounded good but only on the surface. The board could not impose a settlement, and there was no guarantee that board members would favor labor. A scary element gave the board the right to specify wages for workers; for example, once the board was formed, its first act lowered the pay for rail shopmen by 12 percent. In addition, Barkley's amendment to the House version ended up being cut by the conference committee.[35]

Barkley had wanted the Interstate Commerce Commission to have some flexibility when it came to determining profit margins. Instead, the final bill specified a precise 6 percent return on the aggregate value of railroad property. It would provide railroads an additional net operating income of (a then staggering) $140 million over the 1919 figure. Wall Street smiled; stock prices rose. An angry Barkley stated: "I protest against making the American people, who are already overburdened with taxes and expenses, pay tribute to past inefficiency or dishonesty by legislating hot house values into railroad securities, water and all. I protest against compelling millions of people to pay unreasonable and unnecessary railroad rates in order to guarantee dividends and success to every railroad investment." Despite Barkley's efforts, the railway bill passed the House on February 21 by a vote of 250–150. Surprisingly, several Democrats joined the majority in approving the legislation—a surprise because a few, like Sam T. Rayburn of Texas, came from rural districts where farmers and ranchers relied on modest rail rates to transport the products of their labor and secure needed supplies. Part of the reason for the lopsided vote had to do with the nation's cultural environment. The bill was debated and enacted near the height of America's first Red Scare (1919–1920). US attorney general A. Mitchell Palmer conducted his famous raids rounding up some four thousand suspected Communist radicals in thirty-three major cities in January 1920. It should be understood that many congressmen feared the connections between unions and some of these radicals and were willing to vote against the interests of rail workers. Other legislators opposed the expected creeping socialism should the transportation bill fail and the government end up owning and operating what had been private railroad companies. A few asserted that this might be the first step in the creation of Bolshevik America.[36]

Clearly, Barkley's life as a person, a politician, and a legislator changed because of events associated with World War I and its immediate aftermath. He followed German strategies and Wilson's response and moved from peace and neutrality to war. Ranging from buying Liberty Bonds to approving wartime legislation, he avidly endorsed US participation in the conflict. He acquired significant knowledge about those steps needed to put the nation on a war footing; later, he applied that knowledge as Senate majority leader during World War II. Meanwhile, he visited Europe and the front lines and discovered firsthand the nuts and bolts, horrors and heroics of battle. As the war ended, he both warned against and witnessed a president who made political blunders that cost him his health, his leadership, and the League of Nations. All this occurred at a time during which Barkley's party shifted to minority status and an oppositional role. Thus, the congressman had the less familiar experience of legislative failure as seen in the railroad bill. Even with this type of adversity, three results of the period brightened his future. He nailed his relationship with farmers and laborers, improved tremendously his understanding of international relations, and realized unmistakably his role as a figure of consequence in his home state.

8

"Normalcy" and
the Tale of Two Elections

Through his continued support for farmers and workers, Barkley had fired the starting pistol in what he hoped would be a victorious Democratic race to win the fall elections. Fortunately for him in the short term, the Red Scare hysteria that falsely linked unionism with communism abated quickly after February 1920. The new public media of radio, along with Prohibition, Jack Dempsey, Babe Ruth, and the sporting chances of presidential candidates in the upcoming conventions, replaced communism as subjects for the national conversation. Even such stalwart anti-Reds as Senator Warren G. Harding (OH) and the author-editor William Allen White denounced the lower house (the Assembly) of the New York state legislature for excluding five duly-elected assemblymen who belonged to the Socialist Party. Barkley had nurtured the farm-labor vote in the Esch-Cummins transportation bill debate. Similar tactics had kept him in office, and he trusted that his effort would also boost the chances for the election or reelection of Democrats in sufficient numbers to retake control of Congress and hang on to the White House.[1]

Barkley's quest to strengthen his party became a common theme promoted by many of his colleagues on both sides of the aisle. Presidential politics and a diminished leadership from the White House resulted in the passage of just a few pieces of notable legislation by Congress in 1920. Besides the railway measure, the best examples include the Merchant Marine Act and the Federal Water Power Act. The former repealed emergency war legislation related to US shipping; the latter established the Federal Power Commission to regulate waterways and license dam sites for electric power. Otherwise, Congress often became the bully pulpit from which members could tout and publicize their political visions to influence the upcoming electoral campaigns. Barkley eagerly participated in this activity. On April 24, Scott Ferris (OK), who chaired the Democratic Congressional Campaign Committee, asked him to prepare and deliver a speech in the House that was designed purely to be used in whole or in part as Democratic campaign propaganda. The title, "The Partisan Plot against the President," gives a clear picture of the substance of his talk.[2]

When Barkley delivered his prepackaged presentation before the House on June 2, 1920, he may have expected or at least anticipated the possibility that Woodrow Wilson would run for a third term as president. This was, after all, before 1951, when the Twenty-Second Amendment to the US Constitution limited the office to two terms. Unbeknownst to Barkley, there was serious drama being played out at the White House that might have subdued his rhetoric. In his speech, he compared favorably Wilson to Washington and Lincoln but stated that current Republican "methods [were] more contemptible than any ever attempted by any similar organization of political buccaneers and freebooters in the history of the Republic." Indeed, Wilson wanted to serve again and convert the presidential campaign into a crusade that would resurrect the twice-defeated Treaty of Versailles and give new life to American membership in the League of Nations. While Edith Wilson sided with her husband and both plotted to create press reports proclaiming his recovery, they could not quell the more realistic, behind-the-scenes revelations. On April 13, Wilson held his first cabinet meeting since his stroke. Alarmed cabinet members saw firsthand a president who sagged on his left side, could not stand without help, and failed to fathom the issues under discussion. He was a mental and physical invalid. In fact, his physician recommended that he resign and subsequently told party leaders that a third term would be, in essence, a death sentence.[3]

It is easy therefore to guess that Barkley would not be entirely pleased with the end result of the Democratic national convention. He attended the meeting, which opened in San Francisco on June 28, as a delegate at-large. Secretary of State Bainbridge Colby was slated to place Wilson's name in nomination, but the president's physician, Dr. Cary T. Grayson, and party leaders blocked the effort. Barkley then turned to William G. McAdoo, who was one of three serious candidates remaining after early balloting had winnowed out the nominations of favorite sons. McAdoo, however, had three strikes against him. His prohibition stand, pleasing to Barkley, cost him the votes of urban Democrats, who enjoyed a glass of beer, wine, or something a bit stronger. As Wilson's son-in-law, the former Treasury secretary and director of railroads carried the unflattering sobriquet "Crown Prince" among those Democrats who were tired of Wilsonianism. Those still enamored with the president understood that the heir apparent had been denied an endorsement from or even an interview with his father-in-law before the convention. And McAdoo had to compete against arguably America's best-known administration figure, Attorney General A. Mitchell Palmer. By the summer of 1920, however, his fame had soured to notoriety. In the words of the historian Thomas A. Bailey, Palmer had "treated the country to an obscene orgy of red-baiting." The triumvirate's third serious candidate, Governor James M. Cox of Ohio won the nomination on the forty-fourth ballot. Although a wet, Cox promised vociferously to uphold the laws of the land. His running mate was Assistant Secretary of the Navy Franklin D. Roosevelt.[4]

Barkley's name would later be linked closely to Roosevelt's, perhaps as much as that of any other congressional figure during the full range of FDR's multiple terms in the White House. But the Kentuckian had to admit that he really did not know the future president before the 1920 convention. That all changed because of the upcoming campaign. As usual, Barkley had few worries about his own election. He spent time with constituents between congressional sessions and kept in touch with them via the mails and the newspapers. Additionally, he faced no opponent in the Democratic primary and a weak candidate in the general election. Hence, he could and did spend time with Cox and Roosevelt and canvassed for the Democratic ticket especially in Kentucky and Tennessee. He overcame his earlier disappointments that Wilson or McAdoo failed to secure the nomination and accepted Cox's pledge to uphold the Volstead Act. He was even happier that the Democratic candidate for president tagged himself as a progressive. Best of all from Barkley's perspective, on July 18, 1920, Cox and Roosevelt met with President Wilson. Roosevelt stated later that Cox's eyes welled with tears when he heard a weak-voiced Wilson and saw the president's distorted figure in a wheelchair. Small wonder the pair agreed to support another effort to gain Senate approval of the Treaty of Versailles that automatically included membership in the League of Nations.[5]

With Barkley's occasional attendance, Cox and Roosevelt separately crisscrossed the United States, traveled forty thousand miles by train, visited thirty-six states, and delivered hundreds of speeches. Despite this extraordinary effort, the Democratic ticket lost by more than a landslide. Joseph P.

Tumulty, Wilson's private secretary from 1910 to 1921, described the Democratic debacle with the single word *earthquake*. The Republican nominee, Harding, won the electoral votes of all but eleven states, and his popular vote total of 60.2 percent was the largest majority in US history since the time of George Washington. The contrast in activity displayed between Cox and Harding could not have been greater. At least initially, Harding conducted the campaign on the front porch of his Marion, Ohio, home. His running mate, Governor J. Calvin Coolidge of Massachusetts, did make some speeches in the Midwest as well as in Kentucky and Tennessee, but his audiences grew smaller as he talked longer. Nevertheless, Harding captured the vote not only because he was handsome and looked presidential but also because he captured the deep-seated longing of the American people. Just before the Republican national convention, held in June in Chicago, he delivered a speech that became his campaign's theme. He told a Boston group: "America's present need is not heroics, but healing; not nostrums, but normalcy; not revolution, but restoration; not agitation, but adjustment; not surgery, but serenity."[6]

Normalcy became a watchword for the campaign and helped lead Harding to his inauguration. He was sworn in as president by US Supreme Court chief justice Edward D. White on March 4, 1921. Barkley and his eldest daughter, Marian (nicknamed Sis), watched the parade and swearing-in ceremony. He would not attend another until his own participation in the 1949 inaugural parade. Clearly, Barkley was not attracted to the ceremony by Harding, who at the Capitol appeared healthy and strong compared with Wilson, who looked stooped and frail. Barkley, of course, wanted to see the man he revered. At the event's conclusion, father and daughter walked with other well-wishers to Wilson's home on S Street. (Wilson had recently purchased the house near the Library of Congress so that he could use its sources to write a book. He never finished more than a dedication page to his wife.) Mrs. Wilson recognized Barkley among those standing outside the home and invited him and Marian to come inside to see her husband. "Sis stood in the background solemnly and silently," Barkley remembered, "while I groped to find a few words to say to the great wartime leader. That day was the end of an era."[7]

For Barkley and his fellow Democrats, "the end of an era" really had come the previous November in the general election. It marked the start, according to the historian John D. Hicks, to the period of Republican ascendancy. It was an era representing an alternate trend; Harding, the presidential victor, often compared himself with such nineteenth-century conservatives as President William McKinley. And the Sixty-Seventh Congress most clearly defined this ascendancy when it opened on April 11, 1921. Republicans dominated the legislative function of government to such an extent that the Democrats were hard-pressed to perform even a minority role as a serious opposition party. In the fall elections, the GOP gained sixty-three seats in the House and, thus, possessed a supermajority of 303 votes out of a total of 431; it also acquired ten more seats in the Senate and carried a strong majority of fifty-nine votes out of a total of ninety-six there. Barkley had become more sensitive to this issue because of what happened in Kentucky. Not only had Black lost the governor's race in 1919 to the Republican Edwin P. Morrow, but the Republican Richard P. Ernst unseated the Democratic senator Beckham, a prohibitionist, in 1920.[8]

All this bad news for Barkley did not mean that he could not enjoy an occasional legislative victory. From time to time he worked with congressional survivors of the progressive movement as well as rural representatives who banded together in a farm bloc to promote agricultural interests. Both ad hoc groups contained individuals from the two main political parties and championed separate agendas not specifically identified as being sponsored by Republicans or Democrats. The first progressive measure to gain Barkley's vigorous approval was a resolution introduced in April in the Senate by a progressive Republican, William E. Borah (ID). The senator had actually introduced it the previous December, but the resolution never came to a vote. Borah called on the president and his administration to negotiate a reduction in warships and naval expenditures with Great Britain and Japan. For Barkley and most war-weary Americans, whether Democrats or Republicans, progressives or conservatives, a naval disarmament conference was exactly the right step to promote peace, especially in view of the fact the United States had not joined the League of Nations. Grotesquely, a little over two years after the Great War ended, Great Britain, Japan, and the United States were engaged in a senseless and expensive, if not dangerous, arms race to build up their navies.[9]

Barkley had argued against a US naval buildup in the House during the final session of the Sixty-Sixth Congress. In his speech endorsing the Borah resolution in the new Congress on April 25, 1921, his main argument centered on the notion that a warship arms race was likely to spiral out of control, leading to higher taxes and larger naval fleets. The latter would diminish security and increase the likelihood of global war. Fascinatingly, the resolution was tied to a naval appropriations bill that received an over-whelmingly favorable vote. President Harding signed it into law on July 12, and Secretary of State Charles Evans Hughes and his staff arranged for the Washington Naval Disarmament Conference. The day before the con-ference opened on November 12, 1921, delegates from nine nations (Bel-gium, China, France, Great Britain, Italy, Japan, Netherlands, Portugal, and the United States) met on Armistice Day to witness a moving ceremony for the burial of the Unknown Soldier at Arlington National Cemetery. By the time the conference ended on February 6, 1922, it produced sev-eral important agreements and treaties, including one that seriously reduced and limited the building of capital ships—vessels over ten thousand tons. Regrettably, Japan destroyed the work of the conference after 1930 when it openly violated agreements to restrict the size of its navy and respect Chi-na's sovereignty.[10]

According to the *Washington Post* journalist Constance Drexel, Bark-ley played an important part in the passage of another forward-looking measure—the Sheppard-Towner Maternity and Infancy Act. In fact, the legislation was the most progressive bill to make it through Congress and be signed into law during the 1920s. It provided states some seed money from the federal government in order to improve the welfare and hygiene of mothers and their infants. Barkley felt especially comfortable working for the bill because of his earlier association with Senator Morris Sheppard to make the District of Columbia free of liquor. In the maternity bill, Shep-pard shared cosponsorship with Horace Mann Towner (IA), who served as House Republican Conference chairman. Barkley, however, exercised some leadership over the bill because by 1921 he had become the ranking minor-ity member of the Interstate and Foreign Commerce Committee, which held hearings on the proposal. Just as he had employed his leadership posi-tion to secure Democratic support for the noncontroversial establishment of a veterans' bureau in August, he also rallied Democratic representatives to favor the Sheppard-Towner measure on the House floor. The bill sought to lower the dreadfully high infant mortality rate by creating maternal and infant health services in each state.[11]

During his speech in the House, Barkley defended the maternity bill on the basis of the general welfare clause of the US Constitution. Discussions in hearings and on the House floor revealed his view of the federal gov-ernment's role as the organizational framework upholding American soci-ety. When, for whatever reason, society did a poor job—in this case, in promoting the health and well-being of expectant mothers and newborn babies—the framework needed an adjustment. Barkley thus felt that the federal government was justified in adding a brace here or a column there to shore up the framework and correct an obvious societal shortcoming. His visible and vocal leadership in support of the Sheppard-Towner bill partly explained its passage in a lopsided House vote of 279–39 taken on November 19, 1921. Since it already had passed the Senate, the measure required only the president's signature four days later to become a statute. Not Harding but his successor, President Calvin Coolidge, felt uncomfortable dispensing federal funds for a program that he felt should be maintained exclusively by individual states. He allowed the funding to lapse before the end of his administration in 1929. Barkley made a failed bid to revive the program during the presidency of Herbert Hoover, but success had to wait for a new president and the New Deal.[12]

In terms of the farm bloc, it is true that Barkley often sided with the group. For instance, he joined the bloc in voting for the (Kansas senator Arthur) Capper-Volstead cooperative marketing bill that President Harding signed into law on February 18, 1922. The statute exempted agricultural associations and cooperatives from the antitrust laws. On the other hand, it would be wrong to identify Barkley as a consistent, card-carrying member of the congressional farm group. A clear example occurred when he voted against the emergency agricultural tariff bill, which was strongly endorsed by the farm bloc, approved by Congress, and signed by the president on May 27, 1921. Incorporated the next year into a broader tariff bill, the temporary act added prohibitive tariff charges on twenty-eight imported farm products ranging from corn to wheat. It was a cheap way for Republicans to placate the farm bloc, whose constituents suffered at war's conclusion a serious, ongoing economic decline that preceded and later merged with the nation's Great Depression after 1929.[13]

The steep drop in American farm prices ultimately resulted from a major expansion in the amount of crops, livestock, and acreage that occurred between 1914 and 1918. In that period of time, the estimated value of farm produce rose from $4 billion to $10 billion. The European conflict magnified the need for US foodstuffs to meet both the boosted number of calories consumed by Allied soldiers and food deficits caused by the destruction or occupation of European fields, pastures, and storage facilities as well as the conscription of farmers and farm laborers into armies. By the time Harding had become president, *normalcy* for US farmers meant excessive production that fueled declining prices as rural Europe recovered from war. Also, a branch of the Ford Motor Company manufactured by the hundreds of thousands the small, inexpensive Fordson tractor beginning in 1918. The result was a rapid decline in the need for horses and mules that freed thirty million acres for crops that otherwise had been used to raise oats and hay to feed work animals. Monetary values collapsed by 50 percent for wheat, corn, meat, and cotton. Thus, Barkley simply rejected the notion that the emergency agricultural tariff bill would help. He knew that the real solution involved one or more aspects of expanded marketing, delayed marketing, and reduced production. Each year, as US farmers raised, for example, more wheat in order to keep the same cash flow as the previous year, they competed largely against each other and rarely against foreign imports. Except for sugar and wool, the temporary tariff did little to raise the depressed worth of agricultural products.[14]

A key to understanding Barkley's opposition to the temporary tariff was his correct perception that Republicans cleverly connived to secure a commitment from the farm bloc to vote for a permanent tariff with high rates once bloc members enthusiastically backed a protectionist piece of legislation for agriculture. Ordinarily, farmers liked the idea of a lower, general tariff because it had the potential of reducing prices on goods and equipment. The farm bloc consisted of progressive Republican senators from western states and Democratic representatives from rural districts in the South. This "third party," in the words of the contemporary journalist William Allen White, could not ignore the fact that the new general bill embraced elements of the agricultural tariff. Barkley, however, was not blind to the fact that Republicans simply wanted to nullify the Democratic Underwood-Simmons Tariff of 1913. The replacement legislation (like all money bills) began in the House and, in this case, in the hands of Joseph W. Fordney (IN), chair of the Ways and Means Committee. When finally signed into law by President Harding, the new tariff set a record for the time it took to create the statute. Fordney began hearings in January 1921 during the last session of Congress. The open meetings were followed by secret discussions among committee members, excluding Democrats. It would not be until June 29 that Fordney submitted a bill to the House.[15]

It will be recalled that Barkley's first speech in Congress supported the 1913 lower tariff. It was only natural that the high rate increases proposed in the Fordney bill persuaded Barkley to speak sharply against the measure in the House debate on July 14, 1921: "Without regard to the character of the ills that beset the Nation, the Republican party always comes forward with the same remedy—a high, prohibitive, protective tariff. It does not yet realize that the world has undergone a tremendous change. It does not realize that our position as a nation has been reversed from a commercial standpoint, and that we are a great creditor nation, with other countries indebted to us enormously, and with no power to pay that indebtedness except by the exchange of their goods for ours, or for cash." Barkley appreciated what a majority of his colleagues chose to ignore. International trade is essentially barter. A country can buy abroad only to the extent that it can sell abroad; otherwise, its purchases require loans or investments from the seller or a favorable trade balance with a third-party nation that has a hard (exchangeable) currency. As mentioned earlier, Barkley knew that his constituents who raised dark tobacco and cotton needed robust sales abroad to get a good price for the products of their labor. Foreign sales to the United States would help make that possible.[16]

Notwithstanding Barkley's earnest attempt to rally colleagues against the tariff proposal, the House easily passed the Fordney bill on July 21 by a vote of 289–127. Several commentators on this period of American history have observed that the vote not only reflected support from the farm bloc but also marked the growth of nationalistic and anti-European sentiment that after World War I evolved into a form of deep-seated isolationism. The captivating and contrasting characteristic about Barkley is that he emerged from the Great War, in the words of Selig Adler, who authored *The Isolationist Impulse,* as a "moderate internationalist." The proof occurred in August when he traveled to Stockholm, Sweden, to attend a meeting of the Inter-Parliamentary Union. The conference concluded on August 20 with a royal banquet hosted by Sweden's King Gustavus V. Barkley then went via Denmark to Germany where he spent several days visiting cities such as Berlin and Frankfurt. His last stop was Coblenz (Koblenz after 1926) at the confluence of the Mosel and Rhine Rivers, which until 1923 served as the US Army headquarters for American occupation troops in Germany's Rhineland.[17]

By the time Barkley returned to the United States on board the Red Star liner *Kroonland* on September 12, the Fordney bill was being considered by the Senate Committee on Finance, chaired by Boies Penrose (PA) and then, after Penrose's death, by Porter J. McCumber (ND). What happened might appropriately be considered something between extraordinary and silly. Business interests bombarded the Senate with arguments for increasing the Fordney bill's already high rates even more. Members of the Finance Committee accepted many of the arguments and reconstructed the bill by tacking on the mountainous number of 2,082 amendments. These additions invigorated protectionism to historic heights. In the midst of this process, Barkley delivered a Jefferson-Jackson Day address on January 10, 1922. Democrats held this particular annual gathering at an in-your-face location—President Harding's hometown of Marion, Ohio. Barkley blasted the Harding administration for its "abnormalcy" and judged most legislation of the Republican-controlled Congress to be a "tragedy." He saved his sharpest comments, however, for what became the Fordney-McCumber tariff bill. The latter, still in process, was the "most cumbersome, bunglesome, unscientific piece of Jazz legislation of which any legislative body was ever guilty."[18]

McCumber did not report the tariff bill out of the Finance Committee until April 11, 1922. Lengthy debates ensued to the extent that the final version was not approved by the Senate until August 19. The vote was 48–25, with Democrats accounting for most of the negative votes. A House-Senate conference committee then massaged the bill since the Senate significantly altered the original House measure. The revised variant then went back for reconsideration by the House and the Senate. Their favorable votes in September enabled Harding to sign the Fordney-McCumber Tariff into law on September 21. The act did include a provision that allowed presidents some discretion in raising or lowering rates by as much as 50 percent. President Coolidge was the one who made thirty-seven changes between 1923 and 1929. All but five—cresylic acid, live quail, millfeeds, paintbrush handles, and phenol—involved raising rates. "One suspects," the Coolidge biographer Robert H. Ferrell states, "that the president's puckish sense of humor had a hand in choosing the items for reduction." Regardless, the new tariff was then the highest in American history. It wreaked havoc on international trade and made all but impossible the repayment of Europe's war debts to the United States. European debt payments to America, then, depended on German reparations, and those, in turn, depended on US investments. This ridiculous financial roundabout failed with the start of the Great Depression in 1929.[19]

For Barkley and his congressional colleagues in both the House and the Senate, the tariff took up much of their legislative time in 1922. The new act did help American businesses make money without fear of foreign competition, but it also limited foreign sales and did virtually nothing to diminish the money doldrums endured by American farmers. Officially enacted at the start of fall, its conclusion as a completed congressional bill marked the start to the campaign season. Barkley enjoyed a worry-free reelection. He had no primary competition from his own party, and the general election handed him a majority vote in all the First District's thirteen counties. He devoted most of his campaign energy to speaking on behalf of other Democrats in Kentucky and nearby states. Results of the national general elections pleased Barkley and surprised the GOP. Republicans suffered casualties especially among representatives and senators responsible for the Fordney-McCumber Tariff. For instance, neither Joseph Fordney nor Porter McCumber returned to Congress. The Democrats remained a minority but gained six more senators and seventy-seven more representatives. The GOP was so stunned that grumbles could be heard among some party members over whether Harding should be nominated for a second term in the White House.[20]

While Republicans reeled from their losses, their electoral troubles encouraged Barkley to consider a move up in the political world by seeking statewide office. Just three days after winning another two-year term in Congress, he announced his candidacy for the office of governor in Louisville's Seelbach Hotel. The commonwealth's constitution provides the officeholder with only a single four-year term. With such a restriction, most candidates want the post either as a rewarding honor before retiring from politics or as a launching pad for higher office, namely, one of the two Kentucky seats in the US Senate. Barkley had no intention of challenging Democratic senator Augustus O. Stanley in 1924, but he did want to unseat and replace Republican senator Richard P. Ernst in 1926. For Barkley, the strategy was safe because, even if he lost either the 1923 primary or the general election, he still held his position as First District congressman.[21]

In fact, Barkley was in a win-win situation. Win or lose, he could form across the commonwealth both a strong, favorable presence and a viable political organization. It would give him an excellent opportunity to shape a successful campaign for the 1926 senatorial election. For the governor's race, he chose a program that made him highly visible, if not controversial, as a moralist and reform-minded politician. On January 15, 1923, he proclaimed a twelve-point platform that zeroed in on issues ranging from agriculture to taxation and included long-term Barkley concerns for building roads and promoting good government. In one sense, the latter became the organizing principle behind the campaign. Several commentators on

Kentucky politics have discussed the formidable impact of the "biparti-san combine" composed of businessmen and politicians, Republicans and Democrats, in the Bluegrass and eastern portions of Kentucky. Businesses financially supported politicians who opposed regulation and progressive measures and also enhanced the split in the Democratic Party outlined in the previous chapter. Barkley argued that he would restore good, combine-free government to the people. He stated bluntly that his base in the Jack-son Purchase region of western Kentucky made him free of the corruption, power, and money of the combine.[22]

Among the businesses associated with the combine, Barkley focused his attention and rhetoric on the two most visible and powerful players in Ken-tucky politics—the coal and horse-racing lobbies. The National Association of Coal Operators served the interests of the former; the Kentucky Jockey Club represented the latter, which was composed of race tracks and horse breeders. Barkley orally assaulted both groups by advocating a coal tax and repealing legalized betting on horse races. The profits enjoyed by these com-bine members allowed them to grease the palms of Kentucky politicians in the legislature. As Barkley claimed in speeches, anytime a road needed to be built by a schoolhouse, legislators had to consult first with the coal or race-track lobby before approving an appropriation. A severance tax on coal and repeal of legalized gambling would reduce the financial and hence the political clout of these interest groups and restore good government under the control of the commonwealth's citizens. Naturally, coal-mining opera-tors and Jockey Club members threw support to and dumped cash into the campaign of Barkley's Democratic opponent in the August primary, Con-gressman J. Campbell Cantrill of Kentucky's Seventh District (eliminated after 1993 because of relative changes in national population).[23]

In his life, views, and behavior, Cantrill posed a contrast to Barkley. Born and eventually buried in his hometown of Georgetown, he lived in the center of the Bluegrass region. Its rolling hills housed Kentucky's urban areas, educational centers, industrial sites, and, with a substructure of lime-stone, excellent farmland for grazing horses and cattle and growing burley tobacco. He did not share Barkley's populist/progressive heritage, as seen in his opposition to prohibition and alignment with horse racing and coal mining. Moreover, Barkley delivered dynamic and forceful speeches and seemed the antithesis to Cantrill, who addressed audiences in a dignified and calm manner. Cantrill also showed skill in organizing a well-financed political campaign. And Barkley helped his opponent. The Paducah politician's call for the end to gambling on horses hurt him in the Bluegrass; his coal tax proposal handed votes to Cantrill from Kentucky's eastern and western coalfield regions. To be sure, Barkley had a strong base in the Jackson Purchase, but the region was smaller, less populous, and less affluent than the eastern half of Kentucky. These limitations, of course, explained exactly why he jumped into the statewide race for the post of governor.[24]

While Cantrill allowed veteran party leaders from central Kentucky to conduct the bulk of his campaign, his opponent worked personally and diligently to gain notice and votes. Historians have remarked that Barkley was not as clever as his opponent in organizing a campaign. But, in the 1923 primary race for governor, he certainly made some good decisions and gained attention despite a limited budget. He chose Louisville to be his headquarters, which he financed initially out of his own pocket. Elwood Hamilton served as his campaign manager, and William "Percy" Haly helped construct his platform. (Hamilton was a partner in the law firm of the prohibitionist Beckham; Haly directed a political machine in Louisville that had aided Beckham in winning the governor's post and later a seat in the US Senate.) Barkley also asked his First District friend Seldon R. Glenn to oversee the campaign in the Jackson Purchase. By summer, he obtained the endorsement of Robert Worth Bingham, who owned and published Kentucky's largest and most widely read newspaper, the *Louisville Courier-Journal*. He integrated the aid of these important individuals with his vigorous speaking tour of the commonwealth. After Congress recessed in the spring, he drove a Model-T Ford around the state delivering five or more addresses a day and stopping at every village along the way to speak and shake hands with voters. His hard-driven pace earned him the sobriquet "Iron Man of Politics."[25]

Before his on-the-road canvass of the state moved into high gear, Barkley started his campaign early. He used the same approach as when he ran for county attorney, county judge, and congressman. Thus, he began the effort to win the August primary by delivering his opening address in Danville on February 19, 1923. The location was symbolically important for several reasons. The seat of government for Boyle County, Danville anchored the southwest border of the Bluegrass. Its progressive side was exemplified by housing the Kentucky School for the Deaf; the institution was the first of its kind in the United States. Danville also had a reputation for the advancement of education and a theological connection with the Presbyterian Church. The latter influenced the early formation and development of

Centre College—proud of its famous graduates and victory over Harvard College in 1921, winning the national collegiate football championship. And this religious connection prompted most Danville citizens to praise the prohibition reform and recognize Barkley's leadership in that movement. Indeed, Barkley often presented himself as reform minded, claiming, for example: "Woodrow Wilson drove the crooks and corruptionists out of New Jersey, Governor [Gifford] Pinchot is driving them out of Pennsylvania, and if I am elected Governor of Kentucky I promise to drive them out of Frankfort [Kentucky's capital]."[26]

Barkley connected reform with good government. Early in his Danville speech he stated: "Here in Kentucky we are confronted with the obligation to make our government effective and progressive." Moreover, he expected to apply "business methods to the business affairs of the state." This idea merged seamlessly with the concept expressed by the newspaper publisher Bingham, who hoped for a "Business Men's Candidate" for governor. Barkley's rhetoric prompted Bingham and his newspaper in June to decide publicly that the First District congressman was that candidate. Barkley asserted that he could save money for businesses as well as farmers and all property owners by exempting real estate from all state taxes except those for roads and schools. The reduction in revenue would be made up by streamlining government and imposing a special tax on coal. The implication, of course, was that reducing the revenue of the mining industry would also limit the financial power of the coal lobby to influence legislators in Frankfort. In short, one of the major "corruptionist" groups in Kentucky would be thwarted.[27]

Barkley pointed out that in 1922 coal production reached approximately forty million tons. Since the average price per ton at the mine was about $4.00, the total value of Kentucky coal weighed in at a figure close to $160,000,000. The amount was actually higher than the assessed valuation of all coal property in the commonwealth. Obviously, the coal industry enjoyed relatively low taxes. Additionally, Barkley revealed statistics from the Kentucky Department of Commerce indicating that 88 percent of the coal ended up in markets outside the state. He then discussed various ways in which revenue might be secured from the mineral but made it clear that he did not favor double-taxing coal. From his list of strategies, he settled on the production (severance) tax. It would be levied as a small percentage of the selling price as fixed at the mine. That way the tax would be equitable for different grades of coal, whereas a straight tonnage tax would be patently unfair.[28]

Barkley did spend time in Danville highlighting other issues found in his January platform. He deplored, for example, the low ranking Kentucky had in expenditures for public education. In terms of institutions of higher learning, he wanted to upgrade the University of Kentucky to make it one of America's best state universities. Another item that required additional funding was the state's highway system. Barkley always advocated good roads to make certain that his farmer friends had easy access to the markets and cultural benefits of urban areas. He also mentioned proposals that saved money or cost very little. By way of illustration, he wanted to place at least one farmer on every state board "which has to do with the assessment, collection, or expenditure of public funds." Another recommendation would switch the selection of county and state officials from odd to even years to coincide with national elections for Congress and the White House. And, typical of many progressive politicians beginning with President Theodore Roosevelt, Barkley hoped to establish a conservation policy for the commonwealth. Finally, he met head-on the issue of his ambition for higher office. While he claimed (speciously) that he might not seek a seat in the US Senate, he stated: "But I do not feel that any man, in order to be allowed to perform the service that is at hand, should be required to bar himself from any future service that the people might wish him to perform."[29]

The Danville speech proved to be unique. Starting with the address in Frankfort on March 24, Barkley's presentations tended to focus on the two main themes discussed above but under the rubric of good government. For example, his campaign talk on April 2 at Lebanon, Marion County's seat of government, nailed coal for taxes and horse racing for gambling. In Lebanon, Barkley emphasized that the coal tax would be paid primarily by people outside Kentucky. It would not add, he noted, "a dollar to the annual coal bill of a single home in the state, but it would enable the state to reduce by more than thirty percent the tax burden which it now levies on every home in Kentucky." In terms of the gambling issue, Barkley remarked how he loved horses and attended races. But he also pointed out that all other forms of gambling were, according to Kentucky statutes, illegal and that those who gambled were identified as criminals. Such discrimination violated democratic principles. Barkley went on:

> But if this were all, it might not be so alarming. The Kentucky Jockey Club has played for other stakes than those ordinarily wagered on horses. It has played for control of the government of Kentucky. It

and its allies have polluted the very citadel of free government. It has gnawed at the foundations of Kentucky's government like a rat at a corn crib. It has not hesitated to approach the halls of legislation, to hire those who were sent there for nobler purposes. It and its corrupt allies have hung over the desks of legislators, and have swarmed around the state capital, to control legislation, to choke the stream of good government, and to work to increase the burdens borne by honest men and women.[30]

As might be expected, the moralistic tone of Barkley's campaign attracted the support of some extremist groups on the outer fringes of society, including the Ku Klux Klan. On the other hand, the First District representative gained favorable attention among a wide assortment of mainstream citizens. Despite his meager financial resources compared with those available to Cantrill, Barkley's incredible exertions on the hustings allowed him to come within ten thousand votes of beating the combine candidate in the August primary. He carried every rural county west of Louisville and Lexington; his opponent dominated the eastern portion of the state, which often voted Republican in general elections. For what happened next, it must be recorded that, except for prohibition, the two candidates often worked together on a friendly basis in Congress. As a result, and quite unlike modern politics, neither candidate attacked the other. Thus, not only could Barkley congratulate sincerely his opponent for the electoral victory, but he also proceeded to campaign actively on behalf of Cantrill.[31]

Naturally, Barkley impressed Cantrill's political organization. It was a smart activity based on a resolution that he probably made months before he lost the primary. Another wise decision clinched his election to the US Senate in 1926. It was based, unfortunately, on what happened after what was for Barkley an unforeseen tragedy. Cantrill suffered from poor health and had spent much of the final month of the primary campaign in a bed. Close friends suspected he was dying, and, indeed, he passed away from a ruptured appendix on September 2, 1923. The state Democratic Committee had responsibility for selecting a replacement candidate. Many, of course, fully expected Barkley to be that person; however, the party interests that defeated him in the primary controlled the committee. Furthermore, James B. Brown, the head of the National Bank of Kentucky, a member of the bipartisan combine, and a heavy contributor to the Democratic Party's Sinking Fund Commission, pressured the committee to pick William

J. Fields to run against the GOP candidate, Charles I. Dawson. Barkley chose for good reason to campaign energetically for Fields. "Honest Bill from Olive Hill" beat the Republican by nearly fifty thousand votes in the general election. The net result of these events earned Barkley the plaudits of both Democratic Party factions. By the end of 1923, he had a loyal following of Democrats in every commonwealth county. And he knew that he could count in the future on the strong help of Cantrill's political organization. Finally, the Iron Man of Politics understood that the coal and racing lobbies would be partially neutralized in the 1926 Senate race.[32]

Given the 1923 campaign, Barkley was so confident of his future in Washington that he chose this moment to purchase a house in the nation's capital. He moved his family from their apartment to a three-story home at 3102 Cleveland Avenue, not too far from the US Naval Observatory (since 1974 the official residence of the US vice president). The five-member family needed more living space, and the house was big enough for modest entertaining as well as providing room for a visiting guest or relative. The larger domicile prompted Barkley to hire a man to take care of the yard and a woman to help Dorothy with cooking and cleaning. David, Marian, and Laura Louise (nicknamed "Wahwee" from when she first tried to say her own name) loved the home and described it as filled with warmth and fun. The two constants in family life centered on sharing evening meals and taking Sunday drives around the countryside and often visiting sites of historical interest. Of the three children, Marian was the one who suffered childhood health problems. She had such severe sinus discomfort that she underwent corrective surgeries. One must cringe at such procedures when reflecting on the limitations of medical technology in that era. Her sinus complications were so serious that she missed two years of school and ended up in the same grade in school as her younger sister. Unlike her siblings, she never participated in her father's political campaigns.[33]

By contrast, David in 1923 and Laura Louise in 1926 and 1932 accompanied their father on selected road trips during his canvass of the commonwealth. The one in 1926 proved different because Governor Fields and Democratic leaders made certain that Barkley would not have to spend time and money contesting another Democrat in the senatorial primary election. This was one of the dividends earned from his actions for the party and its unity in 1923. With this assurance, Barkley announced in Paducah on April 23, 1926, his candidacy to oppose Ernst in November's general election. In addition to the strategies he employed in the 1923 campaign, the congressman took several steps to improve his chances for victory. Via the Senate Campaign Committee, and with contributions from the financier Bernard Baruch, he secured a slush fund to pay for his travels around the state. Second, he selected Congressman Frederick M. Vinson (Kentucky Fourth District), a future Chief Justice of the US Supreme Court, to head his campaign. Vinson possessed close ties with the coal lobby. If getting rid of Barkley from state politics was not enough, Vinson could encourage the coal lobby to limit its support for Ernst. As the *New York Times* observed: "'If Barkley is defeated for the Senate,' say those who are against him because of his proposals concerning race-track betting and coal, 'he will get the Gubernatorial nomination in 1927, and, if he's elected Governor, he'll put racing out of business and will hurt the coal industry tremendously by the tonnage act. Perhaps the best thing we can do, in spite of the fact that we prefer Ernst, is to vote for Barkley and kick him upstairs into the Senate, thus getting rid of him as a potential Governor.'"[34]

Third, Barkley captured votes from farmers and laborers owing to his exertions on their behalf throughout nearly fourteen years in the US House of Representatives. He reinforced his ties to workers via the Railway Labor Act, signed into law on May 20, 1926, just a few months before the Senate campaign moved into high gear. It will be recalled that Barkley had opposed the Esch-Cummins Transportation Act, in part because it created the Railway Labor Board, which, in terms of wages, favored corporate management rather than railroad employees. By 1924, Barkley introduced a bill to abolish the misnamed labor board. His effort failed temporarily but inspired the creation and approval of the 1926 measure. It abolished and replaced the Railway Labor Board with a board of mediation; it also provided for the formation of railway unions. Along with the Sheppard-Towner Maternity and Infancy Act, the 1926 railroad statute represented one of the few pieces of progressive legislation approved during the 1920s. Barkley drummed up votes with his persuasive oratory for the railway labor bill on the House floor. His speech was so effective and included such a rich history of railroad laws that the Order of Railroad Telegraphers published it in its monthly magazine.[35]

One of Barkley's stops on his automobile canvass of the commonwealth was Ravenna on September 23. Located close to Irvine, the seat of government for Estill County, the area was considered Republican territory in eastern Kentucky. The congressman spoke in the Lynwood Theater and was introduced by John F. Ryan, the foreman of the nearby Louisville and

Nashville railroad shop. Over a hundred voters had to be turned away from the presentation. It takes little imagination to figure out that many of those who filled the theater to capacity worked for the railroad. The candidate had an enthusiastic reception and spoke at length on his congressional efforts to help those who labored. Estill County's hills also had bottomlands that allowed tobacco, alfalfa, and some livestock to be raised. So the audience had more than a sprinkling of farmers. Barkley played up to that portion of the audience as well. In the Bluegrass and regions to the west, he often adjusted his speeches to place an emphasis on agriculture. He described farm life as immersed in an economic depression. Indeed, prices for major cash crops had fallen to ruinous levels, causing distress and bankruptcy in rural areas in Kentucky and across the nation.[36]

Barkley, who ignored the key issue of overproduction, blamed the farmers' economic misery solely on the Fordney-McCumber Tariff, which Senator Ernst eagerly endorsed. Just as Ernst would lose votes among World War I veterans owing to his opposition to the veterans' bonus bill of 1924, he muddied the waters in his relationship with farmers. He claimed in speeches that the Republican tariff actually protected all farm products against foreign competition as it placed most agricultural implements on the free list. In his response at Elizabethtown on October 2, Barkley countered that a number of imported farm products were on the tariff-free list and contributed to lower American prices and a loss of farm revenue; at the same time, high US tariffs on metals raised the expense of equipment that farmers had to buy. Barkley rebuked the senator: "I ask you, Senator Ernst, whether woolen goods are on the free list. I ask you if cotton goods are on the free list. I ask you if the sugar that sweetens our coffee and is used in our desserts is on the free list. I ask you if every plow and hoe, and every cultivator and buggy and wagon and spade are not taxed by the tariff on iron and steel."[37]

Barkley, however, had not begun his campaign at Ravenna or any place else in September. When he spoke to audiences in McLean and Hopkins Counties on October 12, he admitted that he had started his quest for a seat in the US Senate the moment Congress had adjourned on July 3. He then bought a car and started driving the first of thousands of miles over the state to consult with party leaders on the county level as well as Vinson on the state level. This preliminary effort set up his speaking engagements, which began in Republican sections to the east. In coal counties, Barkley attacked Ernst for speaking about Republican prosperity when coal prices had dropped to depression levels of $1.37 a ton. By the time he had driven west to Dawson Springs in Hopkins County, he had visited and/or spoken in 90 of Kentucky's 120 counties. He would finish in Paducah having literally covered the entire state. In the second half of October, Dorothy joined her husband on the hustings closer to home. At the same time, Senator Joseph T. Robinson (AR), the future Senate majority leader and Barkley's mentor, had entered the commonwealth to speak on behalf of the First District congressman. Finally, as Barkley was on the last leg of his campaign in western Kentucky, the widow of J. Campbell Cantrill and representatives of Cantrill's 1923 political organization went on the road in eastern Kentucky to urge citizens to vote for Barkley, wending their way through such towns as Morehead, Sharpsburg, Flemingsburg, Brooksville, Greenup, and Mt. Sterling.[38]

The incredible effort Barkley made to win the election paid off on Tuesday, November 2, 1926. He demonstrated such strength and stamina that his 1923 moniker reappeared. He was sometimes introduced and often referred to in print and conversation as Iron Man Barkley. As it turned out, this man of iron had to expend every ounce of energy, flex every muscle, and collect every political debt from 1923 in order to take the Senate seat away from Ernst. He won by slightly more than 20,000 out of a total of 553,654 votes. In fact, the Associated Press refused to declare a winner in the race until Wednesday evening after all the votes had been counted and reported. Interestingly, Ernst picked up more votes than expected in the First Congressional District, and the same could be said for Barkley in the Seventh. One could justifiably argue that Cantrill's widow and political organization clinched Barkley's victory. The *New York Times* pointed out most Democratic senators who won election or reelection in 1926 did so because of state, not national, issues. Barkley, however, won by assailing normalcy; Harding's successor, President Calvin Coolidge, who needed Ernst; and Republican prosperity. The latter worked best for businesses, banks, industries, and financial markets northeast of Kentucky. It left commonwealth farmers in economic straits, coal miners impoverished or unemployed, and other workers locked into the pecuniary role of second-class citizens whose underconsumption soon led to serious problems for manufacturers, first in the auto industry, and then retailers. These were national, not exclusively Kentucky, problems. Barkley understood from his heritage and home in the Jackson Purchase that the grossly uneven nature of 1920s prosperity created disturbing and dangerous characteristics in America's economy.[39]

9

Senator Barkley from Coolidge to Depression

Between the 1923 and the 1926 elections, dramatic events took place that had an impact on Senator-Elect Alben W. Barkley and the presidential leadership of America. Warren G. Harding took a lengthy trip to Alaska and the West Coast. It was part vacation and part preparation for his 1924 bid to win reelection and keep a residence for four more years in the White House. Before his departure, he painfully realized that several cronies he had appointed to high office had betrayed him by taking advantage of their positions for financial gain. It did nothing to allay his history of high blood pressure to learn that the head of Veteran Affairs (VA) accepted kickbacks for the sale of surplus medical supplies and for the purchase of future VA hospital construction sites; meanwhile, the secretary of the US Department of the Interior exploited for money the US Navy's oil reserves at Teapot Dome, Wyoming, and Elk Hills, California. The president told the Republican journalist William Allen White: "I can take care of my enemies all right. But my friends . . . they're the ones that keep me walking the floor nights." When Harding arrived by ship in Seattle from Alaska on July 27, he delivered a listless speech, met the local press club, and then collapsed after eating a meal. Two of three doctors who attended him suspected cardiac malfunction. Scheduled stops on the train ride from Seattle to San Francisco were canceled, and heart specialists waited for Harding's arrival. He was taken to a suite of rooms in San Francisco's Palace Hotel, where he seemed to respond favorably to treatment for cardiac problems accompanied by bronchopneumonia. Nevertheless, early in the evening of August 2, he suffered a fatal heart attack.[1]

Calvin Coolidge, who succeeded Harding, was born in Vermont but chose to live in Massachusetts after graduating from Amherst College. He read law and passed the bar exam but used his status to create for himself, through diligence, service, and luck, a remarkable political career. The lawyer prudently and patiently climbed the political ladder from local and state offices until he finally achieved the post of governor. After the 1919 Boston police strike, Governor Coolidge sent a widely published telegram to the American Federation of Labor (AFL). Samuel Gompers, the AFL president, had asked for Coolidge's help in getting the striking police officers reinstated after they were fired. The governor responded in the negative and proclaimed: "There is no right to strike against the public safety by any body, any time, any where." It turned Coolidge into a national hero and launched him into presidential politics in 1920. After the fall elections, he landed in the position of US vice president. While he had a keen eye and strong ethics, Coolidge was also a shy and taciturn man who performed poorly as a public speaker. He seemed to believe that most successful, wealthy individuals shared his belief in saving money, hard work, and service to people. Thus, the dangers of underconsumption caused by underpaid or unemployed laborers and impoverished farmers completely eluded him as well as the chicanery of holding companies and investment trusts. The latter spiked the stock market to unsustainable heights using paper credit on margin. No wonder contemporary and even recent commentators criticize Coolidge for not giving serious attention to cooling off overheated speculation. The situation began to implode several months after he left office when the stock market collapsed in October 1929. The crash heralded the opening round of the Great Depression.[2]

Meanwhile, like most Democrats Barkley thought that the party would have a good chance of regaining control of both Congress and the White House in 1924. The Harding administration scandals reached a fever pitch in February of that year and threatened to cause a voter backlash against the GOP in the fall elections. Several things happened, however, to neutralize and then reverse Democratic fortunes. First, one way or another, key culprits left office, and that allowed the scandals to recede from the front pages of newspapers by May. Second, everyone knew that Coolidge had nothing to do with Harding's appointments of friends. It was also clear that he had not in any way benefited unethically in his position as vice president. Except for fine cigars, Coolidge had no taste for luxuries, not even owning an automobile; he did maintain the family's residence in Northampton, Massachusetts, but it was just one side of a duplex he rented for thirty dollars a month. Indeed, he looked and acted like a dour, seventeenth-century Puritan, as one biographer described him. Moreover, the president managed via luck and calculation to dispose of potential rivals and control his party's nominating process when the Republican national convention met in June in the newly completed Cleveland Public Auditorium.[3]

Finally, when the Democrats gathered late in June at Madison Square Garden to select the two men who would challenge Coolidge and his running mate, Charles G. Dawes, they shot themselves in the foot. Barkley and many other delegates wanted the prohibitionist William G. McAdoo to be their presidential candidate; almost an equal number of especially urban delegates worked to select the antiprohibitionist Governor Alfred E. Smith of New York. Both men were widely known, and each would attract a number of votes nationally, but for opposite reasons. Perhaps the winning combination would have been a McAdoo-Smith ticket, assuming that the two gentlemen could agree on giving no more than a wink and a nod to the issue of booze. What happened, of course, is all too obvious. In the heat of summer before air-conditioning, and broadcast over a national radio hookup, the convention deadlocked in bitterness and dragged on and on, ballot after ballot without a victor. While greatly pleasing most Republicans, the deadlock demonstrated painfully for many Americans that Democrats were irreparably divided over the issue of alcoholic beverages. On the surface, that was not the case for the GOP's national ticket and platform, both of which upheld the Eighteenth Amendment to the Constitution.[4]

After nearly one hundred ballots between McAdoo and Smith, the convention's permanent chairman, Senator Thomas J. Walsh (MT) asked Barkley to come up to the platform before the microphones and preside over the convention for an hour or so so that he could get a little rest. The congressman was not shy; in fact, he was frequently described as a showman before an audience. Barkley possessed a commanding baritone voice of depth and resonance that allowed him to take charge of the balloting procedure quite easily. Two days later, the extremely well-rested Walsh returned to the platform just before the 103rd ballot nominated a compromise candidate after McAdoo and Smith withdrew their names from consideration. The delegates chose John W. Davis, a former congressman, US solicitor general, and US ambassador to Great Britain. Barkley had conducted such a smooth operation as temporary chairman that Walsh asked him to preside over what initially appeared to be a wide-open selection of a person for the second spot on the presidential ticket. After twenty-three "favorite sons" and one "favorite daughter" (Mrs. Leroy Springs of South Carolina) had been placed in nomination and voting had begun, Davis made known his preference for the candidate who had received the most votes at that point before the first ballot was finished. The person with the most votes was Charles W. Bryan, brother of the three-time presidential candidate William Jennings Bryan. As Davis's views blanketed the convention, eighteen state delegations that had already voted for someone else jumped to their feet demanding recognition to change their votes to Bryan. Amid the clamor and shouting, Barkley thundered: "Damn it, can't you wait?" His colorful and forceful outburst returned order to the scene as Bryan secured the vice presidential nomination on the first ballot. The convention, filled with exhausted, conflict-weary delegates, abruptly ended five minutes after Bryan's victory at 2:25 in the morning of July 10, 1924.[5]

As a loyal party member, Barkley campaigned actively for the Davis-Bryan ticket, but to no avail. In blunt terms, Davis lacked national standing, and even he knew that he had little chance of occupying the White House as anything other than a visitor. He served as a symbol of a deeply divided Democratic Party that appeared bereft of leadership. And his running mate contributed little to help Davis overcome his shortcomings. Bryan, unfortunately, failed to resemble his famous brother, William Jennings. By contrast, Charles was tall, had a mustache, wore rimless oval glasses, topped his bald head with a black skullcap made of silk, and spoke in an irritating staccato style. He seemed one or more steps removed from normal. On the other side, Coolidge, who could not begin to match Barkley's spirited phraseology and folksy humor, sent Dawes across America by train to deliver speeches. The president made a few set-piece addresses closer to home. The result of all this enabled Coolidge-Dawes to trounce their opponents by a nearly two-to-one popular vote and a colossal electoral count of 382–136 ballots (the Progressive Party candidate, Robert M. La Follette, took the remaining 13 ballots). Years later, Barkley had to admit that Coolidge would have won the election no matter what because he was "a man of integrity" and he "fit what the American people liked." On top of everything else, the president received a number of sympathy votes. Just before the election campaign got under way in July, his younger son, Calvin Coolidge Jr., died from blood poisoning caused by the infection of a ruptured blister on his toe. In many ways, Coolidge Sr. never recovered from this tragic loss.[6]

Barkley's toss-away comments on the newly elected Coolidge administration (1925–1929) characterized the period as one of "calm" and described congressional accomplishments as "little." Neither comment is completely accurate. During the lame-duck session in the winter of 1927, when Senator-Elect Barkley was still a representative in the Sixty-Ninth Congress, he capped his career in the House with the passage of a major bill for the First District appropriating funds for the construction of a bridge across the Ohio River at Paducah. In addition, he and other rural representatives, along with western Republican senators, tried to find a way to ease the plight of farmers. One effort approved by Congress in February was the McNary-Haugen farm bill sponsored by Senator Charles L. McNary (OR) and Representative Gilbert N. Haugen (IA). The complicated legislation would create a government corporation to buy surplus farm commodities and dump them on the world market in order to raise domestic prices. Farmers would be charged an equalization fee (a tax), but, if the system worked as planned, the elevation of prices would be enough to increase farmer purchasing power and relieve some of the serious economic distress in rural America.[7]

President Coolidge did everything possible to defeat McNary-Haugen in Congress. His efforts failed, and the measure traveled to his desk, only to receive a thumbs-down. One Coolidge biographer noted: "When the President finally vetoed the McNary-Haugen Farm Bill, he used such emotional language that the message cracked with malicious static." Essentially, the president felt that the bill was price-fixing (indeed) and both unsound (which it was) and unconstitutional (perhaps). Regardless, many representatives and senators, including Barkley, were committed to finding a way to bolster the depressed agricultural sector of the economy. Congressional leaders with farming interests from both political parties met in St. Paul, Minnesota, in July at a conference called together by the American Council of Agriculture, which was composed of forty-nine farm organizations. Speakers such as Barkley vowed to carry on the fight until "some president" signed a bill into law to help rural America. From his perspective, dumping commodities abroad would only antagonize foreign countries and would not be as effective as restructuring the tariff. Nevertheless, during his speech before the meeting, he argued in favor of the popular (among farmers) notion to use "the Government to control [farm] surplus so that it might be fed to markets as the need of consumption requires." Such a government-funded "ever normal granary," however, would be costly to construct and to operate. In terms of evaluation, it would inflame, not rectify, the real issue: the overproduction of major crops ranging from corn and cotton to wheat.[8]

Obviously, the McNary-Haugen farm bill or a similar substitute would not go away. Moreover, when Barkley was sworn in as senator at the open-ing of the Seventieth Congress on December 5, 1927, he joined six other freshmen senators who had taken seats away from Republicans. Given the fact that one senator belonged to the Farmer-Laborite Party, the forty-seven Democrats stood as a formidable group against the forty-eight Republicans. Several of the latter were old progressives who voted with Democrats on cer-tain issues such as those related to agriculture. In short, Coolidge confronted a hostile Senate. Hence, a second, modified version of the McNary-Haugen bill passed Congress in May 1928. The majority vote was not, however, a two-thirds majority or enough to overcome a presidential veto. Coolidge, who had indicated that he would not run for president in 1928, felt com-pletely free to deliver an unpopular second veto of the farm bill. Despite his action, many Americans did recognize that something needed to be done to alleviate the economic problems endured by most farmers. This nation-wide sentiment, stronger in rural than urban America, explains why in the upcoming presidential election both major political parties responded by selecting candidates and writing platforms that pledged aid to agriculture. In short, each party wanted to win the farmer/rural vote.[9]

During the interim, Barkley settled into his position in the US Senate. He possessed, of course, experience far beyond that of a first-time freshman senator. He carried with him fourteen years of writing and debating legis-lation in the House of Representatives. He not only knew Congress inti-mately but also possessed a widely known reputation for his speaking ability and prohibition leadership. These attributes and the minimal majority held by Republican senators facilitated his initial assignment as a member of the important Banking and Currency Committee and the Finance Committee as well as the interesting but less significant Library Committee. Two years later, he received an appointment to the Interstate Commerce Committee, a logical step considering his years of effective service on the House ver-sion of that Senate group. By pure coincidence, then, these committee posi-tions would place him at the center of New Deal legislation in 1933. Back in December 1927 and the winter of 1928, as committees and the congres-sional session got under way, he soon arranged his professional life into a daily pattern.[10]

For the new senator, mornings centered on answering mail, help-ing constituents, and preparing for committee meetings, which were held before lunch. At noon, Barkley would frequently take commonwealth visi-tors to the Senate dining room to sample a bowl of its famous bean soup.

Afternoons were reserved for the discussions, debates, and votes of the full Senate. Unlike during the New Deal era, when evening sessions sometimes occurred, Barkley could generally make it home in time for dinner with the family. He often spent evenings reading reports and legislative proposals. One thing that changed in life at home was the traditional, family-shared evening meal. By 1928, the size of the family had already started to shrink and would continue until Barkley's bride, Dorothy, remained his only dinner companion. Each of their children graduated from high school, then in birth order left home to attend one or two years of college before becoming a pilot and in 1927 joining the US Army Air Corps (David), marrying in 1929 the Washington lawyer Max O'Rell Truitt (Marian), and marrying in 1934 the career diplomat Douglas MacArthur II, a nephew of the future five-star general of the US Army (Laura Louise).[11]

In the same period when the household presence of his children declined one by one, Barkley's status as an important political figure climbed. There is no more than a whimsical connection in this observation. Regardless, Vice President Charles G. Dawes acknowledged Barkley's growth in stature when, on May 1, 1928, he appointed the Paducah politician to the five-member Senate Select Committee to Investigate Presidential Campaign Expenditures. Its purpose was to bring to light any real abuses and false myths that might be linked to campaign spending by candidates. When, however, the committee was formed at the start of that month, it would focus most of its attention on only two individuals, the leading Republican and Democratic hopefuls, Secretary of Commerce Herbert Clark Hoover and New York governor Alfred Emanuel Smith. Not unexpectedly, Barkley gave Hoover, the GOP candidate, a hard time when the committee convened and hearings began on May 9. The senator did not expose any wrongdoing, but his questions and Hoover's difficulty answering them revealed how little the commerce secretary knew about political campaigns; indeed, he had never run for political office before.[12]

As it turned out, Barkley himself would be caught up in the presidential politics of 1928. It was not completely, however, a satisfying moment in his life. Shortly after the select committee finished its business and Congress ended its first session, it was time for state and national party conventions. Barkley returned to the commonwealth to serve as temporary chairman and deliver the keynote address on June 14 at the state Democratic convention held in the Bluegrass city of Lexington. He used that occasion to plead for the two Democratic factions to come together in unity. The previous year, all Democrats who ran for statewide office won except the head of the ticket, J. C. W. Beckham. Democratic leaders in Louisville and Lexington and even the Democratic governor had supported Republican Flem D. Sampson, who took the governorship. Barkley's rhetoric seemed to succeed at least temporarily. His reward for helping unify the state party occurred on a train that carried the Kentucky delegation to the Democratic national convention in Houston, Texas. Party leaders such as Fred Vinson convinced him that he should allow his name to be placed in nomination for the office of vice president.[13]

By the time the train pulled into Houston, delegation members had convinced themselves that Barkley had the best chance of securing the second spot on the Democratic presidential ticket. And they had good reason to be optimistic. It was certain that Governor Smith would be the party's nominee, but he clearly possessed a series of handicaps that raised serious questions about his ability to secure enough electoral votes to win the White House. Among his several liabilities, he was literally the product of Irish immigrants, was politically associated with New York City's corrupt Tammany Hall machine, was religiously a Roman Catholic in a Protestant country filled with people who mildly, if not militantly, distrusted "popery," publicly favored altering prohibition to allow state or local options, and was unfortunately a person who spoke with an East Side twang that grated on the ears of most Americans west of Jersey City. Barkley seemed to be the exact opposite of Smith and, hence, would perfectly balance the ticket into a victory.[14]

For starters, the senator was rooted in a border state with ties to both the Midwest and the South; the New York governor typified only the urban areas of the Northeast. Indeed, Smith personified city life, while Barkley symbolized rural America. Finally, Smith's handicaps proved to be the senator's strengths. Barkley was a child of American colonial ancestors, a politician who lacked any connection with a corrupt party boss or machine, a Methodist who fit comfortably within Protestant America, a supporter of the Volstead Act, and a speaker with a slight drawl that pleased the ears of most citizens except those east of Jersey City. With those thoughts in mind, Kentucky lieutenant governor James Breathitt Jr. and two delegates, John Murphy and James Garnett, headed for the Al Smith headquarters after the train reached the Houston station; the rest of the delegates checked into their rooms at the McAtee Hotel. The Smith camp welcomed the small group from Kentucky and listened, without making a commitment, to the argument that Barkley would be the ideal person to balance a Democratic ballot led by Smith.[15]

Breathitt and his two companions left the Smith headquarters with the understanding that Barkley would at least be considered for the vice presidency. One would think that Kentucky politicians realized that politics is politics. Naturally, the Smith camp gave the commonwealth delegates the hopeful possibility that Barkley might be tapped for the second spot on the ticket and did so in order to keep Kentucky's twenty-six delegate votes for the governor's nomination. Smith, however, had actually requested Senate minority leader Joseph T. Robinson to be his vice presidential candidate before the convention opened. Nevertheless, to make certain that the Kentucky delegation remained loyal, Barkley was asked to deliver one of three seconding speeches for Smith. Even though news spread around the hotels and at the Sam Houston Hall convention site that the governor favored Robinson, the Kentuckians remained optimistic about Barkley's chances. He just seemed to balance Smith so perfectly that the delegates opened a campaign headquarters, plastered "Al and Al" cards and banners around hotel lobbies, developed slogans such as "Embark with Barkley," buttonholed Smith's Tammany chieftains, and searched for votes among delegates from various states.[16]

In this circus atmosphere, Barkley hastily prepared a seconding speech. His efforts were complicated by the fact that the platform committee was in the process of writing a plank that in essence supported prohibition. Smith's open opposition to the dry movement prompted five southern states to stay out of a pro-Smith demonstration during the morning of Barkley's evening speech. On the other hand, the southern protest encouraged the Kentucky delegation by confirming how Barkley could strengthen the presidential ticket. Thus, the Iron Man struggled to produce an oration that would bring the party together and lighten the controversial baggage that loaded down Smith. The unspoken third aim of his address sought to move Smith to sponsor a wide-open contest for the nomination of a vice presidential candidate. Barkley accomplished only the first two objectives. Wednesday night, June 27, the festivities got under way when Franklin D. Roosevelt delivered an eloquent tribute to Smith; the future governor of New York nominated the current governor of New York as the party's presidential candidate.[17]

Roosevelt's polio-stricken legs forced him to lean on the lectern, but he was greeted by yells and a standing ovation by everyone across the cavernous chamber. The political reporter for the *New York Times* described FDR as "pink cheeked, full of glow of health," and noted that, when he spoke, "his voice rang out with clarity and strength that carried it across the acres which Sam Houston Hall covers." After Roosevelt finished, there were cheers and demonstrations by Smith supporters that lasted over twenty minutes before the three seconding speeches could be delivered. When Barkley's turn came and he was introduced, there were expressions of genuine surprise by many delegates and especially gallery spectators. It seemed strange, if not bizarre, for a notable dry to deliver a seconding speech for the nomination of a famous wet. Some audience members simply did not realize the level and extent of communication by third parties between the Smith camp and Barkley beginning with the Kentucky delegation. In fact, the Smith convention floor manager, Roosevelt, took a friendly interest in Barkley as early as 1920. Indeed, in a preconvention meeting of New York party notables, it was FDR who acknowledged Barkley as a leader and even as a potential candidate to join the Smith ticket. For Roosevelt and the Smith camp it made perfect political sense to have Barkley endorse Smith.[18]

At the rostrum, Barkley sought to unite the delegates on at least one topic; he rhetorically panned the Republican administrations of the 1920s. He then addressed the two big problems that caused some delegates to question and others to oppose a Smith nomination. In terms of the nominee's Roman Catholicism, he reminded his hall and radio listeners of the First Amendment and Article 6 of the US Constitution, which guaranteed freedom of religion and prohibited a religious test to qualify for any public office. He personalized the discussion by revealing his college and current association with the Methodist Church. After that he proudly raised his voice for the nomination of a man who shared the same right to faith as all Americans, including the person giving the seconding speech. He next turned to the other controversy made problematic by the fact that the Democratic Platform Committee endorsed prohibition by supporting the Constitution. He recognized that the 1928 platform served as a guide for the party and its candidates. But he minimized the matter by pointing out that Smith joined the late, great President Woodrow Wilson in holding a different view of the Eighteenth Amendment. Furthermore, he did not want one issue to obscure all the other problems, ranging from agriculture to tariffs, that needed the serious attention of the next presidential administration.[19]

Regardless, a Smith victory was a foregone conclusion. The next morning the New York governor's floor manager, Roosevelt, replaced the convention permanent chairman Joseph T. Robinson at the rostrum. The switch served as a clear message to each of the eleven hundred delegates that the Arkansas senator was Smith's choice for the second spot on the Democratic presidential ticket. Including Robinson, eight men and one woman were nominated for the vice presidency. The head of the Kentucky delegation, the former governor and senator A. O. Stanley, did the honors for Barkley, who came in a distant second with 77 votes to Robinson's 914. Immediately, Barkley mounted the rostrum and changed Kentucky's votes to Robinson. This prompted many other state delegations to shift their votes to the winner, who officially received a near unanimous endorsement. Barkley, of course, could not be terribly upset. His brief candidacy marked his elevated standing within the party and impressed many of his commonwealth constituents. Besides, Robinson was a dry who had campaigned unselfishly for Barkley in his 1926 successful bid to secure a seat in the US Senate. Finally, the head of the Democratic ticket (who had not attended the convention) sent a telegram that pleased Barkley. Smith stated that the saloon was a dead institution and pledged that, if sworn in as chief executive, he would defend earnestly the Constitution and all statutory laws while working to make "fundamental changes in the present provisions for national prohibition." He felt that the latter should be replaced "by the application of the Democratic principles of local self-government and States' rights."[20]

Smith also sent Barkley a telegram, this one thanking him for his stirring speech seconding his nomination. The presidential candidate, however, kept close to his vest a future surprise for the senator. When in August Barkley and his family vacationed on board a ship that sailed from East Coast to West via the Panama Canal, Smith, without prior consultation with Barkley, announced that he had picked him to manage his Kentucky campaign and join his national advisory committee. The Paducah politician first learned of these appointments when he and his family reached California near the end of the month. Whether he wanted such honors or not, the loyal Democrat expressed his enthusiasm for the presidential ticket and informed the press on August 27 that he would establish a Smith headquarters in Louisville shortly after he and his family returned home from California; the headquarters opened on September 4. Unfortunately, after the fact, Barkley could paint the remainder of the 1928 campaign only in the darkest of colors.[21]

In the first instance, many dry voters sent messages to Barkley expressing everything from disappointment to threats because he managed the state's campaign on behalf of a wet presidential candidate. It became clear that the senator would likely lose if he had had to run for reelection in 1928 rather than 1932. The second shoe to drop was the hatred held by many for the Roman Catholic Church. So much bigotry erupted that one of the few positive things to come out of this ugly election season was the formation of the National Conference of Christians and Jews. It was founded by open-minded religious and societal leaders who wanted to counter the appalling intolerance that stained America. As one contemporary commentator pointed out right after the election: "It is impossible to determine when the anti-alcoholic feeling ceased and the anti-Catholic feeling began." Honestly, then, it made no difference how hard Barkley worked on the campaign, such as his organizing a sizable, tumultuous reception for Smith when the candidate visited Kentucky on October 13 and 14. The GOP victor, Herbert Hoover, still took almost 60 percent of the state's votes in the November election. Obviously, considering the large number of registered Democrats, many of them either stayed home or voted Republican.[22]

Barkley, of course, wanted to forget about the 1928 election; he could only hope that Kentuckians would experience a memory lapse concerning the politics of that year. Fortunately for him, but not for the country, that is exactly what happened because of the tragic economic and social consequences of the Great Depression. Meanwhile, neither Smith nor anyone else in the party blamed Barkley for what happened in Kentucky. The commonwealth actually fared better in garnering votes for Smith than did many other states. Nationally, Hoover's victory reached historic proportions as he took slightly more than 70 percent of the popular vote and received 444 of 531 electoral votes. By contrast, Smith failed to win his own state of New York and this despite the fact that Roosevelt won the governor's race. Besides Massachusetts and Rhode Island, Smith won in only six former slaveholding southern states that were still glued to the Democratic Party, which had supported the Confederate States of America during the Civil War and in 1928 upheld racial segregation.[23]

It must be noted, however, that issues related to alcohol and religion merely start to explain Smith's defeat. The other side of the lopsided election equation is that Smith lost to one of the most popular, indeed heroic, figures of the 1920s. A Quaker and a graduate of Stanford University, Hoover applied his mining engineering degree in work and consultation at excavations around the world. He acquired wealth and an international reputation as a brilliant administrator. When the Great War broke out, he applied the latter skill to the philanthropic effort of food relief. He led the Commission for Relief in Belgium and in 1917 joined President Wilson's government as the US food administrator, in charge of US food supplies for both the civilian and the military sectors as well as provisioning the Allied nations. The end to the conflict found Hoover in the role of director general of the American Relief Administration, which ultimately saved the lives of millions of East Europeans. Just as thirty years later with General Dwight D. Eisenhower, both major political parties considered Hoover to be presidential material. In 1920, however, he admitted his commitment to the GOP. In that year he campaigned for Warren Harding. The newly elected president offered, and Hoover accepted, the post of secretary of commerce, an office he continued to hold with distinction until his own inauguration as president on March 4, 1929.[24]

As Barkley returned to Washington, he was painfully aware that Hoover's overwhelming victory was not the only troubling result of the 1928 elections. The Democrats suffered a serious drubbing across much of the country. In March 1929, Republicans in both houses of Congress would exercise supermajorities over the Democrats, 267–163 in the House and 56–39 in the Senate, with one Farmer-Laborite in each chamber. Before Hoover's inauguration, the lame-duck session of the Seventieth Congress approved few notable measures. It served as a fitting end to the Coolidge era. In terms of Barkley's evolution, however, two legislative items gained his attention and illustrated his active interest in foreign policy. He spoke and voted for the treaty negotiated by US secretary of state Frank B. Kellogg and French foreign minister Aristide Briand; it was signed in Paris by fifteen nations on August 27, 1928, and ratified by the United States in January 1929. Signatories of the Kellogg-Briand Pact pledged to renounce war and seek peaceful settlements to disputes. The pact has not enjoyed a good press over time because of World War II and the fact that Germany and Japan both signed it. At least it did get Kellogg a Nobel Peace Prize and served as the basis for the trials and executions of German and Japanese war criminals after 1945 when the second global conflict ended.[25]

Barkley championed the treaty because it was popular among the American people—only one senator voted against it. It also put the United States on the high ground occupied by nations that seemed at least in this period to favor peace. The document matched perfectly the senator's interest in and association with the Inter-Parliamentary Union, which sought to resolve conflict between nations by replacing warfare with mediation. Barkley, however, was not so naive as to believe that a piece of paper would automat-

ically outlaw war on a permanent basis. He proved this by his oral endorsement of and subsequent vote in mid-February 1929 for a new shipbuilding
program for the US Navy. Only a month after the Senate had approved
the Kellogg-Briand Pact, the upper chamber then passed legislation for the
construction of fifteen new cruisers. For Barkley, his approach to this naval
program represented a dramatic shift in position. Except during US participation in the Great War, he had consistently opposed any enlargement of
the sea service from the time he first entered Congress in 1913. His altered
view reflected a more realistic and measured view of foreign affairs.[26]

The change in Barkley's attitude toward the US Navy occurred for two
reasons. First, a year and a half before the Senate voted, the Geneva Naval
Conference simply failed to increase the number of cruisers. To his credit,
Coolidge had called on the principal naval powers to meet again and complete the work of the Washington Naval Disarmament Conference of 1921–
1922. The latter had restricted total battleship tonnage to 525,000 each for
the United States and Great Britain, 315,000 for Japan, and 175,000 each
for France and Italy. No limits, however, were placed on the total tonnage
of smaller ships and boats such as cruisers or destroyers and submarines.
Regrettably, Japan had engaged in a building program in the smaller categories of ships and boats by middecade. Coolidge hoped the conference
in Geneva would address the issue and put a stop to a naval arms race. The
Geneva gathering in the summer of 1927 proved, however, to be a terrible disappointment. France and Italy chose not to attend; Japan absolutely
refused to reduce its naval construction in the categories below battleships.
On top of everything else, the British and American delegations squabbled
bitterly; the United States wanted heavy and England favored light cruisers. The total collapse of the Geneva meeting prompted Barkley to support
the US Navy's acquisition of fifteen heavy cruisers. He felt that it was the
only logical way to pressure other naval powers to consider serious talks on
broad-based naval limitations. Second, he and others argued that the lack of
a powerful cruiser presence had weakened the ability of the United States to
respond strongly to Europe's economic warfare when America was neutral
during the Great War.[27]

Barkley may have been partly right about the pressure the United States
could exert by building fifteen additional cruisers. They would reach the
maximum allowable weight of ten thousand tons and carry hefty, eight-
inch guns. With these muscle ships literally in the works, newly inaugurated President Hoover had strong talking points in his conversations with

J. Ramsay MacDonald in 1929. The British prime minister agreed to invite the five major naval powers to another conference, this time in London in January 1930. It resulted in Britain, Japan, and the United States signing a treaty that did, indeed, limit the tonnage of smaller craft (France and Italy never ratified the agreement). However temporary, this success in foreign affairs was accompanied by the extraordinary change in US relations with Latin America. Hoover personally initiated the good neighbor policy. He withdrew American troops from Nicaragua, overturned Teddy Roosevelt's Corollary to the Monroe Doctrine that had enabled the United States to exercise police powers in Latin America and repudiated President Wilson's policy of taking sides in a revolution and withholding de facto recognition. The latter position prompted the stridently anti-Communist Hoover to admit publicly that he also considered recognizing Soviet Russia in 1929. He never, however, moved beyond the consideration phase.[28]

The occasional good points that Hoover scored in foreign relations were overshadowed and all but obliterated by domestic crises. Barkley admitted that Hoover gave every indication of being genuinely concerned about the severe economic problems confronting the nation. Eventually, however, he and many of his colleagues in Congress became frustrated by Hoover's tendency to rely on volunteerism to deal with, or to blame Europe for, the sufferings of the American people. Even his revisionist biographers, such as Martin L. Fausold and Joan Hoff Wilson, who correctly highlight his progressive background and caring approach to the country's terrible plight, have to admit that Hoover clung to traditional notions that the federal government had no responsibility for providing direct aid to the citizens it governed. Fausold revealed a quote that Hoover apparently prized from President Grover Cleveland (1885–1990, 1893–1897): "The lesson should be constantly enforced that though the people support the government, the government should not support the people." Hoover managed to compound his problems with Barkley and other members of Congress by keeping himself aloof from the legislative branch of government. Part of this attitude reflected his interpretation of the separation of powers in the Constitution. The other issue was mentioned earlier, that he had never ran for political office before 1928 and had failed to acquire a serious understanding of the political process, including congressional politics.[29]

A perfect example of how Hoover approached the subject of aid can be observed in the Agriculture Marketing Act, which the new president signed into law on June 15, 1929. The process actually began near the end of the Coolidge administration with another version of the twice-vetoed McNary-Haugen bill. Hoover, however, made it clear to Senate majority leader Charles L. McNary (who also chaired the Agriculture Committee) that, as the farm bill wended its way through Congress, it must not offer any kind of direct subsidy to help farmers. Barkley and a majority of senators, including thirteen Republicans, ignored the president's charge by adding an export subsidy provision to the marketing legislation. When Barkley argued in favor of the export debenture plan, he understood fully that the proposal was questionable economically. But he felt strongly that something had to be done; the export subsidy seemed to be the only thing available to put on the plate that might actually feed a little more cash to desperate farmers. Incidentally, Hoover had a chance to avoid what journalists called with cute alliteration the Republican Revolt, but in typical fashion he distanced himself from most members of Congress and refused to negotiate or play politics with senators by trading patronage for votes. Luckily for Hoover, the House saved him from further embarrassment. It passed a marketing bill without the debenture plan. And in the conference committee it refused to budge. It forced the Senate to accept the House measure or face the devastating indictment of not wanting to help the American farmer.[30]

Hoover took great pride in the marketing legislation. He thought that the act's Federal Farm Board would regulate commodities just like the Federal Reserve Board regulated currency; best of all, no government dole went to individuals in either case. The farm board advanced commodity markets through agricultural cooperatives and stabilization corporations. A revolving fund allowed the latter to buy and store commodities for resale at an optimum time for good prices. Nonsalaried advisory committees for each major commodity were responsible for securing farmer cooperation in production control, which included eliminating the use of marginal lands. The whole effort ended up a colossal failure. First, the Federal Farm Board lacked the muscle to compel farmers and cooperatives to do anything. Second, the act threatened the existence of private financing, marketing, processing, and distributing agencies associated with rural America's products. Third, the Department of Agriculture continued to do everything in its power to help farmers expand production via better seeds, chemicals, and technologies, yet overproduction served as the key explanation for the decline in commodity prices. Finally, the Great Depression knocked the bottom right out of commodity markets—to such an extent that by 1933 the program's revolving fund was over $370 million in the red. At that moment, no one on the farm or in Congress had a kind word to say about the 1929 legislation.[31]

While Barkley was involved with the agriculture marketing bill, he took a much more visible leadership role in the lengthy process revamping the tariff. Interestingly, both parties had made comments about tariff reform during the recent presidential campaign, but neither featured the issue. But, once President Hoover fulfilled a campaign pledge by calling a special session of Congress to address agricultural problems, representatives and senators from predominantly rural districts or states sought to couple the marketing bill with a tariff that would help farmers. Except over the issue of retaining the Fordney-McCumber Tariff's flexibility clause, Hoover remained relatively quiet and unobtrusive as Congress plowed with gusto into tariff revision. The chair of the Senate Finance Committee, Reed Smoot (UT), cosponsored the tariff bill with Willis C. Hawley (OR), who chaired the House Ways and Means Committee. Smoot recognized the leadership position exercised by Barkley among Democrats. He noted, for example, that Senate minority leader Robinson had recently asked Barkley to fill a Democratic vacancy on the Senate's prestigious Interstate Commerce Committee when the Seventy-First Congress opened. Hence, he chose Barkley to serve as one of the minority-party members on his special subcommittee conducting initial hearings on tariff schedules beginning on June 14, 1929. The altered tariff would be signed into law on June 17, 1930. Clearly, legislation absorbed for a year most of the energy and effort expended in both chambers of Congress.[32]

It was no secret Barkley wanted a lower tariff. Regardless, manufacturers and representatives of whole industries lined up before the subcommittee to plead their cases for more protection against the products of foreign competitors. Barkley managed to show restraint in expressing his contrary views. Instead, he often raised pointed questions of a factual nature that seriously reduced or totally undermined the rationale for higher tariff rates. For instance, the metal industry wanted to see the duty on pig iron increased. Through his queries, Barkley exposed the fact that pig iron imports had sharply declined—by 68 percent—between 1925 and 1928. So why was it necessary to raise the schedule on pig iron? What was the point in elevating rates on a product from another country that simply did not threaten US industry? Barkley could use these questions and their weak answers when in the early fall the Senate debated specific amendments to the House bill regarding tariff rates. A coalition of Democrats and progressive Republicans joined him in forming a majority of senators willing to vote against tariff increases and against handing the White House the same tariff flexibility found in the Fordney-McCumber Act. Too bad for Barkley and his allies, the special session of Congress ended on November 22 before a finished version of the Hawley-Smoot bill could be hammered together.[33]

The regular session of the Congress opened less than two weeks later in December. At first, the coalition led by Barkley, Minority Leader Robinson, and the Republican insurgent Borah could regroup and successfully amend and whittle down the high tariff rates found in the House bill. But several events conspired to cause the coalition to fall apart over time. The keynote was sounded two months earlier in October when the implosion of paper credit hit the stock market. Ignoring their own culpability, leaders in business and finance blamed Congress for the crash because of uncertainty over the tariff. This criticism mounted as the shock waves from the collapsed stock market invaded and buffeted the broader economy. Nervous congressmen started to repeat the unthinking mantra of manufacturers that a highly protective tariff would save jobs. The coup de grâce appeared in the form of Joseph R. Grundy, who had recently been appointed by Pennsylvania's governor to fill an unexpected vacancy in the Senate. Before he took his seat in the upper chamber on December 12, 1929, he had been president of the Pennsylvania Manufacturers' Association. Under his direction the association had over the past five years donated more than $2 million to GOP political candidates. Additionally, he had served as the most aggressive and effective high-tariff lobbyist in the nation's capital. He used his new position in Congress to negotiate a tariff deal with insurgent Republican senators. He would work to advance rates on agricultural products in return for their votes to raise duties on industrial articles. Although on an individual basis it did not always hold up, the deal worked well enough to win the highest tariff in American history.[34]

On Wednesday, June 11, 1930, Barkley delivered his last address on the cynically named Grundy-Hawley-Smoot Tariff. The Senate would approve the final version two days later, but by the narrow margin of 44–42 votes. Barkley knew the head count, so he pulled out all the stops in a speech that he realized would be his last chance to change the minds of two senators. The Kentuckian also understood the deals that had been made with those senators, who wanted to protect US agriculture. So, in his presentation to the chamber, he asked those colleagues to remember the effect of the higher rates embedded in the earlier Fordney-McCumber Tariff that supposedly guaranteed prosperity for rural America. Instead, they resulted in depressed prices, bankruptcy, and foreclosures for many farmers. Why, he wondered, would even higher tariff rates be better? With few exports to America, other nations could not buy US barley, corn, cotton, oats, tobacco, or wheat, yet these staples needed a healthy global market to generate a decent price. What would be generated, Barkley predicted correctly, would be an international tariff war against the United States that would reduce even further America's export trade in both farm and factory goods.[35]

The argument about the collapse of America's export trade reduced to a fallacy the idea held by most of the remaining senators who had convinced themselves that higher duties would protect American jobs and, hence, their Senate seats at election time. Barkley dropped the rhetorical bomb that should have exploded the myth. He pointed out that nine million jobs could be linked to US sales abroad. Because US trading partners would most assuredly raise their duties in response to the new tariff, one might as well add those millions to the four million workers who had already lost their jobs after Wall Street dropped the financial ball. Simple math promised a first-class economic depression in the near future. He reminded his listeners that important industrialists such as Henry Ford (of the Ford Motor Co.) and Harvey S. Firestone (of the Firestone Tire and Rubber Co.) opposed the tariff because of the economic calamity it would spark among companies engaged in foreign trade. Finally, besides farmers, workers, and manufacturers, he also mentioned the tariff's negative impact on every adult US citizen/voter. As he had done in an April speech delivered to women in New York City's Carnegie Hall, he asserted that the lack of competition from imports would force consumers collectively to pay hundreds of millions of dollars more for the goods that they would purchase.[36]

Barkley ended his remarks by wishing that either the Senate would vote the tariff down or, if not, President Hoover would experience an epiphany and veto it. Neither happened. Once the Hawley-Smoot average ad valorem rate of slightly more than 40 percent went into effect, Barkley's predictions were fulfilled. And he was not a lonely prophet. One thousand thirty-eight members of the American Economic Association also pleaded with Congress and Hoover not to enact the new tariff. The law did ignite an international tariff war; US foreign trade plummeted in dollar value from $9.6 billion in 1929 to $2.9 billion in 1932. Worker unemployment mounted sharply, an already depressed agricultural sector declined further, and some consumers and many industrialists suffered as well. While in the tariff struggle Barkley enhanced a reputation for political leadership that had grown exponentially in the last half of the 1920s, he was nevertheless very disappointed in the result of this hard-fought legislative battle. He had convinced himself and many others that a moderate, carefully constructed tariff could be one of the better indirect ways to help the workingmen and -women of the commonwealth and the nation. This defeat had other consequences for his future. Decades later, when the Iron Man's opinion of Republican opponents had mellowed, his comments on Hoover remained cool and reserved. In the short term, between 1930 and 1932, the devastating depression and Hoover's inability to address the real sufferings of millions of people opened Barkley to the idea that the federal government could and should take a more active role in providing direct aid to the country's citizens.[37]

10

Senator Barkley from Depression to the Announcement of a New Deal

Not long after Congress adjourned, Alben W. Barkley sailed to England. He was in the company of, and presided over, the American delegation that attended the Assembly of the Inter-Parliamentary Union (IPU). He and the delegation arrived in London on July 17, 1930, in time to attend the afternoon session. When the conference of global legislators concluded its proceedings, Barkley went to Berlin and in early August joined a party of thirty Americans for a two-week tour inside the Soviet Union. The author and YMCA leader Sherwood Eddy arranged the trip through the USSR Chamber of Commerce for the West. The insurgent Republican senators Burton K. Wheeler (MT), Peter Norbeck (SD), and Bronson W. Cutting (NM) accompanied their friend the Kentucky senator. Interestingly, all four were critics of President Herbert C. Hoover. Obviously, the four men were not part of a political junket. They paid their way just like such notable companions as Francis B. Sayre, one of President Woodrow Wilson's sons-in-law, and Charles P. Taft, one of President William Howard Taft's sons. The previous year the American-Russian Chamber of Commerce sponsored an excursion extravaganza to the Soviet Union for ninety-four business executives, socialites, and journalists.[1]

It may seem strange that a Communist country not recognized diplomatically by the United States had suddenly become something of an exotic tourist attraction. Part of the explanation is related to the fact that in the fall of 1928 the Soviet Union abandoned the New Economic Policy in favor of a Five-Year Plan designed to industrialize the country rapidly. For Barkley and other tour members, the Soviet Union had recently gained a bright reputation for its economic activity and development at a time when the United

States had entered a dark period of economic decline. Moreover, the first Five-Year Plan required the acquisition of Western technologies and capital goods needed to enhance the manufacturing process. It spiked trade with America, which supplied 25 percent of all Soviet imports in 1930. When Hoover was still secretary, the US Department of Commerce responded to this trade activity by easing credit restrictions on Soviet purchases and issuing for the first time bulletins on Soviet economic conditions as a service to American businesses. The other issue was the time frame; 1929–1930 preceded all the horrors associated with purges, gulags, and famines. Rapid, forced collectivization of peasant farms caused the latter. These catastrophes led to the deaths of millions of Soviet citizens under the tyrannical rule of the Procrustean dictator Joseph V. Stalin (Dzhugashvili).[2]

Thus, one must appreciate why, when Barkley and his tour companions reached Moscow on August 11, they looked forward to meeting Stalin. His promised appearance, however, did not occur. Regardless, the entire Eddy group enjoyed a reception sponsored by the USSR Chamber of Commerce for the West and then a tour of the Kremlin, viewing, among other sights, the crown jewels of the Romanov family, which had ruled Russia before the 1917 revolution. The senators then participated in a different agenda. Barkley, Cutting, Norbeck, and Wheeler had interviews with members of the State Planning Committee and the All-Union Central Council of Trade Unions, headed by Nikolai Shvernik. Next, they were taken for a two-day drive into the countryside in American-built Model-T Fords. Accompanied by Russian drivers and interpreters who were undoubtedly Unified State Political Administration security police agents, the loaded cars stopped at rural villages and state farms. This apparently was Barkley's greatest time in Soviet Russia. At one farm he helped thresh grain, and at another he handled one end of a crosscut saw to attack a block of wood. Peasant workers were thrilled to have beside them an American visitor who actually knew and respected farm life and labor.[3]

The senators then rejoined the larger group, took a train, and visited Leningrad (the former and future St. Petersburg) before leaving the Soviet Union and pausing briefly in Western Europe. The tourists arrived back in New York City on board the *Leviathan* of the United States Lines on September 3, 1930. They were greeted by the press. Wheeler and Norbeck told journalists that diplomatic relations with the Soviet Union were needed as a way to promote US business interests and sales at a time when America desperately needed markets for its products. Barkley's answers to the questions of newspapermen were more cautious. He admitted only that his great prejudice against the Soviet system had been somewhat modified by the economic activity generated by the government. Cutting came home on a later passenger ship, but in comments written to his mother he seemed to capture the views of most of those who had visited Moscow and Leningrad. He noted that the "spirit and enthusiasm" associated with the Five-Year Plan had to be balanced against the "lack of Freedom and the general discomfort" experienced by Soviet citizens.[4]

When he and his family returned home to Paducah during the second week of September, Barkley experienced a different kind of discomfort from the one Cutting had described Soviet citizens as suffering. The commonwealth was in the midst of a serious drought that would last into the next year. In the Bluegrass region of central Kentucky, rainfall totals plummeted from a normal annual amount of forty-four inches to a low of twenty-five. South of Paducah in Graves County, where Barkley was born, the county seat of Mayfield did not receive a drop of rain in the month of July, yet it sweltered in hundred-degree daytime heat that dried and destroyed plants. More than a few Barkley supporters in the countryside across the state lost their crops, their livestock, and then their farms. The senator knew that the Hoover administration would be reluctant to recommend federal assistance for drought relief. And he was right. It infuriated him that Hoover belatedly supported a paltry $25 million for drought victims, but only for loans, not grants, to farmers. He decided to spend part of the fall election season campaigning for Democrats seeking congressional seats and the state's remaining post in the US Senate. He felt that, if enough "right-thinking" Democrats populated Congress, there might be a chance to pressure the Republican administration to deal more forthrightly with the environmental and economic disasters confronting the American people.[5]

Before he collected his dwindling family from their Washington residence for the trip to Paducah, Barkley had already begun an attack on the GOP and the Hoover White House. In a major interview article on the front page (and beyond) of the *New York Times,* he grabbed the attention of a large audience that included the president and his cabinet. During the IPU conference, he had had conversations with an unnamed "high British official" later identified as David Lloyd George, who had served from 1916 to 1922 as Great Britain's prime minister during both the Great War and the Versailles Peace Conference. It is true that in 1930 George spent his free time writing what would turn out to be his published, multivolume memoirs. On the other hand, his lengthy public service in top positions left him with numerous political connections that allowed him to know current trends in the British government. Thus, Lloyd George could share newsworthy information with the senator. It appeared likely that the extremely protectionist Hawley-Smoot Tariff would terminate British repayment of war debts to the United States. And the former prime minister knew what he was talking about because it was related to a policy issued by his administration in 1922.[6]

On August 1 of that year, and on behalf of the Lloyd George government, the senior British official Arthur Balfour circulated a note making it clear that London would pay its war debts to Washington, but with funds from those countries indebted ($8.7 billion) to Great Britain. These wartime allies, including Great Britain, owed the United States a total of $9.45 billion. The flow of debt payments, however, began with Germany. The Treaty of Versailles not only blamed Germany for starting the Great War but also required the defeated country to pay damages. In 1921, the Reparations Commission handed Germany a bill for what was at that time the incredible amount of $33 billion. There were two main avenues open to Germany for acquiring the transferable currencies needed to pay the huge tab— foreign investment and favorable trade. In essence, Lloyd George told Barkley that the Depression closed off foreign investment and the Hawley-Smoot Act placed a barrier around favorable trade. Indeed, Barkley discovered at the IPU conference that the barrier would soon be expanded with protective tariffs around most European countries. As a result, Germany would be forced to end reparation payments to Allied Powers, which, in turn, would end paying war debts to the United States.[7]

In the interview article, Barkley did not ignore the issue he had argued so forcefully in the Senate. Since trade is an exchange process, a country that imports something from the United States normally needs to sell something to the United States to keep the account balanced. The usual alternatives in an unbalanced exchange are to buy goods through financing or to transfer funds, for example, from favorable trade with other countries. Barkley used Switzerland to show the dysfunctional impact of the recently enacted tariff. Switzerland sold in America mainly high-quality watches and clocks that were virtually banned by the US tariff. "Does anybody suppose," Barkley asked, "that the people of Switzerland can continue to buy $40,000,000 worth of our goods produced by our labor out of our own materials when we have enacted a law that shuts them out of our market for a type of goods we do not even produce?" The unstated answer, of course, was no. And the result would be the loss of some jobs by those American workers who had produced the $40 million worth of products that Switzerland had annually purchased in the United States before the Hawley-Smoot Tariff.[8]

The Barkley article proved so effective and tight with arguments and data about the detrimental nature of the tariff that it prompted the Hoover administration to respond through a statement issued by Ogden L. Mills, undersecretary and future (1931–1933) secretary of the treasury. Mills attempted to minimize the damage from Barkley's comments by first pointing out that he had rehashed "all of the old generalities that were urged repeatedly during the tariff discussions in the Senate." The implication, of course, was that Barkley's arguments must be faulty because a majority in Congress in essence had voted down his position. Mills was correct about rehashed ideas, but he made no effort to counter Barkley's focus on the exchange of goods between the United States and other countries. From Barkley's perspective, the key to selling products abroad was the fact that those goods were made by the hands of American farmers or workers who received payments or wages for their labors. Such trade kept US families employed, housed, and fed—nothing else mattered.[9]

Additionally, Mills made two errors that Barkley could jump on. First, he used 1929 data to undergird his statement; second, he pointed out that Barkley had neglected other areas that help balance international payments. He then mentioned US investments abroad and touted at length the expenditures of American tourists in foreign countries. Barkley judged the statement by Mills to be somewhere between "evasive" and downright "amusing." He noted in response 1930 data showing that new investment and tourist travel had declined. As for tourist spending, he considered the notion to be a joke when compared with trade in products. He wondered how many tourists it would take to save jobs or farms when it was difficult to sell US products from land and factory to other countries. He proved his point by citing recent US Department of Commerce trade figures for the month of July 1930 showing that exports fell by over $136 million when juxtaposed with those for July 1929. Regardless, Lloyd George and Barkley were, indeed, prophets. Not only did the US tariff cause a tariff war that crippled trade, but reparations and war debt payments ended. Two events triggered a Central European panic in May 1931 that matched the one in America in October 1929. Austria's largest bank failed, prompting a run on gold held by Germany's Reichsbank. President Paul von Hindenburg of

Germany sent Hoover a moving message pleading for help on June 18, 1931. Two days later, the US president responded with a call for a one-year moratorium on both German reparations and war debts. Except for Finland, which repaid its US loan, the moratorium continued forever.[10]

Though it took nine months to happen, Barkley was proved absolutely correct in his newspaper debate with Mills. Meanwhile, right after his reply to the Treasury undersecretary, the senator strengthened his ties with commonwealth workers by giving an address on September 16, 1930, before the Kentucky Federation of Labor, a branch of the American Federation of Labor. He told his audience: "The supreme problem of Government of our time is to find a wise and permanent solution [to] the problem of unemployment." The solution, he noted, required "statesmanship." Since the GOP controlled "Government" (Congress, the White House, the cabinet) and had not solved unemployment, his listeners could connect the dots. The other political party should get their votes in the forthcoming election. In October, Barkley traveled and spoke on behalf of Kentucky Democratic candidates for Congress. Such a canvass also kept his name and face in front of his constituents, which would certainly help his reelection two years later. In addition, the Iron Man spent time at the state's Democratic Party headquarters in Louisville, where he communicated by phone and telegram with individuals who could bolster the vote for the party. Economic and weather conditions across the commonwealth guaranteed that his efforts would not be in vain. Democrats won big in November. One of them, Marvel M. Logan, an elected justice on the Kentucky Court of Appeals, would defeat the Republican John M. Robsion and join Barkley in the US Senate.[11]

Given the circumstances of depression and a serious drought in the Mississippi valley, it was perfectly understandable why the Republican Party experienced losses, not just in Kentucky, but nationwide in the November elections. Indeed, the surprise may have been the fact that the GOP initially seemed to have kept control over both chambers of Congress, the House breakdown being 218 Republicans, 216 Democrats, and 1 Farmer-Laborite and the Senate breakdown 48 Republicans, 47 Democrats, and 1 Farmer-Laborite. Before the Seventy-Second Congress convened on December 7, 1931, however, several House Republicans died, and their seats were won by Democrats, whose party then had the votes to organize the chamber. Moreover, with insurgent Republicans often voting with Democrats in the Senate, Minority Leader Joseph T. Robinson was in reality the de facto majority leader. This situation was so obvious that even President Hoover generally chose to discuss legislation with Robinson rather than Majority Leader James E. Watson (IN). Still, it must be recognized that neither party could dominate Congress. Only an extraordinarily popular issue (an example is discussed below) could overcome a presidential veto. In most cases, then, Hoover could prevent legislation from becoming law if he so desired.[12]

Meanwhile, when the last session of the Seventy-First Congress opened in December 1930, the Republicans still dominated the national legislative body. As a result, Barkley's frustration with the Hoover administration and a "do-nothing" Congress only intensified. He strongly supported the failed attempt to resurrect the lapsed Sheppard-Towner Maternity and Infancy Act of 1921. The measure actually gained the approval of both chambers of Congress. After the House passed the revised version worked out by a House-Senate conference committee, it died in the Senate. A filibuster by an Oklahoma senator over an oil resolution ended the Seventy-First Congress early in March 1931 without a final vote on the maternity bill. Earlier, Barkley and others introduced bills to allow Great War veterans to cash in at full value the bonus certificates approved by Congress in 1924. The certificates would not mature until 1945, though veterans could borrow up to 22.5 percent of the authorizing documents' face value. Barkley's bill was watered down significantly with a final compromise measure that, nevertheless, attracted overwhelming congressional approval. The compromise dropped giving veterans 100 percent of the bonus; instead, they could borrow up to 50 percent of the documents' worth. Considering the revision, Barkley found it incredible that Hoover vetoed the legislation. Congress responded quickly to overturn the president's veto by a vote of 328–79 in the House and 76–17 in the Senate.[13]

The capstone to Barkley's condemnation of Hoover came when the president sought only a relatively small sum of money to be dispensed as loans to drought victims across the Mississippi valley. In Hoover's defense, it should be pointed out the president hoped that a voluntary group, the American Red Cross, could help victims of the drought, which touched forty of the forty-eight states. In fact, he led a national campaign that did raise over $5 million for this purpose, but the amount was not nearly enough to ease the massive losses caused by the dry weather. On February 28, just a few days before Congress adjourned, Barkley openly expressed his deep disappointment with the Hoover administration on the Senate floor. Since the stock market crash, the administration seemed to behave like an "ostrich with its head in the sand," "unwilling to offer any real remedy for the situation." He felt that it was imperative the president call a special session of Congress, which otherwise would not meet until December, leaving the US "Government helpless in the midst of this great tragedy, and powerless to render any real relief." Just as bad, the nine-month absence of Congress would result in the elimination of "a public forum where the situation can be aired."[14]

President Hoover had absolutely no intention of calling a special session of the national legislature. He spent the final moments of the Seventy-First Congress in the presidential room just off the Senate chamber in the Capitol Building. He anticipated signing last-minute pieces of legislation from the weary House and filibuster-bound Senate. The filibuster prevented not only the passage of three bills (including the maternity measure) but also the appointment of the customary committee that would officially notify the president of the congressional adjournment. Because the two years since his inauguration had been filled with congressional strife over his policies, Hoover was all smiles to hear unofficially that Congress had finally adjourned. He knew that the continued pressure of insurgent Republicans, bolstered by an expanded number of Democratic representatives and senators, would not make life easy for him in the Seventy-Second Congress. Hence, a special session was simply out of the question. It would only seat immediately all the newly elected Democrats and promote quickly all the troubles he expected in December. Hoover chose nine months of peace and tranquility rather than legislative battles and agitation.[15]

Barkley remained in the nation's capital for two weeks after Congress adjourned. He cleaned up last-minute correspondence and also took steps necessary to close up the residence on Cleveland Avenue. The family planned to spend time in Paducah, where the senator could strengthen his Kentucky connections and give thought to his future canvass of the commonwealth in the course of next year's reelection campaign. While Barkley stayed in Washington, his wife, Dorothy, motored to St. Louis in the company of Marie Miles Gregory. Marie's husband, William, grew up in Graves County and served in Barkley's former position as Kentucky's First District congressman. Along with Laura Louise Barkley, the ladies visited Marian Barkley Truitt, the January bride of Max, who then had a law practice in St. Louis. In 1935, Max and Marian and their growing family—eventually four sons—moved permanently to Washington. Truitt served as counselor to several government agencies before returning to private practice with the law firm of Cummings, Truitt and Reeves.[16]

Once he and his family were reunited in Paducah, Barkley rested but also engaged in a number of activities, including the preparation of several speeches he planned to give in the spring and summer. He wrote, for example, "Whose Business Is Business" for the June 24 meeting in Boston of the National Association of Credit Men. Besides this onetime address for a specific group, he prepared an all-purpose talk on Russia that he could give to a variety of audiences. In June, he drove leisurely east from Paducah in his Ford roadster on his way to the Boston event. He stopped at several places in Kentucky and made presentations about the Soviet Union. These were based, in part, on his personal observations from the tour he had taken the previous August. One of his venues was the chapel exercises held in the Hiram Brock Auditorium at Eastern State Teachers College (today Eastern Kentucky University) in Richmond, the seat of government for Madison County. While he could not predict whether the "Russian experiment" would succeed, he went on to discuss the physical size of the world's largest country, the impact of the Great War in leading to the Russian Revolution of 1917, and the advent of Marxian socialism. Fitting for an audience of students who grew up on farms or lived in farming communities, he also talked about Soviet agriculture, noting from his own experiences that US machinery (Fordson tractors and International Harvester combines) could be found on some state farms.[17]

Barkley, however, never made it to the Boston meeting. Two days before his scheduled presentation, he fell asleep at the wheel and struck a telephone pole near Parkersburg, West Virginia. That was his later admission; for contemporaries, he used impression management and claimed that loose gravel on the road caused him to skid out of control and into the pole. Still, the impact vaulted him out of the car through the windshield. Fortunately, windshields in that era were normally weak and manufactured out of a simple, single plate of glass; today, they are produced with a sheet of plastic laminated between two hardened plates. To be sure, he sustained some serious cuts on his head and shoulders but not a life-ending crushed skull. Otherwise, when he landed, the blow to his body fractured a wrist and a knee and also produced multiple bruises. He was taken to the hospital in Parkersburg.[18]

Early on, the hospital categorized Barkley's condition as critical. But, within six days, the cut, bruised, and fractured Iron Man had recovered enough to arrange for a telegram to be sent to Hoover. The senator congratulated the president for proposing a moratorium on war debts and reparations owed by the Great War's participants. Moreover, he issued a press release that in part stated: "The real benefit in this proposal lies in the recognition of the inseparable economic relationship existing among all nations of the world and the willingness to act in accordance with that relationship." This message, which basically extolled international cooperation, did not exactly match Hoover's agenda. For one thing, the president refused to acknowledge any connection between German reparations and the ability of the Allied Powers to repay their war debts to the United States. Furthermore, he wanted to free Germany of its public debts to Allied Powers so that it could more readily repay private debts to Americans. Finally, he tried to protect—even isolate—the United States from the European run on gold that might force countries with exchangeable money to give up using gold as the best standard for the measurement and stable worth of national currencies.[19]

Barkley was able to go home to Paducah at the start of July. His correspondence reveals that the healing process, especially for his knee, required a lengthy period of recuperation. His friend Senator Connally from Marlin, Texas, had sent a get-well telegram to the Parkersburg hospital on June 25, 1931. Barkley did not reply until he had been at home for nearly two weeks. "I should have written sooner," he told Connally, "but have been unable to do any writing or engage in any other activity since the accident." He expressed gratitude for the fact that there should be "no permanent bad effect" from the crash. Still, it was clear that it would be weeks or months before he could walk normally and resume comfortably all activities. Hence, he did not play a major role in the 1931 Kentucky governor's race. And he did not need to make a large number of campaign appearances. The Democrat Ruby Lafoon easily won the Frankfort office, beating his Republican opponent by over seventy-two thousand votes. GOP administrations in both Frankfort and Washington seemed deficient in their response to depression and drought. Such lackluster reaction guaranteed a Republican defeat in the state. Perhaps the most important result of the 1931 election was the victory of another Democrat, the commonwealth's rising political star Albert Benjamin "Happy" Chandler, who succeeded to the post of lieutenant governor.[20]

Despite his limited participation in the election campaign, Barkley received in November a warm letter from New York governor Franklin D. Roosevelt, congratulating him on the recent Democratic victory. The governor invited the senator to join him in Warm Springs, Georgia, before the December 7 start to the Seventy-Second Congress. Roosevelt had in the mid-1920s discovered the healing benefits of the buoyant spring water from Pine Mountain that poured into a warm pool of eighty-eight degrees. Crippled in his legs, the future president had turned Warm Springs into a major treatment center for those who, like he, suffered as victims of polio. In this particular instance, Barkley had to turn down the kind offer, but he promised to visit FDR in the governor's office in Albany, New York. After the 1928 Democratic national convention, Roosevelt and Barkley kept in touch with each other. On one level, they simply liked each other, but there were also mutually beneficial political reasons for maintaining a close relationship. FDR expected to seek his party's presidential nomination in 1932 and wanted Kentucky and its powerhouse orator on his side; the senator appreciated the fact that in victory President Roosevelt could help him and Kentucky with favors that would enhance and benefit both Barkley's career and his state.[21]

Before Barkley returned to Washington for the opening of the first session of the new Congress, Minority Leader Robinson had asked his friend Senator Thomas J. Walsh for his views on what should be the Democratic legislative program. From their correspondence, it is clear that neither man wanted to announce an agenda publicly. True, the Democrats possessed just enough votes to elect John Nance Garner (TX) speaker of the House but failed by one vote to organize the Senate. Under these circumstances, Republicans could easily thwart Democratic initiatives and/or uphold a presidential veto. Logically, Walsh recommended that they should quietly help the House prepare bills that, whenever possible, might also be introduced in Senate committees by minority members. Walsh concluded his lengthy message with an interesting list of eight areas Democrats needed to address: (1) fund public works to relieve unemployment, (2) consider proposals to prevent or ease future unemployment, (3) use bonds and taxes to cover deficits, (4) revise the tariff that had worsened the Depression, (5) end stock market gambling, (6) reduce or end bank loans to stock brokers, (7) provide farm relief, and (8) base foreign war debt relief on reduced spending on military armaments.[22]

Except for the last entry on the list, the other seven were handled one way or another after Hoover left office. Barkley understood only too well the views of the latter and the limitations of a politically divided Congress. The prospects for serious steps to be taken to overcome the country's economic disaster in his view ranged unfortunately somewhere between slim and nil. "Hoovervilles" had emerged in large numbers across the nation by 1932. Often located near city dumps, they were populated by dispossessed citizens who lived in tarpaper shacks, packing boxes, and abandoned automobiles. Millions of unemployed had their own cynical expressions for rabbits (*Hoover hogs*), newspapers (*Hoover blankets*), and empty pockets turned inside out (*Hoover flags*). Midwest farmers burned corn to keep warm, destroyed unprofitable crops and milk, and formed mobs to prevent foreclosures on neighboring farms. While the US Communist Party gained only a modest number of new members during the Great Depression, it enjoyed some success. The party attracted crowds of people for its hunger marches and enlisted Alabama sharecroppers and Kentucky coal miners in its unions. The highly visible victims and catastrophic results of the economic collapse prompted Barkley to speak of his frustration over the inability of the White House and Congress to come to grips with this American tragedy.[23] On January 12, he spoke bitterly before his colleagues on the Senate floor:

> All our remedies here are temporary. All of them are merely scratching the surface. Nothing has been done yet by Congress, nothing has been suggested by this administration, which deals with the fundamental difficulty under which our country is laboring, which lays the ax to the root of our troubles. We are now dealing only with temporary expedients, only with palliatives, only with sugar-coated pills which may keep the patient alive until somebody will have enough vision and statesmanship . . . [and can] undertake to eradicate the difficulties and the causes of the difficulties which now engulf us in this disaster.[24]

President Hoover did stretch his philosophy on federal government aid by signing into law on January 22, 1932, a revised form of the War Finance Corporation from the Wilson era—the Reconstruction Finance Corporation (RFC). It sought to protect the nation's credit structure by providing emergency loans to banks, life insurance companies, building and loan societies, farm mortgage associations, and railways. Those institutions, however, were in the hands of wealthy individuals, so critics pondered how much of the loans would trickle down to help the thirteen million who had no wages in 1932. For many critics, in the words of Barkley, the RFC was simply another "sugar-coated pill." Just like Walsh had recommended in November, Senator Robert G. Wagner (D-NY) worked with House speaker Garner on a bill that would have expanded RFC funds and the list of those who could receive government loans. Interestingly, it also included $100 million for the federal government to give, not loan, to needy individuals and $200 million in loans to states that could then disburse cash to distressed citizens. President Hoover vetoed the bill. He felt that money should be loaned and go exclusively to institutions under state or federal regulation. Cash to the unemployed or loans to sundry companies and individuals completely violated his notion of the US government's responsibility in the Depression crisis.[25]

It should be noted, however, that Hoover did sign into law on July 21, 1932, the Barkley-supported Emergency Relief and Construction Act. It increased by $2.12 billion the operating funds of the RFC. The legislation authorized $300 million for relief loans, $322 million for federal public works, and $1.5 billion in loans for state-sponsored public works. Since the measure resembled the Hoover-rejected Garner-Wagner bill, the interesting question is why the president gave his approval to this version. There are several explanations for Hoover's decision. First, and perhaps most importantly, the Emergency Relief and Construction Act complied with his stricture against awarding federal funds to individuals as some type of dole. Second, regardless of party, most members of Congress had authored or endorsed some type of public works program. Hoover knew that his veto had zero chance of being upheld in another congressional vote. Third, the country was in the midst of a political campaign for the presidency; the White House occupant wanted to reside there for another four years. His signature converting the relief bill into law would garner votes.[26]

Unfortunately for the president, there was a tragic episode unfolding that marred his campaign for reelection. When the Republican national convention opened in Chicago on June 14, the Bonus Army had already established and built shacks in a typical Hooverville located southeast of the Capitol Building in Washington's Anacostia Flats. Composed of unemployed veterans and their families, army members demanded full payment for their wartime bonus certificates. To be sure, GOP delegates in Chicago, minus any enthusiasm, selected Hoover as the party's nominee for another presidential term. But one week after he had received plaudits for signing the Emergency Relief and Construction Act, the president inadvertently reduced further any chance he had to win in the November elections. He called on the Washington police and the US Army to clear the Bonus Army out of the business section of the nation's capital. As veterans were evicted from otherwise empty buildings along Pennsylvania Avenue, Chief of Staff General Douglas A. MacArthur chose to expand the presidential order by moving army units against the main encampment on Anacostia Flats. The operations succeeded but also produced three martyrs, including Bernard Myers. Tear gas killed the eight-week-old baby, who gained life and suffered death in Washington's Hooverville. This deplorable blunder handed serious ammunition to those opposed to Hoover's reelection.[27]

Chief among the millions of Hoover's opponents was Governor Roosevelt. And Barkley served an important role in advancing the governor's prospects for securing the Democratic nomination for president. As early as December 1931, FDR speculated about Barkley's role with Robert W. Woolley, the former publicity director for the Democratic National Committee who had also been an interstate commerce commissioner under President Wilson. Woolley and Roosevelt agreed that Barkley could help cripple Al Smith's "Stop Roosevelt" movement. (New York's former governor wanted the nomination for himself.) They believed that Kentucky's nationally known senator could dampen Smith's efforts and promote FDR's nomination through a public statement endorsing his bid to be president. In his talks with Woolley, the governor mentioned that he thought he could secure for Barkley the position of temporary chairman of and keynote speaker at the Democratic national convention if the Iron Man actually announced his support. Woolley remarked and FDR concurred that the latter would not be revealed to Barkley until after he delivered the endorsement. To do anything else, Woolley claimed, "would offend him."[28]

Early in 1932, Roosevelt asked Woolley to seek Barkley's support. It was a good choice because Woolley shared the Kentuckian's favorable memory of Woodrow Wilson. Barkley immediately expressed to Woolley his enthusiasm for championing the governor's nomination. The senator neither asked for nor expected any favors. Woolley impressed on him that Roosevelt hoped that the public statement would come sooner rather than later, yet Barkley chose to wait until March 23. One reason for the delay is that he faced a delicate problem and needed time to work through it. Some Democrats in the Bluegrass region had joined Al Smith's "Stop Roosevelt" movement and wanted the state's delegates to the upcoming convention to pledge their votes to the nomination of Barkley for president. The situation presented an interesting conundrum. On the one hand, such a "favorite son" nomination would give Barkley valuable publicity. And he was concerned about his own future; it had been forty-two years since a Kentucky senator had won reelection to a second term. On the other hand, his support for Roosevelt might cost him votes in the November general election preceded by Democratic challengers for his Senate seat in the August primary. He was certifiably correct about the latter—he would face four opponents in the primary.[29]

In mid-March, Barkley expected to hand a statement for publication to Ulrich Bell, the Washington correspondent for the *Louisville Courier-Journal*. But, just at that moment, rumors erupted claiming that he was about to endorse Roosevelt and in return would be appointed temporary chairman of and keynoter for the upcoming national convention. The rumors shook Barkley so much he delayed his plans for a week in the hope of disconnecting any link to a deal that the Al Smith camp described hyperbolically as a "corrupt bargain." Thus, March 23 was the date his declaration finally appeared in a number of major newspapers. It came in the form of a letter to his friend James H. Richmond, the Kentucky state superintendent of public instruction. Barkley asked Richmond to inform party members at the state Democratic convention in April that he declined to be the delegation's favorite son nominee for president. In the senator's words, the national election was too important to "waste our energy" or "clutter up the situation." The current economic disaster required a united effort by the Democratic Party behind "real leadership, [with] real understanding of the people's needs, and the ability to crystallize them into action and relief." He continued:

In my opinion such a leadership is offered in Gov. Franklin D. Roosevelt. I have known Mr. Roosevelt since he was Assistant Secretary of the Navy under Woodrow Wilson. I have worked with him in national conventions and elsewhere. I have watched his career as Governor of the State of New York. I have been thrilled by his heroic, yet fair and just and patient fight for clean and honest government. The people have confidence in his integrity, his high purpose and his progressive and constructive statesmanship. Instead of attempting to stop a nomination which manifestly the people favor, we ought to unite to bring it about.

That he will be nominated at the Chicago convention I earnestly hope and believe, and that he will, when nominated, be overwhelmingly elected I have not the slightest doubt. I trust the Kentucky State convention will instruct its delegates to vote for and help procure his nomination.[30]

Two days later, Homer S. Cummings, the future attorney general (1933–1939), came to Washington on behalf of Roosevelt. He asked and received Barkley's permission to nominate him for appointment to the significant office of opening the party's Chicago convention. The issue came up on April 4 during a session in the Windy City of the Arrangements Committee of the Democratic National Committee. An unexpected shock hit the Roosevelt camp. Jouett Shouse, the national committee's new chairman, wanted the post for himself. The really troubling aspect of the chairman's self-nomination was the fact that he had close ties to Al Smith and the "Stop Roosevelt" movement. Harry Flood Byrd, a former governor of and future senator from Virginia, proposed a compromise that seemed to make everyone happy. Barkley received the post of temporary chairman as Roosevelt commended (rather than recommended), Shouse to be the permanent chairman. What was the catch? Convention delegates, not the committee, had to approve the permanent post. Since Roosevelt had a majority of delegates, his forces selected Senator Walsh, not Shouse, to be the convention's permanent chairman. Unlike what Shouse might have done, neither Barkley nor Walsh made any rulings that impinged on Roosevelt's nomination.[31]

The Democratic national convention opened in Chicago on Monday, June 27, not long after the Republicans had ended their melancholy meeting. Chicago's streets and hotels, however, had filled with hopeful delegates in a festive mood for several days before the conference began. Unlike their GOP counterparts, these delegates were convinced that they were about to pick the next president of the United States. In the morning of the twenty-seventh, the hall held eager delegates and bystanders to such an extent that the crowded aisles refused to yield to demonstrations and snake dances. At noon, it took more than twenty minutes to quiet the people before the retiring chairman of the Democratic National Committee, John J. Raskob, succeeded in gaveling the convention to order. Commander Evangeline Booth of the Salvation Army delivered the opening prayer, which was followed by two of the four verses of the recently adopted national anthem, "The Star-Spangled Banner," sung by Rose Zulalian. She was succeeded by Mayor Anton J. Cermak, who welcomed the delegates to Chicago. Then Raskob gave his swan-song speech, after which Isidore B. Dockweiler of the party's national committee recited Thomas Jefferson's first inaugural address.[32]

Finally, clad in a white linen suit, and accompanied to the podium by a rendition of "My Old Kentucky Home," the Iron Man began to deliver in his powerful, soft-accented baritone voice one of the longest keynote speeches in history. "We meet today," he began, "in the midst of a solemn responsibility. . . . We meet to fulfill an appointment with Destiny." Barkley went on to assault the three Republican administrations elected in the 1920s. He labeled the Harding era as the "darkest chapter of public betrayal in the history of this or any other nation"; like some contemporaries and recent commentators, he blamed Coolidge for the "orgy of speculation and inflation that had no foundation in real values." For Hoover, as might be expected, he reserved his criticism for the "exorbitant and indefensible rates" of the Hawley-Smoot Tariff. He also called for measures to strengthen the banking system, bring relief and aid to farmers and workers, reduce federal expenditures, and change the leadership in the White House, which was "incomparably short-sighted and bereft of true statesmanship . . . and incapable even now in the midst of its fearful havoc of understanding the extent of its own mischief."[33]

What proved to be the most startling aspect of Barkley's speech, the one that ignited a rousing demonstration of support from the delegates, was his call for a resolution that would repeal the Eighteenth Amendment to the Constitution. Because of his national reputation as a spokesman for the dry position, the commotion (and controversy) over his call also spread across the country via radio and newspapers. Moreover, the excited cheers, afternoon heat, and length of his talk caused many delegates and journalists to miss the nuance of the call for repeal. Barkley's full position stated that, if repeal failed, prohibition must be strictly adhered to by law-abiding citizens and strictly enforced against violators. And, even if it passed, he cautioned, "then let every branch of national government exercise all the powers they possess to protect the states in the observance and enforcement of the laws which they shall enact to control, regulate or prohibit the traffic in intoxicating liquors." There are good reasons why Barkley shifted away from his dry stance. It was disturbing to witness so many Americans violating the Constitution and to see criminal elements growing in strength and expanding their revenue by adding the sale of alcoholic beverages to their other illicit activities. As importantly, Barkley understood that the amendment's repeal would create jobs, especially among Kentucky distilleries, which produced the bulk of America's bourbon and other whiskies.[34]

Partially because of the call for a resolution to repeal prohibition, the convention's delegates relished Barkley's keynote speech. The humorist Will Rogers captured in a jocular newspaper article the essence of why, across the nation, all those who castigated the Hoover administration would like the whole, lengthy address:

> Now comes Senator Barkley with the keynote. What do you mean "note"? This was no note. This was in three volumes. Barkley leaves from here to go to the Olympic Games to run in the marathon. He will win it, too, for that race only lasts three or four hours.
>
> But it had to be a long speech, for when you start enumerating the things that the Republicans have got away with in the last twelve years you have cut yourself out a job.
>
> He touched on the highlights of their devilment. He did not have time to go into detail. This is one keynote speech you can forgive the length, for when you jot down our ills you got to have a lot of paper. He had it all over the Republican keynoter, for this fellow was reading facts while the other fellow had to read alibis! Barkley did a fine job of delivering and, too, he was on his feet at the finish.[35]

Shortly after Barkley's keynote speech, the convention adjourned for the day. The next day the Iron Man had his hands full. First, he dealt with the seating of rival delegations from both Louisiana and Minnesota. In each case, the pro-Roosevelt delegation won a majority of votes from the convention floor. After these delegation issues had been resolved, a vote was taken to approve the convention's permanent chairman. FDR's convention manager, James A. Farley (the future postmaster general), helped line up the pro-Roosevelt forces. The final tally elected Walsh, who secured 626 votes to 528 for Shouse. Naturally, the Roosevelt camp had mixed feelings about the results. An ally became the convention's permanent chairman, but the vote totals proved that the "Stop Roosevelt" minority could prevent the two-thirds majority that FDR needed to gain his party's nomination. "On one thing the convention is agreed," stated the journalist Arthur Krock, "the effective temporary chairmanship of Senator Alben Barkley of Kentucky. Through the difficult day he controlled the delegates firmly and courteously, adding the salt of humor and good taste to the proceedings." When he turned the gavel over to Senator Walsh, Barkley received a prolonged outburst of cheers and applause as the convention organist played "For He's a Jolly Good Fellow."[36]

Among the shouts of delegates could be heard calls for Barkley to be the vice presidential nominee. It would not happen. In the first place, the Kentuckian's endorsement of FDR had been repaid when he received commonwealth and nationwide recognition as one of the party's top leaders. It occurred because of his two-day exposure on national radio plus enough newspaper ink spilled around his name to cover a battleship. The key to FDR's decision on a vice presidential candidate centered on the crucial effort to secure eighty-seven votes that would carry him above the two-thirds mark and to victory. After the third deadlocked ballot, Roosevelt through Farley offered House speaker John Nance Garner the second spot on the Democratic ticket. At that point, Garner had ninety votes pledged to him from Texas (which had forty-six delegates) and California (which had forty-four). On July 1, during the fourth ballot, it was announced that California and Texas would switch their votes from Garner to Roosevelt. It broke the deadlock, caused all but five delegations to jump on the bandwagon, and handed the nomination to the New York governor.[37]

The next day Garner gained the convention's unanimous support to join Roosevelt on the national ticket for the November election. Meanwhile, FDR informed Walsh and, hence, the convention that he was going to break with tradition. Instead of waiting for a formal ceremony of notification at his office in Albany or his home in Hyde Park, he decided to fly from Albany to Chicago and deliver an acceptance speech directly to the delegates. His use of an airplane and appearance at the convention symbolized his willingness to dismiss established practice and employ new ideas and technologies to accomplish goals. Samuel I. Rosenman, Roosevelt's speechwriter, prepared drafts of the acceptance speech. It certainly contained different rhetoric from the Barkley-written keynote address, but it included many of the same basic elements. The orations of both men were long in criticism of Republican shortcomings and lacked specific steps outlining how to heal the half-dead economy of the nation. Fortuitously, however, the New York governor moved from the fourth to the last page of the speech Rosenman's famous peroration that served as the hallmark for an era in American history. Roosevelt concluded his acceptance speech with the phrase: "I pledge you, I pledge myself, to a new deal for the American people." Barkley's role in the New Deal era can best be understood by the fact that Kentucky's senator and New York's governor had reached identical stages in their thinking: the federal government absolutely must expand and supply direct action to help its citizens overcome economic distress.[38]

Marvin College. Author's collection.

Barkley as a young lawyer.

Dorothy Brower as a young lady.

Newly elected Congressman Barkley, wife Dorothy, son David, and daughters Laura and Marian. Courtesy of the Kentucky Historical Society.

Senator Barkley (*left*) and Senate Committee Investigating Campaign Expenditures, presidential candidate Al Smith seated in front, 1928.

Assistant Senate majority leader Barkley supporting the New Deal in a radio address, 1934.

President Roosevelt, Happy Chandler, and Senate majority leader Barkley in open car, 1938.

President Roosevelt campaigns for Senate majority leader Barkley, 1938.

Vice President Wallace, House speaker Rayburn, Senate majority leader Barkley, and House majority leader McCormack after a White House conference, 1941.

Senate majority leader Barkley resigns over President Roosevelt's veto, 1944.

President Truman and Senate majority leader Barkley shortly after their party's nomination for president and vice president, 1948.

President Truman, Vice President Barkley, Senate majority leader Lucas, House speaker Rayburn, and House majority leader McCormack after meeting, 1950.

Clark Clifford, Jane Barkley, Alben Barkley, and Marny Clifford soon after the Barkley marriage.

Barkley statue. Courtesy of the Kentucky Historical Society.

11

The Assistant Majority Leader and the New Deal

Shortly after the convention, campaigns began for the reelection of the Kentucky senator and the election of the New York governor for the presidency. Neither case proved difficult. Despite several opponents in the August primary, Alben W. Barkley swept them away by securing close to two-thirds of the votes cast. In a less troubled time, he might have faced a serious general election contest in November from the Republican Maurice H. Thatcher. A former US attorney, Panama Canal Zone governor, and counsel to his home city of Louisville, Thatcher was serving in his fifth term as a congressional representative when he sought the Senate seat held by Barkley. Thatcher, a prohibitionist, focused his campaign on the fact that Barkley had shifted away from a strict dry position. On October 1, 1932, when Barkley had begun "the vocal part" of his campaign in Cynthiana (the seat of government for Harrison County), the Iron Man chose to dwell on the economy. And it worked. The senator batted the economic ball for a winning home run. He zeroed in on the fact that Republicans controlled the government leading up to the Great Depression and then "doggedly resisted . . . the whole program of relief" after economic disaster struck. In terms of prohibition, Barkley limited his few comments to the fact that he was personally a dry but "disappointed with the measure of its observance and enforcement" during Republican administrations. He felt that only the American people could decide "whether they wish to retain or remove the 18th Amendment to the Constitution."[1]

In the general election, Barkley won overwhelmingly with 575,077 votes to Thatcher's 393,865. As Lowell H. Harrison and James C. Klotter point out in their *New History of Kentucky,* the vote for Barkley was simply one example of the party's dominance in the state. Republicans were crushed as they lost to Democrats all nine of the commonwealth's congressional seats in the House. This dominance would last for most of the twentieth century. And what occurred in the state reflected a powerful trend across the country. Roosevelt, for example, won all but six states, attracting close to 70 percent of the vote. Because several of those states, such as Delaware, New Hampshire, and Vermont, each contained a small population, Roosevelt absolutely swamped Hoover in the Electoral College with a tally of 472–59. What happened in the Kentucky and the presidential elections was replicated nationwide in polls for congressional candidates. Democrats captured twelve Senate seats from the GOP to control the upper chamber fifty-nine to thirty-six (plus one Farmer-Laborite); they also enjoyed a nearly three-to-one edge in the House.[2]

The decisive Democratic victory in November meant nothing to the lame-duck last session of the Seventy-Second Congress when it opened on December 7, 1932, and continued unproductively until March 3, 1933. Because the Hoover administration had reached the philosophical limits to what it perceived as the appropriate response to the Great Depression, Congress was literally stuck in time. Any initiative that moved beyond Hoover's position bumped against an ironclad veto. While the Twentieth Amendment to the Constitution had been ratified by the required three-fourths of the forty-eight states, it did not go into effect until February 6, 1933. Thus, only in the future would the president take office at noon on January 20 and the newly elected Congress begin at noon on January 3. Meanwhile in 1933, the lame-duck Congress operated in what has been described as an interregnum of despair as unemployment soared and banks collapsed in a nationwide panic. In the absence of a federal response, the US economy plummeted to hellish depths.[3]

Shortly after the Seventy-Third Congress convened on March 9, 1933, Democrats organized both the House and the Senate. By then, of course, John Nance Garner had exchanged his position as speaker of the House to become president of the Senate. This was mandated by Section 3 of Article 1 of the Constitution since Garner had been elected US vice president. His place in the House went to Representative Henry T. Rainey of Illinois. The Senate's very experienced minority leader, Joseph T. Robinson, won the acclaim of his Democratic peers to head their majority. Initially, Robinson received the help of Senator John B. Kendrick, an honest-to-gosh cowboy from Wyoming. Unfortunately, the seventy-six-year-old

Kendrick suffered a fatal uremic coma later that year. Out of recognition of Barkley's stature as a national party leader experienced in preparing and debating congressional legislation, Robinson used him informally in the post of assistant majority leader until Senate Democratic colleagues made it official. Even before then, Barkley had played a key role in the first one hundred days of the Roosevelt administration because of his membership on those Senate committees central to the production of most early New Deal measures.[4]

But just what was the New Deal? A reading of Roosevelt's Inaugural Address of March 4, 1933, reveals little in the way of specifics that could be easily turned into a fully developed program. He blamed "moneychangers" for the Great Depression, employed military imagery in response to the economic crisis, and resorted to a carrot-and-stick approach to assert executive leadership over Congress. And his most famous phrase, "the only thing we have to fear is fear itself," came from Louis Howe, a Roosevelt aide and speechwriter responsible for the third draft of the address. The overall impact of the speech on the American public revealed the president's resolution to take immediate, vigorous action to stem the brutal results of the economic collapse. The next day Roosevelt lived up to this image when he issued two edicts. First, he called on Congress to convene in a special session on March 9. Second, he confronted the downward spiral and rampant bankruptcies among American banks. With a wink at legitimacy, he used the 1917 Trading with the Enemy Act to halt gold transactions and start a national bank holiday that failed to be festive.[5]

During the first day of the special session, March 9, Barkley strongly endorsed the passage of the emergency banking relief bill. It legally backed the president's dubious decision to use wartime legislation to meet the banking meltdown. Somewhat over seven hours were needed to approve the measure. Signed by Roosevelt right after Congress voted, the new law permitted sound banks to end their holiday and reopen under license of the Treasury Department. It also provided managers for those financial institutions still in trouble. Finally, it handed the president discretionary power over credit, gold, silver, and foreign exchange transactions. The record-setting quick completion of such a comprehensive measure proved the New Deal to be more than vague phrases in a speech. In fact, months before Roosevelt's inauguration, the journalist James Kieran of the *New York Times* identified what became known as the president-elect's Brain Trust. It was led by Raymond Moley, a professor of law at Columbia University, and composed of, among others, the Columbia professors Rexford Guy Tugwell (economics) and Adolf A. Berle (law).[6]

Brain Trust members recommended speechwriters and programs to the president-elect. They also shared ideas for legislation with future members of the Roosevelt administration and Democratic congressional leaders such as Barkley. Thus, in the historically unprecedented production of laws in FDR's first one hundred days, the actual content of bills came from the White House or Congress or a mixture of both. For example, the emergency banking relief bill originated, via a banker and Treasury Department officials, with the administration. Congressional members quickly accepted the bill precisely because it responded effectively to the dire circumstances associated with bank failures and the run on gold. On the other hand, Congress had layer on layer of legislation in desk drawers that the Republican White House had opposed. When Roosevelt recommended to Congress the approval of the Tennessee Valley Authority (TVA), the measure had already been voted on favorably in an earlier form, not once, but twice as the Muscle Shoals Project. President Coolidge pocket vetoed the legislation, and Hoover repeated the veto in 1931 because the public project competed with private companies. Spearheaded by the insurgent Republican Senator George W. Norris (NE), the TVA would build dams, power plants, and recreation areas (and hence jobs) and supply inexpensive electricity to rural areas of the Tennessee River valley.[7]

Barkley, the Wilsonian, would question an aspect or two of a given bill, but in a short time the economic crisis coupled with party loyalty encouraged him to make the transition from New Freedom regulation to New Deal configuration. For instance, he has been credited with playing an important role in shepherding the gold standard repeal bill through the Senate. The legislation, enacted into law on June 5, 1933, canceled the gold clause in all federal and private obligations and provided that all contracts and debts be payable in legal tender. Because of the current run on gold, Barkley's winning argument in obtaining senatorial votes focused on statistics. He pointed out the number of federal bonds that would soon mature and the amount of gold needed to redeem those bonds. Clearly, without the bill, the integrity of the federal government would disintegrate when the US supply of gold disappeared in under a year.[8]

In addition to the gold issue, Barkley contributed time and effort to the other New Deal measures. One special activity was his participation in the Banking and Currency subcommittee that conducted a stock exchange investigation. Newspaper headlines focused on Ferdinand Pecora, an Italian-American jurist and New York City prosecutor who functioned as the sub-committee's counselor. He took the lead in questioning, and sometimes grilling, witnesses. Of the latter, the most famous was John Pierpont Morgan II, who had inherited from his father America's most prominent and powerful bank, J. P. Morgan and Company. When he and the company manager, Leonard Keyes, responded to Pecora's sharp inquiries during the third week in May, it emerged to everyone's astonishment that Morgan and his twenty partners had not paid a penny in income taxes for the past two years. It then prompted Pecora to consider whether lists of wealthy deposi-tors, borrowers, corporations, clients, and especially bank officers would be made public to expose tax evasion and/or unethical transactions. Barkley and Senator Carter Glass (VA) suggested that the matter should be saved for discussion in the subcommittee's executive session. It was decided in the closed meeting to make public only lists of bank officers receiving Morgan loans as well as individuals invited to subscribe to shares of stock floated by Morgan at a cost below the offering price.[9]

Barkley's participation in the work of the subcommittee was mean-ingful service. The early hearings that centered on J. P. Morgan and Company contributed support, if not substance, to important New Deal legislation. For example, the Federal Securities Act required newly issued securities (stocks) to be registered with the Federal Trade Commission (FTC). An even more obvious result of the hearings can be seen in the Glass-Steagall Banking Act. It separated deposit banking from investment and created the Federal Deposit Insurance Corporation. During the first one hundred days of the new administration, Barkley also spoke and/or voted for the other major acts: (1) Economy, which reduced federal employee salaries and veterans benefits as it reorganized agencies to save federal funds; (2) Beer-Wine Revenue, which altered the Volstead Act by legalizing and taxing the sale of beer, wine, and ale; (3) Civilian Conserva-tion Corps, which created conservation jobs for unemployed citizens; (4) Agricultural Adjustment, which stabilized farm prices by controlling sur-plus crops; (5) Emergency Farm Mortgage, which refinanced farm mort-gages; (6) Federal Emergency Relief, which helped states provide relief to the poor and later created the Works Progress Administration; (7) Home-owners' Loan, which established a corporation that refinanced mortgages; and (8) National Industrial Recovery, which exempted fair trade codes of industries from antitrust laws, guaranteed union rights, and created the

Public Works Administration to promote construction projects to stimulate the economy.[10]

When Congress adjourned on June 16, 1933, Alben and Dorothy had the luxury of staying in Washington and enjoying summertime peace and relaxation. Barkley certainly kept doing from a distance all the right things for constituents; he was especially concerned about patronage. It would be, however, five years before he faced reelection in Kentucky and three years before the next national electoral campaign. To be sure, family members would come for a visit, but now David Barkley, a US Army Air Corps reservist, worked for the Aeronautical Branch of the US Department of Commerce. He and his bride, Dorothy Graves, had two children: Dorothy N. and Alben W. II. As noted earlier, Marian Barkley Truitt, her lawyer husband, and their growing family would soon move to the District of Columbia. During the interim and before her 1934 wedding, Laura Louise remained at home with her parents at their spacious Cleveland Avenue residence. She was caught sunbathing by a *Washington Post* photographer at the Annapolis Roads Beach and Tennis Club in July. The next month she joined her parents for a short stay in Atlantic City.[11]

Shortly ahead of the family trip to Atlantic City, Barkley spent time before a radio microphone. He discussed the assistance and advantages that the National Industrial Recovery Act offered to the American people. The Sunday evening broadcast on August 6 went nationwide with a hookup of radio stations linked to the National Broadcasting Company. It was the first of many times that Barkley would be heard over the air when he defended legislation and policies designed to ease and overcome the multiple economic sufferings associated with the Great Depression. Donald A. Ritchie, a former historian with the US Senate Historical Office, described Barkley as Majority Leader Robinson's "chief oratorical" lieutenant who "performed yeoman labor as a spokesman for the New Deal's legislative program during Roosevelt's first term." Because of his frequent presence on radio, Americans nationwide recognized Barkley with his resonating, authoritative voice as one of the New Deal's prime advocates. In this endeavor, he was exceeded only by the president, who also employed the radio waves to great effect in his famous Fireside Chats.[12]

Early in September, Alben and Dorothy attended what turned out to be a major social event in the nation's capital. They joined Eleanor Roosevelt, the president's wife, and Democratic leaders in witnessing and celebrating the wedding of a daughter who belonged to the secretary of the Democratic National Committee. A week later the pair sailed for Europe and then took a short Mediterranean cruise before ending their water adventures in coastal Spain. (Their daughter Laura Louise remained in the United States and attended the National Law School.) On October 4 in Madrid, Barkley attended the opening of the twenty-ninth conference of the Inter-Parliamentary Union. The meeting inadvertently revealed a glimmer of the dark forces that would cause international strife before decade's end. Conversations among representatives of thirty-two countries centered on the fate of Paul Loebe. A German Social Democrat who had presided over a previous union conference, Loebe was currently imprisoned in a concentration camp. He was a victim of Adolf Hitler's victory in establishing Nazi despotism. In fact, Germany and Italy prevented their delegates from attending the Madrid gathering of would-be peacemakers. A few years later, these two countries assisted militarily General Francisco Franco, who, through bloody civil war (1936–1939), converted the Republic of Spain into yet another fascist dictatorship.[13]

The Pecora Committee, with Barkley or his alternate as a member, continued to hold hearings into the regular session of the Seventy-Third Congress, which opened on January 3, 1934. Its revelations of irresponsible speculation on Wall Street kept Barkley and the full Banking and Currency Committee busy preparing legislation such as the securities exchange bill signed into law by the president on June 6, 1934. The act created the Securities and Exchange Commission, an agency to administer the law as well as the Securities Act of 1933. Hereafter, the 1934 measure required registration and disclosure information for all securities; it also regulated purchase margins for stocks. The purpose for all of this was to eliminate insider manipulation and reduce credit borrowing on traded securities. From his participation on the Senate's Banking and Currency Committee, Barkley also directed his legislative energies and oratorical skills toward passing the Gold Reserve Act (January 30, 1934) and the Silver Purchase Act (June 24, 1934). The former impounded gold with the Treasury Department to prevent a run on the precious metal; both laws abandoned rigidity in favor of a managed currency. Roosevelt reduced by 40 percent the value of the dollar by setting the price of gold at $35 an ounce. A specified amount of silver was purchased using silver certificates, thus adding currency to the economy.[14]

Gold and silver legislation promised a degree of controlled inflation to generate economic activity at home and abroad. In terms of trade, slightly cheaper American goods potentially made sales in foreign markets more attractive. The most effective measure to open up international commerce for the United States was the Reciprocal Trade Agreements Act of June 12, 1934, which tripled, for example, US trade with Latin America by decade's end. This legislation repaid Barkley for all his hard, but unsuccessful, work to modify or defeat the 1930 bill. The senator enthusiastically endorsed the 1934 measure, but credit for its development and implementation must go to Secretary of State Cordell Hull, who remained in office until 1944. The act served as a revolutionary amendment to the Hawley-Smoot Tariff. For one thing, it terminated congressional logrolling over individual tariff rates. Moreover, it modified the 1930 tariff in two ways. First, it repealed US penalty rates assessed against countries for automobiles, trucks, motorcycles, wood, and wood products, including paper and books. Second, it empowered the president to reduce US tariff rates by up to 50 percent through reciprocal trade agreements with individual countries. The US State Department soon negotiated lower tariffs with Belgium, Haiti, Sweden, and Soviet Russia, which the United States recognized diplomatically in 1933. Because the Soviet government monopolized foreign trade and had no tariff, a special agreement granted the Soviet Union most-favored-nation tariff treatment in return for specified dollar amounts of Soviet purchases in the United States.[15]

From Barkley's vantage point, the Reciprocal Trade Agreements Act offered the possibility of more US sales abroad, which he had considered in 1930 a potential game changer in terms of improving America's depressed economy. To be sure, the Iron Man favored the current legislation, but it had a significant shortcoming. A lower tariff occurred only one country at a time after the US State Department successfully negotiated and the president approved a reciprocal trade agreement for reduced rates. Barkley knew that the process could (and did) take time and had mixed results at best because of the global economic downturn. All this helps explain why publicly Barkley stated that he felt the National Housing Act to be the most important bill to be developed by Congress during the final Seventy-Third session. Roosevelt signed the bill into law near the end of that session on June 27, 1934. During hearings on the measure in late May before the Banking and Currency Committee, Barkley told Federal Emergency Relief Administrator Harry L. Hopkins that the housing bill possessed "a greater possibility of more good, more employment, and more industrial activity than any thing else we have undertaken so far."[16]

Indeed, people in and out of government shared Barkley's enthusiasm

for the bill's promised help to many American homeowners and unemployed bricklayers, carpenters, electricians, plumbers, and roofers. The act
created the Federal Housing Administration (FHA), an agency empowered
to insure loans made by banks, trust companies, building and loan associations, and private lending institutions. Loans could be used to construct
new homes (the average price at that time was under $3,500) as well as
repair, alter, or improve existing ones. A very important aspect to FHA
authority was, not its $200 million budget, but its ability to raise $2 billion
in bonds. The latter represented more than half the entire federal budget
for 1922–1923. Alone, the FHA's working funds could guarantee enough
loans to build over fifty-seven thousand houses or repair and improve hundreds of thousands of single-family dwellings. Add $2 billion in bonds, and
every homeowner in America who qualified for a loan could have a new or
improved house. Barkley, of course, fully appreciated the fact that many
of his rural Kentucky constituents who consistently voted him into office
could benefit from and would be grateful for his role in getting this bill
through Congress.[17]

In these first two congressional sessions that inaugurated the New Deal
era, Barkley's prominent role in the Senate also brought him into a lengthy
working relationship with Majority Secretary Leslie L. Biffle and Secretary
of the Senate Edwin A. Halsey. Years later, when he was interviewed exten-
sively by Sidney Shalett, Barkley seemed to call every person he knew, Democrat or Republican, "my good friend." But his daughter Marian Barkley
Truitt later admitted that in reality her father had just one close, lifelong
friend and that was Biffle. He came to Washington in 1909 from Arkansas
as secretary to Representative Robert Macon. When Macon retired from
Congress four years later, he made sure his competent and faithful secretary
had a patronage job in the Senate folding room. In 1925, the fellow Arkansas native and minority leader Robinson appointed the diminutive, but gregarious Biffle to the unofficial job of assistant to Minority Secretary Halsey.
In 1933, when Robinson became the Senate's majority leader, Halsey took
the Senate secretary post, and Biffle replaced Halsey.[18]

In the Senate's chamber, Biffle had a desk by the door and waited in
constant readiness to assist Majority Leader Robinson. He ran errands, sent
messages, gathered gossip, and counted noses to see who would vote in favor
of a given piece of legislation. His colleague for eight years, Halsey, had
an office just off the Senate floor; it contained a telephone with a direct
line to the White House. When the Senate did not meet as a commit-

tee of the whole, the office became a hangout for Biffle, Robinson, Barkley, and other Democratic cronies. From time to time, wealthy contributors would stop by and leave some cash, which Halsey used to keep the office well stocked with food, spirits, and cigars. The Colonel, an honorary title bestowed twice on Halsey by Virginia governors, also distributed cash for reelection campaigns. Indeed, he was secretary-treasurer of the Democratic Senatorial Campaign Committee. That role prompted him to keep biographies of Democratic senators as well as files on state politics, funding sources, and campaign speakers. Three years later, Barkley would inherit the expert services and assistance of his close friend Biffle and, most assuredly, his "good friend" Colonel Halsey when the Kentuckian became Senate majority leader.[19]

From July 1934 to the start of the Seventy-Fourth Congress in January 1935, Barkley kept busy delivering speeches and participating in national radio programs in support of Roosevelt and the New Deal. Two special activities also attracted his attention. The baby of the family, Laura Louise, who had driven her father during his reelection campaign, got married on August 21, 1934. Officiated by the Reverend Francis Yarnell, the wedding, along with the postceremony reception, took place in the ample Barkley home on Cleveland Avenue. Laura Louise was the attractive bride of Douglas MacArthur II, a graduate of Milton Academy and Yale. He had successfully passed the foreign service exam and would soon begin his career in the nation's professional diplomatic corps. Their shared lives produced a daughter, Mimi, who became one of Barkley's seven grandchildren. While wedding arrangements occupied the household, Barkley was also absorbed in Kentucky politics. With the encouragement of President Roosevelt, he adopted a strong stand in favor of using primaries to involve citizens in the democratic process rather than party conventions to select individuals for statewide offices. The Kentucky legislature approved the measure in 1935.[20]

As early as May 1934, President Roosevelt outlined his agenda for the opening of the new Congress, now prescribed by the Constitution to start on the third of January. Among other proposals, he suggested that the legislative body should consider old-age pensions and a new labor board. The extraordinary nature of these and the rest of the social and economic reforms approved by the Seventy-Fourth Congress prompted later commentators to label 1935 as the beginning of the Second New Deal. It was also the start of Barkley's official role as the assistant majority leader. In addition, except for the Wagner Act (July 5, 1935), Barkley had a center seat on those committees creating significant legislation. The latter included the Social Security Act (August 14, 1935), which formed a national system of social insurance, including old-age pensions, and the Revenue Act (August 30, 1935), which increased income and estate taxes on wealthier individuals and corporations. And he played an important part in devising a compromise enabling the Public Utility Holding Act (August 26, 1935) to be passed. The act authorized the Federal Power Commission and FTC to regulate interstate transmission of electric power and natural gas; it also limited holding companies to one company and one subsidiary.[21]

In committees, and on the Senate floor, Barkley developed and helped pass the core of legislation defining the Second New Deal. His prominence in Congress matched his distinction outside the Capitol Building where his speeches and radio broadcasts upheld the president and his program. Small wonder that near the end of the first session Roosevelt invited Barkley to spend a weekend, August 10–11, with him, including a cruise on the Potomac River on the presidential yacht *Sequoia*. The two men discussed at length the revenue bill then before the Finance Committee, on which Barkley served. FDR asked Barkley to use his influence with Democratic colleagues to secure a Senate bill in line with the more modest tax increase initiated by the House. On Monday, August 12, Barkley and the Finance Committee accomplished the president's goal. This meant that, after the Senate approved the bill and it went to a conference committee, the two chambers could quickly reach an acceptable compromise, allowing the bill to pass the House and the Senate before Congress adjourned at the end of August.[22]

Roosevelt clearly had confidence in Barkley and was pleased by the Kentuckian's steadfast efforts on his behalf. Thus, without specific evidence, one can speculate that their weekend together may have allowed some conversation about the president's plans for his 1936 reelection campaign and Barkley's role in that endeavor. Regardless, two issues emerged during this session of Congress that foreshadowed later events affecting Barkley. In a famous decision on May 27, 1935, all nine justices of the US Supreme Court declared the National Industrial Recovery Act to be unconstitutional. Subsequently, Barkley debated against the court's decision at the University of Virginia's Institute of Public Affairs. He criticized the justices for holding "a certain type of mind which revolts against anything new or strange or that cannot trace its antecedents to some outworn condition or revered incident or period in past history." Because it also killed the Farm Mortgage

Relief Act, a measure dear to the hearts of Barkley's most loyal constituents, it seemed that the Court journeyed down the path leading to the destruction of the New Deal and, hence, the administration's effort to revive and restore the nation's economy. The available options to overcome the Court's obstructionism seemed to be centered on two distasteful alternatives— water down either congressional bills or the Supreme Court.[23]

Deteriorating foreign affairs served as a second issue that would deeply affect Barkley. Premonition of a troubled future appeared after passage of the Neutrality Act, which was signed by the president on August 31, 1935. The act was rushed through Congress at the last minute because of the conflict brewing between Italy and Ethiopia. The resolution reflected isolationist views held by the many Americans who felt that US arms sales to Allied Powers had drawn the country into the Great War, which cost lives and treasure without making the world "safe for democracy." Weeks later, when Italy attacked Ethiopia, Roosevelt invoked the act, which prohibited the export of US arms, ammunition, and war implements to belligerent countries. The next year the Spanish Civil War led FDR to call for a moral arms embargo against Spain since the internal conflict lacked the required two or more countries fighting each other. Congress soon tightened the Neutrality Act by forbidding the sale of US military hardware to any country experiencing civil strife. Despite good intentions, neutrality legislation facilitated victories by fascist dictators: Benito Mussolini in conquering Ethiopia and Francisco Franco in defeating the Republic of Spain. US inaction in both cases conveniently rationalized the quiescent behavior of Western Europe's great democracies, France and England. It was a fatal indulgence that encouraged militaristic dictatorships to advance their power through armed force.[24]

The second session of the Seventy-Fourth Congress also passed a second Neutrality Act at the end of February 1936. It added loans and credits to the list of items forbidden to belligerents in the 1935 measure. Of course, the winter-spring session produced other legislation, but Barkley and his congressional colleagues failed to stir additional letters into the New Deal's alphabet soup of bills. The Supreme Court helps explain this anomaly. On January 6, three days after Congress opened, the court destroyed the basis of the crop-control program and processing tax of the Agricultural Adjustment Act (AAA). Six of nine justices claimed that farm production was purely intrastate and not interstate commerce. Hence, it could not be subject to federal regulation under the commerce clause of Section 8 of the

US Constitution. This new blow to the New Deal forced Congress and the White House to scurry around and quickly devise an alternative bill before the start of the growing season. Signed into law six weeks later, the Soil Conservation and Domestic Allocation Act omitted the acreage quotas and processing taxes that had raised votes against AAA from the justices. Instead, the new act provided benefit payments for soil conservation that took land out of production and achieved the goal of crop reduction. The latter raised prices and gave farmers a fighting chance to enjoy profitability.[25]

The other element causing a stall in New Deal legislation simply followed from the fact that 1936 was an election year. Naturally, besides the president, all representatives and one-third of the senators faced reelection campaigns. No wonder Barkley, who wanted Democrats reelected, eagerly sought to pay off the adjusted service certificates held by veterans of the Great War. Obviously, bonus recipients and their families would likely express their gratitude by voting for congressional members who had supported the bill. On the Senate Finance Committee, Barkley joined James F. "Jimmy" Byrnes (SC), Joel Bennett "Champ" Clark (MO), Byron P. "Pat" Harrison (MS), and the Republican Frederick M. Steiwer (OR) in preparing the Senate version of the bill. This was the first time that Barkley advocated a measure that President Roosevelt opposed. The bonus bill would cost around $2 billion and open FDR to Republican criticism for expanding the federal deficit. Congress overwhelmingly passed the bill into law two days after the president's veto on January 25. Fortunately for the administration, it could justifiably delay bonus payments until after June 15, in what was then the new fiscal year. The bonus, coupled with the Supreme Court's termination of the AAA processing tax, required another revenue act, which Barkley helped form and defend. Approved on the last day of the congressional session, June 20, 1936, it increased corporate income taxes as it taxed undistributed corporation profits.[26]

Because so many Democratic members of Congress eagerly joined Barkley in passing the bonus bill, the Iron Man suffered no ill will from the president. Moreover, FDR possessed enough political savvy to appreciate the potential benefit for reelection campaigns of distributing cash to veterans, many of whom were impoverished. More than that, Barkley continued in the winter-spring congressional session to attract the president's favorable attention by his steady campaign praising the New Deal via radio and speeches. Additionally, Barkley consistently but softly criticized the Supreme Court justices who had struck down several key pieces of New

Deal legislation. He told, for example, members of the Democratic Woman's Club of Kentucky: "You can't put a robe on a man and make him forget all his preconceived ideas." His talks in the Midwest supporting the administration were so effective that they caught the notice of White House aides and prompted Roosevelt to send him a note that congratulated him for his "grand and effective work" and concluded: "More power to your arm!" The interesting reference to Barkley's "arm" could suggest that he was FDR's paladin. More likely it reflected Barkley's frequent and literally striking gesture of emphasis as a speaker when his elevated right fist would come crashing down to pound on a lectern or slam his outstretched left hand.[27]

His fame as a New Deal speaker, leadership position in the Senate, and working relationship with Roosevelt guaranteed Barkley a major role in the upcoming Democratic national convention. The convention would open in Philadelphia shortly after the Seventy-Fourth Congress adjourned. The president exercised considerable control over his own reelection campaign mainly because the man who officially and unofficially acted as his chief of staff since 1912, Louis McHenry Howe, had suffered serious pulmonary ailments since March 1935 and died on April 18, 1936. Thus, with FDR's encouragement, the Arrangements Committee picked Barkley to be the temporary chairman and keynote speaker. He would be the first person to deliver the opening address at two consecutive Democratic national conventions. Postmaster General James A. Farley, who held the party chairmanship, announced the decision in Philadelphia on April 25. At the same time, Majority Leader Robinson was selected to be the permanent chairman. Roosevelt would be extremely comfortable about leaving the opening address and convention proceedings in the hands of these two experienced men.[28]

While Barkley consulted with the White House on basic content, he gave a preview draft of his address to some seventy members of the National Democratic Council, headquartered in the District of Columbia and chaired by Robert W. Woolley. The group was composed mainly of senators, cabinet officers, "G" men, and other federal employees. That presentation had to be revised because, a fortnight before the Democrats met at Philadelphia's Municipal Auditorium, the Republican national convention had opened in Cleveland. Barkley's colleague on the Finance Committee, Senator Steiwer, delivered the keynote speech on June 9. So, in the two weeks before the Kentucky senator presented his address, he made several changes in his draft text to respond to Steiwer's attack on Roosevelt and the New Deal.

"Our purpose here," Steiwer opined near the start of his speech, "is not only to adopt a platform and to nominate a Republican President—a deeper and thoroughly American purpose is to start the drive and put an American deal in the place now usurped by a self-styled 'New Deal.'"[29]

Thus, in a number of instances, Barkley responded directly to Steiwer's address. While Steiwer "classed as destructive" the New Deal, Barkley proclaimed its benefits. While Steiwer labeled the New Deal as the "poison of politics in the bread of relief," Barkley noted that relief provided jobs to seven million otherwise unemployed workers. Relief of misery was in the Kentuckian's view good, not poison, politics. While Steiwer criticized the new tariff, Barkley dismissed the criticism with data. American foreign trade had jumped from $2.9 billion to $4.3 billion between 1932 and 1936, and that meant more sales and jobs for US industry and markets for farmers. While Steiwer called New Deal debt a "menace to survival," Barkley reminded delegates and his radio audience across the nation that the Hoover administration had increased the federal debt by $4 billion without providing serious relief to the unemployed. And, while Steiwer used hyperbole to link FDR with the decidedly illiberal Soviet Union, Barkley responded in like manner:

Yes we have destroyed a certain kind of liberty in this country. . . . We have destroyed the liberty of a small group to pick the pockets of the American people, of organized greed to pervert the agencies of government. We have destroyed the liberty of the great financial wizards who have engulfed the nation in a wave of frenzied speculation, and we have destroyed the liberty of any powerful or selfish group [e.g., the late Huey P. Long and his Share Our Wealth Clubs] anywhere in the nation to claim that the capital of the United States is located anywhere on this continent except in the city of Washington.[30]

In one of those fascinating moments in the gray area between plan and coincidence, Barkley spoke of those who most stridently backed the GOP. Specifically, he listed "every stock jobber, every monopolist of privilege and power, every propagandist [e.g., the publisher William Randolph Hearst] for the defunct and unconscionable alliance between politics and crooked business." Four days later in Franklin Field, Philadelphia's open-air stadium, Roosevelt's speech accepting the Democratic Party's presidential nomination called for a war on the economic royalists who controlled property, money, labor, and even the lives of people. Described by Senator Harry S. Truman (MO) as a masterpiece, the speech often receives high ratings if only because of its memorable phrases, including: "To some generations much is given. Of other generations much is expected. This generation of Americans has a rendezvous with destiny." Barkley had used "an appointment with destiny" in his 1932 keynote address, but who borrowed from whom in the 1936 keynote and acceptance speeches? The only available answer is that New Dealers in the White House and Congress had reached similar conclusions—entrenched privilege must be diminished to preserve democracy and prevent destitution. This was the destiny sought by those who promoted the New Deal.[31]

Understandably, then, Roosevelt congratulated Barkley in person and by letter for a keynote address that anticipated so well the president's acceptance speech. One of FDR's secretaries, Grace Tully, sent the senator a telegram rating the speech an absolute knockout. In 1941, Tully replaced the ailing Marguerite "Missy" LeHand as the president's personal secretary. Thus, in the future, Tully and Barkley would have frequent communications. Meanwhile, during the convention, Roosevelt's nomination was never in doubt. In the fall campaign, the president faced a Republican ticket headed by Governor Alfred M. Landon (KS) and his vice presidential candidate, the newspaper publisher William Franklin "Frank" Knox. (Roosevelt later appointed Knox to serve as the US secretary of the navy.) Both Republican candidates had been Bull Moose Progressives who actually endorsed portions of the New Deal. It did not help. In addition to the support of regular Democrats, North and especially South, Roosevelt attracted a huge assortment of new, traditionally GOP voters. These ranged from African Americans to farmers and the urban middle class, all of whom benefited from New Deal programs that improved their lives and, literally, their livelihoods.[32]

After the convention, Barkley and Dorothy traveled to Europe, where the Iron Man attended sessions of the Inter-Parliamentary Union in Budapest, Hungary. Back in the United States, the senator campaigned for Roosevelt and congressional candidates in eighteen states from New Hampshire to Colorado. Election results pleased him beyond measure. The Roosevelt-Garner ticket on November 3, 1936, carried every state except Maine and Vermont and, hence, carried the Electoral College by a tally of 523–8. It was the closest thing to a unanimous vote for a presidential candidate since the victory of James Monroe in 1820. Some commentators actually thought that the GOP was dead and might disappear just like the old Federalist Party in the nineteenth century. The Democratic Party overwhelmingly controlled Congress, with 328 votes to 107 in the House and 77 votes to 19 in the Senate. A number of freshmen Democratic senators would have to sit with Republicans across the aisle in the Senate chamber. On the surface, it appeared that, whatever the president and his party in Congress wanted, it would be quickly and easily fulfilled. And that was the good news. The bad news was the fact that, whatever mandate the American people handed to Roosevelt, his administration still stumbled badly in 1937. It was not a unique situation. The same thing had plagued or would plague other presidents who enjoyed major electoral victories: Thomas Jefferson, Andrew Jackson, Lyndon Johnson, and Richard Nixon. For Barkley, the presidential problems of 1937 became his tribulations, especially after he secured the majority leader post. More than that, he may have inadvertently (or purposively) floated as a trial balloon what became the major problem that Roosevelt faced at the start of his second term. Months earlier, in his keynote speech, Barkley had asked and then responded: "Is the Supreme Court beyond criticism? May it be regarded as too sacred to be disagreed with? Thomas Jefferson didn't think so. Andrew Jackson did not think so. Abraham Lincoln did not think so. Theodore Roosevelt did not think so." And the same could be said for Franklin D. Roosevelt.[33]

12

The Majority Leader
in Time of Peace

The Twentieth Amendment to the Constitution had already caused Congress to shift the start of its sessions from March 4 to January 3. It kicked in for the first time in 1937 for the presidential inauguration, now held on January 20. Alben W. Barkley and others teased Senator George W. Norris, who fathered the amendment. Norris repeatedly reminded those who were ribbing him that he was not responsible for January's ugly weather. President Franklin D. Roosevelt did put up a good front, riding to the Capitol Building for the event in a limousine with open windows and returning to the White House in an open car. His inauguration, however, happened on a day that was cold with a blustery wind and a soaking rain. While the national radio broadcast gave the president the largest audience ever for such an occasion, he had a smaller than expected crowd in attendance at the formal ceremony. Despite the terrible weather, those present responded warmly to FDR's speech, though it was one of his weaker efforts. Clearly, the president assumed that government could solve the nation's ills, but he failed to outline specific plans to address those problems. Most troubling, he neglected to mention, let alone describe, how he would deal with the Supreme Court, which seemed to wield a sharp scalpel as it disemboweled the New Deal.[1]

A little over two weeks later, the president sent Congress a message and a sample bill. Both were extraordinary. Supported by a letter from Attorney General Homer S. Cummings, Roosevelt wanted up to fifty new federal judges, including six more Supreme Court justices, to join those sitting judges who had reached the age of seventy or had served ten or more years on the bench. The rationale centered on the idea that older judges could not keep up with their heavy case loads and also suffered "infirmities"—meaning (wink, wink) senility. The national response was swift and strongly opposed as radio commentators and newspaper editors vied with each other in calling the proposal such negative names as the president's "court-packing plan." Republicans in Congress did not have to say much in opposition because Democrats were badly divided over the initiative. For many, the political ploy elicited a foul odor. Frankly, Roosevelt had blundered. His mandate from the American people coupled with the dominance of his political party in the national legislature blinded whatever political savvy he possessed. To prevent leaks to the press, he chose to work in secret with Cummings. Even Barkley admitted later that, if the president as quarterback "had given us the signals in advance of the play, not after he tossed us the ball, . . . we might have covered more ground." In short, had FDR chanced consultation with congressional Democrats and accepted their input, the end result might have been a considerably different bill, one that actually had an opportunity to clear Congress.[2]

The president took heart from the fact that Majority Leader Robinson and Assistant Majority Leader Barkley sided with the White House on this issue, though for different reasons. Despite reservations about portions of the New Deal program, Robinson made no secret of the fact that he wanted to cap his career in public service as a justice on the Supreme Court. And Roosevelt, along with members of his administration such as Postmaster General Farley, had given Robinson ample reason to believe that he would fill the next available vacancy. Barkley, on the other hand, simply accepted FDR's proposal and for two good reasons. First, and most importantly, the Supreme Court had nullified eleven of sixteen New Deal laws. Clearly, it felt that government might modestly regulate but not aggressively engineer the nation's economy. Barkley was especially upset by the Court's attack on agricultural programs designed to raise farm prices or preserve farm mortgages. He helplessly watched it strike down legislation that aided those rural Kentuckians who steadfastly voted him into national office. Second, unlike many Americans who felt that the Constitution made the Supreme Court sacrosanct, Barkley knew better. Yes, Article 3 of that document mentioned a "supreme" court once, but its organization and membership along with the structure of the entire federal court system dropped into the hands of Congress. In fact, over the years, Congress had changed the number of justices on the Supreme Court seven times.[3]

Barkley expressed explicitly his views of the Supreme Court and indirectly his sympathetic interest in FDR's proposal in a speech that he delivered before members of the Federal Bar Association in Washington, DC, on February 22. His address focused on the legacy of Chief Justice John Marshall. During his tenure (1801–1835) on the Supreme Court, Marshall issued decisions on cases that were extremely important for the future of the United States. For instance, he strengthened the power of the federal government over the states in *McCulloch v. Maryland* (1819) and established national supremacy in regulating interstate commerce in *Gibbons v. Ogden* (1824). Barkley speculated that, if Marshall were alive in 1937, he would agree that the federal government had the power and the right to exercise that power in confronting and resolving the country's economic and social problems. "I believe," he concluded near the end of his talk, "that the Constitution of the United States is a living, moving, vital instrument of government not to be preserved in a museum but to be preserved by a fair and liberal interpretation of its powers as well as a progressive and sane interpretation of its implied powers."[4]

Nevertheless, the huge uproar over and strident divisions caused by the court bill were so obvious across the nation that FDR chose to devote one of his famous Fireside Chats to the subject on March 9. It would be his last public (but not private) attack on the Supreme Court. Rosenman wrote the narrative for the radio address from ideas dictated by the president. The speechwriter did a good job; this particular chat has earned higher than average marks. Roosevelt, of course, repeated earlier ideas, but he also made the argument that, by striking down New Deal laws, the Supreme Court established its own policy agenda. In this process, it had usurped the legislative responsibility assigned by the Constitution to Congress. From this vantage point, the president could claim that his bill would actually restore rather than alter the Constitution. Barkley's published assessment of the March 9 Fireside Chat strongly endorsed FDR's position: "The President's address placed the issue squarely before the American people in a frank and intimate way and there can be no misunderstanding with reference to the propriety and wisdom of the action he suggests. His address clarified the proposal and demonstrated beyond question the sincerity as well as the advisability of this step."[5]

No matter how loyal Robinson and Barkley were to the president in terms of court reform, there had to be majority support in Congress for the bill to pass. Instead, the national legislature appeared to be partially paralyzed by the controversy. Moreover, because Representative Hatton W.

Sumners (TX), who chaired the House Judiciary Committee, opposed Roosevelt's court reform, the administration placed all its hope in the Senate's approval of the bill, which might prompt enough House support to pull the measure through Congress. The strategy failed. Barkley's friend Majority Secretary Leslie Biffle repeatedly counted Senate noses and never found more than forty votes in favor of the bill. Meanwhile, in April and May, the Supreme Court upheld two key pieces of New Deal legislation, the Wagner Labor Relations Act and the Social Security Act. Additionally, a swing voter, Justice Owen J. Roberts, shifted to the New Deal, and a conservative, Justice Willis Van Devanter, announced his retirement on May 18, 1937. His FDR replacement would lead to a 6–3 New Deal majority, which completely undermined the real reason for Roosevelt's court reform.[6]

Eventually, Roosevelt could legitimately claim that, while his proposal failed, it actually accomplished his strategy of securing a Supreme Court favorably disposed to the New Deal. And it all had to do with politics. As it turned out, Van Devanter was in touch with the Senate Judiciary Committee and timed his retirement announcement to coincide (on May 18) with the committee's recommendation for the Senate to reject court reform. In short, the justices were also politicians who took steps to sabotage the president's proposal. Since the Senate Judiciary Committee opposed the measure, Robinson could only go to Roosevelt and inform him that the bill had no chance of gaining Senate approval. FDR initially disagreed but in June abruptly changed his mind in favor of a revised measure. His pride had been hurt, and he hoped that some type of bill could be approved to save face. Thus, Barkley encouraged his Kentucky colleague Senator Marvel M. Logan, a member of the Senate Judiciary Committee, to collaborate with Senator Carl A. Hatch (NM) in modifying the court reform legislation.[7]

Barkley's importance climbed dramatically in the eyes of the president and New Deal adherents during the lengthy controversy over the Supreme Court. Roosevelt intended to keep his pledge to appoint Robinson as a justice, but the majority leader behaved in a way that seriously tested the promise. Robinson increasingly expressed conservative views that questioned New Deal programs. In June, for example, he joined such southern Democratic senators as Byron Patton "Pat" Harrison (MS) and James F. "Jimmy" Byrnes (SC) in opposing New Deal expenditures. Robinson refused to support the president by leading the Senate to defeat an amendment that would cut federal monies for relief by requiring local communities to pay a percentage of the costs needed to operate the Works Progress Administration (WPA). The

WPA, directed by Harry L. Hopkins, had become the primary New Deal vehicle providing employment for jobless workers. It was left entirely, then, in the hands of Barkley to beat back the amendment. Small wonder that some commentators began calling the Kentuckian not the assistant but the actual majority leader over the Senate.[8]

This is why the Logan-Hatch bill contained an interesting safety net. It allowed a conservative Robinson to be appointed by the president as a justice without jeopardizing a New Deal majority on the Supreme Court. The revised bill increased the total number of justices to eleven, which matched the number of federal district courts. But, just as Logan-Hatch actually reduced the number of justices called for in the president's proposal, it also advanced retirement ages from seventy to seventy-five. One and only one additional appointment in any given year could be made for a judge who chose not to retire at age seventy-five. Recognizing that his own nomination to join the Court probably would not occur without passage of the Logan-Hatch bill, Robinson went all out to capture its approval. Biffle's final vote tally showed forty in favor and forty opposed with sixteen senators still wavering over the legislation. By pleading with some, collecting political IOUs from others, and making a strong defense of the bill on the Senate floor, Robinson believed that he could win the bill's passage.[9]

Robinson took center stage and railed against opponents during court reform debates in the early portions of July. He became so agitated that his reddened face and trembling body prompted Senator Royal S. Copeland (NY), a physician, to express his concern to the Arkansan. Indeed, the majority leader began experiencing irregular heartbeats. By July 12 and 13, he came to the Capitol Building but had to abandon the Senate floor both days for rest. He left Barkley in charge but ignored his assistant's pleas for him to see a doctor about his heart condition. On the morning of July 14, Robinson's housekeeper found his pajama-clad body face down on the apartment floor. Nearby was an open volume of the *Congressional Record* that he had been reading in preparation for the day's debate before he suffered a fatal heart attack. News of the majority leader's death was met with much grief, but it also threw court reform debate into chaos. Instantly, senators who had pledged their votes for the bill to Robinson out of friendship or obligation understood that their promises vanished with the majority leader's demise.[10]

Worse, Barkley was shocked to discover that, even before Robinson's death could be announced officially on the Senate floor, one member of the chamber advised colleagues not to kill themselves like Robinson had in trying to pass the court bill. Another senator implied that Robinson's death was God's punishment for tampering with the Supreme Court. The assistant majority leader shared these unfortunate pieces of information with Roosevelt. The next day the president sent Barkley a letter, copies of which ended up in newspapers. The message opened: "I am glad you called my attention to certain events of yesterday. . . . I had hoped, with you, that at least until his funeral services had been held a decent respect for his memory would have deferred discussion of political and legislative matters." Since a few senators demonstrated their bad taste in using Robinson's death simply as a continuation of the court reform debate, Roosevelt felt justified in restating the objectives of reform and expressing his support for the revised bill advocated by the late majority leader. The content of Roosevelt's thoughtful letter did not cause a problem; it was the greeting, "My Dear Alben," that caused controversy.[11]

The salutation coupled with a reference to Barkley as the acting majority leader suggested to many senators that the president tried to appoint Barkley to a post that could be decided only by a caucus vote of the Senate's majority party. Before any court reform controversy had taken place, there would have been little doubt about Barkley's successful candidacy for the office. In essence, he had already been tapped by Democratic senators as the assistant leader who logically would fill a Robinson vacancy. The great Democratic coalition in Congress, however, no longer existed. It had fractured during the court reform squabbles into several groupings, especially along geographic or cultural lines—urban versus rural states and North versus South. Contemporaries gently labeled the southern grouping as composed of *moderate* Democrats who often had reservations about the sweep and expense of New Deal legislation. One issue for southern white Democrats was the fact that national legislation tended to be color-blind and favored the city over the countryside. Such Democrats also feared that decisions of a liberal Supreme Court might bring into question some aspect of the South's system of racial segregation.[12]

Thus, Roosevelt's letter angered court reform opponents because Barkley had consistently upheld the president's proposal and the Logan-Hatch revision. The furor raised by the letter was strident enough to prompt FDR to smooth his relations with the Senate by meeting with Harrison. Harrison had taken a passive role in the court reform debate while expressing his general support for the president. Court reform opponents, however, hoped or even expected that Harrison would be selected as majority leader and would delay a vote on the measure or send it procedurally back to the unfriendly Judiciary Committee. In the short term, a number of senators on both sides convinced themselves that Roosevelt intended to try to persuade Harrison to withdraw as a candidate; in reality, the president gave the Mississippian his assurance that neither he nor his administration would take any part in a decision that belonged exclusively to the Senate's Democratic caucus. What that meant was that the congressional memorial service for Robinson on Friday, July 16, as well as the train rides that carried some fifty senators to and from Little Rock, Arkansas, where the majority leader was buried on Sunday, served as background noise. The real focus of the senators was on politicking for votes to gain a victory for one or the other of the two candidates.[13]

The politicking that occurred among the senators was matched by the White House. President Roosevelt lied to Harrison. He asked several members of his administration to encourage Barkley's election among favored senators quietly. Most importantly, he knew that Senator William H. Dieterick (IL) intended to vote for Harrison. FDR asked WPA administrator Harry Hopkins to work on Chicago mayor Edward J. "Ed" Kelly. A political boss largely responsible for Dieterick winning a seat in the Senate, Kelly agreed to talk with his protégé. The mayor wanted the WPA to continue running smoothly in Chicago, thus creating jobs for the jobless and votes for Democrats. Dieterick switched to Barkley. Once the senators returned to Washington from Little Rock, the chamber's entire Democratic body met in the white marble caucus room of the Russell Senate Office Building on Wednesday, July 21. The morning session to pick a new majority leader was extremely tense. With only one vote left to be counted from the hat of Senator Carter Glass the tally stood at thirty-seven to thirty-seven. The last ballot—and Barkley quipped "it looked as big as a bed quilt"—made him the Senate's majority leader.[14]

It would be hard to refute that Roosevelt did, indeed, secure the election of the fifty-nine-year-old Barkley. Additionally, he gained the type of Senate leadership that clearly held the most sympathy for the New Deal. But did he win or lose his battle with the Supreme Court? The answer is mixed. As suggested earlier, the shifting Court and retiring justices allowed some reshaping. In the short term, however, FDR lost and lost badly. Right after the majority leader vote, Democratic senators took steps or made comments to the press suggesting that they wanted to recapture coalition unity. Harrison, for example, immediately called for the close vote to be made officially unanimous and expressed his support for Barkley as the pair shook hands and shared smiles. Despite the warm gesture, the fact remained that, once Robinson died and the pledges to him disappeared, a strong majority of senators absolutely opposed even the Logan-Hatch version of the president's bill. Later that day, Vice President/Senate president Garner, who had bluntly informed FDR that he had lost the battle, conferred about the next steps to be taken with Barkley and Senator Burton K. Wheeler (MT), who led the court reform opponents.[15]

The next day, July 22, was not a particularly happy one for Barkley and proved to be an awful day for the president. In the morning, Barkley, Garner, and Wheeler met with the Senate Judiciary Committee. They explained and the committee accepted a deal worked out with a most reluctant Roosevelt. But, even before the deal could be implemented, the Senate session that opened in the afternoon began with a blow against the president. The chamber easily overrode FDR's veto of a farm mortgage interest reduction bill. Immediately afterward, Senator Logan moved to send the Logan-Hatch court reform measure back to the hostile Judiciary Committee. To help Roosevelt save face, the motion also instructed the committee to prepare within ten days a bill creating a procedural change for the lower courts. That move resulted in August in a law that could add more lower court judges if the volume of work justified enlargement. Senator Hiram W. Johnson (CA) wanted a point of clarification. He asked Logan: "The Supreme Court is out?" When the Kentuckian replied affirmatively in a clear voice, Johnson yelled: "Glory be to God!" The gallery audience responded with shouts and applause. Senate president Garner had to rap his gavel vigorously to restore order. By an overwhelming vote of 70–20 the motion passed. It entombed permanently the dead motion deep in the archives of the Judiciary Committee.[16]

Some heralded Roosevelt's defeat by the Senate as comparable to Woodrow Wilson's inability to get the Senate to approve the Treaty of Versailles and, hence, US membership in the League of Nations. The comparison may be an exaggeration, but the speechwriter and FDR associate Samuel Rosenman later commented that the setback was extremely hard on Roosevelt after his stunning reelection victory and the equally dazzling ascendancy of his party in Congress. Regardless, on August 10, Kenneth McKeller (TN) and Democratic members of his Senate Appropriations Committee sponsored a dinner presided over by Vice President Garner at Washington's

Raleigh Hotel. It honored the newly elected majority leader, Barkley. As a sign of party unity, Harrison joined the Iron Man at the head table and toasted the Kentuckian, who responded by treating his colleagues to a warbling baritone rendition of his favorite song, "Wagon Wheels." The next day on the Senate floor, it was Barkley's turn to endure a setback that was similar to but on a smaller scale than the one suffered by the president.[17]

Instead of working on his agenda, Robert Wagner (NY) caught the attention of Garner and gained the floor before Barkley. He made a motion to consider first the antilynching bill that had recently passed the House by a large margin. The House vote occurred after the violent lynching of two African Americans in Mississippi. It was the kind of ugly event outside the law that happened all too frequently in the South. To be sure, Barkley also favored the bill but knew that southern senators would conduct a lengthy filibuster to prevent a vote. Wagner's motion resurrected the Democratic Party divisions that came to the surface in the wake of the Supreme Court controversy. More importantly, Barkley knew that such a filibuster would simply terminate all hope of passing any legislation before the end of the congressional session. The majority leader immediately exercised the parliamentary procedure of calling for an adjournment, which would dissolve Wagner's motion. Republicans and liberal Democrats defeated Barkley's motion by a vote of 35–27. Minority Leader Charles McNary then moved for a recess, which would keep Wagner's motion alive when the Senate returned. A Democratic colleague, Josh Lee (OK), asked Barkley how he should vote. The Kentuckian replied sharply: "Ask McNary! He's the only real leader around here. That was a hell of a harmony dinner we had last night." McNary's motion carried by a tally of 36–23.[18]

The experienced, knowledgeable, and personable Barkley took two steps to recover fully from the setback. First, he conferred with his good friend (who really was his good friend) Senate president Garner. They agreed to meet for a few minutes before each daily meeting of the body so that Garner would know Barkley's agenda and what the majority leader hoped to present. Thus, Garner would always recognize Barkley first once the Senate had opened for business. This arrangement avoided unwanted surprises. The pair also met regularly to discuss legislation with House leader Sam Rayburn and President Roosevelt—often on Mondays at 10:00 A.M. in the Oval Office of the White House. Second, Barkley met with Wagner. As it turned out, Wagner cosponsored with Henry Steagall the Wagner-Steagall national housing bill, which had won Senate approval several days earlier on August

6. It would create a national housing authority under the Department of the Interior and make long-term loans to public agencies for low-cost housing. Barkley reminded Wagner that there was a problem; the House had not yet approved the bill, and, moreover, its cosponsor, Steagall, had reservations about the Senate version. Thus, the House bill would be different from the one passed by the Senate. It would lead to a conference committee to iron out the differences, and the revised bill would then have to be debated and voted on by both chambers. Naturally, a filibuster against the antilynching bill in the Senate would also kill passage of the housing legislation.[19]

By August 11, it seemed likely that the House might not pass the bill in a later session of Congress. In fact, President Roosevelt would have to put his weight behind the measure to get the lower chamber to support a version of the Senate's national housing bill before the session ended. Barkley's time with Wagner worked since the New York senator understood the dilemma and chose to withdraw his motion on the antilynching legislation rather than surrender the housing bill. Barkley promised that the antilynching measure would come up in the next session. In addition to the Wagner-Steagall National Housing Act, the other important legislation approved before Congress adjourned on August 21, 1937, was the Federal Aid in Wildlife Restoration Act. The catastrophic effect of the court reform controversy in nearly paralyzing congressional activity is seen by the fact that, besides an amendment to an antitrust act, the only other significant New Deal bill signed into law by FDR during this first session of the Seventy-Fifth Congress was the (John H.) Bankhead (AL)-(Marvin) Jones (TX) Farm Tenant Act, which established the Farm Security Administration to provide low-interest, forty-year mortgages to help sharecroppers buy their own farms.[20]

At the end of the session, Barkley was grateful that the sharp thorn of court reform had been extracted, but it left Congress with an infection that would not go away. The North-South, urban-rural split among Democrats continued. Two key New Deal measures passed by an otherwise unproductive national legislature, housing (urban) and tenant (rural) acts, reflected symbolically Senate divisions that continued beyond 1937. Those divisions would pose problems for, if not impediments to, the work of the newly elected majority leader. No one geographic or cultural division had enough votes to dominate the Senate, but seniority handed southern Democrats powerful chairmanships over crucial Senate committees. Selected economic issues held Democrats together; measures touched by race tore the fabric of unity apart. On the other hand, Barkley could take heart from the fact that he had climbed to the pinnacle of the US Senate.[21]

A couple of days after the first session ended, Barkley and House leader Sam Rayburn met for lunch with Roosevelt at the White House. They considered whether the president should call a special session of Congress before the second session began on January 3, 1938. The three men reviewed the pros and cons of the issue as they recognized the need for legislation devoted to farm relief, government reorganization, and worker standards for hours and wages. They made no decision at the time, but FDR later called for a special session in November. Aside from arguing in the press that there had been no breakdown in the president's leadership, Barkley joined his wife in preparing for a sea voyage to Europe. Once they arrived in France, Barkley delivered an address before the Inter-Parliamentary Union (IPU) on September 5, 1937. He asserted that America opposed force and supported diplomacy in foreign affairs. The gathering of legislators had opened in the Versailles Palace, where the treaty ending the Great War was signed. While the IPU continued to preach mediation as the brightest option for peace, the group met in an international scene darkened by the promise of war. Already Germany had repudiated the Versailles Treaty by rearming its military in 1935 and then remilitarizing the Rhineland in 1936. It had also aligned itself with Italy, the armed occupier of Ethiopia, and Japan, the military invader of China in July 1937.[22]

Shortly after Alben and Dorothy boarded the Italian liner *Rex* for passage to New York, President Roosevelt delivered his famous quarantine speech in Chicago on October 5. It was directed obliquely at Japan, but FDR lumped the Nipponese with the "bandit nations" of Germany and Italy. He felt that the contagion of war needed to be contained by peace-loving nations. He told his audience: "When an epidemic of physical disease [war] starts to spread, the community approves and joins in a quarantine of the patients [militaristic powers] in order to protect the health of the community against the spread of the disease." The speech, delivered during the dedication ceremony of Chicago's new Outer Drive Bridge, caused a sensation in America and around the world. The next day the Assembly of the League of Nations in Geneva condemned Japan for its aggression. US public opinion generally favored FDR's comments, but the president also received some jolting, vitriolic attacks from isolationists—several congressmen even spoke of impeaching him. The real question Roosevelt did not and could not answer was: What economic sanctions or specific actions short of belligerency constituted a quarantine of the fascist-militaristic nations? Since neither Japan nor China had actually declared war, the only (in)action Roosevelt took was not to invoke the military trade restrictions found in the Neutrality Act. Had he done so, it would have hurt China more than Japan. Thus, China would be able to buy implements of war in the United States.[23]

Nine days after Roosevelt's interesting but ineffective speech, Alben and Dorothy arrived back in the United States. Almost immediately, they traveled to Kentucky to join the citizens of Lowes, Barkley's birthplace, in celebrating the town's one hundredth anniversary. The event turned into a love fest for the majority leader. Several speakers who shared the podium with him endorsed the senator for US president in the 1940 campaign. Barkley made no comment about these kind remarks, but he really wanted to be reelected to the US Senate in 1938. A potential problem existed that the Iron Man hoped to avoid. Shortly after the Great War, Alben and Dorothy sold their Paducah home and soon purchased their Cleveland Avenue residence in Washington. Thereafter, they rented apartments in Paducah for their several but brief visits to McCracken County each year. Finally, however, they bought the Angles estate near Paducah in 1937, preemptively quashing the embarrassing charge that Barkley owned a home in the nation's capital but not in the commonwealth he represented in the Senate.[24]

Moreover, Barkley would be sixty in November, and, while he had no thought of retiring soon, the pair did want to spend their final years together near where their married lives had begun. Angles had attracted the senator's attention for a number of years. It had an enchanting brick house situated near where three pieces of farmland of multiple acres came together, which explained the property's name. The residence featured eleven large, high-ceilinged rooms all on the ground floor. Alben and Dorothy over time had to add wardrobes for closets as well as running water, a heating system, and electric wiring to modernize the old domicile and turn it into a livable home. They furnished the house with many antiques; the basement eventually held Barkley's papers, photo albums, and numerous souvenirs from his and Dorothy's travels in America and abroad. The senator was especially fond of collecting canes or walking sticks. Even though the couple lived most of the time in Washington, Angles would acquire a permanent resident in their son, David, who managed the farm.[25]

On returning to Washington, Barkley faced a hostile Senate in the brief five-week, November–December special session. He kept his promise to Wagner. The New York senator reintroduced his motion on the antilynching bill. It resulted in a filibuster for a portion of the special session and for six weeks in the regular session that began in January. No major bill passed in the special session, and only by common agreement was the antilynching bill dropped in the regular session. The latter allowed funding bills for existing New Deal programs to be approved. It also led to a significant appropriation for the US Navy, which over time expanded its fleet into a two-ocean security force to protect US shores against an increasingly dangerous and belligerent world. But, other than a modification of the 1906 Pure Food and Drug Act, the only serious New Deal legislation approved by the end of the regular session was the fair labor standards bill. President Roosevelt signed it into law and praised it in a Fireside Chat several days after the Seventy-Fifth Congress ended on June 16, 1938. The new law established a minimum wage, initially of twenty-five cents an hour, and a forty-four-hour workweek—reduced to forty hours one year after the bill was enacted.[26]

The brief description offered above summarizing Barkley's first year as majority leader strongly suggests that this was nowhere near being one of the high points of his political career. His troubles led to the unflattering "bumbling Barkley" alliteration that stuck to him long after any remote justification for the label existed. He made mistakes, but he learned from them. In reality, he understood and effectively used parliamentary rules. He soon received credit for streamlining the Senate's legislative program. Additionally, he kept his committee assignments to participate and remain current in the bill-writing process; he also absorbed vast amounts of information about each major measure to help him authoritatively defend or defeat its passage. In his maturity, he had become an expert at speaking extemporaneously as he mastered effectively embedding stories and jokes in his comments. Darrell St. Claire, Leslie Biffle's assistant and the secretary of the Senate Democratic Patronage Committee, thought that he was an absolute "show horse on the Senate floor."[27]

Despite these excellent attributes, Barkley suffered two other setbacks that disturbed Roosevelt in the last session of the Seventy-Fifth Congress. Conservative Democratic senators, especially, though not exclusively, from the South, prevented the new majority leader from securing the president's programs for taxes and government reorganization. The same group nearly killed the fair labor standards bill and forced compromises to keep, for example, a low minimum wage. Southern politicians hoped that low wages might attract desperately needed new industries to their region. Roosevelt did not blame Barkley for these issues; instead, he tried to initiate a purge of the Democratic Party. In his Fireside Chat of June 24, 1938, he called on the American people to vote for liberals in the upcoming primaries for congressional offices. Why primaries? In the South, only Democrats won elections. Thus, Roosevelt literally asked citizens to vote in favor of New Deal adherents in primaries; they would then be candidates in November's general election. He stated that he did not care whether voters picked Democrats or Republicans or members of other parties as long as they sided with the New Deal. Otherwise, he claimed neutrality by stating: "Nor am I, as President, taking part in Democratic primaries."[28]

Roosevelt lied, or, to put it more gently, he changed his mind. Barely a week after his Fireside Chat, he and his entourage took a special ten-car train that steamed across America. He then boarded a US Navy ship in San Diego and sailed to the Atlantic Ocean via the Panama Canal. In August, he devoted his attention to the South. During both journeys, he campaigned for pro–New Deal Democrats who were candidates for upcoming primaries. Above all, he wanted to make certain that the majority leader he helped elect, the loyal Barkley, would keep his seat and post in the US Senate. Barkley had an unusually strong opponent in Kentucky's Democratic primary—the young (forty years old before July 14), energetic, and popular Governor Albert Benjamin "Happy" Chandler. Kentucky historians would likely agree with Lowell H. Harrison that Chandler had one of the most successful and productive administrations in the state's history, at least up to the 1930s. Through higher excise and income taxes, he funded improved schools, health and welfare programs, rural roads, and penal institutions; he also instituted a program providing free textbooks to schools, a retirement system for teachers, and a more efficient government while reducing the commonwealth's debt. Nevertheless, from FDR's vantage point, Happy Chandler had three strikes against him: he was the only Kentucky Democrat with a chance to beat Barkley at the polls, he shared with southern politicians certain reservations about the New Deal, and, if he succeeded in defeating a nationally known figure like Barkley, he might be vaulted into presidential politics in 1940.[29]

As early as January 22, 1938, Barkley received clear warning that he would face Chandler in the August primary. The governor had turned down an invitation to be a guest at a testimonial dinner held on that date in Barkley's honor at the Brown Hotel in Louisville. Hundreds of supporters attended, including FDR's aide, Barkley's fellow Kentuckian Marvin McIntyre, who delivered a message of praise from the president. Barkley was joined at the head table by five senators: Joseph Guffey (PA), Sherman Minton (IN), Matthew Neely (WV), Lewis B. Schwellenbach (WA), and Harry S. Truman (MO). Hours before the testimonial dinner began, Chandler conspicuously announced at a separate luncheon: "If I run for any other office, I won't need the help of any Northern Senators or any other Senators." The comment suggested Chandler's plans (fulfilled in February) and referred to the senatorial guests who would soon join Barkley at the evening's event. The next day, after the special dinner, Barkley announced officially that he would be a candidate for reelection. He selected the Louisville attorney Shackelford Miller, who headed the city's Democratic Party, to be his statewide campaign manager.[30]

Barkley began his formal campaign for the August primary on Saturday, June 18, at Lexington. The venue was the trotting track of the Kentucky Trotting Horse Breeders Association. Its grandstand was packed with over two thousand people as hundreds of others jammed the areaway in front of the grandstand. The Iron Man, of course, attracted crowds wherever he spoke because as a national celebrity his voice, comments, and picture entered most Kentucky homes on a regular basis. His lengthy opening address did not focus on his opponent; instead, he spent time exploring his record, the New Deal, and the Hoover versus Roosevelt approach to the Great Depression. Near the end of his well-received speech, the majority leader made his request for the votes of those in the audience: "In asking the people of Kentucky to return me to the Senate, I shall make no appeal to any special class. I have tried to be a servant of all the people regardless of section, party, color, religion or occupation. When I have been upon or have had an opportunity to serve the humblest or the most powerful citizen in this state or this nation, I have not asked his politics or his religion. If I shall again be honored by your suffrage and your confidence, I shall follow the same course in the future."[31]

What should have been a highlight for the Barkley campaign came on July 8, 1938, when President Roosevelt stopped, not once, but three times (in Covington, Louisville, and Bowling Green) to bolster voter support in the commonwealth for the Senate majority leader. The big surprise, however, is that Barkley's opponent, Chandler, boarded the president's special train in Cincinnati, Ohio, and managed to insert himself in every picture taken of FDR. In Covington, the president took an open limousine from the train station to the Latonia Race Track, where he was to speak. At the station, the polio-afflicted president was seated, of course, in the back on the right side of the vehicle. Before Barkley entered the vehicle, Chandler vaulted himself into the rear seat next to FDR and, thus, occupied the middle seat between the president and the majority leader. Barkley later characterized Happy's behavior as "pure unadulterated nerve." While Barkley and Chandler also sat near Roosevelt on the podium at Latonia, the "neutral" president made clear during the speech his preference for Barkley's reelection: "I have no doubt that Governor Chandler would make a good Senator from Kentucky, but I think he would be the first to acknowledge that as a very junior member of the Senate it would take him many, many years to match the national knowledge, the experience and the acknowledged leadership in the affairs of our nation of that son of Kentucky, of whom the whole nation is proud, Alben Barkley."[32]

Frankly, the Barkley-Chandler campaign was ugly from the standpoint of both candidates; each went to his grave with evil thoughts about the other. The governor lost but in the process he delivered personal attacks on the senator. The forty-year-old Chandler called the sixty-year-old Barkley "Old Alben." The Iron Man shamed and surprised Happy by making anywhere from five to fifteen vigorous speeches a day as he outpaced the younger man in the hustings. It also seemed to be a good thing Alben and Dorothy bought a farm and house near Paducah. Chandler did like to dwell on the fact Barkley had spent so much time in Washington and abroad that he had lost touch with Kentucky; the governor actually went so far as to criticize the senator's daughters for marrying and living outside the commonwealth. The majority leader responded quickly and captured his fair share of votes from parents when he replied that he was proud of the accomplishments of his offspring. Finally, both men challenged ethical behavior by gaining support and votes from state (Chandler) and federal (Barkley) workers. The situation in Kentucky seemed to be so much out of control and representative of some campaigns in other states that it led to a Senate resolution creating the Senate Committee to Investigate Campaign Expenditure and Use of Government Funds. Morris Sheppard—the same Texas senator associated with the Sheppard-Towner Maternity and Infancy Act of 1921—chaired the committee. The investigation resulted in the Seventy-Sixth Congress approving and FDR signing the famous Hatch Act sponsored by Senator Carl A. Hatch of New Mexico. It prohibited federal employees from using their authority and resources to influence the outcome of elections for national office.[33]

The interesting question about the campaign asks whether Roosevelt's visit to Kentucky actually helped Barkley. In his autobiography, published two years before his death in 1991, Chandler claimed that FDR was completely responsible for Barkley's lopsided victory. And FDR's secretary, Grace Tully, argued in her book *Franklin Delano Roosevelt, My Boss* that Chandler "was opposing Barkley and making a tight race of it until FDR went into Kentucky to speak on behalf of his loyal Senate lieutenant." The implication of Tully's comment is that, like Chandler, she felt that the president made a significant difference in the race and, perhaps, was responsible for Barkley's victory. Such an implication is simply nonsense. George Gallup's American Institute of Public Opinion released survey results of Kentucky Democrats shortly before Roosevelt's visit on July 8. Barkley had a commanding 64 percent–36 percent lead over Chandler. The institute's polling of Democrats two weeks after the president's trip showed that Barkley still had an overwhelming lead of 61 percent–39 percent. But, if anything, the polling indicated that Barkley had the election sown up without Roosevelt's help. Indeed, the public opinion survey actually suggested that the president's visit helped Chandler more than it did Barkley. Everywhere the governor went during the campaign, he could show pictures of himself with Roosevelt and repeat as a mantra the president's statement that Chandler "would make a good Senator from Kentucky."[34]

Happy, however, did not have a chance of winning. And his chances diminished even further Thursday evening, July 21, when he became ill after drinking a large amount of ice water in his room in Louisville's Kentucky Hotel. He was on the campaign trail in what was considered Barkley territory. The governor's physician and his appointed Kentucky health commissioner claimed belatedly that the patient drank poison that had been slipped into the ice water. There was, however, no evidence because the water container had been removed and cleaned. Also, no culprit could be identified, but, since Chandler was in a Barkley stronghold, there was an automatic link by the governor's camp to Happy's opponent. The event was and remains very suspect. The next day members of Chandler's entourage admitted that Chandler suffered stomach pains for a week before the ice water episode; he apparently had bad eating habits. Moreover, the Weeter Pathological Laboratory tested Chandler's body fluids but found no trace of poison. Bluntly, Louisville's police chief, John Malley, called the governor's health problem "a political bedtime story," and Chief Detective Joseph Stewart dismissed it as a "publicity stunt." Under these highly questionable circumstances, Barkley turned the matter into a joke. He regaled his audiences with stories that he had enlarged his staff with a food taster and an ice water guard, or he would pick up a glass of water, visibly shudder and shake his head, and put the glass down to the hearty laughter of his listeners. Chandler's lengthy recovery from whatever ailed him only made him look weak when compared to the strength of the Iron Man. In an interview held nearly thirty years later, the former governor had to admit that no one could have beaten Barkley in 1938.[35]

With well over seventy thousand more votes than Chandler, Barkley solidly won the Democratic primary on August 6, 1938. Having already canvassed much of Kentucky, he could afford to take a lengthy vacation before the general election. On August 17, he and Dorothy boarded the French liner *Normandie* and embarked for Europe. Among other activities, the majority leader took part in a meeting of the IPU in The Hague, the capital city of the Netherlands. It was a very dangerous and unsettling moment in European affairs. A few months earlier, Hitler's armies had audaciously seized the country of Austria. When the IPU opened, a general European war seemed likely because the German Wehrmacht had prepared itself for an invasion of Czechoslovakia, which had military alliances with France and the Soviet Union. The issue of peace or war still hung in the balance after Alben and Dorothy arrived back in the United States on the liner *Washington* on September 15.[36]

Ignoring Soviet Russia, the Munich Conference of England, France, Germany, and Italy agreed at the end of September that Czechoslovakia had to turn over to Hitler's Third Reich the Sudeten region, strategically vital to the country's defense on the border with Germany but populated with many Germans. The führer's victory at Munich led to only a temporary peace as it emboldened Hitler to threaten or use force rather than diplomacy to expand the interests and territory of the German realm. As these events transpired, Barkley traveled and spoke around the commonwealth and won reelection to the US Senate on Tuesday, November 8. He took a whopping 62 percent of the total vote in defeating the Republican John P. Haswell, a Louisville judge. The majority leader's national reputation, New Deal identification, and farmer heritage helped him win the Kentucky contest. He scarcely mentioned international relations in the electoral race, yet, within months of his victory, he would be focusing much of his attention in the Senate on concerns related to America's national defense and foreign affairs.[37]

13

The Majority Leader from Neutrality to War

Alben W. Barkley's solid victory in Kentucky proved to be one of the few success stories in Roosevelt's well-publicized strategy to maintain and strengthen congressional backing for the New Deal. The attempt, for example, to purge from Congress the conservative Democratic senators Walter F. George (GA), Guy M. Gillette (IA), Ellison D. "Cotton Ed" Smith (SC), and Millard Tydings (MD) failed miserably. And FDR did not endear himself to moderate Democrats who were upset by his quest to reshape the party around his philosophy. Some contemporary commentators considered the purge a fiasco, yet opinion polls continued to register Roosevelt as an immensely popular figure. Regardless, the serious economic recession of 1938 partly explained, along with unique issues and personalities of each campaign, why the GOP enjoyed a revival with eighty new Republicans in the House and eight in the Senate. Still, Democrats of whatever stripe vastly outnumbered the GOP and, thus, organized and dominated both congressional chambers. But the added Republican members strengthened the Democrats who wanted to modify, if not dismantle, the New Deal. The Hatch Act represented the work of this new coalition.[1]

As a result, the now-experienced majority leader still faced a daunting task in upholding the New Deal in the first session of Congress in 1939. Typical of the problems Barkley encountered was the relief fund of $875 million requested by FDR for the Works Progress Administration (WPA). Not just in Kentucky, but throughout the president's purge campaign, the WPA took a political role in supporting Roosevelt. Not surprisingly, then, a coalition of Republicans and moderate or conservative Democrats in the House, where appropriations begin, cut FDR's request by $150 million. Barkley urged his senatorial colleagues to sustain the president, but by one vote, 47–46, a Senate coalition approved the House cut on January 27. Shortly afterward, Roosevelt sent Congress a message asking for the $150 million to be restored. Eventually, the House approved a deficiency appropriation for the WPA of $100 million in April. This time, recognizing that he worked for both the White House and the Senate, Barkley consulted with some twenty senators and chose to respect their views and rebuff the president. On April 11, 1939, the Senate voted 49–28 in favor of the House version, which deleted $50 million from FDR's request. Barkley stood behind the majority and considered the compromise to be a matter of, in his words, "common sense."[2]

The only new legislation that might be considered somewhat progressive was the reorganization bill, which Roosevelt signed into law on April 3, 1939. This bill has sometimes been ignored by historians of this period because it was a watered-down version of a measure the president had earlier proposed and Congress rejected, making it seemed to be less important. The *New York Times* characterized it as "a compromise which can frighten nobody." For example, the Republican-Democratic coalition struck down a proposed department of welfare out of fear that New Deal relief agencies would become permanent. The final bill empowered the president only to reorganize bureaus and agencies below the department level and with the approval of at least one of the two chambers of Congress. The law added six new assistants to the White House staff and led to the creation of the Executive Office of the President as well as the powerful Bureau of the Budget. Frank Freidel, the author of the magisterial biography *Franklin D. Roosevelt: A Rendezvous with Destiny,* describes the legislation as nothing less than a revolution in federal administration.[3]

What is fascinating about the history of this bill was the influence of foreign events on it as it wended its way, in fits and starts, through the congressional system. The seemingly weakened reorganization measure was partially the product of a deep concern by some members of Congress that FDR aspired to create a dictatorship mimicking Europe's fascist governments. Following the pattern established first by Italy and then by Germany, fascism had become downright trendy during the insecure 1930s as a number of European countries from Spain to Bulgaria adopted despotic governments resembling those headquartered in Rome and Berlin. Unfortunately, in the case of Germany, Hitler had promised as early as 1925 in *Mein Kampf* that his national socialist movement would use the military to expand German living space at the expense of Slavic peoples (Russians, Poles, Czechs, Slovaks) to the East. No wonder that, as Nazi Germany started to rearm in 1935, Soviet Russia began to upgrade its hardware for the Red Air Force via the United States as early as 1936. It bought plans, planes, and manufacturing rights to modern military and transport aircraft from such American firms as the Douglas Aircraft Company, the Glenn L. Martin Aircraft Company, the Seversky Aircraft Corporation, and the Vultee Aircraft Company.[4]

Soviet purchases in the United States confirmed that America had reestablished its importance in the design and manufacture of advanced aircraft. Indeed, airplanes also served as the first of two legislative issues that caused foreign affairs to intrude and soon dominate the agenda of Senate majority leader Barkley and his congressional associates. The first issue emerged on November 14, 1938, when President Roosevelt opened a White House meeting, later publicized, of his personal and military advisers. FDR took the occasion to respond to the military used by Germany, Italy, and Japan to expand their territory in Europe, Africa, and Asia. He recommended a policy to match German airpower of six thousand combat planes by expanding US Army Air Corps strength by a factor of eight with the purchase of thousands of new aircraft, thus addressing potential problems should it become necessary to defend the Philippines against Japan and the Panama Canal and portions of the United States against Germany if the latter successfully invaded one of several European countries possessing colonies in the Caribbean region. When legislation implementing the president's policy reached Congress and entered debate in February and March 1939, Barkley faced a bump in the road on the way to gaining congressional approval.[5]

At the end of February, as the Senate considered the Army Air Corps expansion bill, which the House had already approved, a dozen isolationists led by the Republican Gerald P. Nye (ND) tried to turn the conversation into a debate on national defense. They wanted to resurrect a version of the famous (Louis Leon) Ludlow (D-IN) Amendment, which the House barely defeated (209–188) in January 1938 and would have required a national referendum with a majority favorable vote in order to conduct a war overseas. During Nye's arguments for the referendum and against the bill, he dismissed the notion that war was likely in Europe and claimed: "All the gains that have been made by the dictatorships . . . have been by bluff, pure and simple bluff." Barkley recognized that, if countries did not challenge the "bluff" of dictatorships, it was because they lacked the necessary war materiel and combat soldiers. For this reason, he wanted to help Europe's democracies; he also wanted the United States to be able to protect its possessions in the Pacific Ocean from Japan and European colonies in the Caribbean region from Germany. Thus, he responded to Nye that, if the democracies lacked war materiel and "the readiness to meet the bluff," "how long [would it] be before we would either have to stand and fight or to yield and retreat."[6]

Barkley literally had the last word on the Army Air Corps expansion bill when he spoke for nearly two hours immediately before the Senate voted on the measure on March 7. Because Democratic secretary Leslie Biffle had informally polled the senators, and, because a trial vote on an amendment had easily passed the previous day, Barkley already knew that the chamber would approve the bill. As a result, the majority leader also spent time expressing his views as well as those of the administration on the related subject of neutrality legislation. The laws of 1935 and 1936 and the resolution of January 1937 had been combined into a "permanent" Neutrality Act of May 1, 1937. The latter had a temporary cash-and-carry provision that favored the naval powers of France and Great Britain rather than Europe's dictatorships, but that provision expired on May 1, 1939. Barkley reminded senators that, while US foreign policy centered on maintaining a peaceful Western Hemisphere, it also tried to "make some contribution to the preservation of peace in other parts of the world." He noted that the neutrality legislation of 1935–1937 had done little, if anything, to advance the cause of peace around the globe. Hence, he initiated in the Senate what turned out to be a lengthy and bitter debate over revisiting and revising America's 1937 Neutrality Act.[7]

After Barkley concluded his comments, the Senate passed the Army Air Corps expansion bill by the lopsided margin of 77–8. It contained an amendment approved the previous day adding five hundred planes to the fifty-five hundred aircraft in the House version. During the House-Senate conference committee meetings ironing out differences between the two chambers, German troops entered Czechoslovakia. This military action on March 16, 1939, encouraged the conference committee to accept the Senate bill and also increase to six thousand aircraft the fighting strength of the US Army Air Corps. The $358 million appropriation approved by Congress on March 22 also included funds to bolster Panama Canal defenses. In Europe, the invasion of Slavic peoples destroyed the Franco-British policy of appeasing Hitler by allowing the Third Reich to acquire lands occupied predominantly by Germans. Thus, when Hitler made demands for Polish territory, Great Britain and France guaranteed the territorial integrity of Poland. Meanwhile, Italy's dictator, Benito Mussolini, decided that his country had to match Germany's land grab, so his military seized the small country of Albania. From this point in the spring of 1939, knowledgeable people around the world expected that a major war would soon erupt in Europe.[8]

Roosevelt worked privately through Barkley and others to promote the notion that a revised neutrality bill was needed from Congress before the cash-and-carry portion of the 1937 act expired on May 1. German troops on the ground in Czechoslovakia in mid-March, however, prompted him to go public in a press conference in which he commented that the act's revision was imperative. Initially, FDR placed his hope for legislation on Key Pittman (NV), who chaired the Senate Foreign Relations Committee. The diplomatic historian George C. Herring, the author of *From Colony to Superpower,* bluntly noted that the president had "entrusted the task to the inebriated, infirm, and inept Senator Key Pittman, who predictably bungled it." In Pittman's defense, it must be pointed out that his committee was almost evenly divided on the makeup of the neutrality bill, which led to delays and the conduct of lengthy hearings that went past the May 1 deadline.[9]

At the end of June, after the House by a margin of only two votes adopted a piece of neutrality legislation but with an amendment that kept an embargo on arms and ammunition, Roosevelt turned once again to Pittman. He convinced the Nevada senator to convene his committee, take its draft cash-and-carry bill out of the desk drawer, and vote to release it to the Senate. On July 11, 1939, the group of twenty-three, including Barkley, met, with eleven committed to approving the bill, ten opposed, and two uncommitted—Democratic senators Walter George and Guy Gillette. Understandably, the uncommitted Democrats hated FDR, who had tried to purge them from the party in 1938. When the meeting first got under way, the isolationist Missouri senator Bennett Champ Clark, the son of former House speaker Champ Clark, moved to postpone neutrality legislation until the January 1940 session of Congress. The motion to delay carried by a vote of 12–11; George and Gillette joined the ten isolationists in order to embarrass President Roosevelt. And they succeeded only too well.[10]

Obviously, Barkley, a member of the Foreign Relations Committee, voted against the motion. Afterward, he conferred with Secretary of State Cordell Hull, who informed him that the news from US diplomats in Europe confirmed that war was imminent. Barkley tried to come up with a quick solution, but even a neutrality repeal amendment attached to a popular bill required an uncertain majority vote. At a press conference, Roosevelt made it clear that he still wanted action on neutrality legislation, though he offered no specific steps by which to achieve it. Barkley encouraged the president to talk with congressional leaders in an attempt to find out whether Congress could do something, anything, before adjournment, slated for August 5. FDR asked congressional leaders and key cabinet officers including Secretary Hull to meet with him at 9:00 P.M. in the White House on July 18. Accompanying the majority and minority leaders of both chambers were Senators Pittman, William E. Borah (ID) and Warren R. Austin (VT).[11]

From the president's perspective, the whole point of the meeting was to find a way to amend or, as Barkley suggested to Hull, repeal neutrality legislation so that the United States could send war materiel to Great Britain and France after the outbreak of hostilities. To FDR, timing was everything. If the policy were set before combat began, the United States would present to the world at least the appearance of being a bonafide neutral. Moreover, after Germans marched into Prague, Czechoslovakia's capital, public opinion surveys noted a shift in American views that supported the great democracies at Germany's expense. Nevertheless, the evening conference did not go the way the president had hoped. Isolationist congressmen thought that conflict either would be long delayed or could be avoided altogether. Senator Borah, for example, argued that his European "sources" knew that there would be no war. Secretary Hull responded by inviting the Idaho senator to read the latest dispatches from US diplomats that spoke otherwise. Borah answered that he trusted his sources (an English newsletter) over the professional observations of US officials abroad. Shortly after midnight, when it became clear that no common agreement on amending or repealing neutrality could be reached, Roosevelt turned to Barkley and asked whether he had the votes to change the current legislation. Barkley had to admit that he would not be able to muster a majority. His unspoken judgment focused on the fact that the nighttime conference had failed to change the minds of Senate minority leader McNary and Borah, the ranking member and former chairman of the Foreign Relations Committee. It meant that neither that committee nor the Senate as a committee of the whole would overturn the July 11 decision to revisit neutrality no sooner than January 1940.[12]

Two events, one bizarre and the other tragic, forced the US government to revisit the neutrality controversy before 1940. On August 23, 1939, the unthinkable occurred when two countries that despised each other, Hitler's Germany and Stalin's Russia, signed a nonaggression treaty popularly known as the Nazi-Soviet Pact. In return for giving Germany the freedom to engage in hostilities without fear of conflict, Soviet Russia received Germany's blessing to absorb the countries of Estonia, Latvia, and Lithuania plus eastern portions of Poland and the Romanian province of Bessarabia. Deplorably, on September 1, the German Wehrmacht massively invaded Poland on several fronts and bombed the capital, Warsaw, almost killing the US ambassador. Two days later, France and Great Britain fulfilled their pledge to preserve Polish territorial integrity by declaring war on Germany. That evening, President Roosevelt proclaimed on national radio America's neutrality and his intention (fulfilled on September 5) to implement the arms embargo on belligerents as specified in the 1937 Neutrality Act. He noted, however, that the United States had a responsibility to protect the Western Hemisphere and adjacent seas and, thus, keep the war from spreading to European possessions. And, unlike Woodrow Wilson in 1914, he did not ask Americans to be neutral in thought as well as action. "Even a neutral," the president remarked, "has a right to take account of facts. Even a neutral cannot be asked to close his mind or his conscience." Not long after this Fireside Chat, FDR called Congress into an emergency special session to reconsider neutrality legislation.[13]

The special session would keep Barkley busy for its duration. He even supervised the arrangements that enabled Roosevelt to address a joint assembly of the reconvened Congress on September 21. The president asked for a quick repeal of the arms embargo, which would return the United States to the principles of international law. He claimed that it would be the surest safeguard against America being drawn into conflict. The repeal would also increase US industrial employment as it ended the paradox of selling unfinished materials to belligerents who would then manufacture them into war goods. Only two hours after the president delivered his message, twenty-four senators met in the office of Republican Hiram Johnson (CA). The group pledged to fight and defeat FDR's neutrality program, as Republican Robert M. La Follette Jr. (WI) forcefully stated, "from hell to breakfast." That pledge helps explain why it took five weeks and added over a million words in debate to the *Congressional Record* before the Senate approved what was essentially an amendment to the 1937 Neutrality Act shortly before 9:00 P.M. on October 27. And Barkley played a major role in the whole process.[14]

Two reasons account for Barkley's significant participation in the attempt to pass the neutrality measure. First, it was understood that the Senate and its majority leader, rather than the House and its majority leader, would take on the task of preparing and securing the legislation. Second, FDR was taken aback by the loud and abusive outcry about his proposal from isolationists. Even though the isolationists represented a minority, White House advisers agreed with Roosevelt that he would be better off remaining aloof from the issue. Just in case revision failed, the president did not need to be the commander who lost yet another battle with Congress. At this point, FDR could not decide whether to enjoy the peace and honor of being an ex-president or to protect the New Deal by violating tradition and running for a third term in 1940. He did not, however, want the neutrality issue to make that decision for him. Thus, it was Barkley who worked closely with Pittman and Tom Connally (TX) as they prepared the legislation. The draft repealed the arms embargo clause of the 1937 Neutrality Act and allowed belligerents to purchase war materiel in the United States, but only if they paid cash and used their own ships to carry the goods. Barkley contributed an amendment that penalized any foreign vessel that flew, obviously for deceptive purposes, the US flag. During debate, he often seemed evenhanded, but he also delivered a powerful, substantial address in support of the bill.[15]

Despite the lengthy and sometime acrimonious deliberations on the Senate floor, the measure passed by over a two-to-one margin of 63–30. It made the House approval that much easier on November 1. And, because the House accepted the Senate bill almost in its entirety, it took the conference committee only four hours to iron out minor differences and forty minutes total for the two chambers to approve the conference report by the lopsided votes of 55–24 (Senate) and 243–172 (House) before Congress adjourned the special session at 6:30 P.M. on November 3. Roosevelt was extremely pleased with both the result of the session and Barkley's role as facilitator. Journalists commented that the White House and Congress seemed to be working together again, but under new circumstances. When the president signed the bill into law at noon the next day, he asked Barkley and the other congressional leaders to remain in Washington to consult with him on foreign policy issues related to the European war. By November, however, while the war at sea continued, the land war ceased except for the brief conflict between Finland and Soviet Russia. Poland was defeated and literally disappeared under German and Russian occupation.

The French forces that had barely invaded Germany retreated five miles to defensive positions on the Maginot Line before the end of October. Hence, the German blitzkrieg had been replaced by the sitzkrieg.[16]

Before his death in January 1940, Senator Borah called the sitzkrieg a *phony war,* a label that became popular especially to the delight of other isolationists. Germany, of course, complained bitterly about the cash-and-carry aspect of the recent Neutrality Act as by its presence the British navy swept away German transport vessels from the Atlantic Ocean. On the other side of the coin, France and Great Britain took full advantage of the legislation. Their orders and purchases of not only munitions but also complex technologies such as aircraft expanded US employment and enhanced the nation's industry. In 1940, during the third session of the Seventy-Sixth Congress, Barkley's strong leadership helped advance this process with increased appropriations for national defense and authorization for the Reconstruction Finance Corporation to fund loans to US arms manufacturers. The monies went to upgrade machinery and facilities to produce in abundance quality goods for domestic as well as foreign sales. The result of this economic activity helped increase national income from $38 billion in 1932 to $71 billion in 1940. The Great Depression started to travel down the path toward Memory Lane.[17]

The sitzkrieg/phony war enabled Barkley to have time for issues or events other than the European conflict. For instance, he was once again elected by his colleagues to lead the US delegation to the 1940 meeting of the Inter-Parliamentary Union, scheduled to be held in Oslo, Norway. It never happened because of the war. On the other hand, a different occasion found Barkley returning to the radio microphone. He debated the New Deal with Minority Leader McNary as they spoke over the American Forum of the Air on the Mutual Broadcasting System (defunct after 1998). The debate occurred on the eve of the seventh anniversary of Roosevelt's presidency. McNary pointed out that the Republican Party rejected an activist New Deal philosophy that is defeatist and promotes abundance through scarcity. "Instead," he continued, "[the GOP] reaffirms its faith in our historic system of free enterprise." In sharp contrast, Barkley spurned the "historic system" with a dramatically different view of government compared with the laissez-faire style that characterized the 1920s. He countered: "During the seven years of the Roosevelt Administration, [US citizens] have come to realize their government is their servant, their agent, their organized and collective instrument, and that in order to justify itself it must place its experience, its prestige and its power at their disposal and their services in solving their daily problems in so far as government can or ought to do it."[18]

The next day on the Senate floor, Barkley delivered an address that summarized all the accomplishments of President Roosevelt during his seven years in the White House. It was exactly the type of speech that could be printed and used to inaugurate a campaign for the election or reelection of a presidential candidate. Barkley affirmatively added his voice to those who speculated that FDR would seek a third term. Roosevelt himself seemed to be conflicted. While he planned a presidential library to hold his papers and memorabilia at his New York home in Hyde Park, he also maneuvered to secure loyal delegates for the upcoming Democratic national convention. On the same day that Barkley appeared to be a herald for Roosevelt's candidacy, FDR's aide Early would neither confirm nor deny a published report that the president would not be a candidate unless the war in Europe got much worse. And it did get much worse a month later. Between April 9 and June 22, the German blitzkrieg resumed victoriously to defeat the countries of Belgium, Denmark, France, Luxembourg, Netherlands, and Norway. Only Great Britain remained at war with Germany in Europe; naturally, most everyone expected that the island kingdom would soon be invaded and controlled by Hitler. Would Germany then take over the colonies of the defeated nations on the northern coast of South America and among the Caribbean islands, and what would happen to the Commonwealth of Canada, which shared with Great Britain a king?[19]

The news from Europe shocked many US citizens. In the third week in May, when several countries had already fallen and France was reeling on the ropes from German blows, a Gallup poll revealed that 85 percent of Americans thought that the US armed forces needed to be strengthened. The nightmare results of Europe's war tended to unite Republicans and Democrats in their common desire to bolster the nation's defense. On Thursday, May 17, two days after the Dutch army had surrendered and Queen Wilhelmina of the Netherlands created a government-in-exile in London, FDR addressed a joint assembly of Congress in the Capitol Building. He requested over a billion dollars to expand the US Army, Navy, and Marine Corps. By September, Congress had approved ten times that amount on the basis of the president's additional requests. Meanwhile, FDR specifically argued that the country's annual production of military aircraft must be increased to fifty thousand planes because the effective German use of airpower proved crucial to Wehrmacht victories. Finally, the disaster in Europe, with its potential to spill over into the Western Hemisphere, justified the president in thinking that now was not a good time for the US federal government to undergo major changes in leadership.[20]

Intentionally, Roosevelt played the part of the reluctant candidate right up to the opening on July 15, 1940, of the Democratic national convention in Chicago. He understood that not just Republicans but also many Democrats frowned on violating the two-term tradition for US presidents established by George Washington. Nevertheless, he had done everything possible to secure loyal delegates who might draft him for the nomination rather than one of those individuals who had publicly sought to head the Democratic ticket in November: Vice President Garner, Postmaster General Farley, and Senator Wheeler. Additionally, he made certain that his paladin, Barkley, controlled the convention on his behalf as the permanent chairman. Also, he even called Barkley before the majority leader delivered his address on July 16 and asked him to relay to the convention delegates his attitude toward a third-term nomination at the end of his speech. Barkley obeyed but departed from his text by adding a bonus during his presentation. While he discussed how over the past seven plus years government had restored the American system and preserved democracy under "our great President," he abruptly shouted, "Franklin D. Roosevelt!"[21]

The instant Barkley bellowed the president's name, a roar went up from the delegates on the floor as well as in the galleries filled with pro-Roosevelt Democrats who had been placed there by Chicago's Mayor Kelly. For twenty-nine minutes the band played, people cheered, and a parade of state standards wove around the convention floor. It was Barkley who reinvigorated a lackluster convention and aroused the delegates in favor of a third-term nomination. Finally, Barkley had to call an end to the hoopla and request that delegates return to their seats. (In the joyous mayhem, a woman suffered injury and required aid from a physician.) The Kentuckian then continued his speech, praising funding for national defense and blistering former president Herbert Hoover for his speech at the Republican national convention. He finished his address by delivering Roosevelt's message: the president did not desire to continue in office, but delegates were free to vote for any candidate. The message prompted another demonstration. It was punctuated by the voice of Chicago superintendent of sewers Thomas G. Garry. Before a microphone hooked up from the basement to convention loudspeakers, Garry shouted: "Illinois wants Roosevelt. . . . New York wants

Roosevelt [as did other states]. . . . America wants Roosevelt. . . . The world wants Roosevelt."[22]

And so did most, but not all, delegates. The interesting part of the Democratic national ticket was the vice presidential candidate. Roosevelt dropped Garner, who had four strikes against him. He was a southerner, he opposed FDR's third term, he possessed mixed feelings about the New Deal, and he wanted the presidential nomination for himself. Instead of Garner, Roosevelt tapped Henry A. Wallace as his running mate. The editor of a farm journal, Wallace had served since 1933 as US secretary of agriculture. Roosevelt wanted him as a liberal balance to party conservatives and as a way to secure rural votes. Strangely enough, the president's Republican opponent, Wendell L. Willkie, had voted for Roosevelt in 1932. The GOP candidate attacked the New Deal, not so much for what it did, but for the government red tape associated with the program. In addition, both candidates advocated national defense and British aid. In fact, as the campaign heated up, Republicans joined Democrats in sponsoring and approving the Selective Service Training Act in September along with the additional military funding mentioned above. That same month, communications between Roosevelt and British prime minister Winston S. Churchill led to the exchange of fifty older US destroyers for ninety-nine-year leases on air and naval bases on British territories in the Western Hemisphere. In essence, the United States at that point abandoned neutrality.[23]

Because enough Republicans and Democrats found common ground in supporting national defense in 1940, Barkley was enabled to enjoy such success that his effective leadership in directing and streamlining the legislative process was noted by the *American Political Science Review*. These same commonalities that smoothed the work of the majority leader were also shared by the two main presidential candidates; it may have harmed the GOP national ticket. Willkie was left with weak arguments such as promoting the two-term tradition, claiming to be a better manager, and promising new blood and ideas for a stale administration. As Barkley discovered on the hustings, however, a number of voters felt uncomfortable changing the country's leadership in the midst of a major crisis. And he used that argument effectively as he campaigned in Kentucky and a number of midwestern states speaking on behalf of FDR and Democratic candidates seeking seats or trying to keep their seats in Congress. Earlier, he also traveled to St. Louis and Kansas City for Missouri's August primary. He helped Truman in his reelection bid for the Senate at a time when his campaign coffers were nearly empty. Of course, such activities enhanced his ties with senatorial colleagues and created IOUs that he could collect when needed on the Senate floor. In this case, it also strengthened the majority leader's ties to Roosevelt's replacement as the next US president.[24]

Both Truman and Roosevelt won resounding victories on Tuesday, November 5, 1940. FDR ended up with 449 of the 531 available votes from the Electoral College. A little over a month after the election, he received an urgent message from Prime Minister Churchill. Great Britain was running out of liquid capital or the cash needed to complete the purchase of US military supplies. Moreover, the (Hiram) Johnson Act of 1934 forbid American loans to any foreign government in default on (war) debts to the United States; as mentioned earlier, Hoover's one-year moratorium on war debt payments, in essence, lasted forever, but that was the decision of the debtors. Roosevelt, however, recognized that, with its powerful navy and heroic air force, Great Britain posed the only threat to Germany and prevented the Third Reich from reaching out and taking over European holdings in the Western Hemisphere, some of which either had or would soon have US military bases leased from Great Britain. During a December 17 press conference, Roosevelt mentioned that, instead of leaving unpaid-for British supplies in warehouses, it would be better to lease or loan them to the island kingdom. He used the folksy example that, if the house next door caught fire, would a neighbor not want to loan a hose to help put the fire out, especially if it might spread. By the same token, loaning or leasing military supplies might extinguish the fire of war or at least prevent it from radiating to the United States.[25]

Later that same month, in one of his Fireside Chats, Roosevelt asserted that America must become "the great arsenal of democracy." More specifically, he mentioned aid to Britain, which guarded the Atlantic Ocean and, hence, defended the United States against German expansion. He followed up on his nationally broadcast radio message with a recommendation for definite legislation when he presented his annual State of the Union address to Congress on January 6, 1941. Among other points, he outlined his famous Four Freedoms as war aims for a future world. They were the freedom of speech, the freedom to worship God, the freedom from want, and the freedom from war. These freedoms, along with the arsenal of democracy concept and a promise that no American blood would be shed, laid the ideological foundation for his Lend-Lease legislation. He and his advisers benignly packaged the measure as a "Bill to Promote the Defense of the United States." Four days later, Majority Leader Barkley in the Senate and Majority Leader John McCormack in the House introduced the bill as cosponsors. It would grant the chief executive the right to sell, transfer, exchange, lend, or lease arms and goods to any country deemed vital to America's defense.[26]

Lend-Lease involved money, so the lower chamber was the one that gave it a designation—cleverly out of sequence and patriotically charged as House Resolution 1776. Opinion polls over the 1940–1941 winter revealed that slightly more than three-fourths of Americans favored US aid to Great Britain, but a somewhat greater percentage wanted America to stay out of the war. For good reason, then, Lend-Lease created extreme controversy across the country. Destroyers for military bases two thousand miles from Europe was one thing, but loaning or lending war materiel to a belligerent turned the United States into a de facto ally of Great Britain and its dominions. Critics correctly understood that such legislation would vault America much closer to combat. Germany, for example, would certainly be justified in declaring war against the United States. The two sides of the legislative issue had already organized in 1940 and, thus, led the national Lend-Lease debate in 1941. Isolationists had joined the America First Committee, whose chief spokesman was the world's most famous aviator, Charles A. Lindbergh; those supporting Britain had formed the Committee to Defend America by Aiding the Allies under the newspaper editor William Allen White. Most disturbing to isolationists, a faction of the latter under Senator Carter Glass and the Episcopal bishop Henry W. Hobson broke away from White's group early in 1941 to create the Fight for Freedom Committee.[27]

These organizations presented their opposing views on radio and in print media to produce a cacophony of scathing argumentation that served as a backdrop to the debate in Congress. Despite all this, the House easily passed House Resolution 1776 on February 8 by a mainly partisan vote of 260–165. It was then up to Barkley to guide the House bill as cleanly as possible through the Senate against opposition led by Senators Nye, Wheeler, and Robert A. Taft (OH). Barkley, representing the Foreign Relations Committee, began senatorial consideration of the matter by delivering the first speech on February 17. He made, of course, a number of different points and observations in his effort to encourage his colleagues to support the measure. One of his most striking arguments came in the form of quotes from Hitler. The führer made clear his intent to create what would be literally a new world order fashioned around national socialism and controlled by German masters (*Herrenvolk*). And, yes, the quotes revealed Hitler's desire to spread German hegemony overseas and apply Nazi ideology throughout the Western Hemisphere. "National socialism alone," the führer stated, "is destined to liberate the American people from their ruling clique."[28]

During the course of his address, Majority Leader Barkley responded both to Hitler's actions as conqueror and his threats for the future:

> There are two things which in my judgment the American people desire to preserve. One is the peace of this nation and of this Hemisphere. The other is the freedom and independence of this nation and of this Hemisphere. They want to preserve them both at the same time, if this is possible. If they cannot both be preserved at once and simultaneously, then our history has belied our character if they are not willing to make whatever effort is essential and undergo whatever sacrifice is required to preserve the freedom and independence of this nation and this Hemisphere and the method of life and the form of culture which they have established. . . . There is but one way to stop a conqueror. That way is to defeat him. The only way to stop Hitler is to defeat him, and if we do not help Great Britain and other [Commonwealth] nations now fighting him to defeat him over there, we shall some day have to surrender to him or defeat him over here.[29]

Barkley proved to be a skillful guide for the legislation. He also enjoyed a degree of good fortune because the dreaded filibuster never occurred. That may have been due to the strongly favorable House vote and the fact that most senators—even those opposed to the bill—wanted some type of aid to go to Great Britain. Opponents often focused on the discretionary powers of the chief executive to select without congressional approval the recipient countries receiving US aid. Regardless, Barkley assured senators that anyone who wanted to speak for or against the measure would have the floor and ample time to present his views. Sixty-one hours of speechmaking were taken up by thirty-seven senators. In between these formal addresses, there were plenty of spontaneous and sometimes testy debates conducted between Barkley and George of the Foreign Relations Committee and Taft and Wheeler of the isolationists. On the other hand, to make certain that the debate would end in timely fashion, committee meetings and hearings ended as Barkley scheduled a series of full daily Senate sessions for the aid bill. Assistant Secretary of War John J. McCloy, who followed the measure's progress through Congress, remarked on his respect for the way in which the majority leader handled the process. He was especially impressed by how Barkley "refused to yield on proposed amendments" that were often designed by opponents to alter the legislation drastically. Only two weeks after the debate began, the Senate voted by nearly a two-to-one margin, 60–31, its approval. Roosevelt signed the Lend-Lease Act on March 11, 1941.[30]

Before long, the administration had to confront a troubling issue related to Lend-Lease. On June 22, 1941, Nazi Germany invaded Soviet-held territory. Immediately, a desperate Great Britain and its conservative, anti-Communist prime minister welcomed the Soviet Union as an ally. Under different circumstances, the realpolitik approach would have been for the United States to extend Lend-Lease aid to the Russians, but Stalin and company had turned that into an awkward decision for the Roosevelt administration. Soviet Russia had fought a war with Finland, absorbed three Baltic countries, and taken Polish and Romanian lands while enjoying the blessings of a nonaggression treaty with Hitler. Small wonder that some members of Congress had a hard time making any type of distinction between the two dictators. Thus, in the short term, FDR failed to identify the Soviet Union as a Lend-Lease recipient for fear Congress might react by cutting funds and, hence, war supplies to Great Britain and the Commonwealth nations. Militarily, of course, it made perfect sense to aid the Soviet Union. To be sure, Britain was a great sea power and possessed an air force with the proven ability from the Battle of Britain of being able to fight the German Luftwaffe effectively. It lacked, however, an army large enough to challenge Germany's ground forces. By contrast, the Soviet Union could muster forces that exceeded, at least in numbers, the German Wehrmacht. Churchill and Roosevelt realized that, as long as the Russians continued to battle the Germans in the East, there was absolutely no danger of an attempted invasion of Great Britain by Nazi Germany.[31]

This is the reason that on June 24 Roosevelt agreed with Churchill that aid must go to the Soviet Union, but not Lend-Lease aid. Hence, the US Treasury Department bought Soviet gold at the legal price of $35 an ounce and released $39 million in Soviet assets that had been frozen because of territorial acquisitions and military actions in Eastern Europe. Moreover, FDR failed to invoke the Neutrality Act and, thus, did not name the Soviet

Union as a belligerent, which meant that US ships could sail to Soviet ports. Finally, the Reconstruction Finance Corporation opened a $100 million line of credit to Soviet Russia against future imports into the American market of manganese, chromium, and platinum. All these steps allowed the start of the immense transfer system that by 1945 sent from the United States to the Soviet Union seventeen million tons of war materiel valued at nearly $11 billion. Late in October 1941, the Red Army and bad weather managed to stop the otherwise victorious German Wehrmacht outside Moscow. To celebrate and encourage Stalin not to consider a peace treaty with Hitler, Roosevelt added the Soviet Union to the list of Lend-Lease countries on October 30. The decision was made public on the November 7 anniversary of the 1917 Bolshevik Revolution.[32]

November 7, 1941, was also a memorable day for Barkley, but not because of Lend-Lease aid to Soviet Russia. The Kentuckian and the Senate took the lead in introducing and approving legislation that modified the Neutrality Act of 1939. President Roosevelt had requested on October 9 that the act be changed to allow US armed merchant vessels to carry goods to belligerent ports. Barkley directed the battle for the administration in Congress. A series of events required the change as Lend-Lease naturally expanded America's interests deep into the Atlantic Ocean. The United States sought to protect American products being shipped to Great Britain from German submarines. As part of this process, the US military ended up occupying Greenland and Iceland. By September, the US Navy started protecting convoys of ships from America to Iceland, where merchant vessels were turned over to the guardian warships of the British navy. On September 4, an American destroyer, the USS *Greer,* managed to escape damage from a torpedo attack by a submarine. Thus began an undeclared war between the US Navy and the German navy. Opposed by Senators Clark, Tydings, and others, Barkley worked effectively debating for the passage of a bill that, in essence, made the United States a cobelligerent with the British. In November, Majority Secretary Biffle counted senatorial noses and assured Barkley that the measure would secure majority approval. The vote, 50–37, sanctioned the revised neutrality bill on November 7. Prompted by the Senate, six days later the House dramatically passed the Senate bill by an incredible tally that exceeded a two-to-one margin.[33]

Barkley, like many of his contemporaries, recognized that the naval conflict in the Atlantic might evolve into an official war between Germany and the United States. The focus on Europe added to the absolute shock and dismay when, a month after the Senate vote, Japan conducted a surprise aerial assault on Pearl Harbor, the Hawaiian headquarters for the US Navy's Pacific Fleet. The attack sank or disabled nineteen warships, destroyed 152 military aircraft, and killed close to twenty-four hundred servicemen and civilians. Japanese aggression against the United States had its short-term origins in the defeat of Japan by Russia in 1939. The two countries had a brief but fierce war along the border between Soviet Siberia and Japanese-held Manchuria. Japan's defeat prompted Tokyo's heavily militarized government to shift its territorial ambitions away from eastern Siberia toward Southeast Asia. The war in Europe and America's Eurocentric response to the conflict there virtually invited Japan, which had to import almost all its industrial raw materials and energy supplies, to gain these items through colonial lands from countries either defeated by or absorbed with concern over German power. Territories seemingly ripe for the picking included British Malaya and Hong Kong, French Indochina, the Dutch East Indies, and the US islands of Guam, Midway, the Philippines, and Wake.[34]

The first wave of Japanese aircraft attacked Pearl Harbor Sunday morning at 7:50 A.M., which was early afternoon in Washington. Admiral Harold R. Stark, the chief of naval operations, soon began to telephone regularly updated reports to the White House. Grace Tully, the president's secretary, took the calls and typed up the information for the president. Later, Barkley joined cabinet members and congressional leaders at the White House for an evening meeting with Roosevelt. FDR gave the executive group the latest information on the day's horrific events and shared a draft of a short speech that he had dictated to his secretary. He wanted to deliver his request for a declaration of war to Congress as soon as possible. Barkley helped arrange for the joint session that opened the next day at 12:30 P.M. By then, Roosevelt had to add to his speech the fact that Japanese aircraft, ships, or troops had also bombed, shelled, or landed on Guam, Hong Kong, Malaya, Midway, the Philippines, and Wake within hours after the attack on Pearl Harbor. Most famously, his address before Congress began: "Yesterday, December seventh, 1941—a date which will live in infamy—the United States of America was suddenly and deliberately attacked by naval and air forces by the Empire of Japan."[35]

Shortly after the speech, Congress voted for the war resolution. Except for Representative Jeanette Rankin, an avowed pacifist and the first woman to serve in the House, the vote was unanimous. Barkley and biparty leaders of both congressional chambers brought the resolution to the White House.

The majority leader and his colleagues witnessed the president sign the document while press photographers shot pictures. Barkley received one of the pens used to make official the declaration of war against Japan. Because America's now official enemy had also attacked British possessions in Asia, there was no doubt that Parliament would quickly vote for war against the Japanese. By telephone, Churchill and Roosevelt and their aides actually tried, but failed, to synchronize their declarations so that the United States would be the first to complete the process. Three days later, Germany and Italy declared war on the United States. The German note to the US chargé d'affaires in Berlin based the Third Reich's action, not on the alliance with Japan, but on US violations of neutrality. (Despite Japan's membership in the Tripartite Pact, the empire strictly upheld its nonaggression treaty with the Soviet Union.) Regardless, in the space of four days, the United States was suddenly thrust into a global conflict.[36]

14

The Senator in a Time
of Troubles and Triumphs

Winston S. Churchill and his military leaders arrived in the United States on December 22, 1941. It would be Alben W. Barkley who arranged for the prime minister to speak before a joint session of Congress on December 26. The address was memorable as the prime minister spoke eloquently of Anglo-American unity in the face of shared enemies. Conferences between Churchill and Roosevelt and their military staffs lasted until January 14, 1942 and produced three major decisions. First, they drafted a military alliance, the Declaration by the United Nations, signed initially by representatives of twenty-six nations, including China and Soviet Russia, on January 1. Second, the United States and Great Britain created the Anglo-American Combined Chiefs of Staff, which attempted, not always smoothly, to coordinate military activity. Third, the two allies resolved to contain Japan but first defeat Nazi Germany. American naval airpower contained Japanese expansion in the Pacific when Douglas SBD Dauntless dive-bombers sank four Japanese aircraft carriers during the Battle of Midway on June 4, 1942. The beginning of the end for German power occurred over the winter of 1942–1943 when Anglo-American forces took North Africa away from Axis control, going on to invade Italy, and the Soviet Union utterly destroyed the German Sixth Army at Stalingrad.[1]

Meanwhile, Barkley's life—at least in his official role as majority leader—became somewhat easier in wartime. Despite the reduction in numbers of Democratic senators from seventy-six in 1937 to fifty-eight after November 1942, everyone wanted to win the war. Thus, Selective Service Acts (December 1941 and November 1942), War Powers Acts (December 1941 and March 1942), the Emergency Price Control Act (January 1942), and several funding bills for the military passed with ease. Between January 6 and December 16, 1942, in the second session of the Seventy-Seventh Congress, most bills gained approval with less than an hour's debate in the Senate. The conservative trend in Senate and House had little or no effect on war issues. President Roosevelt seemed to have more control over and support from Congress than at any time since the serious strife over the Supreme Court. What had happened to resurrect this positive relationship between the White House and Capitol Hill was the fact that FDR generally abandoned the New Deal. It was quite simple for a conservative coalition of Republicans and Democrats to kill, for example, the Works Progress Administration and the Civilian Conservation Corps. Such job-creating agencies were no longer needed. With millions of men drafted into or volunteering for the military, and with industries operating at full capacity producing war materiel, there was a terrific shortage of workers. Fortunately, women ably filled many factory positions normally reserved for men.[2]

Barkley's work in Congress—at least in 1941 and 1942—generally went so smoothly that he garnered praise from both the president and journalists such as Allen Drury (a United Press correspondent and future novelist) and Arthur Krock (a *New York Times* writer and political analyst). Unfortunately, the majority leader's personal affairs took a turn for the worse as the war progressed. Dorothy Barkley survived a heart attack in 1942, but the doctor gave her a maximum of two years to live. She continued to suffer shortness of breath, fatigue, and chest discomfort. Modern invasive procedures to address the problem did not exist until years later. At the time, the best hope for life to continue was a quiet existence with rest and a diet filled with salads. Obviously, she needed to avoid climbing stairs in their multistory residence. Logically, the Barkleys sold their Washington home on Cleveland and moved to an apartment at 2101 Connecticut Avenue. Over time, Dorothy became a complete invalid and required three years of round-the-clock nursing care. The additional medical expenses took all of Alben's salary; he had to seek paid speaking engagements evenings, weekends, and during breaks between congressional sessions to pay all the bills. He amazed the *New York Times* journalist William S. White because he could deliver an impressive off-the-cuff speech on the Senate floor "after flying in at three o'clock in the morning red-eyed from some dreary lecture."[3]

In the midst of these doleful circumstances, and at a time Barkley was busy supplementing via speeches his annual salary of $10,000 and chairing a special Senate committee, his mother, Electa, died on December 22,

1945. She was eighty-nine and had outlived her older husband, John, who had passed away thirteen years earlier at age seventy-eight. President Harry S. Truman out of caring respect for the majority leader loaned him the White House plane, *Sacred Cow,* and its crew of five to fly him from Washington to the Paducah-McCracken Municipal Airport to attend the funeral. He was the only passenger on the large, four-engine aircraft. Less than a year later, Barkley's wife suffered a stroke and never rallied. Near the end of February 1947, she lapsed into a coma and died ten days later on March 9; Alben and his eldest daughter, Marian Truitt, were at her bedside in her last moments. At that time, Laura MacArthur was in Paris, France, with her diplomat husband, and the Barkleys' son, David, was in Kentucky taking care of the Angles farm. Despite her husband's lengthy ties with the Methodist Church, Dorothy always kept an active, if often a long-distance, membership in Paducah's First Christian Church, where the Barkley family attended funeral services on March 12. Burial occurred at the Mt. Kenton Cemetery. Subsequently, Barkley, who had been Dorothy's guardian angel in her final years, donated money to advance the treatment of heart disease to what is today the University of Louisville School of Medicine.[4]

Despite these very personal trials and the special circumstances of war, Barkley still generally provided excellent leadership over the steady operation of a productive Senate. At the same time, he kept the goodwill and respect of most colleagues on both sides of the aisle. This is not to suggest that conflicts and problems disappeared in the chamber or that Barkley always agreed with and supported the president. For example, in the spring of 1942, as the federal government through the Office of Price Administration began to set up a gas-rationing-card system, a proposal was introduced in the Senate that would prohibit senators from acquiring X-Cards, which allowed holders to purchase gasoline without restrictions for their automobiles. The proposed bill infuriated Barkley, who chose to uphold the dignity of the chamber and the ethics of its members. "Our constituents," he bellowed sarcastically, "ought to send some honest men here if we cannot be trusted to buy only the gasoline we need in the performance of our duties." The next day the Senate aligned itself, Republicans and Democrats, with Barkley and defeated the proposal on May 15 by a nearly unanimous vote.[5]

By contrast, an event later in 1942 went very much against Barkley. On November 13, he brought before the Senate an anti–poll tax measure recently approved by the chamber's Judiciary Committee. The bill would eliminate poll taxes from all elections for federal office. The levies disenfranchised impoverished African Americans and poor whites in Alabama, Georgia, Louisiana, Mississippi, South Carolina, Tennessee, Texas, and Virginia. Immediately, to prevent the bill's passage senators from southern states initiated a filibuster that lasted until November 23. On that date, Barkley had had enough and moved to impose cloture on the filibuster. Senate rules at that time required a two-thirds vote to end debate (today it is sixty out of one hundred votes). While a majority supported the motion, their forty-one votes to the opponents' thirty-seven failed to achieve the needed supermajority. Barkley had to shelve the anti–poll tax bill in order to proceed with wartime legislation. In the process, he directed some comments at southern Democrats. He felt that repeal of poll taxes must occur if the basis of the Democratic Party, founded by the Virginian Thomas Jefferson, were to be upheld. The party, he argued, "has lived because it served the cause of the common man, and if its members now believe it can be kept alive only by taxing the right of humble men to vote, its future is dim."[6]

The poll tax controversy in wartime resurrected the ugly division among Democratic senators over race and region that had bubbled to the surface during the Supreme Court dispute. It points to the fact that the Roosevelt administration served as the beginning of the amazing transposition that altered American politics in the space of several decades. Most African Americans who had been Republicans from the time of President Abraham Lincoln would switch to the Democratic Party; a majority of southern whites who had been diehard Democrats would join the GOP. After Barkley's death, two compelling issues promoted this change: segregation versus integration and states' rights versus federal governance. Meanwhile, in the 1940s, Barkley had to deal with the developing split among Democrats, several of whom continued to have misgivings about the president and the depth of federal intervention in domestic affairs. These were the ones who subtly criticized Barkley as a "White House gift"—a majority leader who felt that his first priority was to facilitate the Senate's approval of the president's program.[7]

While some of his advisers believed that Barkley should be more assertive and demanding and not so convivial and easygoing with senators on both sides of the aisle, Roosevelt genuinely appreciated the majority leader's earnest and steadfast support of the administration. After all, there had to be times when Barkley needed votes from both political parties. The Iron Man continued to meet with FDR on Mondays during congressional sessions. Clearly, the pair had become, not social buddies, but good working friends. Over the winter of 1942–1943, a Supreme Court vacancy prompted several senators to recommend Barkley for the justice position. As an expression of his high regard for the Kentucky senator, Roosevelt carefully considered him as a candidate. On January 8, 1943, he sent Barkley a kind and forthright explanation for why he chose someone else to be the justice nominee:

> Dear Alben:
> I do not know whether you will be disappointed or not in the Supreme Court matter. Personally, I would not be. I had really thought a lot about sending your name up but two things happened. First of all, there was no question that your ability, learning and liberality fitted you in every way for the Court. The other consideration, however, tore me apart because of the fact that you are such a very old and close friend of mine.
> It related to the fact that the country really needs you just where you are—a good, hard-hitting, yet just, leader of democracy—democracy both with a large "d" and a small "d." You are a sort of balance wheel that has kept things moving forward all these years—and that's that. I had to come to the conclusion that there are nine Justices but only one Majority Leader in the Senate—and I can't part with him in that capacity.
> Affectionately,
> Franklin D. Roosevelt[8]

This is not to say Barkley followed so closely the president in friendship that he never thought to criticize the administration. Quite the contrary, on February 11, 1943, he joined Senator Truman in speaking out against the policies of the War Production Board (WPB). Truman headed the Senate Special Committee to Investigate the National Defense Program. As it was popularly known, the Truman Committee has been recognized by various commentators as one of the most successful, objective, and respected investigative committees in congressional history. It is not too far-fetched to claim that the committee was one of the main reasons Truman ended up on the second spot of the Democratic presidential ticket in 1944. He and his group guarded the costs, quality, and effectiveness of war materiel bought with taxpayers' money for national defense. Barkley and Truman spoke against the WPB's failure to cooperate with the Smaller War Plants Corporation (SWPC). Congress had intended that an equitable share of military contracts would go to smaller companies. Most contracts, however, had been offered to America's one hundred largest corporations. Thus, Barkley and Truman worked together to pressure the WPB to work consistently with the SWPC in awarding government orders for military supplies.[9]

Barkley balanced this limited criticism a few weeks later with effusive praise for President Roosevelt. His prepared speech marked and celebrated "a decade of achievement" since FDR's first inauguration. The "delivery" of Barkley's lengthy "address," however, seemed to expose a characteristic behavior of the Senate during much of World War II. Because senators had eagerly jumped, with some variations, on the war wagon, they logically handed the president enormous powers to lead the country to victory by directing the nation's productivity to meet the needs of a valiant and massive citizen-military. The Senate thus played second fiddle to the chief executive's virtuosity. This backseat role resulted in a degree of apathy and culminated in attendance problems. More than once, Barkley had to ask the sergeant at arms to gather enough senators to make a quorum when the Senate met as a committee of the whole. Not surprisingly, then, the address in question was simply hand-delivered to the offices of the *Congressional Record* for publication rather than being actually presented on the Senate floor before a relatively empty chamber.[10]

As discussed above, the war distorted not only the behavior but especially the voting of senators as it tended to hide the chamber's serious divisions. These features merged with background events to defeat Barkley's effort to sustain Roosevelt's June 11 veto of an antistrike, antiunion bill sponsored by Senator Connally and Representative Howard W. Smith of Virginia. Both southern Democrats opposed urban colleagues who sought to strengthen unions. The legislation made it illegal for unions to strike war industries as it enhanced presidential powers to seize plants threatened by strikes, required unions, at companies not essential to the war, to observe a thirty-day cooling-off period before calling a strike, and outlawed monetary contributions by unions to political candidates and campaign organizations. It had its origins in 1942 when Congress deliberated the second War Powers Act. Barkley, whose political base in Kentucky consisted of farmers and workers, deplored the antiunion nature of the bill and managed to use his position to first delay and then postpone its consideration.[11]

The background event that gave new life to the Smith-Connally antistrike bill erupted in a major national walkout that began in the spring of

1943. John L. Lewis, the head of the United Mine Workers' Union, led the work stoppage to raise the hourly wage for miners. But note the three distinct reasons why the Senate (and the House) voted on June 25, 1943, to override FDR's veto. The combination simply made it impossible for Barkley to sustain the president's action. First and foremost, senators understood that coal literally kept America in the war. Electricity powered war industries, and most generating plants used coal as the heat source to move fluids through turbines that mechanically produced the current. Coal distilled via heat into coke also became the heat source used to convert iron ore into steel through the Bessemer process. The latter was the foundation product for heavy ordnance and most land and sea machines of war. Second, regional differences between urban and rural members of Congress normally found senators from rural states against unions. Finally, a number of senators and representatives from both political parties disliked Roosevelt either for personal (Democrats) or for political (Republicans) reasons. These individuals supported the United States in war but took every available occasion to vote against the president. The antiunion bill worked perfectly to uphold the American military and defeat the chief executive.[12]

Unlike the antiunion legislation, most bills were cut-and-dried, with the possible exception of those connected with funding the war. There was, however, another war-related problem that absorbed Barkley's attention—the fate of European Jews within the areas occupied by the Third Reich. The majority leader had taken a special interest in Jewish history as a young man when he attended Sunday school at the Methodist Church. He renewed this interest in the 1930s when he and Dorothy visited British-controlled Palestine. He also maintained a special friendship with his fellow Kentuckian Louis D. Brandeis, the first Jew to sit as an associate justice on the Supreme Court. Small wonder that he received and gladly accepted invitations to address dozens of Jewish groups. Even before the United States exchanged war proclamations with Nazi Germany, he had become an early advocate in America of implementing the famous 1917 Balfour Declaration made by British foreign secretary Arthur J. Balfour that Palestine should become a Jewish homeland. As a member of the American Palestine Committee, Barkley spoke in favor of the Jewish homeland before a gathering of thirty-five hundred Zionists in Carnegie Hall on November 1, 1941, the twenty-fourth anniversary of the declaration. Dr. Stephen S. Wise, the chairman of the Emergency Committee for Zionist Affairs, had convoked the meeting.[13]

By 1943, various sources, including information collected by the US

legation in neutral Switzerland, made clear that the stridently anti-Semitic
Nazi government of Germany had in 1942 moved from unrelentingly mis-
treating Jews to barbaric genocide. Naturally, a number of groups and individuals hoped that Roosevelt and Churchill would order the bombing of the
death camps, but what targets could bombardiers aim for to avoid the collateral deaths of Jews? Postwar study of US bombing sites revealed that targets were missed by a thousand or more feet 70 percent of the time. Wisely,
the Anglo-American leaders wanted to save Jewish lives by winning the war
as quickly as possible. Nevertheless, on March 5, 1943, Barkley introduced a
resolution in the Senate calling for the punishment of those guilty of atroci-
ties against Jews. By the end of the year, he worked with a group of senators
led by Guy Gillette in sponsoring a resolution that called for a government
rescue agency for Jews. This proposal, along with pressure from Treasury
secretary Henry Morgenthau Jr., resulted in Roosevelt issuing an executive
order on January 22, 1944, creating the War Refugee Board. Before the end
of the war in Europe, the board managed through various and sometimes
intriguing ways to save the lives of about 200,000 Jews. The order's pream-
ble stated: "It is the policy of this Government to take all measures within
its power to rescue the victims of enemy oppression who are in imminent
danger of death and otherwise to afford such victims all possible relief and
assistance consistent with the successful prosecution of the war."[14]

Many congressional members applauded the formation of the WRB
as well as the work of the president's War Relief Control Board. The latter had co-opted the National Refugee Service to help those who escaped
Nazi persecution find a haven in the United States. But, even when it came
to these benign agencies, there were members of Congress who held anti-
Semitic views and/or resented any potential opening of US doors to immigrants beyond the numbers specified in the highly restrictive Immigration
Act of 1924. In short, these apparently humane endeavors worried just that
many more members of Congress who were already divided over Roosevelt
and the enormous powers he held because of the war. The president did not
help matters during his State of the Union message delivered on January
11, 1944. There was, however, at least some good news. The allies who had
signed the Declaration by the United Nations were clearly winning the conflict with Japan and Germany and the associated small powers of Bulgaria,
Finland, Hungary, Romania, and Slovakia. Italy switched sides in October
1943, but German troops contested US and British forces for control of the
country.[15]

Accompanying the good news about the war was the bad form demon-strated by Roosevelt in assailing the "noisy minority" members of Congress for their "bickering and self-seeking partisanship." FDR centered so much of his attention on the global conflict that he neglected to notice the needs and complaints of representatives who prepared money bills and the sena-tors who revised and approved them. At the time of the State of the Union, he had placed before Congress a request for a sharp increase of $10.5 bil-lion in taxes to help pay for domestic expenses and the war. But Congress had already taken several steps to increase revenue, including an expanded taxpayer base and the creation of withholding taxes. What Roosevelt for-got to consider was the fact that in 1944 all House members were up for reelection, as were one-third of the senators. Vulnerable politicians did not want to face constituents who were unhappy or angry over the issue of such a dramatic rise in taxes. The president, however, felt that it was imperative for the federal government to dampen inflation through taxation. Also, in his speech, he employed a softer, family-oriented argument that the increase would "reduce the ultimate cost [debt] of war to our sons and daughters," and, thus, he could state that his revenue request was for "a realistic tax law." Congress subsequently did approve a conference committee report reconcil-ing House and Senate versions of a tax bill. The final bill, however, passed by the legislative body on February 7, 1944, raised only $2.3 billion—a sum a little over one-fourth of the amount requested by the president.[16]

It is important to note that Barkley, a member of the Finance Commit-tee, helped frame the Senate version of the tax bill. While he was not happy with the radical cut, he had signed the final conference committee report that both chambers approved. Unlike Roosevelt, he understood perfectly why his colleagues supported legislation that lopped off nearly 75 percent of the tax revenue requested by the president. On the Monday mornings of February 14 and 21, Barkley joined House speaker Rayburn, House major-ity leader McCormack, and Vice President/Senate president Wallace for their regular meeting with Roosevelt in his White House bedroom. FDR obviously wanted his initial proposal for $10.5 billion fulfilled; he was fol-lowing the recommendations of his advisers, especially those from the Trea-sury Department. Wallace kept quiet, but the three legislators urged the president to sign the bill into law. If he vetoed it, there might not be enough votes to override, and the result would be no new tax revenue at all. As it turned out on both occasions, the meetings became a dialogue between Barkley and Roosevelt. The first one remained pleasant, though no agreement was reached. By the second meeting, Roosevelt indicated that he had made up his mind to veto the legislation. Barkley argued persistently against this course of action but to no avail. Before leaving, he stated that he would be compelled to speak against the president's action in the Senate.[17]

Barkley left the meeting with Vice President Wallace and in a depressed mood that was unusual for the majority leader. He had no idea how he might respond in the Senate to the veto. When it formally arrived at the House the next day with a notifying message to the Senate, the tone and arguments Roosevelt used in explaining the veto shocked Barkley. FDR attacked Congress for an assortment of tax problems. He employed cute passages and glib phrases to chastise the legislative body for approving what he considered to be a shortsighted bill. For instance, he stated: "Having asked the Congress for a loaf of bread to take care of this war for the sake of this and succeeding generations, I should be content with a small piece of crust." The most memorable, if not notorious, flip comment that FDR inserted in his message was the following: "It is not a tax bill but a tax-relief bill providing relief not for the needy but for the greedy." Roosevelt actually authored the latter. Most of the rest of the speech was written by Benjamin V. "Ben" Cohen, an original member of the New Deal Brain Trust. Cohen was supervised by James F. "Jimmy" Byrnes, then the head of the Office of Economic Stabilization and often referred to as Roosevelt's assistant president.[18]

That evening, after consulting with his invalid wife, Barkley spent a sleepless night preparing a speech in response to Roosevelt's insolent comments. It proved to be not only his declaration of independence from the White House but also possibly a life-changing event that altered his career and American history. On Wednesday, February 23, accompanied by Democratic secretary Biffle, he entered the Senate chamber for the session that began at noon. Senate president Wallace recognized him, and he then spent forty-five minutes on the floor delivering a speech that shredded every point the president made in his veto message. Near the end of his protest of Roosevelt's veto, he declared:

> I thank Heaven that my future happiness does not depend upon whether I shall retain the post of majority leader of the Senate for another hour. As proof of that, Mr. President [Wallace], and in confirmation of this statement, I have called a conference of the Democratic majority for 10:30 o'clock tomorrow morning in the conference room of the Senate Office Building, at which time my

resignation will be tendered and my services terminated in the post which I now hold at this desk. . . .

Mr. President [Wallace], let me say, in conclusion, that if the Congress of the United States has any self-respect yet left it will override the veto of the President and enact this tax bill into law, his objections to the contrary notwithstanding. [Prolonged applause on the Senate floor, senators rising.][19]

Roosevelt, who was then out of Washington, heard about Barkley's speech in detail. He sent a telegram later that day to the White House with a message for Barkley. He asked his assistant, Stephen T. "Steve" Early, to hand-deliver the telegram to the majority leader's apartment. In his telegram, FDR claimed that he did not intend to attack members of Congress. Moreover, he hoped that, if Barkley resigned, his colleagues would not accept his resignation or would reelect him. Roosevelt ended his telegram: "Certainly your differing with me does not affect my confidence in your leadership nor in any degree lessen my respect and affection for you personally." The next day, after he resigned and Democratic senators unanimously reelected him as their majority leader, Barkley prepared a letter for the president. In his pleasant response, he generously noted, among other issues, "that sometimes language in a written document carries with it connotations not intended by the writer." (He knew, of course, that Roosevelt had not written most of the message.) He kindly mentioned that his and the president's "personal and official relations" were "a source of infinite pride." He concluded: "I fervently trust that this incident may be instrumental in bringing the Executive and Legislative Departments closer together in fullest cooperation to the end that we may win this terrible war at the earliest possible moment."[20]

Barkley's speech against the veto and recommendation for the Senate to override it were just as important as the assurance that Democratic senators demonstrated in his leadership via their unanimous vote. On Friday, the House (292–95) and Senate (72–14) voted the war revenue bill into law. There is little doubt that Barkley's address had an impact on both congressional chambers. The day before, Democratic secretary Biffle's nose count revealed that the Senate, and hence Congress, would not override the veto. Obviously, the other result of the speech and reelection was Barkley's relationship with Roosevelt. No one could now claim that the Kentucky senator held the majority leader position as a mere cipher of the president.

Indeed, for the next several months, there were only two legislative meetings between the two men. When they did see each other, Barkley observed an "intangible reserve" on the part of the president. Like a number of insiders, he knew about Roosevelt's tendency to hold grudges against those who crossed him.[21]

While he would not admit it publicly, Barkley did make an effort to reestablish good relations with Roosevelt. One example occurred in the spring when he wrote an article, "Why I Support Roosevelt," for *Collier's,* a high-circulation magazine of the period. The piece promoted and anticipated FDR's nomination for a fourth term during the July Democratic national convention in Chicago. By the same token, Barkley eagerly accepted the invitation from Robert E. "Bob" Hannegan, who chaired the party's national committee, to nominate Roosevelt as head of the party's national ticket in the upcoming election. In his nominating speech on July 20, 1944, he endorsed Roosevelt with high praise by comparing his attributes with Thomas Jefferson's intellect, Andrew Jackson's courage, Abraham Lincoln's patience, Grover Cleveland's integrity, and Woodrow Wilson's vision. In the time leading up to and including this speech, the Senate leader appeared to have had an agenda concerning the vice presidency. A large number of conservative Democrats let Roosevelt know that they opposed Wallace returning to the second spot on the November ballot. Because Barkley was the new hero who had foiled FDR's tax proposal, his name cropped up more and more before the convention as a viable candidate for the vice president post.[22]

The key, of course, was whom did Roosevelt want as a running mate? In short, who could best help him win reelection? Normally, convention delegates automatically picked for vice president the person designated by the presidential nominee. But this was a problem for FDR. He wanted to keep Wallace, who, unfortunately from the president's standpoint, attracted major opposition from southern delegates owing to his strong support for racial equality. At this point, Roosevelt focused his limited time and energy on winning the war and preparing for peace; he had no need or desire to engage in a political battle on the convention floor. Heavy media presence guaranteed that the nation's attention would be drawn to such an internal clash. And the fight would only delight Republicans and alert voters to the deep division that weakened the Democratic Party. At first, the president pursued and then abandoned a solution that would have allowed a wide-open selection process, but that would also likely have highlighted sectional issues. Logically, he needed a border state individual who was favored by or who at least would satisfy most delegates. Barkley fit that description perfectly. Roosevelt, however, literally struck his name from the short list of potential vice presidential candidates during an evening meeting with advisers on July 11.[23]

Roosevelt told his advisers that, at age sixty-six, Barkley was simply too old. The comment was prompted by the fact that, at their convention, the Republicans had just selected New York governor Thomas E. Dewey as their presidential candidate; Dewey was only forty-two, and his running mate was the fifty-one-year-old Ohio governor John W. Bricker. FDR expressed concern that age might be a campaign issue. On the other hand, Eleanor Roosevelt had to admit that, at least then, her husband looked healthy and vigorous. (He was neither.) Moreover, the sixty-two-year-old president ended up picking a sixty-year-old running mate. This seems to suggest that his criticism of Barkley's age was nothing but a toss-away comment. Additionally, his thank-you telegram to Barkley, after his favorable nomination speech, appeared to capture the president's "intangible reserve" toward "his" majority leader. The sixteen-word message, minus any indication of warmth, fondness, or camaraderie, ended: "It made me very happy. Franklin D. Roosevelt." The message must have given the Kentucky senator frostbite when he opened the envelope.[24]

Could it be that Roosevelt crossed Barkley's name off the vice presidential list because the majority leader had crossed him? Regardless, on July 19, one day before Barkley's convention speech, FDR handed party chairman Hannegan a note showing his preference for Truman or the Supreme Court associate justice William O. Douglas. Truman, like Barkley, fit the bill. The Missouri senator was well liked by delegates from both sections of the country and had received plaudits in the media across the nation for his committee's rigorous oversight of military spending. As importantly, he resembled Barkley in being a scrappy and energetic campaigner out on the hustings. Considering Roosevelt's concentration on the war and his physical and health conditions, he needed the second spot on the ticket filled by someone eager to do the widespread public appearances necessary to win the election. Through loyal contacts, FDR communicated his strong preference for the senator to several political bosses and delegation leaders on the convention floor. Truman won the party's nomination on the second ballot. While hard evidence does not exist, there is a strong possibility that Barkley's role in the tax revenue episode prevented him from inheriting the White House after Roosevelt died in April 1945.[25]

Once the convention ended, Barkley had to begin his own campaign for reelection. He faced six candidates in the August Democratic primary but won easily against an opposition composed of individuals with few credentials or holding little public esteem. He had to be a bit more concerned about his Republican adversary in the November election. The previous year, the GOP regained the commonwealth's governorship with a victory by Simeon Willis. On the surface, it appeared that Democratic dominance over Kentucky politics might be on the wane. While Willis had served with distinction on the court of appeals, he had, according to the Kentucky historian Lowell H. Harrison, faced a relatively weak Democratic opponent. By contrast, in 1944 Barkley squared off against a highly respected Lexington attorney, James Park. As a result, he took seriously the campaign not only for himself but also for President Roosevelt. He began his personal appearances and addresses on September 30. Typical of his speeches was the one delivered in Glasgow (Barren County). He compared the Republican and Democratic responses to the Great Depression and used that as the basis for arguing that the Democrats would be better than the Republicans in terms of winning the war and restoring the peace.[26]

The Iron Man blanketed the state, delivering over seventy major speeches, and conducting numerous other appearances. His campaign ended with a motorcade through the First District right before the November 7 election. The vigorous effort he displayed was rewarded with a victory of nearly 55 percent of the vote—slightly better than that of the president. The level of Barkley's energy caught the attention of Capitol Hill. Vice President/Senate president Wallace sent the majority leader a letter of congratulations that stated in part: "They tell me you did one of the most remarkable jobs of campaigning ever seen in the State of Kentucky. The way in which you threw yourself into this campaign is a great encouragement to 'tired old men.'" And Roosevelt easily won his fourth term. While his popular vote was "only" a respectable 53 percent, he won enough states that he gained an incredible Electoral College majority of 432 votes to Dewey's 99. The election successes of both men coincided with an improvement in their relationship. In December, Barkley had to visit the Naval Medical Center at Bethesda, Maryland, to get treated for a cornea ulcer in his left eye. FDR sent Barkley another telegram. This time he concluded his message: "Take care of yourself. Affectionate regards. Franklin D. Roosevelt."[27]

Later the following month, Barkley had to return to the Naval Medical Center. The distance of time makes it difficult to speculate about procedures and treatments for the eye problem. What is known is that Barkley briefly had to wear a patch over his left eye, prompting colleagues to jokingly compare him with characters from the past such as Blackbeard (Edward Teach) and Dead Eye Dick (Richard W. Clarke). Before this new addition to his daily wardrobe, Democratic senators had unanimously reelected him majority leader on January 5, 1945, shortly after the Seventy-Ninth Congress opened. Unfortunately, at the very moment near the end of January when he was receiving medical treatment, he had to work his way around a controversy. Troubled by his decision to back Truman for the vice presidency, Roosevelt asked Wallace to name the consolation position he wanted in his fourth administration. Wallace chose the Commerce Department. There were two serious obstacles to Senate approval of this appointment. A competent Jesse H. Jones headed the department, and a number of senators did not want him removed. And, of course, southern Democrats disliked Wallace because he opposed racial segregation.[28]

On January 26, 1945, by a vote of 14–5, the Commerce Committee rejected Wallace's nomination as commerce secretary. An early ballot by the full Senate would only confirm the Commerce Committee's decision. With the help of Vice President/Senate president Truman, who met with Barkley before each daily session of the Senate, the majority leader delayed a vote on Wallace. In essence, he juggled the schedule of bills by moving ahead of the Wallace appointment a popular resolution sponsored by Senator George. The George bill (S. 375) would remove loaning agencies, including the Reconstruction Finance Corporation, from the purview of the Commerce Department. Barkley then negotiated a compromise between Democratic senators and President Roosevelt, who opposed the bill. Through long-distance communication (FDR was on his way to Yalta for what proved to be his last wartime conference with Churchill and Stalin), he got the president to change his mind about the bill. He would forgo a veto in exchange for a favorable Senate vote on Wallace. The compromise worked. After his return from the Soviet Union, Roosevelt signed the George bill into law on February 28; the next day, the Senate confirmed Wallace as commerce secretary by a vote of 56–32.[29]

The day, March 1, that Wallace became commerce secretary, Roosevelt delivered his report on the Yalta Conference to a joint session of Congress. He chose to come personally rather than send a typed copy or have the message read by a surrogate to a small handful of representatives and senators who might show up. The president had an agenda beyond the substance of his speech. He wanted to squelch the rumors about his bad health that emerged from pictures and newsreels taken of him during the meeting in Crimea. Beyond Congress, the president's words went to a national radio audience, and newsreels of his performance were later viewed by millions of Americans at local movie theaters. Unfortunately for Roosevelt, his voice and image only confirmed the rumors. This was a rare moment, the first for Congress, when the president did not hide the effects of his struggle with polio. He entered the House chamber in a wheelchair and sat for the nearly hour-long speech; beforehand, he even apologized for not standing because of the ten pounds of steel that braced his legs. The journalist John H. Crider, who covered the event for the *New York Times,* remarked that Roosevelt had an uneven delivery as he lost his place several times in reading the text. "Members of Congress," the newsman reported, "[had] noted that he was grayer, thinner and considerably aged since he last appeared in the House two years ago."[30]

Indeed, in the days following his Yalta speech, Roosevelt spent too much time on tasks in his effort to catch up with the work he had missed during his lengthy absence. His leisurely trip to the Soviet Union began on January 20, and he returned late in February. The extra chores he engaged in caused him to experience alarming blood pressure swings, continuing weight loss, and nagging fatigue. Before the end of March he was forced to go home to Hyde Park and then spend time at Warm Springs, Georgia, for rest and recuperation. By then, the Secret Service had been alerted and had assigned bodyguards to protect Vice President Truman. (Harry took pleasure in successfully eluding them.) The situation appeared so grim to insiders that Barkley told Truman he wondered whether Roosevelt would return to Washington alive. His concern was correct. FDR was pronounced dead by his doctor at 3:35 P.M. local time (4:35 in Washington) on April 12. Shortly before 5:00 on Capitol Hill, Barkley moved for the Senate to recess for the day. Truman came down from the dais and left the chamber for Speaker Rayburn's office, where he and several friends would unwind with mixed drinks.[31]

An aide in the vice president's office had called Rayburn with an urgent message for Truman to call Steve Early. When he did, Early told Truman that he had to come to the White House immediately and without telling anybody. There, Truman learned that the president had died (of a cerebral hemorrhage). Staff contacted government officials and Chief Justice Harlan Stone for the oath of office ceremony to be held at seven o'clock in the Cabinet Room. Truman asked for congressional leaders to attend by calling

Leslie Biffle. He also called his wife and daughter, Bess and Margaret, who came and witnessed him being sworn in as the thirty-third president of the United States. Barkley and Senator Connally had gone to the White House and Eleanor Roosevelt's study as soon as they heard about her husband's death. Instead of going to the Cabinet Room for the ceremony, the two senators chose to stay and console the widow as she prepared for her evening flight by government plane to Warm Springs.[32]

President Truman continued the practice of having meetings when needed with Barkley and the other congressional leaders. They were held, not in a White House bedroom, but in the mansion's executive offices. The only change in the close relationship between Barkley and Truman was that Alben told Harry to stop calling him "boss." The former senator, not the majority leader, was now the presidential boss. Naturally, because of Truman's years in the Senate and his brief role as the president of the upper chamber, everyone expected good relations between 1600 Pennsylvania Avenue and Capitol Hill. The new president, however, was humble and deprecated his ability to match Roosevelt. In his first meeting with President Truman, Barkley told him: "Have confidence in yourself. If you do not, the people will lose confidence in you." The majority leader decided to reinforce his advice. On April 19, Barkley asked Democratic senators in a party conference to join him in preparing a resolution expressing confidence in Truman's leadership.[33]

A few days later, Barkley chaired a bipartisan committee of a dozen House and Senate members that flew to Europe. The military commander for Western Europe, General of the Army Dwight D. Eisenhower, asked for a congressional group to visit several German death camps recently liberated by Allied forces. He felt that the almost indescribable conditions had to be witnessed by civilians and their findings sent to the upcoming meeting in San Francisco for the establishment of a permanent international organization to promote peace by signatories to the Declaration by the United Nations. Barkley and the American delegation, which included journalists and publishers, visited Buchenwald, Nordhausen, and Dachau. Only seven days after war in Europe ended on May 8, 1945, Barkley delivered his committee's shocking report to the Senate as Representative R. Ewing Thomson (D-TX) did the same in the House. All members, Republicans and Democrats, signed the Barkley-written eyewitness account, which concluded that the Nazi extermination of individuals represented a horrifying crime against humanity.[34]

A grim, absolute silence reigned during Barkley's presentation. Since the meeting that formed the United Nations lasted from April 25 to June 26, delegates did have access to Barkley's report. It served as one small part of the broader background leading to the Nuremberg war crimes trials. The latter, however, took place, not because of the United Nations, but because of decisions reached by the main Allied countries during the Potsdam Conference from July 17 to August 2. It was Truman's first and only meeting with Stalin. A lesson in democracy occurred when, in the midst of Potsdam, British elections led to the newly minted prime minister, Clement R. Attlee, replacing Churchill. Not long before Truman flew to Europe for this last wartime meeting of what he called the "big three" (Japan had not yet surrendered), he sent Barkley a personal message on July 5 to do everything he could to get the Bretton Woods legislation passed quickly. He felt that, if the United States became the first significant power to approve the measure, it would strengthen his hand at Potsdam as well as the nation's international position.[35]

At Bretton Woods, New Hampshire, in the summer of 1944, forty-four nations agreed to an Anglo-American proposal creating the International Bank for Reconstruction and Development (the World Bank) and the International Monetary Fund. These financial institutions were intended originally to promote peace and revive infrastructure as a counter to the massive disruption and destruction caused by war. Among other provisions the agreement would stabilize international exchange rates and peg national currencies to the US dollar. Obviously, the United States had become the center of world finance. Because the Bretton Woods Agreement was not a treaty and involved funding, both chambers of Congress had to approve it. The initial US commitment involved several billion dollars. In the Senate, the fight for passage (July 12–19, 1945) was headed by Barkley and Senator Wagner, who chaired the Banking and Currency Committee. Residual isolationists led by Senator Robert A. Taft (OH) tried to kill the bill through postponement. Their motion failed on July 18; the next day the Senate voted 61–16 in favor of the legislation. Barkley delighted Truman by fulfilling his request. Officially, the president signed the Bretton Woods Agreement into law on July 31 during the Potsdam Conference.[36]

Successful passage of the Bretton Woods Agreement paved the way for Senate consideration of the UN Charter prepared in San Francisco the previous month. During five days of debate that started on Monday, July 23, Barkley delivered a major address on Tuesday. He defended the charter and

US membership. Like other contemporaries, the Wilsonian majority leader deeply regretted the Senate's failure to approve the Treaty of Versailles. In his heart, but not in his speech, he shared a notion held by a number of contemporaries that US membership in the League might have altered history and prevented the Second World War. But he did state: "It is not my purpose or my province, nor would I think it useful to this discussion, to undertake to assess the blame on either side for the failure of the United States to ratify the Treaty of Versailles and the Covenant of the League of Nations. We can profit by the mistakes of that day only if we seek to avoid them now." He pointed out that the measure had attracted bipartisan support. It was actually introduced to the Senate by Connally, who led the Foreign Relations Committee, and by one of its Republican members, Arthur H. Vandenberg from Michigan, who became an important GOP internationalist. And most of the fifty-eight senators who spoke on the charter endorsed the bill. On July 28, it passed by the extremely lopsided vote of 89–2.[37]

Shortly before the Senate approved the United Nation's Charter, Barkley's eighth anniversary as majority leader was celebrated by his colleagues from both sides of the aisle along with a message of congratulations from Truman in Potsdam. The president said:

Dear Alben:
     Today marks the eighth anniversary of your service as Majority Leader of the Senate. I understand that this is twice as long as any of your predecessors have served. These years have been eventful ones. They have been years of great moment to the United States and to the world.
     In all of the recent events which have meant so much in shaping the future of our civilization you have played an important and effective role. Not only have you helped to fulfill the ideals and principles of our party, but you have been willing and anxious to lay aside all semblance of partisanship or desire for party advantages whenever the welfare of our nation required it.
     I congratulate you on your past service as Majority Leader, and also on your thirty-three years of service in the Congress. The nation is grateful to you for your patriotic share in the accomplishments of these years, and I know that the years to come will be equally fruitful.

With all best wishes for your continued health and success from your old friend,
Very sincerely yours,
Harry S. Truman[38]

15

The Iron Man Becomes a Veep

World War II finally ended with the surrender of Japan as announced in a recorded message on radio by Emperor Hirohito at noon local time on August 15, 1945. Unlike Germany, which succumbed to Allied ground forces supported by airpower, Japan's four home islands did not experience a combat invasion by US troops. Instead, they faced isolation from the larger empire thanks to the US Navy and Marines. Thus, Japan's surviving military industries were literally in the process of dying out from the lack of vital raw materials for fuels and metals. Japan also suffered utter devastation from the US Army Air Force bombing of factories and military installations and the destruction of sixty cities before the employment of atomic devices to do the identical thing to Hiroshima and Nagasaki. The use of standard bombs on Tokyo actually proved to be more destructive but not as infamous. For Alben W. Barkley, however, the war did not end in August 1945; it simply collapsed back in time to December 1941. As the majority leader worked to restore America's peacetime economy, aid allies in their recovery from war, contain the Soviet Union in the developing Cold War, and deliver speeches for money to keep his wife alive, the Iron Man, despite his age, possessed enough strength and stamina to take on another major task. On September 6, the Senate approved his resolution to chair and establish a joint congressional committee to investigate the Pearl Harbor catastrophe.[1]

The catalyst for this step erupted into sensational newspaper headlines on August 30. The previous day the US Army and Navy had released for publication reports on the military interpretation of the Pearl Harbor disaster. Both armed forces placed the blame mainly on several authority figures. The navy pointed its finger at Admiral Husband E. Kimmel, the commander in chief of the Pacific Fleet, and Admiral Harold B. Stark, the chief of naval operations. Similarly, the army criticized Major General Leonard T. Gerow, the chief of the War Plans Division, and Lieutenant General Walter C. Short, the commander of the Hawaiian Department, but also Secretary of State Cordell Hull and Army Chief of Staff and General of the Army (five stars) George C. Marshall. The last two individuals listed as responsible for the disaster simply shocked, among many others, both Barkley and President Truman. Hull received the Nobel Peace Prize for his work during the war; Marshall's outstanding military career and superb wartime leadership placed him in a category that approached the status of Mars, the ancient Greek god of war. At the time of the report, Hull was retired, and Marshall was US ambassador to China.[2]

What also disturbed Barkley and Truman was the fact that some GOP members of Congress wanted to use Hull and Marshall as links to the recently deceased president and, thus, blame Roosevelt for Pearl Harbor. They therefore decided that a rigorous congressional investigation must be made of the December 7 tragedy. Such an effort would, it was hoped, reveal military shortcomings, suggest corrections for the future, and eliminate both the myths and the misconceptions that had emerged about the Japanese attack. Including Barkley as chair, the special joint congressional committee contained five senators and five representatives, six of whom were Democrats and four Republicans. The hearings, which lasted seventy days, began on September 18 and ended with a final report on July 20, 1946. Between these dates the committee heard the testimony of forty-four individuals, recorded over fifty-five hundred pages of testimony, and reviewed over 14,500 printed exhibits. It upset Barkley that the Republican senators Owen Brewster (ME) and Homer Ferguson (MI) inserted partisan politics into the hearings. The committee's Republican counsel, William D. Mitchell, and his entire staff eventually quit after Owen and Ferguson spent four days grilling General Marshall and an entire month on only eight witnesses in a fruitless effort to condemn Franklin D. Roosevelt.[3]

Two other Republicans joined six Democrats in signing the majority report. It ended up as a very meticulous and exhaustive congressional investigation. The Republican counsel to the committee admitted that he had access to all pertinent records and received complete cooperation from all government departments and agencies. The final report became the fountainhead of documents and interviews used by historians writing about the start of World War II for America. Two of the twelve summary statements on responsibilities captured the essence of that part of the conclusion:

4. The committee has found no evidence to support the charges, made before and during the hearings, that the President, the Secretary of State, the Secretary of War, or the Secretary of Navy tricked, provoked, incited, cajoled, or coerced Japan into attacking this Nation in order that a declaration of war might be more easily obtained from the Congress. On the contrary, all evidence conclusively points to the fact that they discharged their responsibilities with distinction, ability, and foresight and in keeping with the highest traditions of our fundamental foreign policy.

7. Virtually everyone was surprised that Japan struck the Fleet at Pearl Harbor at the time she did. Yet officers, both in Washington and Hawaii, were fully conscious of the danger from air attack; they realized this form of attack on Pearl Harbor by Japan was at least a possibility; and they were adequately informed of the imminence of war.[4]

The conclusion also listed twenty-five recommendations based on the narrative found in the body of the report. They explore and explain the answer to the question as to why the Pearl Harbor debacle took place. It occurred despite the fact that the US military in Washington and Hawaii knew that war with Japan seemed likely and that US forces across the Pacific Ocean had been alerted to be prepared for military action. Barkley's committee, then, focused on the deficiencies in organization and administration that existed in the army and navy. For example, given the fact that Japan could attack Pearl Harbor only by sea or with seaborne aircraft, thorough, persistent, and widespread US reconnaissance by sea and air should have occurred. But such determined activity required coordination between army and navy—two organizations that competed with each other on athletic fields and over congressional funds. The US Navy and Army Air Forces each had three bases for military aircraft, but rivalry and separate commands kept them apart. When push came to shove on December 7, 1941, fragmentation of the services added nothing to the possibility of an integrated American aviation response to the Japanese air assault.[5]

Despite the burdens, personal and professional, that Barkley had to carry from September 1945 to July 1946, he did not lose his sense of humor.

With a sigh of relief at the end of the committee's work, he joked: "I feel numb, just as if a fat woman had been sitting on my lap for a year!" While his joint committee busily dug into the tragic causes of the Pearl Harbor attack, he also facilitated the Senate in developing, debating, and approving a bumper crop of important pieces of legislation. These included acts that provided the appointment of representatives to the United Nations, established the President's Council of Economic Advisors, authorized federal matching grants to states and cities for airport construction, assisted states in subsidizing nonprofit school lunch programs, provided a multi-billion-dollar loan to help Great Britain recover from war, created the Fulbright Scholars program, transferred atomic energy development from the military to the civilian Atomic Energy Commission, streamlined congressional standing committees, and required registered lobbyists to report their expenses.[6]

At the close of the last session of the Seventy-Ninth Congress, Democratic senators and President Truman gave a dinner party to honor Barkley at the Raleigh Hotel on July 29. Senators praised the majority leader's patience under the stress and strain of an extremely busy and sometimes contentious congressional session. Truman admitted that he did not know of anyone who could have been more effective than Barkley. The president felt that his administration simply could not have functioned without his help. The next month Barkley flew to Europe and attended a meeting of the Executive Committee of the Inter-Parliamentary Union (IPU) in St. Moritz, Switzerland. The IPU could not meet during the Second World War. Barkley and the other presidents of national delegations met as a group for four days to plan the first postwar IPU gathering, scheduled for 1947. After two weeks in Europe, Barkley flew on September 7 into New York's La Guardia Field at noon and then transferred to another aircraft for a flight to Washington's National Airport. Soon he would prepare to campaign for several congressional Democrats in the upcoming November election.[7]

Indeed, Barkley was a sought-after campaigner who usually enlivened his talks with folksy humor. The Democratic Speaker's Bureau admitted that the majority leader received the most requests for his services. A survey conducted by the widely read magazine *Look* confirmed Barkley's general popularity. He took second place nationwide to General Dwight D. Eisenhower as the country's most fascinating American. But for a variety of reasons the 1946 election proved different. The Iron Man had to cut his campaigning short because his wife took a turn for the worse. Dorothy suffered a stroke in October. Barkley's early removal from the hustings was not the reason explaining the Republican victory in November. GOP slogans, "had enough?" and "to err is Truman," worked well on Americans tired of wartime restrictions, residual rationing, economic inflation, and a paralyzing railroad strike. For the first time since 1931, Republicans controlled both chambers when the Eightieth Congress opened on January 3, 1947. Republicans controlled the house 246–188 and the Senate 51–45.[8]

A few days after the election, one could observe some gray prickly hairs emerging on Barkley's upper lip. To his startled colleagues, the senator explained: "The voters have just said they wanted something different. I'm giving them the mustache." Six weeks later, however, he shaved it off. With a twinkle in his eye, he then commented: "I just found out the people were wrong about wanting change." The *Washington Post* reporter Sam Stavisky found the brief mustache episode prophetic for what would happen at the polls in 1948. During the interim, Minority Leader Barkley had been replaced by Republican senator Wallace H. White from Maine, a quiet figure who held the majority leader post in name only. The Senate's real leader was Robert A. Taft, who chaired the GOP Policy Committee and the Senate Labor and Public Welfare Committee, served as ranking Republican on, but not chair of, the Senate Finance Committee, and led the group that allocated GOP committee assignments. Taft, quite conservative and an avowed isolationist, never earned Barkley's favorable opinion.[9]

In 1946, Taft delivered a speech at Kenyon College attacking the war crimes tribunals in Germany and Japan. The Ohio senator noted that defendants were being tried under an ex post facto statute that would be illegal under American law. This prompted Barkley to respond that Taft "never experienced a crescendo of heart about the soup kitchens of 1932, but his heart bled anguishedly for the criminals at Nuremberg." By contrast, Barkley genuinely appreciated Arthur H. Vandenberg, who embraced Truman's international perspective as Taft undermined the president's domestic policies. The Michigan senator served as the upper chamber's president (there was no US vice president), chaired the Senate Foreign Relations Committee, and shared similar values on foreign affairs with Barkley. The pair, for instance, collaborated in April on a bill to aid Greece and Turkey. The latter helped implement what became known as the Truman Doctrine, one of the centerpieces in containing Soviet expansion in the early phase of the Cold War. Truman presented his concept before a joint session of Congress on March 12, 1947—the same date Barkley attended his wife's funeral in Paducah.[10]

In his memoirs, Truman identified the key phrase in his doctrine. "I believe," he told Congress and his radio audience, "that it must be the policy of the United States to support free peoples who are resisting attempted subjugation by armed minorities or by outside pressure." The statement laid the groundwork for his request from Congress for a bill that would provide $400 million in aid and military assistance to Greece and Turkey. The Greek government fought Communist insurgents who wanted to add the country to the Soviet Russian Empire. At the same time, the Soviet Union pressured and threatened Turkey in order to secure joint control over the straits leading from the Black to the Aegean and Mediterranean Seas. A Communist victory over both countries would give the Soviets an opening to the Middle East and Western Europe. The Truman Doctrine served as a major initial step in the administration's containment policy toward the Soviet Union. Its author hoped to sign a bill by March 31, but the chambers failed to agree on legislation until May 9.[11]

As House and Senate committees began framing the bill at the start of April, Barkley left the country. He presided over the ten-member congressional delegation attending the Cairo, Egypt, conference of the IPU. The official nature of the delegation, coupled with limited airline service to Cairo, prompted use of a transport plane from the US Army Air Forces (the US Air Force after September 1947). It took off for a flight to North Africa from Bermuda on the evening of April 4. During the IPU conference, Barkley delivered an address supporting the United Nations despite criticism from smaller nations over the veto power held by the five permanent countries (China, France, Great Britain, Soviet Russia, and United States) on the UN Security Council. After the conference, the delegation visited Greece and Turkey before reaching Paris on April 15. Barkley and other delegate members announced their unqualified endorsement of President Truman's request for $400 million to aid the two countries the group had just visited. In the French capital, the minority leader had a chance to visit his daughter Laura Louise, her diplomat husband, and Barkley's granddaughter, Mimi. He flew home in time to be one of eight senators speaking in favor of the Greek-Turkish aid bill. It easily passed the Senate on April 22 by a vote of 67–23; the House needed seventeen more days before it also approved the measure.[12]

In the Senate, the Greek-Turkish aid bill was a legislative issue that brought Republicans and Democrats together despite its origin as a request from the Democratic president. Vandenberg, as chair of the Foreign Relations Committee, introduced and sponsored the bill. And the GOP accounted for over half the sixty-seven passing votes. For years afterward, anti-Communist statutes attracted the votes of both parties. Unfortunately, from Barkley's perspective, a majority of Democrats also joined Republicans in approving, 54–17, the Taft-(Fred A.) Hartley (NJ) bill on June 6, 1947. It prohibited closed shops, jurisdictional strikes, secondary boycotts, union contributions to political campaigns, and Communists holding union offices; it also required union public finances and a sixty-day moratorium before a strike could be called against a company operating across state lines. The measure weakened the labor movement as it undermined the New Deal's National Labor Relations Act. It gained, however, a significant number of Democratic votes partly because of the anti-Communist nature of the legislation and partly because many voters were upset by the postwar eruption of labor disputes and strikes along with a beef embargo by cattle ranchers.[13]

Barkley had been the last person to speak for the opposition before the vote was taken. The *New York Times* reporter William S. White noted that senators "listened intently" to the respected minority leader's objections to the legislation. These included the difficulty employees would have in negotiating a union shop, the opportunity states would have to pass antiunion legislation not reversible by existing federal law, and physically removing the conciliation service from the US Labor Department. Truman vetoed the bill on June 20 and the next evening went on national radio to explain his action. Clearly, he wanted workers across America to appreciate (and perhaps remember in the 1948 elections) the Roosevelt-Truman position that embraced labor. Along with his veto message to Congress, the president read on the Senate floor a letter to Barkley that in closing stated: "I want you to know you have my unqualified support, and it is my fervent hope, for the good of the country, that you and your colleagues will be successful in your efforts to keep this bill from becoming law." Despite the president's letter and Barkley's effort, the Senate overrode the veto with a remarkably strong 68–25 vote.[14]

Barkley, a consistent champion of the worker on farm or in factory, had to swallow the disappointment of Democratic defections in the passage of Taft-Hartley. Fortunately, he enjoyed a satisfying victory the following month. Exactly one year after his special Pearl Harbor committee issued its report, Congress approved and Truman signed the National Security Act. It placed America's military under a single administrative structure, soon named the US Department of Defense. It also created the Central Intelligence Agency and the National Security Council. This piece of legislation fulfilled the very first and most important recommendation of the Barkley committee, which stated: "Operational and intelligence work requires centralization of authority and clear-cut allocation of responsibility." Moreover, Barkley was gratified by continued Republican support for Truman's foreign policy in the Cold War. Despite an otherwise "do-nothing" reputation, in January 1948 Congress passed the US Information and Education Exchange Act. The latter formed a State Department cultural/propaganda service that included the Voice of America. And, a little over two months later, Capitol Hill and the White House agreed to the Economic Cooperation Act, better known as the Marshall Plan. General Marshall, then the secretary of state, initially proposed the idea during his commencement address the previous year at Harvard University. The act established the European Recovery Program to provide economic assistance to sixteen European countries. Economic revival from the war bolstered US commerce as it prevented the spread of communism in Western Europe.[15]

A little over a month after Truman signed the Marshall Plan, Barkley joined the president at the White House Rose Garden on May 8, 1948. An extraordinary triple celebration occurred on a beautiful spring day. It was the third anniversary of the end to the European phase of the Second World War, it was also Truman's sixty-fourth birthday, and Barkley received the prestigious Collier Award for distinguished service in the Senate. Sponsored and publicized by the popular *Collier's* magazine, the tribute expanded Barkley's reputation and enhanced his popularity and name recognition. He was selected for the honor by the recommendations of 244 newspaper editors across the nation. He received an engraved plaque and a $10,000 cash award. (The cash award was the source of the money that, as noted earlier, Barkley donated to the University of Louisville School of Medicine to establish a fund for research in heart disease in honor of his late wife, Dorothy.) His three-and-a-half decades of work in Congress and on behalf of the national Democratic Party, his widespread name recognition, and the publicity he just received from the Collier Award had consequences. Barkley was tapped for the third time to deliver a keynote address at the Democratic national convention, held this time in Philadelphia in July.[16]

On arriving in the City of Brotherly Love on Saturday, July 10, the day before the convention opened, Barkley noted: "I found the most dis-couraged and downcast group [of delegates] I had ever seen. You could cut the gloom with a corn knife. The very air smelled of defeat." A little over two weeks earlier in the same city and its Convention Hall, an exciting and roaring conclave once again nominated New York governor Thomas E. Dewey—but with a different running mate, California governor Earl Warren—to head the GOP national ticket. The spirited and joyful Repub-licans were absolutely certain that Dewey would be the next occupant of the White House and for good reason. The Democratic Party was on the verge of splitting apart. Southerners were furious over the fact that north-ern members wanted to insert a civil rights plank into the party's platform. Furthermore, most Democrats openly believed that Truman, the unelected "accidental" president, could never be elected to that high office in his own right. Several Democratic leaders, including Franklin D. Roosevelt's sons, tried but failed to get General Eisenhower to agree to be the party's presi-dential candidate. To top things off, Truman's only serious choice for vice president, Supreme Court associate justice William O. Douglas, had just turned the president down right before the start of the convention.[17]

The problems Truman faced actually helped Barkley. During the day on Monday, as he glanced over the remarks he would deliver that night, the minority leader decided to call the president in Washington. Leslie Biffle, then secretary to the Senate Democratic Policy Committee, joined Barkley on the line. The Kentuckian asked the Missourian whether he could seek the vice presidential nomination. Truman replied: "It's all right with me." From that brief open-ended statement, Biffle began spreading the word (more pre-diction than fact) among delegations that Barkley would be the president's running mate. Originally, of course, Truman had not given much thought to Barkley for the position. It was partly because of his age (seventy), and partly because of poor eyesight, and most importantly because Barkley and Truman came from adjacent border states that would do nothing geograph-ically to bolster the national ticket. Thus, it would be Barkley's powerhouse keynote speech during the evening session that claimed for him the nomi-nation for the second spot on the ballot. He turned delegates around from glum to gleeful. Despite the first-time special lighting for television cameras that elevated the ninety-degree heat in Convention Hall, a perspiring Bark-ley energetically, enthusiastically, and effectively attacked GOP domination of the Eightieth Congress and extolled the fourteen years when Democrats controlled the federal government.[18]

Barkley rattled off major New Deal legislation and asked a series of rhetorical questions: Did farmers want to surrender price supports or rural electrification, did workers want to surrender collective bargaining or maximum hours and minimum wages, did businesses want to surrender the Reconstruction Finance Corporation or the Reciprocal Trade Agreement, did citizens want to surrender aid to homeowners or Federal Deposit Insurance Corporation guarantees of bank deposits? He then used statistics to compare America's depressed economy of 1932 with the prosperity of 1948 and credited much of the latter to the New Deal. Finally, he spent time, as only a wise and experienced lawmaker could, exposing the shortcomings of recent congressional sessions. His rousing speech drew frequent cheers, applause, and two demonstrations. One of the latter occurred when he pointed out that Dewey proposed "to clean the cobwebs from the government at Washington." Barkley commented: "I am not an expert on cobwebs, but if my memory does not betray me, when the Democratic Party took over the government of the United States sixteen years ago, even the spiders were so weak from starvation that they could not weave a cobweb in any department of the government in Washington."[19]

With spontaneous cheers and applause, delegates thanked Barkley for bringing the convention to life. The celebration continued as the band played "My Old Kentucky Home" and the standards of a dozen delegations came to the rostrum to praise the keynoter. Other delegations raised their standards in tribute. The convention's enthusiastic reaction to Barkley visibly affected him, especially when a banner inscribed "Barkley for Vice President" was brought forward. Indeed, the speech and the expressions of approval by the delegations handed Truman an easy decision as to who should join him on the national ticket for the November 2 election. Early in the morning on July 15, Truman secured enough votes on the first ballot to be nominated to keep his position, while Barkley became the vice presidential candidate by simple acclamation. It was almost 2:00 A.M. before the two men could begin to deliver their acceptance speeches. Given the late hour and the fact that everyone wanted the convention to end as quickly as possible, Barkley's grateful but very brief acceptance of the nomination had to be close to the shortest speech of his political career.[20]

Truman was upset by the fact that his nomination was delayed for a couple of days after Barkley's keynote speech. Convention delegates became embroiled in conflict over the civil rights plank that was added to the party platform. Media coverage of convention discord made the nation very aware of the deep North-South division in the Democratic Party. The civil rights plank, coupled with Truman's defeat of the South's candidate, Senator Richard Russell (GA), prompted the Alabama and Mississippi delegations to walk out of the convention. Subsequently, rebellious southerners met in Birmingham, Alabama, on July 17 and nominated for president J. Strom Thurmond. The South Carolina governor headed the ticket of the States' Rights Democratic Party, whose members were soon renamed by the press the Dixiecrats. Six days later, Democratic liberals who opposed a moderate Truman held a convention in Philadelphia. On July 24 they nominated Henry A. Wallace as the presidential candidate for the Progressive Party. Multiple fractures among Democrats convinced most Americans that the Truman-Barkley ticket simply had no chance of winning the November election.[21]

"Give 'Em Hell Harry" and "Iron Man Alben" were undaunted by the seemingly impossible scenario they faced. During his acceptance speech, Truman blasted the Republican Congress, "which has still done nothing," and convincingly promised that he and Barkley would win the election. At the same time he announced that he was calling Congress into a special session to open on July 26. Finally, he expected the GOP to pass the substance of the platform program approved by the Republican national convention three weeks earlier. The GOP had promised America that the party would halt rising prices, aid education, meet the housing crisis, advance civil rights, and, among other things, extend and expand social security. On the very day the special session began, Truman signed an executive order ending discrimination because of race, color, religion, or national origin in the federal government and the armed forces. The order established the Fair Employment Board within the Civil Service Commission and mandated the head of each department within the executive branch to hire personnel solely on the basis of merit.[22]

When Truman came into the House chamber to deliver his address before the joint session of Congress on Tuesday, July 27, a few congressional members chose not to fulfill the tradition of standing when the chief executive entered the hall. Many more also refused to applaud. After the president's presentation, it soon became clear that Republicans rejected his legislative program as simply election-year politics. And southern Democratic senators, furious at the executive order promoting civil rights, promised to filibuster the two-week special session into oblivion. Cleverly, Republican majority leaders claimed that the president's legislative agenda would be examined and considered next winter rather than on an emergency basis in the short session. As quoted by the journalist C. P. Trussell, GOP majority leaders added: "We do not intend to consider routine legislation or open the Pandora's box of the legislative calendar." In short, they condemned the session. Thus, everything worked in favor of Truman and Barkley. During the campaign, they could point to the chasm between Republican promises and actual performance; they could chastise the GOP Congress as a do-nothing legislature that served only as an impediment to social progress. Moreover, the executive order would help them win votes from those who suffered from discrimination, not only citizens of color, but also at that time Jews, Catholics, and individuals with surnames from countries outside Western Europe.[23]

Truman and Barkley decided to begin their campaign in earnest in mid-September. This timing gave Barkley the opportunity to attend the meeting of the IPU held in Rome earlier that month. Truman, who loved trains, had access to the *Ferdinand Magellan,* which had been used by his predecessor. It was the only private railroad car fitted out by the Pullman Company for the exclusive use by the chief executive. Barkley returned home in time to have his picture taken with Truman on the rear platform of the train on September 16. The next morning the president and a large entourage housed in the seventeen-car train began rolling from Washington on a 21,298 mile whistle-stop campaign across America. When the train departed from Union Station, the latest Roper Poll showed Dewey leading Truman by an "unbeatable" 44 percent to 31 percent. Roper would do no more polls because Dewey had such a lead that he could not lose the November election. Before Barkley had left for Rome, he had to struggle with members of the Democratic National Committee who assumed "old Alben" needed to preserve his health by campaigning at a leisurely pace. But, unlike Truman, Barkley loved airplanes and wanted to conduct the first prop-stop campaign in national politics.[24]

As discussed earlier, Barkley took his first airplane flight in 1918, and his son, David, had been a military pilot before managing his father's farm. The vice presidential candidate had become an occasional air passenger in the latter portion of the 1930s when the Douglas Aircraft Company revolutionized America's airline industry by manufacturing hundreds, and ultimately thousands, of model DC-3 aircraft. By 1938, these planes carried 95 percent of all airline traffic in the United States. The Democratic National Committee rented a DC-3 from United Airlines for Barkley. Named appropriately *The Bluegrass,* the propeller-driven airliner normally carried twenty-one passengers. The redesigned interior contained a bunk bed and special work spaces so that a couple of secretaries could use their typewriters and make copies of speeches for the press on a mimeograph machine. There remained enough room to seat several journalists, advisers, and writers. The plane took off from Washington's National Airport the day after Truman had departed by train. Between his first prop-stop in Wilkes-Barre, Pennsylvania, and his last one in Paducah on November 1, one day before the election, the vice presidential candidate visited thirty-six states (Truman stopped in twenty-eight), delivered 250 speeches, and traveled 150,000 miles. Journalists and Democratic Party workers simply marveled at the Iron Man's strength and endurance. He absolutely thrived in the airplane and on the hustings.[25]

For a variety of reasons, Barkley delivered speeches that were relatively short and very focused when compared with his major addresses on the Senate floor or at the convention rostrum. On the prop-stop campaign, those speeches also varied in length and matched the audience. For example, his speech in Pittsburgh on October 1 had to be slightly less than thirty minutes because CBS radio broadcast it nationally; his comments in Louisville on October 23 lasted longer because he had a large crowd in the formal setting of the city's Memorial Auditorium. Naturally, Barkley told his Louisville listeners how happy he was to be "back in [his] native state"; he reminded the assemblage "in the great industrial center of Pittsburgh . . . that the Democratic Party was a major factor in the growth of the trade union movement." Before Truman and Barkley entrained or enplaned, they agreed not to mention the names of their opponents. In his typed and mimeographed speeches, Barkley kept his word, though he could not resist mentioning Dewey in his ever present extemporaneous remarks. When in Dover, Delaware, rain prompted the vice presidential candidate to cut short his talk. "I don't want you to get wet," he mirthfully told the crowd. "In fact, I don't even want you to get *dewey.*" Frequently, he inserted: "I am a little bit different from Dewey and Warren. I prepare my speeches in the air and deliver them on the ground. They prepare theirs on the ground and deliver them in the air."[26]

Barkley's folksy humor about the airy oratory produced by Dewey struck reality. While the Democratic candidates delivered hard-hitting speeches using informal and direct language, Dewey tried to look presidential and speak presidentially. Too often the GOP candidate's words floated up into pointless clouds of platitudes. Nevertheless, the polls and pundits continued to predict a Dewey victory, though a Gallup Poll taken shortly before the election showed that the New York governor's lead had been cut to only six points. The evening before the election found Barkley reaching Angles close to 6:00 P.M. After a day of campaigning in the Purchase area, the vice presidential candidate was carried in a motorcade to Paducah and the new Arena, where a crowd of fifteen hundred listened to and from which a Kentucky network of seventeen radio stations broadcast Barkley's last campaign speech. Harsh lighting prevented him from reading a script, but his improvised remarks lasted exactly the required broadcast time of fifty minutes. He then rushed home to Angles, where on national CBS radio he introduced President Truman, then in Independence, Missouri. The president began his radio comments: "I want to thank Senator Barkley for his generous introduction, and to say what I have said before—that no candidate for President ever had a finer running mate. The people of this country are everlastingly in his debt for his leadership in their interest. Senator Barkley will go down in history as one of our greatest public servants."[27]

The next day's election led to one of the most incredible upsets in the history of American politics. Despite what opinion polls had indicated and political commentators had believed, Truman beat Dewey by over two million votes and thumped the governor in the Electoral College 303–189. The Dixiecrats and the Progressives, many of whom were registered Democrats, did not have the expected impact on the Truman-Barkley ticket. And, with Barkley as his running mate, Truman actually received a higher percentage of Kentucky votes than Roosevelt had in 1944. Additionally, the effective nature of the Truman-Barkley, train-plane campaign resulted in Democrats regaining control over the national legislature. In the Eighty-First Congress, the House had 263 Democrats and 171 Republicans and the Senate 54 Democrats and 42 Republicans. New Democratic senators included the future president and vice president: Lyndon B. Johnson (TX) and Hubert H. Humphrey (MN). On January 20, 1949, a beautiful but chilly day in Washington, the inaugural ceremony took place in front of the Capitol's East Portico before a live audience estimated at an extraordinary one million people. It was also the first time that the event could be not only heard on radio but also watched on television across the nation. Chief Justice Frederick M. Vinson of Kentucky swore in Truman as president; Associate Justice Stanley F. Reed, also of Kentucky, administered the oath to Barkley as vice president.[28]

In terms of his newly elected position in government, Barkley remembered one of his borrowed anecdotes: "There once was a farmer who had two sons. Both boys showed great promise early in life. But the elder son went to sea and the younger son was elected Vice President and neither has been heard from since." Several of America's founding fathers considered the post superfluous. The US Constitution handed the vice president only the one task of serving as the presiding officer of the Senate and having a vote only in cases of a tie. One individual who served in that role, John C. Calhoun, had so little to do and became so disgusted with the president that he resigned. (Calhoun did not miss being and Andrew Jackson did not miss having a vice president.) On the other hand, Barkley fully understood the one absolutely critical responsibility of the office. Vice Presidents John Tyler, Millard Fillmore, Andrew Johnson, Chester Arthur, Theodore Roosevelt, Calvin Coolidge, and Harry Truman each had become the US president following the death of a chief executive. This point struck home and jolted Barkley on November 1, 1950, when two Puerto Rican nationalists, Griselio Torresola and Oscar Collazo, attempted but failed to assassinate Truman.[29]

Barkley's national reputation and Truman's unfortunate experience as vice president led to a change in the role of that office. In the brief time that Truman served in the second spot under President Roosevelt, the vice president was virtually excluded from the workings of the executive branch of government. Small wonder that Truman deprecated his ability to fill FDR's shoes after he had been left in the dark about presidential problems and procedures before Roosevelt died. Logically, he did everything to counter FDR's mistake by making Barkley an integral part of the administration. In the process, Barkley became the first working vice president in American history. Truman recognized that Barkley's lengthy tenure in both the House and the Senate made him a master of the legislative process and a valuable asset in cabinet meetings. In addition, Barkley served as a member of the National Security Council since strategy decisions reached there sometimes required congressional legislation. He also became the principal spokesman for Truman's Fair Deal program. In the first eight months of the new administration, he delivered sixty major addresses at venues across the country. He continued his close association with airplanes, especially those that belonged to the US Air Force.[30]

Barkley also signed congressional resolutions, appointed several minor Senate committees, selected five candidates each to attend West Point and the Naval Academy, and served on the Board of Regents of the Smithsonian Institution. As the Kentucky historian Thomas D. Clark remarked, Barkley "gave the office a sparkle and usefulness which it had never had before." On top of everything else, he became the last vice president to devote serious time to his constitutional role as the Senate's chief officer. In fact, Harry Truman employed Barkley as the administration's point man in Congress. The vice president consulted with Truman, but he additionally received an enormous number of messages from the president that spelled out precisely hoped for bills or refinements to bills as well as decisions and documents from the administration. Barkley frequently shared this information with his longtime friend House speaker Rayburn and the new majority leader, Scott W. Lucas (D-IL, 1949–1951), and later Ernest W. McFarland (D-AZ, 1951–1953). Truman acknowledged the important part that Barkley played in his administration when he ordered the Heraldic Branch of the US Army to create a special flag, seal, and coat of arms for the Office of the Vice President.[31]

When Barkley first entered the Senate as vice president, he was greeted warmly with applause from both sides of the aisle. Senator Vandenberg, a Republican who had served as president pro tempore in the absence of a vice president, paid tribute to him, noting that, while he "may lack the right of recognition [to speak] on the floor, many other recognitions can never be taken from him." Among these Vandenberg listed unblemished integrity, successful leadership, great courage, marvelous eloquence, much humility, wonderful patience, and good fellowship. All these qualities had made Barkley "one of the greatest senators of his time and generation." Fortunately for Senate president Barkley, most of his actions were tactfully or easily accomplished and greatly appreciated. His most controversial and unsuccessful moment occurred on March 11, 1949. On the evening of that date, he ruled on whether cloture (a supermajority, then of sixty-five votes) applied to a motion to proceed. Southerners had conducted a filibuster for ten days because the motion to proceed would lead to the next proposed bill on the docket—civil rights legislation. Barkley favored the latter and ruled that cloture on a bill could also be applied to a motion. He used humor to soften the ire of his opponents. Before issuing his ruling, he commented: "The Chair feels somewhat like the man who was being ridden out of town on a rail. Someone asked him how he liked it. He said if it weren't for the honor of the thing, he would just as soon walk."[32]

Praise for his ruling from northeastern senators did not spare Barkley from experiencing disappointment. A coalition of midwestern Republicans and southern Democrats, a group that often defeated Truman's domestic agenda, led a 46–41 vote to overturn Barkley's decision. Edgar C. Brown, the director of the National Negro Council, asserted: "The unholy combination of some Senate Republicans with the Southerners will long be remembered at the polls." Executive Secretary Walter F. White of the National Association for the Advancement of Colored People described the repudiation of Barkley's ruling as "a cruel blow." On the other hand, Barkley's letdown over the rejection of his ruling elevated his standing among African Americans, who, in the North, were switching parties in droves. Meanwhile, Democratic and Republican leaders met with key southern Democrats and worked out a deal to drop both the filibuster and the civil rights bill and move on to consider a different agenda item. As a result, southern rancor directed at Barkley soon dissipated.[33]

Two months later, as the antidote for the setback over civil rights, Barkley was honored for his service in promoting the freedoms defined by President Franklin D. Roosevelt before Congress on January 6, 1941. In front of an audience of a thousand guests at New York's Waldorf-Astoria Hotel, the vice president received the Four Freedoms Award. Presiding over the dinner event, New York Supreme Court justice Ferdinand Pecora read a letter from President Truman as part of the ceremony for the award presentation. Truman stated in part: "It is particularly fitting that Alben Barkley has been selected for so signal an honor. There is not in the country today a more zealous or more eloquent advocate of the Four Freedoms than he." On numerous other occasions, the president expressed his high regard for Barkley. One very special moment took place on March 1, 1951. Truman made a surprise visit to the Senate to celebrate the thirty-eighth anniversary of Barkley's first year in Congress. As a token of his admiration for the vice president, Truman gave him a gavel composed of old wood from the White House, which was then undergoing renovation.[34]

Barkley occupied an office reserved historically for the Senate president in the Capitol Building. The room was adorned with Theodore Roosevelt's chandelier, Dolly Madison's mirror, Rembrandt Peale's portrait of George Washington, and a hand-me-down desk formerly used by several presidents, including Barkley's hero T. Woodrow Wilson. Barkley also kept guest books signed by more than twenty-two thousand visitors, including families from every state. In addition, a number of entries belonged to well-known individuals ranging from Winston Churchill and Bob Hope to Jane Russell and the Duke of Windsor. Because he had lost his wife, the vice president asked his daughter Marian Truitt to serve as his official hostess whenever he entertained. He also spent time with the Truitt family, which resided in Washington. It would be the youngest of four sons, Stephen M. Truitt, who suggested at age ten that "gramps" should simplify his long title by inserting two *e*'s between the *v* and the *p* in *vice president*. Barkley proudly mentioned his grandson's idea to a group of reporters, and before long he was known ubiquitously as *the Veep*. This label of endearment became his unique moniker. It transferred neither to Vice President Richard M. Nixon in 1953 nor to later vice presidents. Only in the twenty-first century did the appellation gain new life, but only in the fiction of a television show. Meanwhile, the Veep did add one other singular activity to the post he held. Barkley became the first vice president to marry in office.[35]

16

The Iron Man Keeps His Mettle

On July 8, 1949, Alben W. Barkley joined a party on the presidential yacht the USS *Williamsburg,* renamed unofficially *Margie* after Truman's daughter Margaret. Marny Clifford, the wife of President Truman's legal counsel Clark Clifford, served as hostess during the festivities. She had brought her vacationing Missouri friend Jane Rucker Hadley to the floating party. Jane's late husband, Carleton, had been best man at the Cliffords' wedding. The thirty-eight-year-old widow had taught foreign languages (French and Italian) part-time at Washington University in St. Louis. Raising two daughters (Ann and Jane) without a husband led her to double her salary by accepting a secretarial position with the Wabash Railroad. When Marny Clifford introduced Barkley to Jane Hadley, the Veep was smitten by the attractive and spirited woman. The gregarious Alben soon discovered that he had known Jane's grandfather, Congressman William J. Rucker. The next day Barkley called Marny Clifford to tell her that he hoped to enhance Jane's vacation with some events in her honor. Three days later, he gave a luncheon for Jane in the Senate, followed the next day by a cocktail party in his Connecticut Avenue apartment.[1]

Shortly thereafter, Jane flew back home to St. Louis and her job with the railroad. Intrigued by all the attention she had received from the Veep, she wondered whether she might be only a passing memory to the Kentuckian. Barkley, however, found a number of speaking engagements that he had to make in the Midwest. Somehow, his flight travels always ended up in St. Louis. The couple's developing May-December love affair made headlines in the media; millions followed its progress with the same devotion given by later viewers of the television soap opera "The Guiding Light," which began its multidecade run in 1952. After talking on the phone about their plans with President Truman, on Sunday, October 30, 1949, the pair announced their intention to marry in St. Louis on November 18. Right after the wire services picked up the hot story, the *Washington Daily News* sent a reporter to interview Marian Barkley Truitt. When asked how she felt about losing her job as the Veep's hostess, Marian responded that Jane Hadley was "more than welcome" to replace her. "She'll do a swell job," Barkley's daughter predicted. "She is good looking, charming, poised and intelligent. I think she's going to make him very happy."[2]

On Friday, November 18, the motorcade carrying the happy couple and various dignitaries, including the mayor of St. Louis, wended its way through a cheering crowd of onlookers as the cars approached St. John's Methodist Church. The wedding ceremony took place in the church's Memorial Chapel under the direction of Ivan Lee Holt, Missouri's Methodist bishop. Two days later, the newlyweds began their honeymoon at coastal Georgia's Sea Island resort. At Jane's request, they temporarily interrupted their stay to fly to New York to see Mary Martin perform in the Broadway production of *South Pacific*. When they entered the theater, audience members recognized the Veep and his bride and gave them a standing ovation. At honeymoon's end the couple returned to New York at the beginning of December and attended a $100-a-plate fund-raising dinner at the Waldorf-Astoria on behalf of the Democratic National Committee. Guests included numerous party leaders, entertainers, and administration personalities such as Secretary of State Dean G. Acheson and Secretary of Defense Louis Johnson. The lighthearted event was hosted by the party chairman, William M. Boyle, who, when he introduced Barkley, said: "Our Vice President is returning after winning another campaign." The Veep jovially responded: "I am grateful for the various references tonight to my successful invasion of the state of Missouri."[3]

While the romantic interlude shared by Barkley and Hadley seemed at times to be widely read news—one reporter actually claimed that their engagement announcement produced the planet's top story—in reality America's and the world's consistent long-term concern focused on the expanding Cold War between the United States and Soviet Russia. Shortly before Alben and Jane met for the first time, the Soviet Union's nearly year-long blockade of West Berlin ended in May 1949. With British help, the US Air Force conducted Operation Vittles, a massive airlift that brought 2.5 million West Berliners 2.3 million tons of food, fuel, medicine, and other supplies, defeating the Soviet effort to force the Americans, British, and French to withdraw from their sectors in the former and future capital of Germany. Because the United States did not trust the Soviet Union, the airlift continued and built up emergency supplies into September. By then, the formation of two German states, East and West, was under way; also, on July 21, 1949, the Senate confirmed American membership in the North Atlantic Treaty Organization (NATO). The NATO military alliance contained originally Belgium, Britain, Canada, Denmark, France, Iceland, Italy, Luxembourg, the Netherlands, Norway, Portugal, and the United States. Greece and Turkey soon augmented its membership.[4]

In the same month that Alben and Jane announced their engagement, the Communists enjoyed victory in China's civil war. Mao Zedong (Mao Tse-tung) announced in Beijing (Peiping) the formation of the People's Republic of China (PRC). The Nationalist government of the Republic of China (ROC) under the leadership of Jiang Jieshi (Chiang Kai-shek) moved to the island of Taiwan (Formosa) with its capital at Taibei (Taipei). Because the United States had used special advisers and significant funds to aid, but in vain, the corrupt ROC government, the Truman administration blamed Jiang Jieshi for the "loss" of China. As a result, early in January 1950 the president announced that the federal government would no longer provide military or financial assistance to the ROC on Taiwan. The administration hoped that the public statement ending American intervention in the Chinese civil war might result in the PRC remaining, like Yugoslavia, semiautonomous in its relations with the Soviet Union. On the reverse side of the coin, a week later, on January 12, Secretary of State Acheson delivered a speech before the National Press Club making it clear that the United States would set up a defensive perimeter in Asia and use its armed forces to preserve and protect Japan and the Philippines from any type of PRC or Soviet incursion.[5]

In key locations around the world, people observed that Taiwan and Korea failed to receive US military protection within Acheson's defensive perimeter. Initially, the Truman administration chose not to interfere should the PRC attempt to extend the civil war to Taiwan. Korea, however, represented a different issue. As they did in Germany, Russians and Americans militarily occupied postwar Korea, but divided at the thirty-eighth parallel between North and South. In 1948, Soviet Russia blocked UN efforts to conduct nationwide elections to unite the Korean Peninsula politically. Thus, southern elections resulted in the formation in August of the Republic of Korea (ROK) led by President Syngman Rhee in the capital city of Seoul. The next month in the North a Communist assembly in Pyongyang created the Democratic People's Republic of Korea under Premier Kim Il Sung. That step prompted Soviet Russia to withdraw most of its occupation forces. With limited military resources and firm security obligations in both Asia and Europe, the US Joint Chiefs of Staff had no interest in keeping troops and bases in Korea. The last of the US occupation soldiers left South Korea on June 29, 1949.[6]

Realizing that South Korea lay outside the American defensive perimeter, appreciating the fact that virtually all Koreans wanted the peninsula unified, and receiving the encouragement of Stalin, North Korea chose to send its troops and Russian T-34 tanks crashing across the thirty-eighth parallel and into South Korea on June 25, 1950. Truman understood that, as a Russian client state, North Korea would, if victorious, likely hand the Soviet Union air and naval bases, placing Japan and even Taiwan in harm's way. He consulted with Barkley as well as with congressional leaders but decided to take the "police action" route to save South Korea and Taiwan rather than to seek the authorization of Congress. The seating of the anti-Communist Taiwan diplomat as the official representative of China on the UN Security Council had caused a reversal in US policy toward the island. In protest that Taiwan represented China, the Soviet Russian ambassador, Jacob Malik, boycotted the council. This meant that the Soviet Union could not veto the UN resolution calling on the world's nations to rally in defense of South Korea. Between June 27 and 29, Truman in his role as commander in chief ordered the US Navy's Seventh Fleet to protect Taiwan and General of the Army Douglas MacArthur, head of America's Far East military in Japan, to use all available US forces to save the ROK.[7]

Except for the excessive Communist witch hunt conducted by the Republican senator Joseph R. McCarthy (WI), the war in Korea absorbed most of America's attention for the remainder of the Truman administration. At first, things went well. The United States helped ROK forces establish a successful defensive line around Pusan at the southeastern end of the peninsula. Then General MacArthur and his staff planned a brilliant land, sea, and air attack halfway up the coast at Inchon on September 15. It caught by surprise in the south the bulk of North Korea's army, which suffered serious losses in terms of troops and military hardware. The US/UN and ROK victory in South Korea prompted the UN Assembly on October 7 to approve a resolution recommending that MacArthur's UN forces take "all appropriate steps . . . to ensure conditions of stability throughout Korea." As US/UN and ROK troops moved north above the thirty-eighth parallel, Stalin stridently urged Mao Zedong to bolster the remnants of North Korea's army with Chinese divisions. By late October, several US/UN and ROK units advancing north encountered Chinese "volunteer" soldiers south of the Yalu River, which served as the border between Korea and China's region of Manchuria.[8]

On November 28, Barkley participated in President Truman's emergency meeting in the Cabinet Room of the National Security Council (NSC). By that date, not just Chinese volunteers but at least nine Chinese armies each with multiple divisions had crossed the Yalu and more than matched in numbers their UN opponents. A threefold problem undermined any UN advantage in hardware, training, or airpower. China had a Manchurian reserve of 500,000 men, tens of thousands of volunteers had slipped behind UN lines, and nearly half the 177,000 US soldiers in Korea were stretched all the way south to Pusan as supply and service troops. It gave China somewhere between a three- and a four-to-one edge over American forces. By the evening of November 26, not only had the US/UN offensive stalled, but also some US units had retreated, and three ROK divisions simply disintegrated as the Chinese conducted a counteroffensive. At the NSC meeting on the twenty-eighth, Barkley expressed a deep concern about the US/UN commander despite the fact that his daughter, Laura Louise, had married General MacArthur's nephew. As recently as Friday, November 24, MacArthur had issued a victory communiqué to members of his staff. His US/UN command would initiate on that date a "massive compression envelopment in North Korea against the new Red armies operating there."[9]

MacArthur went on to predict that, by reaching the Yalu River, the US/UN military would end the war and be able to be withdrawn. When handing the communiqué to John B. Coulter, the commanding general of XI Corps, MacArthur said: "Tell the boys. . . . I want to make good my statement that they are going to eat their Christmas dinner at home." In the NSC meeting, Barkley exclaimed: "This is an incredible hoax." The Veep wondered whether MacArthur actually understood what was going on. By November 24, everyone knew about the massive Chinese military presence in North Korea and Manchuria. Truman remembered that Barkley was deeply perturbed and asked the rhetorical question, "How could a man in his position be guilty of such an indiscretion?" He recalled World War I when combatants on both sides claimed that the conflict would be over by Christmas 1914, yet it continued for nearly four more years. Meanwhile, Barkley and the NSC members discussed the Soviet Russian–Communist

Chinese alliance and recognized that, no matter how terrible the crisis in Korea, every effort must be made to avoid allowing events there to flare up into World War III.[10]

A second decision of the NSC was to avoid initially any public statement that might be construed as a criticism of MacArthur even though many NSC members agreed with Barkley that the UN commander had blundered badly with his communiqué and home-for-Christmas statement. Regardless, negative public comments about the general at this point would only enhance the élan of Chinese troops and harm the morale of American soldiers who were in the process of suffering one of the worst military defeats in US history. The good news was the fact that, after more than two months of continuous fighting, the American forces were able to stop the Chinese advance south of the thirty-eighth parallel. Under the leadership of a tough and demanding field commander, General Matthew B. Ridgeway, "Operation Killer" was launched on February 21, 1951. It resulted in an offensive that recaptured South Korea's capital city of Seoul as well as a defensive line above the thirty-eighth parallel except for Kaesong and a small portion of the Korean west coast.[11]

Meanwhile, and understandably, as US troops suffered terrible casualties, MacArthur argued for the US bombardment of China, especially against reserve units and military supplies in Manchuria. He also wanted to "unleash" Jiang Jieshi and Nationalist Chinese forces on Taiwan for an invasion of Communist China. Either step violated the first decision reached by Barkley and the NSC on November 28. Such action would likely cause war with Soviet Russia—a frightening prospect as both the United States and the Soviet Union possessed atomic bombs. Such a quest for total victory made MacArthur such a public opponent of Truman and his policy that early in April the president began consulting with his advisers about relieving him of his command. At that very moment, Barkley underwent another eye operation at Bethesda Naval Hospital. Truman, however, did talk with him over the telephone. Nevertheless, the Veep was released in time to join, on Monday, April 9, 1951, Truman and administration key advisers, including Secretary of State Acheson, General Marshall, and General Omar Bradley, head of the Joint Chiefs of Staff, in coming to terms with MacArthur. Because the latter had defied the commander in chief, Barkley could see no other course than to agree with the advisers' unanimous decision to remove the general from his command.[12]

Truman announced his decision nationwide on April 11. Public opinion against the president magnified when MacArthur flew back to the United States to a hero's welcome. The general then delivered an eloquent, "no substitute for victory" speech before a joint session of Congress on April 19. Some congressional members openly wept at the end of the emotional address. Meanwhile, as Truman stated on April 11, his administration had no thought about using force to reunify Korea. Thus, the war turned into an ugly stalemate filled, to be sure, with bravery but also with death and casualty. Later that year, Barkley expressed support for the troops by visiting Korea. It had to occur to the Veep that a short outline of his life in national politics could be centered on his several travels to American battlefields as representative, senator, and then vice president. This time, on November 24, he celebrated his seventy-fourth birthday near the combat zone by eating military rations with troops and General Ridgeway's replacement, General James A. Van Fleet. Barkley's bride, Jane, had accompanied him to Korea but remained a safe distance from the battlefield. Later, the pair visited wounded soldiers. A more pleasant highlight of their trip occurred when a group of Korean orphans serenaded the Barkleys with "My Old Kentucky Home."[13]

The Iron Man faced an uncertain future as he entered the presidential election year of 1952. The Twenty-Second Amendment to the Constitution had gone into effect on February 27, 1951. It restricted an individual to two elected presidential terms; a person who acted as president for more than two years could be elected only once to occupy the White House. On the other hand, a clause stated that the latter clause did not apply to a person holding the presidential office when the amendment became operative. It literally granted Truman permission to seek, in essence, a third term, but would he? If he did pursue the nomination, would he want to keep Barkley in the second spot? Truman himself struggled over the issue of his candidacy. After the MacArthur episode, opinion polls gave him an approval rating of only 26 percent; a year later he remained woefully unpopular. The low figure suggested that a battle over the nomination would likely erupt at the upcoming Democratic national convention should Truman choose to try for the nomination. Early in the new year, and without publicity, Truman discussed with Governor Adlai E. Stevenson (IL), Barkley's distant cousin, the possibility of becoming a candidate for the Democratic nomination. The president felt that the governor would try to preserve Truman's domestic and foreign policies.[14]

On March 4, Stevenson informed Truman that he had committed to run in November only for reelection as Illinois governor. The president then toyed for a while with the idea of seeking the party's nomination even though many convention delegates would likely prefer an alternative candidate. He consulted secretly with several friends and advisers. The negative opinion polls, coupled with Tennessee senator Estes Kefauver's stunning victory over Truman in the New Hampshire primary (March 11), prompted those he asked to suggest kindly that he look forward to his January 1953 retirement. After a stay at the Little White House in Key West, a tanned and rested president delivered a lively address before fifty-three hundred Democrats at the Jefferson-Jackson Day Dinner in Washington's National Guard Armory on March 29. At the conclusion of his assault on the GOP, Truman announced: "I shall not be a candidate for re-election. I have served my country long, and I think efficiently and honestly. I shall not accept renomination. I do not feel it is my duty to spend another four years in the White House." There were shouts of "No! No!" from the surprised audience, but the die was cast.[15]

Since Barkley worked closely with Truman, the Veep knew that the president had mixed feelings about the matter but generally wanted to avoid trying for a third term. Unlike Clark Clifford, Barkley as vice president could not spend time with Truman in Key West. It was there that Clifford helped the president come to a final decision. Thus, Barkley was almost as surprised as were most Democrats at the dinner when Truman abruptly ended his address with a no-turning-back statement on his future. Before the announcement, Barkley had already resolved that, if Truman chose not to seek the party's nomination, he would be a candidate for the top spot on the national ticket. It must be pointed out that, while Truman had talked with Stevenson and even with Supreme Court chief justice Fred Vinson about seeking the presidential nomination, the man from Missouri failed to suggest the same thing to the Veep who had done so much to help him gain the White House in 1948. Frankly, the good-hearted Truman felt that, at Barkley's age, three months in office would be long enough to kill him. Beyond that, the Veep's eyesight was so bad that he could read only material printed in bold letters an inch tall. How could he possibly review, ponder, and act on hundreds of documents and correspondence each week? Truman wrote in his diary that he had observed Barkley spending up to five minutes just signing his name.[16]

These serious eyesight problems were not widely known, and Barkley easily concealed his infirmity. Decades of experience before different groups allowed him to speak extemporaneously with confidence to any group on any occasion. Moreover, he had a reputation for keeping audiences smiling, if not laughing, by the immense collection of funny tales and folksy stories that he inserted in his presentations. Thus, his eyesight was a nonissue when Truman's announcement freed him to admit publicly that he would be willing to accept, if offered, the party's nomination for president. While he did not state officially that he was seeking or campaigning for the nomination, the District of Columbia Democratic Club, spurred on by Leslie Biffle and several senators, nevertheless formed early in April a Barkley for President Club headed by Senator Guy M. Gillette (IA). The next month the Kentucky state Democratic convention pledged the commonwealth's twenty-six delegates to the Veep's nomination. As soon as Congress adjourned, Barkley took the old-fashioned step for those who hoped to land America's highest office. He and Jane went home to Angles, their large farm near Paducah. While giving the impression that he was quietly sitting at home and waiting to be drafted by the party's Chicago convention, Barkley played a political hand with key figures via telephone and letters. For example, he conversed by phone with Adlai Stevenson's campaign manager and discovered that Stevenson supported him and might even be willing to place his name in nomination. It was not until July 7, however, that Barkley officially stated that he was a presidential candidate.[17]

Three days later, Barkley flew to Washington for a conference with Truman, Leslie Biffle, Chairman Frank E. McKinney of the Democratic National Committee, and several White House staffers. Truman had initiated the meeting after he had read about Barkley's official candidacy. As Barkley already knew, the president had hoped originally that Stevenson would seek the party's nomination. Stevenson, however, continued to refuse to commit himself as a candidate; hence, Truman would back Barkley. The president chose not to make a public endorsement before the convention opened, but clearly the Veep would be the administration's favored candidate. For one thing, Truman promised to instruct the Missouri delegation to vote for Barkley. The president kept his word by sending, on July 16, a note to that effect to Thomas J. "Tom" Gavin, Truman's alternate on the Missouri delegation.[18]

As he and Jane approached Chicago on Friday, July 18, Barkley felt good about his chances to gain the presidential nomination at the Democratic national convention, which would be held in the huge, nine-thousand-seat Chicago (later International) Amphitheater adjacent to the Chicago Stock

Yards. He personified, after all, the party as Mr. Democrat. Truman later admitted that, in July 1952, the Veep "was at the height of his popularity with the people, with the party, and with the Congress." Moreover, except for Kefauver and the South's candidate, Richard B. Russell, most other candidates with delegates were simply favorite sons of individual states. Barkley, by contrast, had the votes of three states: Kentucky, Missouri, and, ostensibly, Illinois. He could also count on votes from a number of northern states that were influenced by unions. He had long been recognized as a consistent ally of labor in Congress. Finally, Truman, who reputedly controlled up to four hundred delegates, could swing those votes to the Veep on, perhaps, the second ballot. It might produce a bandwagon effect that could vault Barkley to victory.[19]

Age, however, threatened to trump all these positive elements. Barkley was seventy-four years old and would be seventy-five on Inauguration Day, January 20, 1953. He knew that the media had played up his age and recognized how this issue worried many of the arriving delegates. As a result, he took three steps to confront and neutralize this apparent barrier to his nomination. First, he and Jane turned down a motorcade ride and instead walked jauntily seven blocks (about half a mile) from Chicago's Illinois Central Railway Station to the Conrad Hilton Hotel, the Barkley for President headquarters. Accompanying the couple was a large crowd that included Jacob Avery, who headed Chicago's Democratic Party, and Governor and Mrs. Lawrence W. Wetherby of Kentucky. Many in the group carried signs that read "North South East West All Agree Barkley Best." With a smile on his face, and waving his white hat to onlookers and members of the press, Barkley literally took in stride, without perspiring, the brisk walk on a hot day. He hoped to demonstrate that he was just as active and healthy as his younger competitors for the nomination.[20]

Second, Barkley followed his spry walk with a televised press conference. Before the media, he readily acknowledged that the one potential handicap to his nomination emerged from the number of years of life he had enjoyed. The Iron Man stated, however, that he was proud of his age, strength, and good health. He reminded the press that there were a number of examples of public figures who performed their tasks effectively at an older age. Among others, he cited William E. Gladstone, who served as British prime minister into his middle eighties, and Oliver Wendell Holmes, who retired from the US Supreme Court at age ninety-one. "I am just 74," Barkley exclaimed. "What do you think I am going to do the rest of my life?" Third, Barkley needed to scotch the old-age issue with labor leaders. They directly controlled something close to one hundred delegates, but, more importantly, they influenced large delegations from northern states. Truman and Barkley had discussed the labor vote during their recent conference. Regrettably, Barkley ignored or forgot or was too busy to implement Truman's advice. The president had urged the vice president to talk with labor leaders one at a time because no single individual would want to make a public commitment in front of the group. On the other hand, if most agreed individually that Barkley's age was not a problem, the entire group would back him.[21]

Instead, during the weekend, Barkley invited sixteen union men to join him for breakfast on Monday morning, July 21, before the convention opened. As Truman anticipated, those invited talked with each other. The American Federation of Labor (AFL) and the Congress of Industrial Organizations issued a statement on Sunday to the press that they had reached a united position on Barkley and would express their views to him at the next day's breakfast. But that Sunday statement also quoted the ranking AFL official among convention delegates, George M. Harrison, who summarized labor's position: "We can't sell Barkley to labor, not because of his record, but his age." It takes little imagination to understand why Barkley suffered a disaster at Monday's breakfast. With encouragement from his wife and several advisers, he told the press that he was withdrawing as a candidate. He also telephoned Truman and told him he planned to leave the convention. The level of disappointment that he experienced can be seen in a statement he issued Monday evening. A key portion of his press release revealed an uncharacteristic vindictiveness. He vented his anger at labor:

> I have never believed, and do not now believe, that anyone of these groups [rich, poor, Negro, Jew, Catholic, Protestant, businessmen, and field or factory labor] should be permitted to dominate or control either of the great political parties of our nation.
>
> However, since arriving in Chicago, I have learned that certain self-anointed political labor leaders have taken it upon themselves to announce their opposition to me as the Democratic nominee for President. They have admitted to me that weeks ago they committed themselves to a program and to candidates other than myself, which would give them greater control of the machinery and policies of the Democratic Party.[22]

To keep the vice president at the convention, Truman telephoned Democratic Party chairman McKinney and strongly recommended that Barkley be given time outside the scheduled agenda for a farewell speech. His swan song came on Wednesday evening. When Sam Rayburn and several senior Democrats led Barkley to the rostrum, spontaneous and lengthy applause took place. The Veep's poor eyesight meant that his speech was unscripted, but from the heart. It proved to be a stunning oration. Truman later commented: "It was . . . one of the most heart-warming and moving speeches ever brought before such a gathering. It was the 'Veep' at his best." Untypically, Barkley failed to go after the Republicans at length. He briefly mentioned that the unnamed GOP presidential nominee (Dwight D. Eisenhower) had promised a "crusade" from the same rostrum a couple of weeks earlier. "We are not," he said, "beginning a crusade. We are continuing a crusade." He went on to describe in detail the Democratic crusade and its accomplishments from Wilson to Truman. The American people, he asserted, needed to be reminded of these achievements so that the results of the 1952 election would be the same as those of the one in 1948.[23]

The applause and demonstrations after Barkley's speech lasted forty-five minutes. During that time, every person from James A. Farley to Franklin D. Roosevelt Jr. who had credentials to get on the platform came up and shook Barkley's hand or patted him on the back. The Veep was overwhelmed by the applause from the floor and the warmth and attention he received from so many party leaders. "It was all," he later remembered, "I could do to maintain my composure, and, when my wife came to the platform to join me as the bands played 'My Old Kentucky Home,' I would not have trusted myself to have attempted to say another word." The journalist Felix Belair Jr. stated that the spontaneous, intensive, and sustained outburst "guaranteed [Barkley] a permanent seat in the Democratic hall of fame." Subsequently, the Veep received over a million letters and telegrams. It took nine secretaries months to acknowledge them all. Meanwhile, the next day, Adlai Stevenson suddenly became a candidate. On the third ballot, he won the nomination. To gain southern votes and avoid resurrecting the Dixiecrats, he picked Senator John J. Sparkman (AL) as his running mate. On election day, November 4, the military hero Eisenhower and his running mate, Richard M. Nixon, triumphed in a landslide victory over Stevenson and Sparkman. It is very unlikely that Barkley or any other Democrat could have beaten the general, though Barkley was better known nationally than Stevenson and might have made it a closer race.[24]

During the presidential campaign, Eisenhower announced in Detroit on October 24 that, after winning the election, he would visit Korea for information and then, as president, give priority to securing an end to the fighting. He fulfilled the first part of his pledge by flying to Korea on November 29. Then several factors merged that allowed him to complete the second part of his pledge. Like Truman, Eisenhower was willing to accept an armistice rather than seek unconditional surrender from the Chinese and the North Koreans. Also, these opponents were worried by the general's battle-tested reputation for success at war, and the US State Department, through India, suggested to China that the United States was considering all military options, which would include atomic weapons, to win the war. Later research revealed that the key to the Korean armistice of July 26, 1953 (July 27 in Korea), was not atomic threats but the death of Stalin in March 1953. The Procrustean dictator had insisted that the Chinese and the North Koreans continue the conflict long after their losses prompted them to consider peace. Stalin loved the Korean War. Because of it America lost thousands of soldiers and billions of dollars. Without touching the Soviet Union's warmaking infrastructure, it weakened the United States and limited its military options elsewhere, especially in Europe. Theoretically, the July armistice stopped active fighting, though it provided nothing more than a multidecade pause in the war.[25]

Barkley, of course, was retired from office when President Eisenhower and his administration struggled for six months to secure an armistice agreement from the North Koreans at Panmunjon. Shortly after January's inauguration, the former vice president started his new life without work in the Bethesda Naval Hospital. He went through two operations to remove a cataract from each eye. Once the operations were over Barkley became restless; he had worked all his adult life and even for much of his childhood. He began to consider job offers from various businesses and industries that wanted to take advantage of his name recognition across the nation. He wanted some type of position because he missed receiving a paycheck and enjoying the personal satisfaction of doing something meaningful. In March, he accepted an offer from the National Broadcasting Company to do a fifteen-minute national television show, "Meet the Veep," each week for twenty-six weeks. Barkley had his job, but he also had plenty of time to take trips around the country with Jane. On television he told stories, explored national issues, and reminisced about his life in Congress. He would be guided through the unscripted show by questions from Earle Godwin, whose lengthy service in broadcasting was acknowledged by his unofficial title, the dean of radio commentators.[26]

In September 1953, NBC abruptly informed Barkley that he would not receive a contract for a second set of twenty-six shows. Jane later spoke harshly about the show's cancellation, but ratings are ratings, and Barkley was neither a comedian like Bob Hope nor a singer like Bing Crosby. Barkley did not miss doing the show, however, because he had his hands full with another project. He was helping prepare his autobiography for publication. As early as 1947, the head of a major publishing house, Alfred A. Knopf, suggested that the then Senate minority leader consider writing a memoir. The notion received impetus at decade's end when a widely read and heavily subscribed magazine, the *Saturday Evening Post,* ran a feature article on Barkley, "Washington's Greatest Storyteller." It prompted the vice president, with secretarial help, to begin composing some ideas for a book. By March 1951, Andrew R. "Drew" Pearson caught wind of Barkley's efforts and publicized the project on his popular NBC radio program "Drew Pearson Comments" on March 11. Radio revelations about Barkley as a memoirist prompted several book publishers, including the Bobbs-Merrill Company and Doubleday and Company, to compete for the manuscript.[27]

Of the eight major publishing houses that contacted Barkley and expressed an interest in printing and marketing his autobiography, Doubleday initially won the competition. The reason is simple. Doubleday's editor in chief, Ken McCormick, offered an advance of $50,000 (then a small fortune) against a satisfactory manuscript in the form of the first six chapters. More than that, McCormick's letter promised a 15 percent straight royalty from the retail price; it also spelled out exactly what would happen with revenue generated from reprint, book club, movie, and TV rights and even foreign sales. The offer resembled the one given to General Eisenhower, then president of Columbia University, for his best-selling book *Crusade in Europe,* also published by Doubleday. Later that year, Barkley provided the firm, not just six chapters, but the entire manuscript of 360 pages. On January 10, 1952, the publisher sent Barkley a summary of the reports from several editors who had read the memoir. The manuscript was not satisfactory. Barkley had spent too much time on his childhood and ancestry, introduced too many people, and buried memorable and readable material in less important passages. The publisher recommended that he edit and rewrite his manuscript with the aid of a professional editor.[28]

Barkley sent chapters over time to two other publishers, Bobbs-Merrill and Knopf, but with results much like those from Doubleday. Nevertheless, Doubleday kept in touch with the would-be memoirist and continued to show interest in helping him with his manuscript. What happened next can best be understood by the fact that Doubleday was a subsidiary of the Curtis Publishing Company, which also published a number of magazines, including the very popular *Saturday Evening Post*. In April 1953, NBC's new but temporary television personality finally agreed to Doubleday's suggestion and accepted the help of Sidney Shalett, a freelance writer who had worked for the *New York Times* and then served as a correspondent for the *American Magazine* as well as a stringer in editing and writing for the *Saturday Evening Post*. The latter loaned Shalett to Doubleday, which paid his expenses and part of his salary for six months beginning in June. Shalett had access to Barkley's original manuscript and spent hours and days at the Barkley apartment in Washington and, after September, in Angles where he tape-recorded at great length Barkley's reminiscences about his life and career.[29]

On the basis of these extensive interviews, Shalett wrote Barkley's autobiography. The subject of the book read Shalett's draft manuscript more like an editor, one who was deeply familiar with its content. All things considered, Barkley's share of the promised $50,000 advance dropped to $30,000, with the remainder going to Shalett. Royalties also changed. The listed author received 80 percent of the royalties, and 20 percent went to Shalett, whose assistance, but not coauthorship, was acknowledged in the book. Barkley, however, received much more money up front because two Curtis subsidiaries collaborated. Before Shalett completed the book at the end of May 1954, he had already prepared a shortened version of Barkley's life in segments that was published by the *Saturday Evening Post*. The series actually served as an advertisement for the sale of the book. Barkley, the listed author, received a generous $65,000 for the serialization. Shalett's compensation came from a regular salary funded by the magazine. Later, the published book appeared on October 13. Aside from distribution to and sales from bookstores across the country, it became the monthly selection or the alternate selection of twelve national book clubs. Even though some reviewers considered it to be shallow—it focused as much on Barkley's stories as on his achievements—all this activity plus Doubleday publicity thrust *That Reminds Me* into the status of a best seller.[30]

Barkley's multiple, widely read 1954 publications partly explain his decision to return to the hustings and seek political office. Thanks to Curtis

Publishing, he was flush with cash, and the activity surrounding his memoirs kept his name before the public. To be sure, he also wanted to prove to certain Democrats—and especially sixteen labor leaders—that he really was not too old for public service. Moreover, he admitted publicly that he was tired of playing the country squire at Angles, where his son, David, actually managed the large farm. He simply wanted to return to the political life he had relished for more than four decades. The inspiration for his decision came from Governor Lawrence W. Wetherby and Senator Earle C. Clements. The pair had surveyed the commonwealth's political landscape and, except for Barkley, could not find a single Democrat with enough fame and a reputation for leadership to prevent the Republican John Sherman Cooper from keeping his seat in the US Senate in an election year. In March Barkley accepted the challenge from Wetherby and Clements to run against Cooper. First, in August, Barkley won the Democratic primary by astronomical proportions against three weak opponents. Then, in typical Iron Man fashion, he canvassed the state frenetically and, incredibly, delivered as many as fifteen speeches a day, beginning with an address in Shelbyville (Shelby County) on September 30, 1954. He struck hard at issues related to unemployment among coal miners, low agricultural prices for farmers, and broken promises from the GOP administration in Washington. In short, he aligned himself with his traditional base of support: farmers, workers, and those disgruntled with the GOP. On election day, November 2, 1954, his total votes exceeded Cooper's by more than seventy thousand. After Alben won his fifth election to the US Senate, he and Jane soon returned to their Washington apartment.[31]

Two months later, on January 3, 1955, Clements, the senior Kentucky senator, accompanied Barkley, the junior Kentucky senator, down the Senate aisle to Vice President Nixon, who administered the oath of office. The brief ceremony ended with Barkley signing the rolls for the twelfth time as a member of Congress. Colleagues, witnesses, and those in the gallery and press gallery gave him a standing ovation. The tenure of his service in the Senate had been broken and cost Barkley his seniority. He entered the upper chamber of the nation's legislative assembly as a freshman. The Democratic senator Harley Kilgore (WV) offered his front-row seat to Barkley, who turned him down. The former vice president took delight in his backbench assignment. He sat between two other Democratic newcomers, Patrick McNamara (MI) and Richard Neuberger (OR). His junior position meant that he would play no leadership role in the formation and approval of legislation. On the other hand, one could argue that his victory against a Republican in November 1954 gave the Democrats a two-vote edge (49–47) over the GOP. It enabled Lyndon B. Johnson (TX) to become the Senate's majority leader. Johnson, as a reward to Barkley for his crucial victory and out of recognition for his years of service, arranged to have him appointed to the important Finance Committee and the prestigious Foreign Relations Committee—assignments often reserved for senators with lengthy, continuous membership in the upper chamber.[32]

As a member of the latter committee, Barkley was able to perform a gracious act on behalf of his recent Republican opponent. President Eisenhower nominated John Sherman Cooper to be America's ambassador to India, then the most important neutral country in the ongoing Cold War era. When Cooper came before the Foreign Relations Committee, Barkley readily endorsed his nomination with his voice and his vote. He also drew smiles from Cooper and his committee colleagues by congratulating the former (and future) Kentucky senator on his recent engagement to the socialite Lorraine R. Shevlin. Outside the political hustings, the two men were actually friends. Despite this incident, Barkley could be a force neither in advancing nor in suppressing specific pieces of legislation. Bills before congress had to be read to him by a staff member. During the recent electoral campaign, most of his speeches were off-the-cuff remarks from basic points he had committed to memory. He did deliver a scripted speech. The twenty-page draft of double-spaced lines took seventy-eight pages of exploded print in the version he read. In the Senate, Barkley was beloved by his colleagues, who treasured his wit and humorous tales. The Iron Man, however, had difficulty speaking with authority about bills he could not read, ponder, and study with care.[33]

By the winter of 1955–1956, the unfortunate was happening. Certainly, the Iron Man continued to feel strong and vibrant after proving his physical and political stamina in winning the hard-fought 1954 campaign. On the other hand, by the start of 1956 it had become obvious that he was going blind. He did not, however, withdraw from life and society but instead expanded his activities to see things and people at least imperfectly before their images disappeared entirely. With the aid of a calendar/diary that she kept to help her sight-impaired husband keep his schedule, Jane could list, for instance, some of her husband's commitments for April 1956. In that month Barkley addressed the Woodrow Wilson Centennial Dinner, delivered a report to senatorial colleagues on the forthcoming meeting of the

Inter-Parliamentary Union in Bangkok, Thailand, attended the Apple Blossom Festival in Winchester, Virginia, joined members of Congress for the annual Press Club party, enjoyed a dinner that celebrated the tenth anniversary of television's "Meet the Press," and picnicked with friends at Senator Harry F. Byrd's Virginia farm.[34]

The final entry in Jane's calendar/diary for her husband's activities was the mock convention at Washington and Lee University, where Barkley delivered the keynote address on Monday afternoon, April 30. When he collapsed at the end of his speech, Jane was among the first to reach him from her front-row seat. She assumed or hoped that the hot weather had simply caused him to faint. As she held his head in her lap, Jane failed to revive him. Francis P. Gaines, the president of Washington and Lee, promptly called the rescue squad and a heart specialist, Dr. Robert Munger. Rescue personnel administered oxygen to the stricken senator, but without effect. He was pronounced dead at 5:25 P.M., though the heart specialist was certain that his death was instantaneous at the moment of his collapse, around 5:15. Funeral services were held at Washington's Foundry Methodist Church on Wednesday. Those attending the service included President Eisenhower, Vice President Nixon, and almost the entire Senate as well as members of the House, the Supreme Court, and cabinet officials. The Reverend Frederick B. Harris praised Barkley as "one of the Republic's best-loved sons." The Methodist pastor noted that the country would be "poorer because his eloquent, passionate voice will be heard no more in its councils, on its platforms and in its national forum."[35]

The next morning Senator Barkley's body arrived in Paducah on a special Chesapeake and Ohio train drawn appropriately by an old-fashioned steam locomotive. It carried more than a dozen senators such as Hubert Humphrey, William Fulbright, and Earl Clements. Among those arriving separately were former president Truman, Kentucky governor A. B. "Happy" Chandler, and three Democratic candidates for president in 1956: Adlai Stevenson, Estes Kefauver, and New York governor Averell Harriman. Even though all schools and most businesses were closed in the town, the visitors could eat in the Irwin S. Cobb Hotel, named for another famous Paducah citizen. After a brief funeral service in the Broadway Methodist Church, the hearse drove to the Mt. Kenton Cemetery. The burial ceremony lasted a short time and was attended not only by the day's special visitors but also by crowds of local families. Other townspeople had shown their respect for Barkley by lining the road leading to the cemetery. After the service, Jane remained in Paducah for two months before going back to Washington, where she secured employment with George Washington University. Barkley's son stayed for the duration at Angles; the senator's daughters, after their husbands passed away, lived in nearby apartments in the nation's capital.[36]

Tributes offered immediately after Barkley's death help measure the life of the man. The former postmaster general and Democratic Party chairman James A. Farley focused on the humble beginnings that Barkley managed over time to transform into the nation's second highest office. Former president Harry S. Truman dwelt on the deceased's effective work in the nation's legislature, first in the House, then in the Senate, and finally as Senate president when he served as one of the greatest vice presidents in American history. President Dwight D. Eisenhower recognized the senator's esteemed accomplishments on behalf of the people of Kentucky and the nation. Vice President Richard M. Nixon remarked that Barkley had the incredible ability to be viewed with fondness and respect by those from both political parties. Governor Averell Harriman felt that what would be missed the most would be the senator's warmhearted nature and wise counsel. Senator Estes Kefauver believed that Barkley embodied the highest qualities one could hope for in a national leader. Senate majority leader Lyndon B. Johnson noted that the senator was beloved by the nation's citizens. The presidential candidate Adlai E. Stevenson admired Barkley's liberal nature. Senator Harry F. Byrd, former vice president John Nance Garner, and House speaker Sam Rayburn celebrated the greatness of the man but expressed grief in their personal loss. Finally, Governor A. B. "Happy" Chandler, a person with unhappy thoughts about the senator who beat him in the 1938 election, inadvertently, but correctly, praised the Iron Man for his remarkable political success. "I always thought," Chandler had to admit, "Senator Barkley was indestructible."[37]

Acknowledgments

Alben W. Barkley was a larger-than-life political personality who first became a national figure in 1918 and who had become a household name by 1950. He was one of the few individuals who could actually compete in popularity polls with the military hero Dwight D. Eisenhower after World War II. Barkley's amazing public career covered the half century from the age of progressivism to Eisenhower's midcentury presidential administration. During this period, the United States moved from a strong agricultural but developing industrial nation to a global power. Barkley's life touched and sometimes influenced all of the era's key events as he moved from local politician to congressman, senator, senate majority leader, vice president, and senator once again. Small wonder that a number of adept and perceptive scholars researched and wrote Ph.D. dissertations about the Kentuckian, but each shied away from attempting more than a portion of his life. Thus, for reasons that may now be obvious, this single-volume, comprehensive biography would simply not be possible without the aid of those scholars and the well-informed professionals who helped me unearth and unravel key sources of information about Barkley.

Certainly, the groundwork for an examination of Barkley's life had to begin in the Breckinridge Research Room of Special Collections at the University of Kentucky. I was assisted by Subject Specialist Archivist Jeff Suchanek, Research Coordinator Matthew A. Harris, and Research Assistant John Wickre. On a research venture years earlier, these three were preceded by Terry Birdwhistell, William Cooper, William Marshall, and Terry Warth. Barkley spent years as a colleague and friend of Harry S. Truman in the US Senate, in the Truman presidency, and in the time he served as Truman's vice president. Many documents in the Truman Presidential Library attest to their close relationship. Those who helped unlock the appropriate contents of this relationship were Supervisory Archivist Sam Rushay, Archivist Randy Sowell, Archives Specialist Jim Armistead, and Audiovisual Archivist Pauline Testerman. For the quarter century from 1920 when Franklin D. Roosevelt was the Democratic vice presidential candidate until his death in 1945 as US president, Barkley had interacted with the squire of Hyde Park. Their association, at times fruitful and occasionally rocky, was revealed in the Roosevelt Presidential Library with the assistance of Supervisory Archivist Robert Clark, Archivist Matt Hanson, and Archivist Mark Renovitch.

A large number of collateral papers, ranging from those of Senator Bronson Cutting to those of President Thomas Woodrow Wilson, are housed in the Manuscript Division of the Library of Congress. Those offering assistance to researchers included Fred C. Coker, Gary J. Kohn, Ruth Nicholson, Mary Ann Roos, and Janis Wiggins. Individuals who provided help with the biography included Richard Baker of the US Senate Historical Office, Sharon Bidwell of the Louisville Courier-Journal Morgue, University Records Officer and Digital Archives Specialist Jackie Couture of Eastern Kentucky University's Crabbe Library, Special Collections Librarian Keith M. Heim of Murray State University's Pogue Library, Archivist Marsha Trimble Rogers of the University of Virginia's Arthur J. Morris Law Library, and James Rush of the National Archives. Special thanks for continuous aid must go to Michael Gallen, the director of Flagler College's Proctor Library, and the librarians Suzanne Eichler, Sue Burkhart, and Elizabeth H. Sterthaus of Embry-Riddle Aeronautical University's Jack Hunt Library— and also to the love of my life, Joyce, who served as my alpha editor. Importantly, I want to express my grateful appreciation to my copyeditor, Joseph Brown, and the anonymous readers associated with the University Press of Kentucky. Each one took thoughtful care in reading the manuscript and recommending improvements as well as alerting me to needed corrections. Remaining problems in the narrative belong exclusively to me. Finally, I need to acknowledge the expert assistance of Cindy Taylor, who gave new life to two old photographs.

Notes

The following abbreviations have been used throughout the notes:

FDR/E. Roosevelt Papers   Eleanor Roosevelt Papers, Franklin D. Roosevelt Presidential Library

FDR/Roosevelt Papers   Franklin D. Roosevelt Papers, Franklin D. Roosevelt Presidential Library

FDR/Tully Papers   Grace Tully Papers, Franklin D. Roosevelt Presidential Library

HST/Barkley Papers   Alben W. Barkley Papers, Audio Tape and Transcript, Harry S. Truman Presidential Library

HST/Truman Papers   Harry S. Truman Papers, Harry S. Truman Presidential Library

LC/Connally Papers   Thomas T. Connally Papers, Library of Congress

LC/Cutting Papers   Bronson W. Cutting Papers, Library of Congress

LC/Wilson Papers   T. Woodrow Wilson Papers, Library of Congress

LC/Woolley Papers   Robert W. Woolley Papers, Library of Congress

UKSC/Barkley Papers   Alben W. Barkley Papers, Special Collections, University of Kentucky

Prologue

1. Harry Bolser, "[House Speaker Sam T.] Rayburn . . . Lauds Barkley at Dedication of Monument in Paducah," *Louisville Courier-Journal,* April 15, 1957; Allan M. Trout, "Statue Enshrines Barkley with Great Kentuckians," *Louisville Courier-Journal,* October 4, 1963; Jim Hampton, "[Senate Minority Leader Everett M.] Dirksen Eulogizes Barkley as Statue at [the University of Kentucky] Unveiled," *Louisville Courier-Journal,* November 24, 1965.

2. Jane R. Barkley, *I Married the Veep* (New York: Vanguard, 1958), 304–8.

3. Alben W. Barkley quoted from "Text of Senator Barkley's Final Address, Washington and Lee University, April 30, 1956" (transcription), p. 1, box 165, UKSC/Barkley Papers; "Barkley, 78, Dies of Heart Attack during a Speech," *New York Times,* May

1, 1956. The contemporary newspaper account is slightly different from the one given later by Jane Rucker Barkley to the author of her memoir, Frances Spatz Leighton.

4. Barkley quoted from "Text of Senator Barkley's Final Address, Washington and Lee University, April 30, 1956," pp. 1, 4 (see also pp. 2–3), box 165, UKSC/Barkley Papers.

5. Ibid., p. 4.

1. Child of the Jackson Purchase

1. Quote from Alben W. Barkley, *That Reminds Me* (Garden City, NY: Doubleday, 1954), 24; interview of Alben Barkley by Sidney Shalett, summer and fall 1953, reel 1, HST/Barkley Papers.

2. James K. Libbey, "Alben W. Barkley," *Louisville Courier-Journal Magazine,* November 20, 1977, 11–17, 54–57, and *Dear Alben: Mr. Barkley of Kentucky* (Lexington: University Press of Kentucky, 1979).

3. J. H. Battle, W. H. Perrin, and G. C. Kniffin, *Kentucky: A History of the State* (Louisville: F. A. Battey, 1885), 3–6; P. P. Karan and Cotton Mather, eds., *Atlas of Kentucky* (Lexington: University Press of Kentucky, 1977), 164–67; Thomas D. Clark, *A History of Kentucky* (Lexington, KY: John Bradford, 1960), 3; Lowell H. Harrison and James C. Klotter, *A New History of Kentucky* (Lexington: University Press of Kentucky, 1997), 23.

4. Battle, Perrin, and Kniffin, *Kentucky,* 6–7. See also Lowell H. Harrison, *The Civil War in Kentucky* (Lexington: University Press of Kentucky, 1975).

5. Malcolm E. Jewell and Everett W. Cunningham, *Kentucky Politics* (Lexington: University of Kentucky Press, 1968), 180; Bela Kornitzer, *American Fathers and Sons* (n.p.: Hermitage, 1952), 106. For example, only in the latter half of the 1970s did the *Paducah Sun-Democrat* drop the party name from its masthead. For a brief monograph on Kentucky journalism, see Herndon J. Evans, *The Newspaper Press of Kentucky* (Lexington: University Press of Kentucky, 1976).

6. Charley A. Leistner, "The Political Campaign Speaking of Alben W. Barkley" (Ph.D. diss., University of Missouri, 1958), 8; Alben W. Barkley to L. W. Arnett, August 22, 1912, box 1, UKSC/Barkley Papers.

7. Battle, Perrin, and Kniffin, *Kentucky,* 57–58; W. F. Axton, *Tobacco and Kentucky* (Lexington: University Press of Kentucky, 1975), 49, 60, 76–77.

8. Gerald S. Grinde, "The Early Political Career of Alben W. Barkley, 1877–1937" (Ph.D. diss., University of Illinois, 1976), 3; reel 1, HST/Barkley Papers. In several publications, Barkley's mother's name is given as Electra. However, Barkley's daughter, Marian Barkley Truit, stated adamantly that her grandmother's real name was Electa. See author interview of Marian Barkley Truitt, June 29, 1980.

9. Grinde, "Early Political Career of Alben W. Barkley," 3; Kornitzer, *American Fathers and Sons,* 105; Fred G. Neuman, *The Story of Paducah* (Paducah, KY: Young Printing, 1927), 217; reel 1, HST/Barkley Papers.

10. Quote from Kornitzer, *American Fathers and Sons,* 94; J. T. Salter, ed., *Public Men: In and Out of Office* (Chapel Hill: University of North Carolina Press, 1946), 243. Interviews conducted by Leistner revealed more faults in John Barkley than just a doting behavior. A few of his contemporaries viewed him as ignorant and shiftless and

claimed that Electa Barkley kept the household running. See Leistner, "Political Campaign Speaking of Alben W. Barkley," 10–11 (narrative and notes).

11. Quote from Barkley, *That Reminds Me*, 27; reel 2, HST/Barkley Papers. Interestingly, the actual first name of both uncles was William. Both were called Willie by friends and relatives rather than the normal and informal Bill.

12. Clark, *A History of Kentucky*, 419–26; Kornitzer, *American Fathers and Sons*, 102; reel 2, HST/Barkley Papers.

13. Quote from Kornitzer, *American Fathers and Sons*, 99. Six Barkley children were born near Lowes in the period 1877–1890, according to Alben Barkley in an article he wrote for the *Hickman County Gazette*, April 30, 1953. The other two children were born near Clinton, Kentucky.

14. Barkley, *That Reminds Me*, 26, 32–33; reel 2, HST/Barkley Papers.

15. First quote from *Louisville Courier-Journal*, July 3, 1937; second quote from Kornitzer, *American Fathers and Sons*, 94.

16. Quote from Kornitzer, *American Fathers and Sons*, 101; reel 1, HST/Barkley Papers.

17. Both quotes from Kornitzer, *American Fathers and Sons*, 88; reel 2, HST/Barkley Papers.

18. Quote from Barkley, *That Reminds Me*, 44; reels 2–3, HST/Barkley Papers.

19. Kornitzer, *American Fathers and Sons*, 89; *Hickman County Gazette*, October 14, 1926; reels 1, 22, HST/Barkley Papers.

20. Quote from Kornitzer, *American Fathers and Sons*, 92; Barkley, *That Reminds Me*, 39, 48.

21. Quote from Kornitzer, *American Fathers and Sons*, 90–91; reel 1, HST/Barkley Papers.

22. Kornitzer, *American Fathers and Sons*, 97; reel 2, HST/Barkley Papers.

23. Quote from Kornitzer, *American Fathers and Sons*, 88 (see also 105). The only supposed exception to the liquor rule occurred when Alben suffered a snake bite at age six. Reel 2, HST/Barkley Papers. On the basis of interviews, however, Leistner states that the family would not allow liquor to be consumed even during that emergency. Leistner, "Political Campaign Speaking of Alben W. Barkley," 14.

24. I have noted from visits that the school Alben attended in Lowes has since been reconverted into a modest home. For discussions of public education in Graves County, see Battle, Perrin, and Kniffin, *Kentucky*, 54; Neuman, *Story of Paducah*, 217; and reel 2, HST/Barkley Papers.

25. Clark, *A History of Kentucky*, 201. See also the discussion of country schools in Thomas D. Clark, *Pills, Petticoats and Plows: The Southern Country Store* (New York: Bobbs-Merrill, 1944), 173–89.

26. First quote from *Hickman County Gazette*, October 14, 1926; second quote from Barkley, *That Reminds Me*, 16. See also *Louisville Courier-Journal*, July 22, 1937; and reel 1, HST/Barkley Papers.

27. Barkley, *That Reminds Me*, 51; Clark, *Pills, Petticoats and Plows*, 19–33.

28. Thomas D. Clark, *Agrarian Kentucky* (Lexington: University Press of Kentucky, 1977), 56; Kornitzer, *American Fathers and Sons*, 98; reels 1–2, HST/Barkley Papers.

When Alben accompanied his father to, e.g., Paducah, the daylong, eighteen-mile trip by wagon forced them to spend at least one night in rooms connected to the town's wagon yard. Evenings were spent with other farmers who entertained each other with their stories and tall tales. Barkley felt that this experience also added to his storytelling ability. Reel 1, HST/Barkley Papers.

29. Quote from Kornitzer, *American Fathers and Sons,* 99; reel 1, HST/Barkley Papers. Barkley claimed that his first girlfriend was Joe Dunn's daughter, Ora, a neighbor girl who walked to school with him. Reel 2, HST/Barkley Papers.

30. Quote from Barkley, *That Reminds Me,* 50; Alben W. Barkley, "Accustomed as I Am to Public Speaking," *Collier's* 127 (June 9, 1951): 20–21, 66–67; Clark, *Pills, Petticoats and Plows,* 297–312.

2. Clinton and College

1. *Hickman County Gazette,* October 21, 1976.
2. *Hickman County Gazette,* April 30, 1953.
3. Richard Hofstadter, *The Age of Reform* (New York: Vintage, 1955), 50–52; Axton, *Tobacco and Kentucky,* 78–81.
4. For examples of errors referred to in the narrative, see Neuman, *Story of Paducah,* 217; and Salter, ed., *Public Men,* 242–43.
5. Quote from *Hickman County Gazette,* October 21, 1976.
6. *Hickman County Gazette,* April 30, 1953.
7. Ibid.; Jackie Caraway and Lucille Owings, *Sesquicentennial Program Booklet* (Clinton, KY, 1971), 18–20.
8. *Hickman County Gazette,* April 30, 1953; Leistner, "Political Campaign Speaking of Alben W. Barkley," 34.
9. Kornitzer, *American Fathers and Sons,* 102–3; Barkley, *That Reminds Me,* 37.
10. Quote from *Hickman County Gazette,* October 14, 1976. See also *Hickman County Gazette,* April 30, 1953; and reel 3, HST/Barkley Papers.
11. Reel 1, HST/Barkley Papers.
12. Ibid.
13. Robert M. Ireland, *The County in Kentucky History* (Lexington: University Press of Kentucky, 1976), 55–56. See also Robert M. Ireland, *Little Kingdoms: The Counties of Kentucky, 1850–1891* (Lexington: University Press of Kentucky, 1977); and reel 1, HST/Barkley Papers.
14. Barkley, *That Reminds Me,* 34–36; reel 11, HST/Barkley Papers. The nexus between the races in rural America was, of course, the farmers' economic plight. In the 1890s, the populist search for a political answer to the common man's problems sometimes led to a direct alliance between whites and former slaves. Several studies have dealt with this issue. See, e.g., C. Vann Woodward, *The Strange Career of Jim Crow* (New York: Oxford University Press, 1955), 60–65.
15. Kornitzer, *American Fathers and Sons,* 93; *Hickman County Gazette,* April 30, 1953; reel 3, HST/Barkley Papers. For a different explanation of the origins of Barkley's nickname, see Salter, ed., *Public Men,* 243.
16. *Hickman County Gazette,* October 28, 1976, and October 14, 1926. There was

also a seventy-five-cent incidental fee charged per term. See *Eleventh Annual Announcement and Catalogue of Marvin College* (Clinton, KY, 1896). The local historian and newspaper correspondent Virginia Jewell of Clinton shared with me her copies of Marvin's catalogs.

17. O. P. Fitzgerald, the editor of the *Nashville Christian Advocate,* dedicated the building. See *Hickman County Gazette,* September 30, 1971.

18. Ibid.; *Hickman County Gazette,* November 11, 1976.

19. *Eleventh Annual Announcement and Catalogue;* memorandum from Virginia Jewell to author, March 15, 1979.

20. *Hickman County Gazette,* April 30, 1953, September 30, 1971, October 28, 1976, and November 11, 1976.

21. Reel 10, HST/Barkley Papers.

22. Quote from Kornitzer, *American Fathers and Sons,* 99–100; reel 10, HST/Barkley Papers.

23. Barkley, *That Reminds Me,* 56–57; reels 2–3, HST/Barkley Papers.

24. Quote from *Hickman County Gazette,* October 14, 1926. See also Salter, ed., *Public Men,* 243; and *Hickman County Gazette,* October 28, 1976. The records and, thus, the grades of Marvin College are no longer extant.

25. *Hickman County Gazette,* October 28, 1976; Barkley, "Accustomed as I Am to Public Speaking," 21; reel 15, HST/Barkley Papers. As was normal for the time, only males could join the Periclean Debating Society. Coeds participated in the Hypatian Literary Society.

26. Quote from Leistner, "Political Campaign Speaking of Alben W. Barkley," 57. See also *Hickman County Gazette,* October 28, 1976.

27. Barkley, *That Reminds Me,* 49–50.

28. Quote from *Hickman County Gazette,* October 28, 1976.

29. Grinde, "Early Political Career of Alben W. Barkley," 18; Salter, ed., *Public Men,* 243.

30. Leistner, "Political Campaign Speaking of Alben W. Barkley," 42–43. While Emory's main campus is now in Atlanta, the school kept a branch in Oxford.

31. *Hickman County Gazette,* April 30, 1953.

32. Ibid.

33. The amount loaned ($175 or $200) and the principal holder of the note (Thomas Kennedy or Nathaniel P. Moss) vary with the sources of information. See, e.g., Leistner, "Political Campaign Speaking of Alben W. Barkley," 44; and Salter, ed., *Public Men,* 243.

34. Neuman, *Story of Paducah,* 217; Barkley, "Accustomed as I Am to Public Speaking," 21; *Hickman County Gazette,* October 14, 1926; Virginia Cain (at the time an assistant archivist at Emory University) to the author, April 29, 1980.

35. *Hickman County Gazette,* April 30, 1953, September 30, 1971, and November 4, 1976.

3. Barkley's Reconciliation with His Roots

1. *Hickman County Gazette,* November 4, 1976.

2. Irvin S. Cobb, *Exit Laughing* (New York: Bobbs-Merrill, 1941), 68.

3. Ibid., 70–77.

4. Neuman, *Story of Paducah,* 217; entry on Wheeler in *A Newspaper Reference Work: Men of Affairs of Paducah and Western Kentucky* (Paducah, KY: Paducah Evening Sun, 1913), n.p.; Joe LaGore (former editor of the *Paducah Sun[-Democrat]*) to author, July 7, 1980.

5. *Hickman County Gazette,* October 14, 1926.

6. Quote from Barkley, *That Reminds Me,* 63.

7. Paul W. Glad, *The Trumpet Soundeth: William Jennings Bryan and His Democracy, 1896–1912* (Lincoln: University of Nebraska Press, 1960), 54–57, 141–46.

8. Charles Morrow Wilson, *The Commoner: William Jennings Bryan* (Garden City, NY: Doubleday, 1970), 230; Hambleton Tapp and James C. Klotter, *Kentucky: Decades of Discord, 1865–1900* (Frankfort: Kentucky Historical Society, 1977), 353–55.

9. Joseph Frazier Wall, *Henry Watterson: Reconstructed Rebel* (New York: Oxford University Press, 1956), esp. ix, xii (Barkley's introduction); *Hickman County Gazette,* April 30, 1953.

10. Barkley, "Accustomed as I Am to Public Speaking," 21; *Hickman County Gazette,* April 30, 1953.

11. Reel 3, HST/Barkley Papers. A different picture of the relationship between Wheeler and Barkley was painted by Wheeler's son, James, when he was interviewed in 1973. See Grinde, "Early Political Career of Alben W. Barkley," 22.

12. Salter, *Public Men,* 243; reel 3, HST/Barkley Papers; Cobb, *Exit Laughing,* 333–35. In a 1926 newspaper article Barkley gave his salary as $15, and in his memoirs he mentioned $12. See *Hickman County Gazette,* October 14, 1926; and Barkley, *That Reminds Me,* 64.

13. H. Levin, ed., *The Lawyers and Lawmakers of Kentucky* (Chicago: Lewis, 1897), 412–13; Fred G. Neuman, *Paducahans in History* (Paducah, KY: Young Printing, 1922), 75. Bishop died in 1902.

14. Grinde, "Early Political Career of Alben W. Barkley," 23. Ollie M. James replaced Wheeler in 1902. See Thaddeus M. Smith, "Ollie Murray James: An Early Twentieth Century Politician" (M.A. thesis, Eastern Kentucky University, 1973), 36.

15. Charles Kerr, ed., *History of Kentucky* (New York: American Historical Society, 1922), 270; Salter, *Public Men,* 243.

16. Reel 16, HST/Barkley Papers.

17. Ibid.

18. Grinde, "Early Political Career of Alben W. Barkley," 28.

19. Quote from Barkley, *That Reminds Me,* 77; reels 20–21, HST/Barkley Papers. Barkley also sang in the Methodist church choir. See reel 4, HST/Barkley Papers.

20. Barkley, *That Reminds Me,* 77–78.

21. Kerr, ed., *History of Kentucky,* 270; Neuman, *Story of Paducah,* 217; Marsha Trimble Rogers (University of Virginia School of Law archivist) to author, April 28, 1980. There were a total of 118 lectures offered to several categories of students. See *Catalogue for 1902,* University of Virginia Summer Law School, 5–8.

22. *Catalogue for 1902,* University of Virginia Summer Law School, 11.

23. The literature on Jefferson is massive. For a brief but authoritative study, see For-

rest McDonald, *The Presidency of Thomas Jefferson* (Lawrence: University Press of Kansas, 1976).

24. Seymour Martin Lipsett, *Political Man: The Social Bases of Politics* (Garden City, NY: Doubleday, 1960), 279–86.

25. Kerr, ed., *History of Kentucky,* 270; author interview of Marian Barkley Truitt, June 29, 1980. Accounts differ on the background of the Brower family.

26. Electa Barkley quoted from *Louisville Courier-Journal,* July 22, 1937.

27. Author interview of David M. Barkley, May 18, 1977; Kerr, ed., *History of Kentucky,* 270.

28. Author interview of David M. Barkley, May 18, 1977.

29. Kerr, ed., *History of Kentucky,* 270; reel 4, HST/Barkley Papers.

30. Cobb, *Exit Laughing,* 335. County attorneys received 30 percent of judgments (fines) in county courts and 25 percent of judgments in district courts. See John D. Carroll, *The Kentucky Statutes* (Louisville: Courier-Journal Printing, 1903), sec. 133.

31. *Paducah Evening Sun,* December 19, 1904. For the flavor of local politics in this era, see James C. Klotter, *Kentucky: Portrait in Paradox, 1900–1950* (Frankfort: Kentucky Historical Society, 1996), 195–201.

32. Leistner, "Political Campaign Speaking of Alben W. Barkley," 82; reel 3, HST/Barkley Papers.

33. Quote from Beverly Smith, "Washington's Greatest Storyteller," *Saturday Evening Post* 222 (July 2, 1949): 17–19, 66–68, 68. See also Campaign Card, box 1, UKSC/Barkley Papers.

34. Smith, "Washington's Greatest Storyteller," 68; reel 3, HST/Barkley Papers.

35. *Paducah Weekly Sun,* March 1, 1905, and March 15, 1905. There were fifteen debates scheduled throughout the county between March 6 and March 21.

36. Barkley secured 940 votes in the county. See *Paducah Evening Sun,* April 5, 1905.

4. From Courthouse to Congress

1. *Paducah News-Democrat,* September 22, 1906, and October 28, 1909; Grinde, "Early Political Career of Alben W. Barkley," 49; Ireland, *Little Kingdoms,* 35; John E. Reeves, *Kentucky Government* (Frankfort: Kentucky Legislative Research Commission, 1973), 100–101. For county attorney duties at the time, see Carroll, *Kentucky Statutes,* secs. 178, 2119, 4333, 4347, 4394, 4440.

2. Ireland, *The County in Kentucky History,* vii; Carroll, *Kentucky Statutes,* secs. 4332–33.

3. *Paducah News-Democrat,* October 28, 1909; Barkley, *That Reminds Me,* 80.

4. *Paducah News-Democrat,* July 29, 1908; *Paducah Weekly Sun,* January 9, 1907, April 3, 1907, and August 7, 1907; Salter, ed., *Public Men,* 144.

5. Neuman, *Story of Paducah,* 60. Elizabeth Sanders has noted: "Despite the common description of the progressive reform leaders as representatives of the urban business and professional classes, the farmers were the most numerous constituents for expanded public power in the southern and midwestern states where the reform movements were strongest." Elizabeth Sanders, *Roots of Reform: Farmers, Workers, and the*

American State, 1877–1917 (Chicago: University of Chicago Press, 1999), 158. Several scholars argue that William Jennings Bryan symbolized the merger of rural populism and urban progressivism. See LeRoy Ashby, *William Jennings Bryan: Champion of Democracy* (Boston: Twayne, 1987), 97–125.

6. Henry B. Hines to Barkley, June 13, 1907, reel 1, David M. Barkley Microfilms, UKSC/Barkley Papers; *Paducah Weekly Sun,* July 17, 1907; Leistner, "Political Campaign Speaking of Alben W. Barkley," 85; *Paducah News-Democrat,* September 3, 1908, and October 10, 14, 30, 1908.

7. *Paducah News-Democrat,* October 25, 1908; William R. Mofield, "The Speaking Role of Alben Barkley in the Campaign of 1948" (Ph.D. diss., Southern Illinois University, 1964), 29.

8. *Paducah Weekly Sun,* February 22, 1905; *Paducah News-Democrat,* October 25, 1908.

9. *Paducah Weekly Sun,* May 5, 1909. Smedley was first indicted on January 16, 1909. See *Paducah Evening Sun,* February 9, 1909. Unfortunately, many county records from this period were destroyed by the 1937 Ohio River flood.

10. *Paducah Weekly Sun,* July 21, 1909, and August 4, 1909. For a thorough and thoughtful investigation, see Gerald S. Grinde, "Politics and Scandal in the Progressive Era: Alben W. Barkley and the McCracken County Campaign of 1909," *Filson Club History Quarterly* 50 (April 1976): 36–51.

11. Quote from Barkley, *That Reminds Me,* 80.

12. See, e.g., Leistner, "Political Campaign Speaking of Alben W. Barkley," 79. The notion that Barkley ran unopposed in the 1909 election first appeared in Kerr, ed., *History of Kentucky,* 269. More than likely Kerr, not Barkley, caused the error in Salter, ed., *Public Men,* 244.

13. For Hazelip, see *A Newspaper Reference Work,* n.p.; and Neuman, *Paducahans in History,* 122–24.

14. *Paducah Evening Sun,* September 25, October 3, 1909.

15. *Paducah News-Democrat,* October 9, 10, 16, 1909; James C. Klotter, *William Goebel: The Politics of Wrath* (Lexington: University Press of Kentucky, 1977), 100–125. For an excellent discussion of the multidecade influence of the assassination, see Clark, *A History of Kentucky,* 436–46.

16. Grinde, "Politics and Scandal in the Progressive Era," 49–50; *Paducah Evening Sun,* November 3, 4, 1909.

17. Barkley, *That Reminds Me,* 81.

18. Ireland, *Little Kingdoms,* 24; Reeves, *Kentucky Government,* 100–101; John D. Carroll, *Kentucky Statutes* (Louisville: Courier-Journal Printing, 1915), secs. 331, 928, 938, 1037, 1057, 1077, 2044, 2103, 2113, 2232–33, 2240, 3925, 4115, 4421, 4868.

19. *Paducah Evening Sun,* January 1, 8, 1910.

20. Ireland, *The County in Kentucky History,* 70–71; *Paducah News-Democrat,* March 31, 1912; *Paducah Evening Sun,* May 4, October 4, and November 1, 1910.

21. Neuman, *Story of Paducah,* 218; *Paducah News-Democrat,* March 12, 1912; Clark, *A History of Kentucky,* 466–67.

22. *Paducah News-Democrat,* March 31, 1912.

23. Quotes from Kornitzer, *American Fathers and Sons,* 97, 104.

24. *Paducah News-Democrat,* December 15, 1911.

25. Klotter, *Kentucky: Portrait in Paradox,* 220–22; *Paducah Evening Sun,* February 6, 1911. For more information on James, see Forrest C. Pogue Jr., "The Life and Work of Senator Ollie Murray James" (M.A. thesis, University of Kentucky, 1932).

26. Leistner, "Political Campaign Speaking of Alben W. Barkley," 87; *Paducah News-Democrat,* March 24, April 23, 27, 1912; *Paducah Evening Sun,* March 25, August 28, 1912.

27. Salter, ed., *Public Men,* 245; *Paducah News-Democrat,* July 18, 30, 1908; Glad, *The Trumpet Soundeth,* 81–109; Donald K. Springen, *William Jennings Bryan: Orator of Smalltown America* (New York: Greenwood, 1991), 202–9, 217–26.

28. Quotes from Barkley, *That Reminds Me,* 84–86; *Paducah Evening Sun,* June 22, July 17, August 5, 1912; *Louisville Times,* June 11, 1912. Leistner argues that the congressional contest revealed Barkley as a superb speaker and politician. See Leistner, "Political Campaign Speaking of Alben W. Barkley," 88–93. Another historian claims that Barkley was the state's best "stump speaker." See Steven A. Channing, *Kentucky: A History* (New York: Norton, 1977), 183.

29. Grinde, "Early Political Career of Alben W. Barkley," 76; Barkley to W. A. Fraser, Sovereign Commander of Woodmen of the World, May 9, 1912, box 1, UKSC/Barkley Papers.

30. Urey Woodson, ed., *Report of the Proceedings of the Democratic National Convention of 1912* (Chicago: Democratic Party, 1912), 376; James Chace, *1912: Wilson, Roosevelt, Taft and Debs—the Election That Changed the Country* (New York: Simon & Schuster, 2004), 146–58; A. Scott Berg, *Wilson* (New York: Putnam's, 2013), 231–48.

31. The final tally was Barkley 9,274, Smith 5,707, Hendrick 3,374, and Corbett 898. There was a two-vote discrepancy in election reports. See *Paducah News-Democrat,* August 4, 1912; and *Calloway Times,* August 7, 1912.

5. Congressman Barkley and the New Freedom

1. Robert I. Blagg to Barkley (re: petition of W. G. Dycus), October 7, 1912, Barkley to Blagg, October 9, 1912, and Barkley to James V. Wear (editor of the *Weekly Advance* in Ballard County), November 15, 1912, all in box 1, UKSC/Barkley Papers; Clark, *Agrarian Kentucky,* 54–55. It was only in 1933 that Amendment 20 of the US Constitution changed the presidential inauguration date to January 20.

2. J. C. Dean to Barkley, November 7, 1912, Ollie M. James to Barkley, August 12, 1912, and Champ Clark to Barkley, November 6, 1912, all in box 1, UKSC/Barkley Papers.

3. Barkley to Champ Clark, November 22, 1912, box 1, UKSC/Barkley Papers; reel 14, HST/Barkley Papers; Arthur S. Link, *Woodrow Wilson and the Progressive Era, 1910–1917* (New York: Harper & Row, 1954), 11–13; Chace, *1912,* 238–40. It should be noted that in 1913 any Democratic president would likely have placed Bryan, the party's three-time national standard-bearer, in a prominent cabinet or ambassadorial post.

4. Quote from Barkley, *That Reminds Me,* 91. For examples of Speaker Clark's leg-

islative opposition to President Wilson, see Ray Stannard Baker, *Woodrow Wilson: Life and Letters,* 8 vols. (New York: Scribner's, 1946), 3:414–15; and John Milton Cooper Jr., *Woodrow Wilson: A Biography* (New York: Alfred A. Knopf, 2009), 47–51. See also Woodrow Wilson, *Congressional Government: A Study in American Politics* (Boston: Houghton, Mifflin, 1885).

5. Link, *Woodrow Wilson,* 12–17; Josephus Daniels, *The Wilson Era: Years of Peace, 1910–1917* (Chapel Hill: University of North Carolina Press, 1946), 47–67; H. W. Brands, *T.R.: The Last Romantic* (New York: Basic, 1997), 710–17.

6. George E. Mowry, *The Era of Theodore Roosevelt and the Birth of Modern America, 1900–1912* (New York: Harper & Row, 1958), 272; August Heckscher, *Woodrow Wilson* (New York: Scribner's, 1991), 256–61; Brands, *T.R.,* 676–77; Link, *Woodrow Wilson,* 20–22.

7. Quote from David Newton Lott, *The Presidents Speak: The Inaugural Addresses of the American Presidents from Washington to Clinton* (New York: Henry Holt, 1994), 236 (see also 233–35, 237); Berg, *Wilson,* 272–76.

8. Quote from Kornitzer, *American Fathers and Sons,* 97–98 (see also 104); reel 3, HST/Barkley Papers; author interview with Marian Barkley Truitt, June 29, 1980.

9. Reels 2, 15, HST/Barkley Papers; Clarence Sherrill to Barkley, June 29, 1916, Barkley to Sherrill, July 5, 1916, Barkley to Kentucky Commissioner of Motor Vehicles, April 11, 1917, and T. S. Byars (Kentucky commissioner of motor vehicles) to Barkley, April 13, 1917, all in box 1, UKSC/Barkley Papers; author interview of David M. Barkley, May 18, 1977; author interview of Marian Barkley Truitt, June 29, 1980.

10. Quote from William C. Adamson to Barkley, September 2, 1916, box 1, UKSC/Barkley Papers; reels 1, 8, HST/Barkley Papers; Karan and Mather, eds., *Atlas of Kentucky,* 60.

11. Barkley, *I Married the Veep,* 18–19; Randall B. Ripley, *Majority Party Leadership in Congress* (Boston: Little, Brown, 1969), 52, 54, 154.

12. Ripley, *Majority Party Leadership in Congress,* 55–56, 58, 63; Cooper, *Woodrow Wilson,* 97–98; Woodrow Wilson, *Constitutional Government in the United States* (New York: Columbia University Press, 1908), 68, 70–72.

13. Barkley, *I Married the Veep,* 44; reel 8, HST/Barkley Papers.

14. George Brown Tindall, *America: A Narrative History,* 2 vols. (New York: Norton, 1984), 2:836.

15. Woodrow Wilson to Barkley, January 26, 1915, reel 141, ser. 3, LC/Wilson Papers; White House Memorandum (re: Barkley and the appointment of W. L. Hale as postmaster), February 4, 1915, reel 263, ser. 4, LC/Wilson Papers; Wilson to Barkley, February 4, 1915, reel 141, ser. 3, LC/Wilson Papers; Wilson to US Postmaster General Albert S. Burleson (re: postmaster appointment for Mayfield), February 4, 1915, reel 263, ser. 4, LC/Wilson Papers; reel 8, HST/Barkley Papers.

16. "Wilson Wins Congress in His Epochal Speech from House Rostrum," *Washington Post,* April 9, 1913; F. W. Taussig, *The Tariff History of the United States* (New York: Capricorn, 1964), 413–15; Baker, *Woodrow Wilson,* 3:104–10.

17. Quote from "Speech of Hon. Alben W. Barkley of Kentucky in the House of

Representatives, April 24, 1913," p. 9, box 149, UKSC/Barkley Papers; "Tariff Guns Roar," *Washington Post*, April 25, 1913; reel 9, HST/Barkley Papers.

18. Quote from "Speech . . . April 24, 1913," pp. 13–14; Steven R. Weisman, *The Great Tax Wars, Lincoln to Wilson: The Fierce Battles over Money and Power That Transformed the Nation* (New York: Simon & Schuster, 2002), 272. For the Payne-Aldrich Tariff, see Taussig, *Tariff History*, 361–408. The tariff was named for House majority leader (the first in history) Sereno E. Payne of New York and chair of the Senate Finance Committee Nelson W. Aldrich of Rhode Island.

19. Quote from "Speech . . . April 24, 1913," p. 16. See also Barkley, *That Reminds Me*, 101–2.

20. Cooper, *Woodrow Wilson*, 216–19; Link, *Woodrow Wilson*, 40–43; Taussig, *Tariff History*, 409–46.

21. "Signed by Wilson, Tariff Is in Force," *Washington Post*, October 4, 1913; Baker, *Woodrow Wilson*, 3:131–202; Link, *Woodrow Wilson*, 48; "Signs Money Bill: Speaks on Peace," *Washington Post*, December 24, 1913; Weisman, *The Great Tax Wars*, 284–85. The expansion of the money supply caused an inflation rate of 20 percent from 1914 to 1916. See Byron Farwell, *Over There: The United States in the Great War, 1917–1918* (New York: Norton, 1999), 129.

22. Leistner, "Political Campaign Speaking of Alben W. Barkley," 180–82; Grinde, "Early Political Career of Alben W. Barkley," 112–14; reels 8–9, HST/Barkley Papers; Baker, *Woodrow Wilson*, 5:100–101; "Signs Rural Credits Bill," *Washington Post*, July 18, 1916.

23. Weisman, *The Great Tax Wars*, 285; Daniels, *The Wilson Era*, 234–36; Baker, *Woodrow Wilson*, 4:370–73; reel 8, HST/Barkley Papers; "Trust Bill Is Adopted: House Sends Trade Commission Papers to President," *Washington Post*, September 11, 1914.

24. Baker, *Woodrow Wilson*, 3:364; Daniels, *The Wilson Era*, 234–35; Heckscher, *Woodrow Wilson*, 324–25; Link, *Woodrow Wilson*, 68–74; "Present Congress Making New Record," *New York Times*, October 18, 1914; "Speech of Hon. Alben W. Barkley in the House of Representatives, June 1, 1914," p. 13, box 149, UKSC/Barkley Papers.

25. Quote from "Speech . . . June 1, 1914," p. 12.

26. Form Letter to Constituents, July 10, 1914, box 1, UKSC/Barkley Papers; "Speech . . . June 1, 1914," pp. 3–16.

27. For sample correspondence on topics covered in this paragraph, see Barkley to Gus P. Green (chair of the Democratic Committee for Graves County), December 8, 1916, Fred G. Stevenson (Paducah public schools) to Barkley (re: medals), June 9, 1916, B. F. Baggy (Hickman College) to Barkley (re: commencement address), May 2, 1916, Barkley to Governor A. O. Stanley (re: position for Will Thomas), June 20, 1916, and Barkley to H. H. Hanks (re: political contribution), March 2, 1916, all in box 1, UKSC/Barkley Papers.

28. "Present Congress Making New Record"; Grinde, "Early Political Career of Alben W. Barkley," 142; reel 8, HST/Barkley Papers.

29. Quote from Wilson to William G. McAdoo as printed in "President Sees a New America," *New York Times*, November 18, 1914; "Present Congress Making New Record."

30. Quote from Link, *Woodrow Wilson*, 80; Herbert Croly, "Presidential Compla-

cency," *New Republic* 1 (November 21, 1914): 7; reel 8, HST/Barkley Papers; Barkley, *That Reminds Me,* 91–105; Wilson and Galt Wedding Invitation to Dorothy and Alben Barkley, box 1, UKSC/Barkley Papers.

31. Author interview of David M. Barkley, May 18, 1977. See also William A. Colledge (Redpath Speaker Bureau) to Barkley, November 27, 1916, and Barkley to Colledge, November 29, 1916, both in box 1, UKSC/Barkley Papers.

6. The Reformer in Time of War

1. Barbara W. Tuchman, *The Guns of August* (New York: Macmillan, 1962), 91–134; Paul F. Braim, *The Test of Battle* (Shippensburg, PA: White Mane, 1998), 3–4; A. J. P. Taylor, *The First World War* (New York: Putnam's, 1980), 13–21; Baker, *Woodrow Wilson,* 4:8; Berg, *Wilson,* 334–35; "President Moves for Mediation," *New York Times,* August 6, 1914.

2. "President Urges Temperate Speech," *New York Times,* August 19, 1914; Link, *Woodrow Wilson,* 148; Daniel M. Smith, *The Great Departure: The United States and World War I, 1914–1920* (New York: Wiley, 1965), 24–25; George C. Herring, *From Colony to Superpower: U.S. Foreign Relations since 1776* (New York: Oxford University Press, 2008), 390–98.

3. Reels 9–10, HST/Barkley Papers. See also James Douglas, *Parliaments across Frontiers: A Short History of the Inter-Parliamentary Union* (London: H.M. Stationery Office, 1975).

4. Smith, *Great Departure,* 6; Link, *Woodrow Wilson,* 149; Baker, *Woodrow Wilson,* 4:104–5; reel 9, HST/Barkley Papers.

5. "Cotton Now Contraband," *New York Times,* August 22, 1915; Baker, *Woodrow Wilson,* 4:104–7, 377–83; Link, *Woodrow Wilson,* 149–50, 170–73; Daniels, *The Wilson Era,* 579; reel 9, HST/Barkley Papers.

6. Quote from William Jennings Bryan to Barkley, telegram, November 9, 1914, box 1, UKSC/Barkley Papers; Smith, *Great Departure,* 42; "Text of British Order in Council," *New York Times,* March 16, 1915.

7. "Full Text of American Note to London Protesting against Trade Interference," *New York Times,* November 8, 1915; "Britain Is Puzzling over Shipping Plan," *New York Times,* November 24, 1915; "Tobacco Growers Protest," *New York Times,* August 29, 1916. See also Axton, *Tobacco and Kentucky,* 28–29, 140 (fig. 8), the latter showing the dramatic decline in price of all types of tobacco during World War I.

8. Reel 1, HST/Barkley Papers; Barkley, *That Reminds Me,* 43.

9. Axton, *Tobacco and Kentucky,* 136 (fig. 4); Pogue, "The Life and Work of Senator Ollie Murray James," 90, 94–95; "Trade Retaliation Weapon for Wilson," *New York Times,* September 1, 1916.

10. Quote from "Speech of Hon. Alben W. Barkley of Kentucky in the House of Representatives, September 6, 1916," p. 8 (see also pp. 1–7), box 149, UKSC/Barkley Papers.

11. "Germany Declares New Tobacco Embargo," *New York Times,* September 6, 1916; Baker, *Woodrow Wilson,* 4:131–32; "House Vote on Ships: Final Roll Call 215 to 121 in Favor of Passage," *Washington Post,* February 17, 1915.

12. "Ship Bill Scotched," *Washington Post*, February 19, 1915; Baker, *Woodrow Wilson*, 4:135; Link, *Woodrow Wilson*, 191–92; "President Approves the Shipping Bill," *New York Times*, September 8, 1916.

13. Farwell, *Over There*, 23; Braim, *The Test of Battle*, 15; Heckscher, *Woodrow Wilson*, 363–70; Smith, *Great Departure*, 54; reel 8, HST/Barkley Papers.

14. Quote from "Speech . . . September 6, 1916," p. 7; reel 8, HST/Barkley Papers. The other passenger ship torpedoed without warning was the *Sussex*. For a complete discussion of the *Sussex* Pledge, see Link, *Woodrow Wilson*, 215–18.

15. Baker, *Woodrow Wilson*, 5:365–73; Link, *Woodrow Wilson*, 252–53; Smith, *Great Departure*, 72–74. In reality, the United States never treated Great Britain as harshly as it did Germany over the violations of neutral rights on the high seas in wartime.

16. Quote from Thomas R. Pegram, *Battling Demon Rum: The Struggle for a Dry America, 1800–1933* (Chicago: Ivan R. Dee, 1998), 167; "Hobson Denies States Would Lose Powers, and Say [*sic*] Loss of Revenue Would Be Slight Compared to Economy Gain," *Washington Post*, December 23, 1914.

17. Quotes from Hofstadter, *The Age of Reform*, 289–90; Jeff Hill, *Prohibition* (Detroit: Omnigraphics, 2004), 26, 150, 187.

18. Hofstadter, *The Age of Reform*, 289–90; Pegram, *Battling Demon Rum*, 86–87; Norman H. Clark, *Deliver Us from Evil: An Interpretation of American Prohibition* (New York: Norton, 1976), 129.

19. Pegram, *Battling Demon Rum*, 89, 130; Clark, *Deliver Us from Evil*, 102–4, 121–22.

20. Quote from Link, *Woodrow Wilson*, 224; Grinde, "Early Political Career of Alben W. Barkley," 154; "Brandeis Is Chosen for Supreme Court," *Washington Post*, January 29, 1916.

21. Marguerite R. Plummer, "Louis D. Brandeis: Pioneer Progressive," in *Great Justices of the U.S. Supreme Court: Ratings and Case Studies*, ed. William D. Pederson and Norman W. Provizer (New York: Peter Lang, 1993), 147–55. See also Melvin I. Urofsky, *Louis Brandeis and the Progressive Tradition* (Boston: Little, Brown, 1981); "Joins Fight on Liquor Here: Representative Barkley Offers Bill to Make District 'Dry,'" *Washington Post*, January 21, 1916; "Will Sign 'Dry' Bill," *Washington Post*, March 2, 1917; Albert E. Shoemaker (ASL executive secretary for the District of Columbia) to Barkley, June 2, 1916, box 1, UKSC/Barkley Papers.

22. "Washington 'Dry' Nov. 1," *Washington Post*, March 1, 1917; "Would Exact Fines for Misbranding: Representative Barkley Offers a Bill Applying 'Pure Food' Principles," *New York Times*, February 1, 1916; Mowry, *The Era of Theodore Roosevelt*, 207–8.

23. Quotes from 53 Cong. Rec. 2033, 2035 (1916). See also "Pass Child Labor Measure," *Washington Post*, February 3, 1916.

24. Tindall, *America*, 2:939, 1094, 1073–74; Kendrick A. Clements, *The Presidency of Woodrow Wilson* (Lawrence: University Press of Kansas, 1992), 63–64.

25. Reel 2, HST/Barkley Papers; 53 Cong. Rec. 7988–91 (1916); "Loan Board Organizes: First Meeting Today to Plan Land Bank Credit System," *Washington Post*, August 17, 1916.

26. "Was a Record Session: Congress Passed Most Important Acts since the Civil

War," *Washington Post,* September 11, 1916; Hofstadter, *The Age of Reform,* 118–19; Clements, *The Presidency of Woodrow Wilson,* 81; reel 9, HST/Barkley Papers.

27. Link, *Woodrow Wilson,* 235–36; Clements, *The Presidency of Woodrow Wilson,* 44, 81. Barkley and his son David served as the official greeters of President Wilson during one of his visits before joint sessions of Congress. Author interview of David M. Barkley, May 18, 1977.

28. Adamson to Barkley, September 2, 1916, box 1, UKSC/Barkley Papers; "8-Hour Bill Is Signed," *Washington Post,* September 4, 1916.

29. "Test of 8-Hour Bill," *Washington Post,* September 3, 1916; Link, *Woodrow Wilson,* 236–37; Clements, *The Presidency of Woodrow Wilson,* 81; Alfred B. Leet (Economic Club, Washington, DC) to Barkley, December 20, 1916, and Barkley to Leet, December 23, 1916, both in box 1, UKSC/Barkley Papers.

30. "Was a Record Session"; Grinde, "Early Political Career of Alben W. Barkley," 177–80; *Lyon County Herald,* August 15, 1916; Barkley to Claude W. Perry (*Louisville Times*) (letter of recommendation for J. C. Utterback), July 16, 1916, Barkley to B. J. Billings (Billings Printing Co., Paducah), March 20, 1916, Barkley to W. A. Sexton (Lyon County Democratic Committee chair), July 21, 1916, and Gus G. Singleton (McCracken County court clerk) to Barkley, August 23, 1916, all in box 1, UKSC/Barkley Papers.

31. Brands, *T.R.,* 767; Barkley to J. Campbell Cantrill, March 10, 1916, Mrs. Desha Breckinridge (Kentucky Equal Rights Association campaign chair) to Barkley, March 12, 1916, and Barkley to Mrs. James Bennett (Richmond, KY), March 15, 1916, all in box 1, UKSC/Barkley Papers. On the Nineteenth Amendment, see Barkley, *That Reminds Me,* 103–4; and Mrs. Madeline McDowell Breckinridge (Kentucky Equal Rights Association president) to Barkley, December 15, 1919, box 3, UKSC/Barkley Papers. See also Melba Porter Hay, *Madeline McDowell Breckinridge and the Battle for a New South* (Lexington: University Press of Kentucky, 2009).

32. Edmund Morris, *Colonel Roosevelt* (New York: Random House, 2010), 457–62; Seward W. Livermore, *Politics Is Adjourned: Woodrow Wilson and the War Congress, 1916–1918* (Middletown, CT: Wesleyan University Press, 1966), 8–9; Cooper, *Woodrow Wilson,* 341–61; Link, *Woodrow Wilson,* 241–43; reel 9, HST/Barkley Papers.

33. Quote from "Convention Roused by James's Speech," *New York Times,* June 16, 1916; Pogue, "The Life and Work of Senator Ollie Murray James," 90–94; Link, *Woodrow Wilson,* 281.

7. The Congressman in War and Peace

1. First quote from Clements, *The Presidency of Woodrow Wilson,* 137 (see also 135–36); subsequent quotes from "Must Be 'No Victory' in Europe's Conflict, He [Wilson] Warns Powers," *Washington Post,* January 23, 1917; Herring, *From Colony to Superpower,* 407–8.

2. Farwell, *Over There,* 32; Link, *Woodrow Wilson,* 266–67; "President Now Faces Break with Germany: Berlin's Promises Are Brushed Aside; Teuton Diplomats Predict War's End in Thirty Days," *Washington Post,* February 1, 1917.

3. Quote from "Text of President's Address to Congress Ending Diplomatic Rela-

tions with Germany," *Washington Post,* February 4, 1917; Herring, *From Colony to Superpower,* 409. For the fascinating explanation of how the British kept secret that they had broken German codes, see Barbara W. Tuchman, *The Zimmermann Telegram* (New York: Viking, 1958), 144–54.

4. Quote from Arthur S. Link et al., eds., *The Papers of Woodrow Wilson,* 68 vols. (Princeton, NJ: Princeton University Press, 1966–1994), 41:523–24; reel 9, HST/Barkley Papers. The House vote on the armed ship bill was 403–13. See the discussion of the bill in Link, *Woodrow Wilson,* 273. The United States became the world's first country to recognize Russia's new provisional government. When the president asked Congress for a declaration of war, the United States also offered Russia $100 million in economic aid. See James K. Libbey, *Russian-American Economic Relations, 1763–1999* (Gulf Breeze, FL: Academic International, 1999), 68.

5. Reel 9, HST/Barkley Papers; Herring, *From Colony to Superpower,* 402–4; 54 Cong. Rec. 375–76 (1917). On Cuba as a US protectorate, see Herring, *From Colony to Superpower,* 325, 500.

6. Schultz Riggs (Paducah district superintendent for the Metropolitan Life Insurance Co.) to Barkley, May 4, 1918, box 1, UKSC/Barkley Papers; "Nation Opens Its Purse," *New York Times,* April 9, 1917; Link, *Woodrow Wilson,* 188; Farwell, *Over There,* 69–78.

7. Clements, *The Presidency of Woodrow Wilson,* 143; Link et al., eds., *Papers of Woodrow Wilson,* 41:522; Farwell, *Over There,* 50; reel 9, HST/Barkley Papers.

8. Quote from 54 Cong. Rec. 1278 (1917); Clements, *The Presidency of Woodrow Wilson,* 144–45; "Army Bill to Wilson: Senate Adopts Draft Measure as Agreed to by Conferees," *Washington Post,* May 18, 1917.

9. Reel 9, HST/Barkley Papers.

10. David J. Goldberg, *Discontented America: The United States in the 1920s* (Baltimore: Johns Hopkins University Press, 1999), 10; Berg, *Wilson,* 486–94; "Suffrage Lacks Vote: Ballot Shows 63 to 33 Senators for [Susan B.] Anthony Amendment," *Washington Post,* September 27, 1918; Baker, *Woodrow Wilson,* 6:463; Tindall, *America,* 2:1000.

11. Edwin C. Dinwiddie (superintendent of the Legislative Department of the Anti-Saloon League) to Barkley, May 11, 1917, box 1, UKSC/Barkley Papers; Hill, *Prohibition,* 27–28; 54 Cong. Rec. 4153–63 (1917); "'Bone Dry' Nation Voted by the House," *Washington Post,* June 24, 1917.

12. "New Deadlock over Food Bill," *New York Times,* July 30, 1917; Livermore, *Politics Is Adjourned,* 50–56; Clark, *Deliver Us from Evil,* 128–29; Grinde, "Early Political Career of Alben W. Barkley," 202–3; 55 Cong. Rec. 458–59 (1917); "Prohibition Wins in Senate, 47 to 8: Concurs in House Resolution," *New York Times,* December 19, 1917; Baker, *Woodrow Wilson,* 6:419.

13. Pegram, *Battling Demon Rum,* 148–49. As Wilson understood even before war was declared, the United States would and did suffer the loss of civil liberties in wartime. See the brief but excellent discussion of this issue in Clements, *The Presidency of Woodrow Wilson,* 152–56. See also Braim, *The Test of Battle,* 14–40. It should be noted that the AEF finished training in France. Normally, US troops then spent time in a

relatively, but not completely, quiet section of the front before moving to battle-active trenches. See, e.g., the experience of a US artillery officer, Captain Harry S. Truman, as related in David McCullough, *Truman* (New York: Simon & Schuster, 1992), 111–23.

14. Taylor, *The First World War*, 215–28; Norman Stone, *The Eastern Front, 1914–1917* (London: Penguin, 1998), 282–301; Braim, *The Test of Battle*, 50.

15. Reels 1, 10, HST/Barkley Papers; author interview of David M. Barkley, May 18, 1977.

16. Reels 1–2, 10, HST/Barkley Papers; "Trip to European Battlefields, 1918," box 2, UKSC/Barkley Papers.

17. Reel 10, HST/Barkley Papers; Taylor, *The First World War*, 37, 74, 187–94; Livermore, *Politics Is Adjourned*, 206–23.

18. Quote from Barkley, *That Reminds Me*, 115; reel 10, HST/Barkley Papers. On the difference between trench warfare and the open warfare that the AEF tried to practice during its St. Mihiel and Meuse-Argonne offensives (September–November 1918), see Braim, *The Test of Battle*, 28–137.

19. Reel 10, HST/Barkley Papers; C. E. Black and E. C. Helmreich, *Twentieth Century Europe: A History* (New York: Knopf, 1963), 80; Taylor, *The First World War*, 196–97.

20. Quote from Barkley, *That Reminds Me*, 114; reel 10, HST/Barkley Papers.

21. Smith, *Great Departure*, 112; Clements, *The Presidency of Woodrow Wilson*, 160; Link, *Woodrow Wilson*, 175–77.

22. Quote from "President's Appeal to Democrats," *Washington Post*, October 26, 1918.

23. Livermore, *Politics Is Adjourned*, 224–47; "Wilson Bound to Be Leader in Decisions at Versailles Affecting Future of World," *Washington Post*, November 17, 1918; Thomas A. Bailey, *Woodrow Wilson and the Great Betrayal* (Chicago: Quadrangle, 1963), 82–83, 149–52. It should be noted that the Inquiry, a secret American peace-planning commission, provided Wilson with excellent background information. See Wesley J. Reisser, *The Black Book: Woodrow Wilson's Secret Plan for Peace* (Lanham, MD: Lexington, 2012), 9–27, 33–41. See also reel 9, HST/Barkley Papers; and Barkley, *That Reminds Me*, 110–11.

24. Herring, *From Colony to Superpower*, 416–35; Bailey, *Woodrow Wilson and the Great Betrayal*, 187–207, 266–70; "All Attempts at Compromise Meet with Failure," *Washington Post*, November 20, 1919; "Ratification Refused; 49 to 35, Senate Vote; Pact Sent to Wilson," *Washington Post*, March 20, 1920.

25. Reel 9, HST/Barkley Papers; Herring, *From Colony to Superpower*, 451; John D. Hicks, *Republican Ascendancy, 1921–1933* (New York: Harper & Bros., 1960), 31; 60 Cong. Rec. 2520–21 (1921); "President [Harding] Ends War: Signs Peace Resolution at New Jersey Home of [Senator] Frelinghuysen," *Washington Post*, July 3, 1921; Clements, *The Presidency of Woodrow Wilson*, 189. For a long-term view of Wilson's influence on US foreign policy, see Reisser, *The Black Book*, 170–73.

26. Reel 3, HST/Barkley Papers; author interview of David Barkley, May 18, 1977; author interview of Marian Barkley Truitt, June 29, 1980; Barkley to Frank B. Smith (special agent in Paducah for the Equitable Life Assurance Society), January 3, 1918

(*sic*), box 1, UKSC/Barkley Papers. Barkley was responding to Smith's letter of December 31, 1918, so the reply should be dated January 3, 1919.

27. "End of Militarism Is Wilson's Plan," *Washington Post,* December 5, 1918; Eugene P. Trani and David L. Wilson, *The Presidency of Warren G. Harding* (Lawrence: University Press of Kansas, 1977), 53; "Text of President Wilson's Address, Submitting Peace Treaty to Senate," *Washington Post,* July 11, 1919; Gene Smith, *When the Cheering Stopped: The Last Years of Woodrow Wilson* (New York: William Morrow, 1964), 50–92; Edwin A. Weinstein, *Woodrow Wilson: A Medical and Psychological Biography* (Princeton, NJ: Princeton University Press, 1981), 355–62.

28. Clements, *The Presidency of Woodrow Wilson,* 198–203; Tindall, *America,* 2:A26; Pegram, *Battling Demon Rum,* 148; "'Drys' Will Fight Efforts at Repeal," *New York Times,* May 21, 1919.

29. Anti-Saloon League of America, *Proceedings of the Nineteenth National Convention* (Westerville, OH: American Issue Publishing, 1919), 136–38; "'Drys' Will Fight Efforts at Repeal"; "Fight Whiskey Hoards: House Drys Will Today Try to Bar Possession in the Home," *Washington Post,* July 21, 1919; R. L. Davis (secretary of the North Carolina Anti-Saloon League) to Barkley, February 18, 1920, box 3, UKSC/Barkley Papers. For one of numerous such letters over time, see Barkley to James C. Utterback (cashier, City National Bank of Paducah), March 28, 1916, box 1, UKSC/Barkley Papers. See also 60 Cong. Rec. 2900 (1921).

30. "Veto of the 'Dry' Bill by Wilson Overridden in the House, 170 to 55: Expected to Meet Same Fate in Senate Today," *Washington Post,* October 28, 1919; Clark, *Deliver Us from Evil,* 131–32; Barkley, *That Reminds Me,* 41. Considering the fact that Wilson was incapacitated in October when "he" vetoed the Volstead bill, it is understandable why some commentators have described the president's wife, Edith Bolling Wilson, as America's first female president. See Bailey, *Woodrow Wilson and the Great Betrayal,* 143–44.

31. Governor James D. Black to Barkley, August 23, 1919, box 2, UKSC/Barkley Papers; James K. Libbey, "Barkley, Alben William," in *The Kentucky Encyclopedia,* ed. John E. Kleber (Lexington: University Press of Kentucky, 1992), 52–54; Lowell H. Harrison, "Beckham, John Crepps Wickliffe," in ibid., 65, and "Stanley, Augustus Owsley," in ibid., 846–47. See also Pogue, "The Life and Work of Senator Ollie Murray James," 112.

32. Lowell H. Harrison, "Black, James Dixon," in Kleber, ed., *Kentucky Encyclopedia,* 83; Grinde, "Early Political Career of Alben W. Barkley," 229–31; Libbey, *Dear Alben,* 37.

33. Barkley to Utterback, January 12, 1920, box 3, UKSC/Barkley Papers; K. Austin Kerr, *American Railroad Politics, 1914–1920: Rates, Wages, and Efficiency* (Pittsburgh: University of Pittsburgh Press, 1968), 142–43; "Wilson by Proclamation, Orders Railways and Express Companies Turned Back to Owners March 1," *Washington Post,* December 25, 1919; Clements, *The Presidency of Woodrow Wilson,* 32, 209–10; Libbey, *Dear Alben,* 32.

34. Clements, *The Presidency of Woodrow Wilson,* 210; 60 Cong. Rec. 8328–34 (1921); Libbey, *Dear Alben,* 33.

35. "House Approves the Railway Bill by 250 to 150; Labor and Farmer Opposition Fails to Weaken Advocates of Bill," *New York Times*, February 22, 1920; Clements, *The Presidency of Woodrow Wilson*, 210–11; Libbey, *Dear Alben*, 33.

36. Barkley quoted from his minority report in "Union Leaders Urge the Defeat of Railroad Bill," *New York Times*, February 20, 1920. See also "The Return of the Railroads: Speech of Hon. Alben W. Barkley of Kentucky, in the House of Representatives," February 21, 1920, box 149, UKSC/Barkley Papers; "I.C.C. Rate Power Is Made Supreme: Conferees on Railroad Bill Agree to Clause Removing Doubt," *Washington Post*, January 3, 1920; "Conferees Agree on Railroad Bill," *New York Times*, February 17, 1920; "6% as Rail Return Lifts Stock Prices," *New York Times*, February 18, 1920; "House Approves the Railway Bill by 250 to 150"; Berg, *Wilson*, 570–671; Robert K. Murray, *Red Scare: A Study of National Hysteria, 1919–1920* (New York: McGraw-Hill, 1964), 210–22.

8. "Normalcy" and the Tale of Two Elections

1. Murray, *Red Scare*, 240–43; Grinde, "Early Political Career of Alben W. Barkley," 249; Tindall, *America*, 2:982.

2. "Americans to Get First Bid on Ships," *Washington Post*, June 3, 1920; "Substituting White Coal for Black: New Water Power Act Opens Up Great Possibilities of Linking Isolated Sources of Energy," *New York Times*, June 27, 1920; Scott Ferris to Barkley, April 24, 1920, box 2, UKSC/Barkley Papers.

3. Quote from Barkley, *That Reminds Me*, 117; Tindall, *America*, 2:A27–A28; Bailey, *Woodrow Wilson and the Great Betrayal*, 308–14; Clements, *The Presidency of Woodrow Wilson*, 203; "Wilson Talks on Campaign Issues: Sees League as the Dominant One; His Condition Described as Improved," *New York Times*, June 18, 1920; Smith, *When the Cheering Stopped*, 150–53; Weinstein, *Woodrow Wilson*, 366–67.

4. Bailey, *Woodrow Wilson and the Great Betrayal*, 318; Clements, *The Presidency of Woodrow Wilson*, 203; "Cox Nominated on Forty-Fourth Ballot," *Los Angeles Times*, July 6, 1920; "Cox Approves Roosevelt," *Los Angeles Times*, July 7, 1920; Weinstein, *Woodrow Wilson*, 368; Frank Freidel, *Franklin D. Roosevelt: A Rendezvous with Destiny* (New York: Little, Brown, 1990), 23, 38.

5. Reel 20, HST/Barkley Papers; Freidel, *Franklin D. Roosevelt*, 38–39; Smith, *Great Departure*, 199–200; Bailey, *Woodrow Wilson and the Great Betrayal*, 321; Smith, *When the Cheering Stopped*, 156.

6. Harding quoted in Robert K. Murray, *The Harding Era: Warren G. Harding and His Administration* (Minneapolis: University of Minnesota Press, 1969), 70; Samuel Hopkins Adams, *Incredible Era: The Life and Times of Warren Gamaliel Harding* (Boston: Houghton Mifflin, 1939), 168–95; Freidel, *Franklin D. Roosevelt*, 39; Trani and Wilson, *The Presidency of Warren G. Harding*, 26, 28; Robert H. Ferrell, *The Presidency of Calvin Coolidge* (Lawrence: University Press of Kansas, 1998), 16–17.

7. Quote from Barkley, *That Reminds Me*, 119; Trani and Wilson, *The Presidency of Warren G. Harding*, 53; author interview of Marian Barkley Truitt, June 29, 1980; Bailey, *Woodrow Wilson and the Great Betrayal*, 346–47; Weinstein, *Woodrow Wilson*, 371–72.

8. Hicks, *Republican Ascendancy*, 24; H. Wayne Morgan, "William McKinley," in *Buckeye Presidents: Ohioans in the White House*, ed. Philip Weeks (Kent: Kent State University Press, 2003), 180–211; Trani and Wilson, *The Presidency of Warren G. Harding*, 28, 59; Harrison, "Black, James Dixon," in Kleber, ed., *Kentucky Encyclopedia*, 83; and "Ernst, Richard Pretlow," in ibid., 297.

9. Hicks, *Republican Ascendancy*, 32–34; Herring, *From Colony to Superpower*, 452–53; "[House] Votes $90,000,000 for Battleships," *Washington Post*, February 15, 1921; "[President-Elect] Harding Backs Big Navy Bill in Senate," *Washington Post*, February 26, 1921.

10. 60 Cong. Rec. 3148 (1921); 61 Cong. Rec. 623–24 (1921); Murray, *The Harding Era*, 142–45; "Agree on Peace Vote," *Washington Post*, April 29, 1921; Thomas G. Paterson et al., *American Foreign Relations*, vol. 2, *A History since 1895* (Boston: Houghton Mifflin, 2005), 144–45; "[Charles Evans] Hughes Outlines Bold Program to Cut Navies Before Arms Conference," *Washington Post*, November 13, 1921; "Will Send Treaties to Senate Friday: President Meanwhile Orders Work Stopped on All Ships Doomed for Scrapheap," *New York Times*, February 18, 1922; Hicks, *Republican Ascendancy*, 33–49.

11. Constance Drexel, "279 to 39 Is Vote on Maternity Bill," *Washington Post*, November 20, 1921; "The Veterans' Bureau," *Washington Post*, August 10, 1921; Trani and Wilson, *The Presidency of Warren G. Harding*, 57–58, 66, 105.

12. 61 Cong. Rec. 7931–36 (1921); Murray, *The Harding Era*, 408; Drexel, "279 to 39 Is Vote on Maternity Bill"; Trani and Wilson, *The Presidency of Warren G. Harding*, 105–6.

13. "Signs Marketing Bill: President Approves Measure Legalizing Cooperative Association," *Washington Post*, February 19, 1922; Taussig, *Tariff History*, 452; Adams, *Incredible Era*, 228; "Proceedings of Congress and Committees in Brief . . . House," *Washington Post*, May 24, 1921; Hicks, *Republican Ascendancy*, 54.

14. Hicks, *Republican Ascendancy*, 18; Taussig, *Tariff History*, 451–53; Trani and Wilson, *The Presidency of Warren G. Harding*, 13, 56; Ferrell, *The Presidency of Calvin Coolidge*, 81–82.

15. Trani and Wilson, *The Presidency of Warren G. Harding*, 73; Taussig, *Tariff History*, 453; Hicks, *Republican Ascendancy*, 55–56; William Allen White, *A Puritan in Babylon: The Story of Calvin Coolidge* (New York: Macmillan, 1938), 262; "The New Tariff," *Washington Post*, September 22, 1922.

16. Quote from 61 Cong. Rec. 3841 (1921); Hicks, *Republican Ascendancy*, 59; Thomas C. Cochran and William Miller, *The Age of Enterprise: A Social History of Industrial America* (New York: Harper & Row, 1961), 301.

17. "House Votes Tariff: Fordney Bill Passes, 289 to 127," *Washington Post*, July 23, 1921; "Backs Washington [Naval Disarmament] Parley: Inter-Parliamentary Union Decides to Help Make It Successful," *New York Times*, August 21, 1921; Goldberg, *Discontented America*, 50; Selig Adler, *The Isolationist Impulse: Its Twentieth Century Reaction* (New York: Collier, 1961), 132, 144; Trani and Wilson, *The Presidency of Warren G. Harding*, 145; reel 10, HST/Barkley Papers.

18. Quote from Jefferson-Jackson Day Address, January 10, 1922, p. 5 (see also p.

4), box 149, UKSC/Barkley Papers; "Four U.S. Delegates Home from Sweden," *New York Times*, September 13, 1921; Hicks, *Republican Ascendancy*, 56; Trani and Wilson, *The Presidency of Warren G. Harding*, 73.

19. Quote from Ferrell, *The Presidency of Calvin Coolidge*, 70 (for war debt failure, see 145–52); Adams, *Incredible Era*, 300–301; Murray, *The Harding Era*, 392–93; "The New Tariff," *Washington Post*, September 22, 1922; Trani and Wilson, *The Presidency of Warren G. Harding*, 73–74; Hicks, *Republican Ascendancy*, 56–59; Taussig, *Tariff History*, 453–88.

20. Hicks, *Republican Ascendancy*, 88–89; Trani and Wilson, *The Presidency of Warren G. Harding*, 79–80; Grinde, "Early Political Career of Alben W. Barkley," 270; "Washington Dazed by Big Reversal," *New York Times*, November 9, 1922.

21. "Barkley's Hat Flung in Ring for Governor," *Louisville Courier-Journal*, November 11, 1922; George W. Robinson, "The Making of a Kentucky Senator: Alben W. Barkley and the Gubernatorial Primary of 1923," *Filson Club History Quarterly* 40 (April 1966): 123–35, 124; Robert F. Sexton, "The Crusade against Pari-Mutuel Gambling in Kentucky: A Study of Southern Progressivism in the 1920's," *Filson Club History Quarterly* 50 (January 1976): 47–57, 53; James K. Libbey, "Alben W. Barkley (1877–1956)," in *The Vice Presidents: A Biographical Dictionary*, ed. L. Edward Purcell (New York: Facts on File, 1998), 314–21, 318.

22. "Barkley Is Out with Platform," *Louisville Courier-Journal*, January 16, 1923; Klotter, *Kentucky: Portrait in Paradox*, 272; Channing, *Kentucky*, 188; Jewell and Cunningham, *Kentucky Politics*, 13; John H. Fenton, *Politics in the Border States* (New Orleans: Hauser, 1957), 48.

23. Reel 11, HST/Barkley Papers; Robinson, "Making of a Kentucky Senator," 128–29; Clark, *A History of Kentucky*, 444; Sexton, "Crusade against Pari-Mutuel Gambling in Kentucky," 53; Tracy A. Campbell, "Cantrill, James Campbell," in Kleber, ed., *Kentucky Encyclopedia*, 160.

24. Reel 7, HST/Barkley Papers; Klotter, *Kentucky: Portrait in Paradox*, 271–72; Orval W. Baylor, *J. Dan Talbott, Champion of Good Government: A Saga of Kentucky Politics from 1900 to 1942* (Louisville: Kentucky Printing, 1942), 80; George Lee Willis, *Kentucky Democracy: A History of the Party and Its Representative Members—Past and Present* (Louisville: Democratic Historical Society, 1935), 461; Karan and Mather, eds., *Atlas of Kentucky*, 8–11; William A. Withington, "Bluegrass Region," in Kleber, ed., *Kentucky Encyclopedia*, 91–92.

25. Klotter, *Kentucky: Portrait in Paradox*, 272; Barkley to Elwood Hamilton, November 28, 1922, and Barkley to Wiley Bryan (Barkley's campaign treasurer) (the letter included a personal check from Barkley), November 28, 1922, both in box 2, UKSC/Barkley Papers; Willis, *Kentucky Democracy*, 461; Samuel W. Thomas, "Bingham, Robert Worth," in Kleber, ed., *Kentucky Encyclopedia*, 80; Thomas H. Appleton, "Haly, William Purcell Dennis," in ibid., 300; James C. Klotter and Freda C. Klotter, *A Concise History of Kentucky* (Lexington: University Press of Kentucky, 2008), 211; Robinson, "Making of a Kentucky Senator," 130; Harrison and Klotter, *New History of Kentucky*, 352.

26. Quote from Sexton, "Crusade against Pari-Mutual Gambling in Kentucky," 54.

See also Neil Dalton, "Compares Lynch to Russian Town," *Louisville Courier-Journal,* June 1, 1923; Alben W. Barkley, "Opening Campaign for Governor," Danville, February 19, 1923, p. 3, box 149, UKSC/Barkley Papers; John W. Hudson, "Kentucky School for the Deaf," in Kleber, ed., *Kentucky Encyclopedia,* 511–12; and Charles R. Lee, "Centre College," in ibid., 177–78.

27. Quotes from Barkley, "Opening Campaign for Governor," pp. 3, 8; Willis, *Kentucky Democracy,* 461; Baylor, *J. Dan Talbott,* 81.

28. Barkley, "Opening Campaign for Governor," pp. 5–8. The weakness in Barkley's revenue scheme is the fact that Kentucky coal has had its dramatic ups and downs. See Klotter and Klotter, *Concise History of Kentucky,* 130–32; and Henry C. Mayer, "Coal Mining," in Kleber, ed., *Kentucky Encyclopedia,* 209–11.

29. Quotes from Barkley, "Opening Campaign for Governor," pp. 11, 14 (see also pp. 8–9, 12–13).

30. Quotes from "Lebanon Speech, April 2, 1923," pp. 3–4, box 149, UKSC/Barkley Papers.

31. Baylor, *J. Dan Talbott,* 81; Fenton, *Politics in the Border States,* 49; Sexton, "Crusade against Pari-Mutual Gambling in Kentucky," 55; Willis, *Kentucky Democracy,* 462; Harrison and Klotter, *New History of Kentucky,* 352–53.

32. Willis, *Kentucky Democracy,* 462; Baylor, *J. Dan Talbott,* 81–82; Harrison and Klotter, *New History of Kentucky,* 353; "Brown, James Buckner," in Kleber, ed., *Kentucky Encyclopedia,* 127–28; "Dawson, Charles I.," in ibid., 257; Paul Hughes, "William J. Fields," *Louisville Courier-Journal,* July 2, 1950; Klotter and Klotter, *Concise History of Kentucky,* 212.

33. Reel 1, HST/Barkley Papers; author interview of David M. Barkley, May 18, 1977; author interview of Marian Barkley Truitt, June 29, 1980.

34. Quote from Richard V. Oulahan, "Election Will Test Kentucky's Status," *New York Times,* October 21, 1926; Barkley, *That Reminds Me,* 74, 137; Governor William J. Fields to Barkley, April 3, 1926, box 3, UKSC/Barkley Papers; "Barkley Announces as Candidate for United States Senator," *Louisville Courier-Journal,* April 24, 1926; Freidel, *Franklin D. Roosevelt,* 60; Daniel Roper (a Washington attorney) to Barkley (re: Baruch), July 10, 23, 1926, box 4, UKSC/Barkley Papers; Richard P. Hedlund, "Vinson, Frederick Moore," in Kleber, ed., *Kentucky Encyclopedia,* 921; Tindall, *America,* 2:1080–81.

35. "Barkley Drops Rail Board Fight," *Louisville Courier-Journal,* June 2, 1924; "Bill for Rail Peace Signed by Coolidge . . . Labor Board Abolished," *Louisville Courier-Journal,* May 21, 1926; Tindall, *America,* 2:1046; Alben W. Barkley, "Speech of A. W. Barkley," *Railroad Telegrapher* 43 (June 1926): 594–620.

36. J. Howard Henderson, "Barkley Cites Labor Record," *Louisville Courier-Journal,* September 24, 1926; Ron D. Bryant, "Estill County," in Kleber, ed., *Kentucky Encyclopedia,* 298; Ferrell, *The Presidency of Calvin Coolidge,* 81–94; J. Howard Henderson, "Voters Crowd in [Warsaw] to Hear Barkley," *Louisville Courier-Journal,* September 28, 1926. See also speeches that Barkley made in Paris and Bowling Green, September 11, 25, 1926, box 149, UKSC/Barkley Papers.

37. Quote from J. Howard Henderson, "Ernst Speech Is Answered by Barkley,"

Louisville Courier-Journal, October 3, 1926; Harrison and Klotter, *New History of Kentucky,* 355; Taussig, *Tariff History,* 471; Donald J. Lisio, *The President and Protest: Hoover, Conspiracy, and the Bonus Riot* (Columbia: University of Missouri Press, 1974), 8; J. Howard Henderson, "Barkley Again Attacks Ernst," *Louisville Courier-Journal,* October 7, 1926.

38. J. Howard Henderson, "Inspired by Trip, Barkley Says," *Louisville Courier-Journal,* October 13, 1926, "Trade in State Held Stagnant," *Louisville Courier-Journal,* October 15, 1926, "Barkley Is Lauded," *Louisville Courier-Journal,* October 19, 1926, and "Barkley Nears Close of Drive," *Louisville Courier-Journal,* October 31, 1926; Klotter and Klotter, *Concise History of Kentucky,* 34–37; Robert M. Ireland, "Counties," in Kleber, ed., *Kentucky Encyclopedia,* 229–31.

39. Klotter, *Kentucky: Portrait in Paradox,* 284; "Kentucky," *New York Times,* November 3, 1926; Richard V. Oulahan, "Coolidge Facing a Hostile Senate," *New York Times,* November 4, 1926; Ferrell, *The Presidency of Calvin Coolidge,* 167–89.

9. Senator Barkley from Coolidge to Depression

1. Quote from Trani and Wilson, *The Presidency of Warren G. Harding,* 183 (see also 176–77); Adams, *Incredible Era,* 366–76; Ferrell, *The Presidency of Calvin Coolidge,* 43–47; Thomas C. Sosnowski, "Warren G. Harding," in Weeks, ed., *Buckeye Presidents,* 270–71; "Body of Harding Starts East," *Los Angeles Times,* August 4, 1923.

2. Quote from Calvin Coolidge, *The Autobiography of Calvin Coolidge* (New York: Cosmopolitan, 1929), 134; White, *A Puritan in Babylon,* 154–66; Ferrell, *The Presidency of Calvin Coolidge,* 1–24, 207. For a more favorable view of Calvin Coolidge, see Robert E. Gilbert, *The Tormented President: Calvin Coolidge, Death, and Clinical Depression* (Westport, CT: Praeger, 2003), 118–30; reel 13, HST/Barkley Papers.

3. White, *A Puritan in Babylon,* 236–66. See also Ferrell, *The Presidency of Calvin Coolidge,* 43–57, 183; Gilbert, *Tormented President,* 135–37.

4. Ferrell, *The Presidency of Calvin Coolidge,* 57–58; Tindall, *America,* 2:1033–34; "Delegates Want Leaders to Quit: Convention Rank and File Hope McAdoo and Smith Will See Need of Withdrawing," *New York Times,* July 6, 1924.

5. Quote from reels 2, 15, HST/Barkley Papers; Leistner, "Political Campaign Speaking of Alben W. Barkley," 409–17; Mofield, "The Speaking Role of Alben Barkley," 52–53, 60; "Davis Is Put over in Wild Stampede," *New York Times,* July 10, 1924.

6. Quotes from reel 13, HST/Barkley Papers; Coolidge, *Autobiography,* 189–92; Ferrell, *The Presidency of Calvin Coolidge,* 20, 59–60; Gilbert, *Tormented President,* 147–70.

7. Reel 13, HST/Barkley Papers; 68 Cong. Rec. 3365–66 (1927); "Day in Congress: House," *Washington Post,* February 8, 1927; "Swift Senate Coup Gives Right of Way to Farm Relief Bill," *New York Times,* February 4, 1927.

8. White, *A Puritan in Babylon,* 262; "Text of the President's Message Vetoing the McNary-Haugen Farm Bill," *New York Times,* February 11, 1927; Barkley quotes from "Farm Leaders Urge M'Nary Relief Plan," *New York Times,* July 12, 1927; "More 'Coolidge Luck,'" *New York Times,* July 13, 1927; Ferrell, *The Presidency of Calvin Coolidge,* 88–93.

9. Oulahan, "Coolidge Facing a Hostile Senate"; Coolidge, *Autobiography,* 239–47; reel 13, HST/Barkley Papers; "Coolidge Vetoes the Farm Relief Bill as a Deceptive, Price-Fixing Scheme," *New York Times,* May 24, 1928; Martin L. Fausold, *The Presidency of Herbert C. Hoover* (Lawrence: University Press of Kansas, 1985), 22–25.

10. Leistner, "Political Campaign Speaking of Alben W. Barkley," 155–56; Libbey, "Alben W. Barkley" (in Purcell, ed.), esp. 318.

11. Reel 12, HST/Barkley Papers; Bill Powell, "David Barkley, 77 Dies at His Paducah Home," *Louisville Courier-Journal,* June 12, 1983; "Engagement Announced of Miss Marian Barkley," *Washington Post,* January 17, 1929; "Vital Statistics: Licensed to Marry," *Washington Post,* August 16, 1934.

12. "Senators Named for Fund Inquiry," *New York Times,* May 2, 1928; "Hoover Resents Queries as to Prices and Promises at Campaign Fund Hearing . . . Barkley Arouses His Ire," *New York Times,* May 10, 1928; "Governor Smith Questioned on His Presidential Nomination Campaign Fund," *New York Times,* May 11, 1928; reel 10, HST/Barkley Papers. See also US Congress, Senate Select Committee, *Investigation of Presidential Campaign Expenditures* (Washington, DC: US Government Printing Office, 1928).

13. "Text of Barkley's Keynote Speech," *Louisville Courier-Journal,* June 15, 1928; Klotter and Klotter, *Concise History of Kentucky,* 46–48; Lowell H. Harrison, "Sampson, Flem D.," in Kleber, ed., *Kentucky Encyclopedia,* 795–96; C. C. Colt, "Kentuckians Urge Barkley for 2d Place: Boom for Senator Given Impetus as Democrats Ride to Houston," *Louisville Courier-Journal,* June 26, 1928.

14. Colt, "Kentuckians Urge Barkley for 2d Place"; Fausold, *The Presidency of Herbert C. Hoover,* 23, 29–30; Tindall, *America,* 2:1047–48.

15. Colt, "Kentuckians Urge Barkley for 2d Place"; Libbey, "Barkley, Alben William" (in Kleber, ed.).

16. James A. Hagerty, "Robinson Slated for Second Place," *New York Times,* June 27, 1928; C. C. Colt, "State [of Kentucky] Seeks [New York City's] Tammany Aid for Barkley," *Louisville Courier-Journal,* June 28, 1928; "Barkley Men Start Second Place Drive: Despite Robinson's Big Lead, They Insist Kentuckian Is the Logical Nominee," *New York Times,* June 28, 1928.

17. "Barkley Men Start Second Place Drive"; Richard V. Oulahan, "Big Smith Demonstration: Huge Crowd Shouts Madly as Delegations March about the Hall [Morning] . . . Carnival Enthusiasm Is Let Loose by Eloquent Tribute of F. D. Roosevelt [Evening]," *New York Times,* June 28, 1928; James MacGregor Burns, *Roosevelt: The Lion and the Fox* (New York: Harcourt, Brace & World, 1956), 99; James Tobin, *The Man He Became: How FDR Defied Polio to Win the Presidency* (New York: Simon & Schuster, 2013), 252.

18. Quote from Oulahan, "Big Smith Demonstration"; Claude G. Bowers, *My Life: The Memoirs of Claude Bowers* (New York: Simon & Schuster, 1962), 186. Bowers gave the keynote address at the 1928 convention.

19. Alben W. Barkley, "Seconding Nomination of Al Smith," box 149, UKSC/Barkley Papers. For the First Amendment and Article 6, see Tindall, *America,* 2:A20, A22.

20. Quotes from W. A. Warn, "Delegates Cheer Message," *New York Times,* June

30, 1928; "Democrats Name Robinson for Vice President on First Ballot: Many States Shift to Him," *New York Times,* June 30, 1928; "Delegates Hasten End of Convention," *New York Times,* June 30, 1928. Stanley is described as bald and brassy with a foghorn voice in Thomas D. Clark, *Kentucky: Land of Contrast* (New York: Harper & Row, 1968), 156.

21. "Barkley Named Manager," *New York Times,* August 28, 1928; reel 4, HST/Barkley Papers; Grinde, "Early Political Career of Alben W. Barkley," 413, 415.

22. Quote from Patrick H. Callahan, "Religious Prejudice and the Election," *Current History* 29 (December 1928): 381–83, 383; reel 4, HST/Barkley Papers; "[Barkley] Finds Smith Slurs Spread in Kentucky," *New York Times,* October 4, 1928; "Smith . . . Acclaimed in Louisville," *New York Times,* October 14, 1928; "Family with Smith as He Gets Returns," *New York Times,* November 7, 1928.

23. Fausold, *The Presidency of Herbert C. Hoover,* 30–31.

24. Ibid. (see also 9–16, 39); Libbey, *Russian-American Economic Relations,* 79–81; Bertrand M. Patenaude, *The Big Show in Bololand: The American Relief Expedition to Soviet Russia in the Famine of 1921* (Stanford, CA: Stanford University Press, 2002), 29–32.

25. Hicks, *Republican Ascendancy,* 212; "Briand Calls Pact Direct Blow to War," *New York Times,* August 28, 1928; 70 Cong. Rec. 1154–62 (1929); "Coolidge Puts Name to Our Acceptance of Anti-War Treaty," *New York Times,* January 18, 1929; "After Nuernburg [Nürnberg]: Convention on War Crimes," *Washington Post,* October 15, 1946.

26. Herring, *From Colony to Superpower,* 478; 70 Cong. Rec. 2607–11 (1929); "Senators Vote $700,000 Fund to Begin Ships," *Washington Post,* February 15, 1929.

27. Ferrell, *The Presidency of Calvin Coolidge,* 152–55; "Cruiser Bill Starts Row: Senate Big Guns as Democrats Champion Coolidge," *New York Times,* February 2, 1929; 70 Cong. Rec. 2607–11 (1929); Ulric Bell, "Navy Bill Is Defended by Barkley," *Louisville Courier-Journal,* February 2, 1929.

28. Fausold, *The Presidency of Herbert C. Hoover,* 172–76; "Senate Ratifies Naval Treaty," *New York Times,* July 22, 1930; Joan Hoff Wilson, *Herbert Hoover: Forgotten Progressive* (Boston: Little, Brown, 1975), 199–202; David Burner, *Herbert Hoover: A Public Life* (New York: Knopf, 1979), 285–88; Joyce M. Libbey, "Herbert Hoover's Latin American Policy: Its Caribbean Tests" (M.A. thesis, Eastern Kentucky University, 1968), 70–74.

29. Quote from Fausold, *The Presidency of Herbert C. Hoover,* 111 (see also 49); reel 13, HST/Barkley Papers; Wilson, *Herbert Hoover,* 140–50.

30. "Hoover Signs the Farm Relief Bill," *Washington Post,* June 16, 1929; 71 Cong. Rec. 900–904 (1929); Steve Neal, "Charles L. McNary: The Quiet Man," in *First among Equals: Outstanding Senate Leaders of the Twentieth Century,* ed. Richard A. Baker and Roger H. Davidson (Washington, DC: Congressional Quarterly, 1991), 98–126; Richard V. Oulahan, "Congress Rifts Widen: Senate Rebuffs Hoover," *New York Times,* May 11, 1929; "Hoover Wins Victory on Farm Relief After He Condemns the Senate's Action in Again Insisting upon Debentures," *Washington Post,* June 12, 1929; Fausold, *The Presidency of Herbert C. Hoover,* 51; Burner, *Herbert Hoover,* 236–44.

31. Reel 13, HST/Barkley Papers; Harris Gaylord Warren, *Herbert Hoover and the*

Great Depression (New York: Oxford University Press, 1960), 168–77. Many sources deal with the legislation discussed in this paragraph, but Warren has a very thorough narrative on the subject.

32. Taussig, *Tariff History,* 490; Fausold, *The Presidency of Herbert C. Hoover,* 53; Warren, *Herbert Hoover and the Great Depression,* 87–97; Donald C. Bacon, "Joseph Taylor Robinson: The Good Soldier," in Baker and Davidson, eds., *First among Equals,* 75–76; "President Uses Six Pens to Sign Tariff," *Washington Post,* June 18, 1930.

33. US Congress, *Tariff Act of 1929: Hearings Before a Subcommittee of the Senate Finance Committee on H.R. 2667,* 2 vols. (Washington, DC: US Government Printing Office, 1929), 2:92–93; Taussig, *Tariff History,* 498; Fausold, *The Presidency of Herbert C. Hoover,* 53–54.

34. Taussig, *Tariff History,* 498; "Tariff Coalition Regains Its Power: Wins in Senate Cutting Duties on Straw Hats and Handkerchiefs under House Bill; Attack Led by Barkley," *New York Times,* January 31, 1930; "Cement Duty Voted by Senate, 46 to 37: Barkley Vigorously Denounces Deals as Rate Is Put at 6 Cents a Hundred Pounds; Shifts by Five Senators," *New York Times,* March 8, 1930; "Urges Saner View of Tariff Issues: Senator Barkley Tells Import Traders Moderated Foreign Trade Attitude Is Needed: Predicts Reaction Abroad," *New York Times,* April 9, 1930.

35. "Tariff Bill Approved: Senate Passes Final Draft Measure Gets 44–42 Vote," *Los Angeles Times,* June 14, 1930; Burner, *Herbert Hoover,* 288–89; Ulric Bell, "Barkley Raps Tariff Bill on Eve of Voting," *Louisville Courier-Journal,* June 12, 1930.

36. Bell, "Barkley Raps Tariff Bill on Eve of Voting"; "Assail Tariff at Meeting," *New York Times,* April 24, 1930.

37. Bell, "Barkley Raps Tariff Bill on Eve of Voting"; Hicks, *Republican Ascendancy,* 221–22; Taussig, *Tariff History,* 518–19; John Barnhill, "Hawley-Smoot Tariff," in *Encyclopedia of World Trade: From Ancient Times to the Present* (4 vols.), ed. Cynthia Clark Northrup (Armonk, NY: M. E. Sharpe, 2005), 2:452–54; reel 13, HST/Barkley Papers.

10. Senator Barkley from Depression to the Announcement of a New Deal

1. Reels 10, 12, HST/Barkley Papers; Hicks, *Republican Ascendancy,* 209; Neal, "Charles L. McNary," 107; Bronson W. Cutting to Phelps Purnam, August 8, 1930, box 9, LC/Cutting Papers; James K. Libbey, *Alexander Gumberg and Soviet-American Relations, 1917–1933* (Lexington: University Press of Kentucky, 1977), 162–64.

2. Libbey, *Russian-American Economic Relations,* 90–91; Michael Kort, *The Soviet Colossus: A History of the USSR* (Boston: Unwin Hyman, 1990), 167–99.

3. "Senators Visit Moscow," *New York Times,* August 12, 1930; "American Senators See Russian Jewels," *New York Times,* August 17, 1930; reel 12, HST/Barkley Papers; Cutting to his mother, August 15, 1930, box 9, LC/Cutting Papers.

4. Quotes from Cutting to his mother, August 27, 1930, box 9, LC/Cutting Papers; "Wheeler Deplores Our Stand on Soviet: Senator Back from Russia Sees Millions Lost Here by Non-Recognition Policy; Barkley's Views Changed," *New York Times,* September 4, 1930; reel 12, HST/Barkley Papers.

5. Klotter, *Kentucky: Portrait in Paradox,* 245–46; Glenn Conner, "Climate," in Kleber, ed., *Kentucky Encyclopedia,* 207; Bacon, "Joseph Taylor Robinson," 77–78;

Burner, *Herbert Hoover*, 263–64; Fausold, *The Presidency of Herbert C. Hoover*, 111; reel 12, HST/Barkley Papers.

6. Quote from "Asserts Our Tariff Will Cause Move to Cut War Debts: Senator Barkley Quotes English Official as Fearing Britain Cannot Continue Payments," *New York Times*, September 8, 1930; reel 12, HST/Barkley Papers.

7. "Asserts Our Tariff Will Cause Move to Cut War Debts"; Black and Helmreich, *Twentieth Century Europe*, 222–23, 300–301; Paterson et al., *American Foreign Relations*, 2:90–91, 120; Herring, *From Colony to Superpower*, 458–59.

8. Quote from "Asserts Our Tariff Will Cause Move to Cut War Debts"; Taussig, *Tariff History*, 517.

9. Quote from "War Debt Prophecy Assailed by Mills: Barkley Rehashes Old Generalities of the Tariff Debate, Says the Treasury Official; Administration Stirred," *New York Times*, September 9, 1930.

10. "Barkley Belittles Tourist Revenue," *New York Times*, September 15, 1930; "Mills Reply on Tariff Hit by Barkley," *Louisville Courier-Journal*, September 15, 1930; Hicks, *Republican Ascendancy*, 245; Fausold, *The Presidency of Herbert C. Hoover*, 186–87.

11. Quotes from "Labor Meeting Hears Barkley: Senator Says Government Must Solve Unemployment," *Louisville Courier-Journal*, September 17, 1930; Klotter, *Kentucky: Portrait in Paradox*, 293; Barkley (in Louisville) to Senator Thomas T. Connally (D-TX), telegram, October 21, 1930, box 92, LC/Connally Papers; "Logan, Marvel Mills," in Kleber, ed., *Kentucky Encyclopedia*, 567–68.

12. Hicks, *Republican Ascendancy*, 239; Warren, *Herbert Hoover and the Great Depression*, 122–28; Bacon, "Joseph Taylor Robinson," 76; Fausold, *The Presidency of Herbert C. Hoover*, 129.

13. "71st Congress Closes Session by Filibuster . . . President Smiles as Tumult Is Ended," *Washington Post*, March 5, 1931; Lisio, *President and Protest*, 28–42; Fausold, *The Presidency of Herbert C. Hoover*, 134; Hicks, *Republican Ascendancy*, 272–75; 74 Cong. Rec. 157–59 (1931); "Bonus Bill Is Vetoed by Hoover," *New York Times*, February 26, 1931; "Senate Votes Bonus Law Overriding Veto 76 to 17," *New York Times*, February 28, 1931.

14. Quotes from 74 Cong. Rec. 6419 (1931); Grinde, "Early Political Career of Alben W. Barkley," 476–77; Bacon, "Joseph Taylor Robinson," 77–79; Fausold, *The Presidency of Herbert C. Hoover*, 110–11.

15. "71st Congress Closes Session by Filibuster"; Fausold, *The Presidency of Herbert C. Hoover*, 137, 145.

16. "Society News: Former Secretary of War Washington Visitor," *Washington Post*, March 5, 1931; Berry Craig, "Gregory, William Voris," in Kleber, ed., *Kentucky Encyclopedia*, 392; author interview of Marian Barkley Truitt, June 29, 1980; "Max O. Truitt Dead; Barkley's Son-in-Law," *Washington Post*, February 3, 1956; "Marian B. Truitt Dies; Daughter of Alben Barkley," *Washington Post*, May 20, 1996.

17. "Whose Business Is Business," n.d. (early June 1931?), box 150, UKSC/Barkley Papers; "Hear Barkley at Eastern," *Eastern Progress*, July 3, 1931, Eastern Kentucky University Digital Archives (the speech was delivered on June 17, 1931); Jackie Couture (Eastern Kentucky University records officer and digital archives specialist) to author,

June 28, 2013; Charles C. Hay III, "Eastern Kentucky University," in Kleber, ed., *Kentucky Encyclopedia*, 278–79.

18. "Senator Barkley Hurt: Kentuckian Is in West Virginia Hospital After Auto Crash," *New York Times*, June 24, 1931; reel 21, HST/Barkley Papers.

19. Quote from "Barkley Hails Debt Plan: Kentucky Senator Notifies Hoover of Support for Suspension," *New York Times*, June 29, 1931; Fausold, *The Presidency of Herbert C. Hoover*, 187–88; Herring, *From Colony to Superpower*, 480–81; Hicks, *Republican Ascendancy*, 245.

20. Quotes from Barkley to Connally, July 14, 1931, box 13, LC/Connally Papers (see also Connally to Barkley, telegram [copy], June 25, 1931, box 13, LC/Connally Papers); Klotter, *Kentucky: Portrait in Paradox*, 285–88, 293–94; Lowell H. Harrison, "Chandler, Albert Benjamin," in Kleber, ed., *Kentucky Encyclopedia*, 179, and "Lafoon, Ruby," in ibid., 529–30.

21. Governor Roosevelt to Barkley, November 12, 1931, and Barkley to Roosevelt, November 16, 1931, both in box 8, UKSC/Barkley Papers; Freidel, *Franklin D. Roosevelt*, 46–47; Tobin, *The Man He Became*, 201–7. See also, e.g., Roosevelt to Barkley, December 26, 1929, and Barkley to Roosevelt, December 30, 1929, both in box 8, UKSC/Barkley Papers; and reel 21, HST/Barkley Papers.

22. Robinson to Thomas J. Walsh, October 31, 1931, and Walsh to Robinson, November 7, 1931, both in box 382, Thomas J. Walsh Papers, Library of Congress, Washington, DC.

23. William E. Leuchtenburg, *Franklin D. Roosevelt and the New Deal, 1932–1940* (New York: Harper & Row, 1963), 2–3; Klotter, *Kentucky: Portrait in Paradox*, 248; Tindall, *America*, 2:1054.

24. Quote from 75 Cong. Rec. 1784 (1932). See also Grinde, "Early Political Career of Alben W. Barkley," 187–88.

25. Fausold, *The Presidency of Herbert C. Hoover*, 162–64; Warren, *Herbert Hoover and the Great Depression*, 143–47; Hicks, *Republican Ascendancy*, 229, 274; "Statement by President on Bill for Idle Relief," *Washington Post*, July 7, 1932.

26. "Big Relief Bill Signed to Help Trade Revival," *Washington Post*, July 22, 1932. The article uses *trade revival* as a generic catchall for invigorating business, increasing employment, and relieving human destitution; the term *trade* has nothing to do with foreign commerce. See also Fausold, *The Presidency of Herbert C. Hoover*, 163–66.

27. "Opening Session Listless: Leaders Are Absent as [Republican Senator Lester J.] Dickinson Lauds the President's Record," *New York Times*, June 15, 1932; Lisio, *President and Protest*, 190–225; Fausold, *The Presidency of Herbert C. Hoover*, 195; "Day's Events in Bonus Battle Front Riots," *Washington Post*, July 29, 1932; Hicks, *Republican Ascendancy*, 275–76.

28. Quote from Robert W. Woolley, "How Barkley Scored for Roosevelt," box 44, LC/Woolley Papers (this is a chapter from Woolley's unpublished autobiography); Link, *Woodrow Wilson*, 242–43; Hicks, *Republican Ascendancy*, 65; Freidel, *Franklin D. Roosevelt*, 67–70.

29. Woolley, "How Barkley Scored for Roosevelt"; "Barkley Urged to Run," *New York Times*, March 6, 1932; Klotter, *Kentucky: Portrait in Paradox*, 299; "Kentucky [Pri-

mary] Vote Today Offers a Repeal [of Prohibition] Test: Barkley's Stand on Democratic Platform Holds Major Interest," *New York Times,* August 6, 1932.

30. Quotes from "Barkley Advocates Roosevelt Delegation: Kentucky Senator Declines 'Favorite Son' Support; Predicts New Yorker's Nomination and Election," *Louisville Courier-Journal,* March 23, 1932. See also "Barkley Declares for Gov. Roosevelt," *New York Times,* March 23, 1932; Woolley, "How Barkley Scored for Roosevelt."

31. Reel 15, HST/Barkley Papers; "Pledge to Barkley After His Statement," *New York Times,* April 7, 1932; Freidel, *Franklin D. Roosevelt,* 71; "Memorandum for the Press Regarding the Selection of Senator Barkley to Chair the Democratic National Convention, April 4, 1932," box 13, FDR/Tully Papers; "Barkley Selected as Keynoter After Democratic Club: Senator Wins Temporary Chairmanship of Convention Despite Shouse Rivalry," *New York Times,* April 5, 1932. Byrd was the brother of the famed aviator and polar explorer Richard E. Byrd.

32. William J. Abbot, "Great Chicago Gathering Expecting 'Big Show' as Sessions Begin," *Christian Science Monitor,* June 28, 1932; "Program for Opening Day," *New York Times,* June 27, 1932; "Will Rogers Says Party Acts Like a Bunch of Republicans," *New York Times,* June 28, 1932. Cermak would be fatally wounded in a February 1933 assassination attempt against Roosevelt. See Freidel, *Franklin D. Roosevelt,* 87–88.

33. Quotes from "Speech of Hon. Alben W. Barkley, Temporary Chairman, Democratic National Convention, June 27, 1932," pp. 1, 3–4, 10 (see also pp. 11–18), box 150, UKSC/Barkley Papers; "G.O.P. Rule Lashed in Keynote Speech," *Washington Post,* June 28, 1932; Richard L. Strout, "Keynote Speech by Senator Barkley Criticizes Administration," *Christian Science Monitor,* June 28, 1932.

34. Quotes from "Speech of Hon. Alben W. Barkley . . . June 27, 1932," p. 19; George W. Robinson, "Barkley and Roosevelt: A Political Relationship" (n.d., typescript), 142, Crabbe Library, Eastern Kentucky University; Flaget M. Nally, "Bourbon," in Kleber, ed., *Kentucky Encyclopedia,* 103–4; Clark, *Kentucky: Land of Contrast,* 192. Hoover's Commission on Law Enforcement and Observance had branded prohibition enforcement a failure the previous year. See Hicks, *Republican Ascendancy,* 262.

35. Quote from "Will Rogers Says Party Acts Like a Bunch of Republicans"; "Keynote Speech Wins Approval in Congress," *New York Times,* June 28, 1932.

36. Quote from Arthur Krock, "Three Triumphs in Day," *New York Times,* June 29, 1932.

37. Arthur Krock, "Roosevelt Vote Is 945," *New York Times,* July 2, 1932; Freidel, *Franklin D. Roosevelt,* 72–73; reel 12, HST/Barkley Papers.

38. Quote from "Acceptance Speech," July 2, 1933, p. 4, PPF box 483, FDR/Roosevelt Papers; Arthur Krock, "[Roosevelt] Family Flies to Chicago," *New York Times,* July 3, 1932; Tobin, *The Man He Became,* 300; Halford R. Ryan, *Franklin D. Roosevelt's Rhetorical Presidency* (New York: Greenwood, 1988), 42–43; reel 5, HST/Barkley Papers.

11. The Assistant Majority Leader and the New Deal

1. Quotes from "Speech of Alben W. Barkley, United States Senator, Opening the Campaign in Kentucky at Cynthiana, October 1, 1932," pp. 1, 15, 20–21, box 150, UKSC/Barkley Papers; "Thatcher, Maurice Hudson," in Kleber, ed., *Kentucky Ency-*

clopedia, 877; "Barkley Urges Work for All," *Louisville Courier-Journal,* September 6, 1932; "Barkley Reply Is Made Public: Senator Willing for Voters to Pass on Prohibition Early as Possible," *Louisville Courier-Journal,* September 30, 1932.

2. "Thatcher, Maurice Hudson," 877; Harrison and Klotter, *New History of Kentucky,* 363; Fausold, *The Presidency of Herbert C. Hoover,* 212; "Victory Is Assured Roosevelt's Plans," *Washington Post,* November 11, 1932.

3. Tindall, *America,* 2:1064–65, A26; reel 16, HST/Barkley Papers; Leuchtenburg, *Franklin D. Roosevelt and the New Deal,* 18–40. Leuchtenburg titled his chapter on this lame-duck period "Winter of Despair."

4. Tindall, *America,* 2:A13; reel 21, HST/Barkley Papers; Robinson, "Barkley and Roosevelt," 148; "Robinson Retains Post," *Washington Post,* March 11, 1933; Bacon, "Joseph Taylor Robinson," 81; Donald A. Ritchie, "Alben W. Barkley: The President's Man," in Baker and Davidson, eds., *First among Equals,* 131; Barkley to Senator Key Pittman (NV), November 28, 1934, box 11, Key Pittman Papers, Library of Congress; "Sen. Kendrick, Wyoming, Dies; Career Varied," *Washington Post,* November 4, 1933.

5. "Inaugural Address," March 4, 1933, box 610, PPF 1820, FDR/Roosevelt Papers; Ryan, *Franklin D. Roosevelt's Rhetorical Presidency,* 76–86; Freidel, *Franklin D. Roosevelt,* 73; Leuchtenburg, *Franklin D. Roosevelt and the New Deal,* 42.

6. 76 Cong. Rec. 53–65 (1933); Alan Lawson, *A Commonwealth of Hope: The New Deal Response to Crisis* (Baltimore: Johns Hopkins University Press, 2006), 66–67; "Bank Bill Is Enacted: Emergency Program Put through in Record Time of 7½ Hours," *New York Times,* March 10, 1933; James Kieran, "The 'Cabinet' Mr. Roosevelt Already Has: The Group of Advisers Who Assist Him in Plotting His Course on Political Seas," *New York Times,* November 20, 1932. Originally, Kieran used the term *brains trust.*

7. Kieran, "The 'Cabinet' Mr. Roosevelt Already Has"; Raymond Moley, *After Seven Years* (New York: Harper & Bros., 1939), 5–148; reels 16, 18, 21, HST/Barkley Papers; Leuchtenburg, *Franklin D. Roosevelt and the New Deal,* 43; "Bank Bill Is Enacted"; Ferrell, *The Presidency of Calvin Coolidge,* 118–20; Fausold, *The Presidency of Herbert C. Hoover,* 134–36.

8. Grinde, "Early Political Career of Alben W. Barkley," 565–68; "Would Legalize Fact Existing in Gold Embargo," *Washington Post,* May 27, 1933; "Roosevelt Signs Gold Clause Ban," *New York Times,* June 6, 1933; reel 19, HST/Barkley Papers; 76 Cong. Rec. 4892–4913 (1933).

9. "The Man Who Will Question Morgan: Pecora, Former New York Prosecutor, Has a Style of His Own in Boring for Facts," *New York Times,* May 21, 1933; "Morgan Inquiry Stirs Washington," *New York Times,* May 22, 1933; "Senate Committee to Reveal Lists of Morgan's Favored Clients and Loans to Bank Officials," *Wall Street Journal,* May 24, 1933.

10. Leuchtenburg, *Franklin D. Roosevelt and the New Deal,* 41–62; Lawson, *Commonwealth of Hope,* 107–10.

11. Barkley, *That Reminds Me,* 146; "Obituaries: David M. Barkley," *Washington Post,* June 12, 1983; author interview of David M. Barkley, May 18, 1977; "Sunning at Annapolis Roads," *Washington Post,* July 11, 1933; "Society News," *Washington Post,* August 17, 1933.

12. Quotes from "Alben W. Barkley: The President's Man," 131; "Society News," August 17, 1933; Lawson, *Commonwealth of Hope,* 84–85; "For Business Men Who Listen In: On the Radio Today," *Wall Street Journal,* August 5, 1933 (the listing was for August 6). For a thoughtful discussion of FDR's Fireside Chats, see Ryan, *Franklin D. Roosevelt's Rhetorical Presidency,* 27–33.

13. "Mrs. Roosevelt Witnesses Morgan-Coonley Wedding," *Washington Post,* September 6, 1933; "Spain's President Opens Conference on World Laws," *Christian Science Monitor,* October 5, 1933; Felix Gilbert with David Clay Large, *The End of the European Era, 1890 to the Present* (New York: Norton, 1991), 301–3.

14. Reels 18, 20, HST/Barkley Papers; "73rd Congress," *New York Times,* January 1, 1935. The latter gives a list and descriptions of all major bills passed by Congress between March 1933 and June 1934. See also "Roosevelt Signs Exchange Curb Bill," *New York Times,* June 7, 1934; "Money Bill Signed: Reserve Bank Gold Goes to Treasury," *New York Times,* January 31, 1934; Lawson, *Commonwealth of Hope,* 68; and Leuchtenburg, *Franklin D. Roosevelt and the New Deal,* 80–83, 90.

15. "Roosevelt Signs Reciprocal Tariff," *New York Times,* June 13, 1934; Herring, *From Colony to Superpower,* 500–501; reel 14, HST/Barkley Papers; Cynthia Clark Northrup, "Reciprocal Trade Agreements Act of 1934," in *The American Economy: A Historical Encyclopedia* (2 vols.), ed. Cynthia Clark Northrup (Santa Barbara, CA: ABC-CLIO, 2003), 4:1–709, 241; Libbey, *Russian-American Economic Relations,* 110.

16. Quote from US Congress, Senate Banking and Currency Committee, *A Bill to Improve Nation-Wide Housing Standards, Provide Employment and Stimulate Industry: Hearings on S. 3603* (Washington, DC: US Government Printing Office, 1934), 179; Northrup, "Reciprocal Trade Agreements Act of 1934," 241; "Housing Bill Signed, Lumber Prices Cut: Early Building Revival Is Predicted," *New York Times,* June 29, 1934.

17. "Housing Bill Signed"; Hicks, *Republican Ascendancy,* 51–52.

18. Reels 1–22, HST/Barkley Papers; "Leslie Biffle, Secretary of the Senate, 1945–1947; 1949–1953," http://www.senate.gov/artandhistory/history/common/generic/SOS_Leslie_Biffle.htm; "Edwin A. Halsey, Secretary of the Senate, 1933–1945," http://www.senate.gov/artandhistory/history/common/generic/SOS_Edwin_Halsey.htm; author interview of Marian Barkley Truitt, June 29, 1980.

19. Reels 1–22, HST/Barkley Papers; "Leslie Biffle, Secretary of the Senate, 1945–1947; 1949–1953," http://www.senate.gov/artandhistory/history/common/generic/SOS_Leslie_Biffle.htm; "Edwin A. Halsey, Secretary of the Senate, 1933-1945," http://www.senate.gov/artandhistory/history/common/generic/SOS_Edwin_Halsey.htm.

20. "Today on the Radio," *New York Times,* July 3, October 17, 1934; Ulric Bell, "Barkley Hoots G.O.P. Criticism," *Louisville Courier-Journal,* July 4, 1934; "Vital Statistics," *Washington Post,* August 16, 1934; "Troth Announced of Laura Barkley," *New York Times,* August 14, 1934; Roosevelt to Barkley, August 1, 1934, PPF file 3160, FDR/Roosevelt Papers; Ulric Bell, "Barkley, Logan Ask 'Single' Primary," *Louisville Courier-Journal,* February 19, 1935; Jack Goldstein, "Elections," in Kleber, ed., *Kentucky Encyclopedia,* 288–90.

21. "President to Ask Congress for Far-Reaching Reforms, Both Social and Eco-

nomic," *New York Times,* May 18, 1934; Freidel, *Franklin D. Roosevelt,* 169; "Kentuck-
ians' Vote on Bills Is Reviewed," *Louisville Courier-Journal,* August 29, 1935; reel 19,
HST/Barkley Papers; "Roosevelt Signs Wagner Bill as 'Just to Labor,'" *New York Times,*
July 6, 1935; "Social Security Bill Is Signed," *New York Times,* August 15, 1935; "Utili-
ties Bill Made Law," *New York Times,* August 27, 1935; "President Signs Tax Bill," *New
York Times,* August 31, 1935.

22. "Barkley Defends New Deal [at Jefferson Day Dinner]," *New York Times,* April
28, 1935; "Barkley Hits at 'Croakers' [at the University of Virginia Institute of Public Affairs]," *Louisville Courier-Journal,* July 12, 1935; "Today on the Radio," *New York
Times,* March 5, 1935; "Radio Programs Scheduled for Broadcast This Week," *New
York Times,* April 14, June 23, 1935; "Senators Retreat on Taxes," *New York Times,*
August 13, 1935; Barkley to Roosevelt, August 16, 1935, PPF file 3160, FDR/Roo-
sevelt Papers.

23. Quote from Winifred Mallon, "Debate Decision of Supreme Court," *New York
Times,* July 12, 1935; Tindall, *America,* 2:1079; Frank Freidel, "The Sick Chicken Case
[re: the National Industrial Recovery Act]," in *Quarrels That Have Shaped the Constitution,* ed. John A. Garraty (New York: Harper & Row, 1988), 233–52; reel 14, HST/
Barkley Papers.

24. "Neutrality Law Is Signed," *New York Times,* September 1, 1935; Leuchtenburg,
Franklin D. Roosevelt and the New Deal, 220–23; Herring, *From Colony to Superpower,*
506–8.

25. "Roosevelt Renews Plea against Profits in War: He Signs Neutrality Bill," *New
York Times,* March 1, 1936; "Farm Act Is Swept Away," *New York Times,* January 7,
1936; "Roosevelt Signs New Farm Aid Bill," *New York Times,* March 2, 1936; Tindall,
America, 2:A15; Freidel, *Franklin D. Roosevelt,* 191–92.

26. "Veto for Bonus," *New York Times,* January 26, 1936; "Bonus Bill Becomes
Law," *New York Times,* January 28, 1936; "Congress Ends Its Session: New Tax Measure
Enacted," *New York Times,* June 21, 1936; "Tax Bill Signed," *New York Times,* June 25,
1936; Leuchtenburg, *Franklin D. Roosevelt and the New Deal,* 171.

27. Barkley quote from Bennett Roach, "Chandler, Barkley Heard by State Democratic Woman's Club," *Louisville Courier-Journal,* April 18, 1936; Roosevelt quote from
Roosevelt to Barkley, February 27, 1936, PPF file 3160, FDR/Roosevelt Papers; S. H.
Ourbacker (president of the Democratic Club) to Marvin McIntyre (White House
appointments secretary), March 21, 1936, box 75, UKSC/Barkley Papers. For an
extended discussion of Barkley's speaking style, see Leistner, "Political Campaign Speaking of Alben W. Barkley," 147–54, 409–17.

28. "Louis M. H. Howe, Roosevelt Friend, Dies at Capital," *New York Times,* April
19, 1936; Freidel, *Franklin D. Roosevelt,* 197–98; Ulric Bell, "Keynote Job Is Proposed
for Barkley," *Louisville Courier-Journal,* April 21, 1936; "Barkley Again Named Democratic Keynoter," *Louisville Courier Journal,* April 26, 1936.

29. Quote from "The Keynote Speech: Text of the Keynote Speech of Senator
Steiwer, Assailing Record of the New Deal," *New York Times,* June 10, 1936; Woolley
to Barkley, May 16, 1936, and Barkley to Woolley, May 23, 1936, both in box 2, LC/
Woolley Papers.

30. Steiwer quotes from "The Keynote Speech . . . of Senator Steiwer"; Barkley quotes from "The Keynote Speech: Senator Barkley's Keynote Speech as Temporary Chairman of the Convention," *New York Times*, June 24, 1936. The newspaper published the stenographic report of the speech. It is far more accurate than the printed copy issued to the press. The latter had been changed with last-minute deletions and additions along with the removal of material to keep the address within the sixty minutes allotted by the national radio networks. On H. P. Long, see Tindall, *America*, 2:1078.

31. First Barkley quote from "The Keynote Speech [of Barkley]"; Ryan, *Franklin D. Roosevelt's Rhetorical Presidency*, 47–48; Roosevelt quote from Freidel, *Franklin D. Roosevelt*, 202; second Barkley quote from "Speech . . . June 27, 1932," p. 1, box 150, UKSC/Barkley Papers. See also "Acceptance Speech," June 27, 1936, pp. 1–11, PPF box 879, FDR/Roosevelt Papers.

32. Roosevelt to Barkley, June 30, 1936, box 60, UKSC/Barkley Papers; Grace Tully to Barkley, telegram, June 25, 1936, box 1, FDR/Tully Papers; Grace Tully, *Franklin Delano Roosevelt, My Boss* (New York: Scribner's, 1949), 246. For a summary of FDR's 1936 campaign, including a discussion of his coalition, see Burns, *Roosevelt*, 264–88.

33. Quote from "The Keynote Speech [of Barkley]"; Grinde, "Early Political Career of Alben W. Barkley," 648–49; "Barkley Talks in Maryland," *Louisville Courier-Journal*, September 18, 1936; Leuchtenburg, *Franklin D. Roosevelt and the New Deal*, 195–96; Tindall, *America*, 2:1085–86.

12. The Majority Leader in Time of Peace

1. Tindall, *America*, 2:A26–A27; reel 16, HST/Barkley Papers; Arthur Krock, "President Speaks," *New York Times*, January 21, 1937; Ryan, *Franklin D. Roosevelt's Rhetorical Presidency*, 86–91; "Second Inaugural Address," box 1030, PPF 1820, FDR/Roosevelt Papers.

2. Quote from Barkley, *That Reminds Me*, 153; "President's Message: Texts of Roosevelt's Court Message, His Proposed Bill and Cummings's Letter," *New York Times*, February 6, 1937; Bacon, "Joseph Taylor Robinson," 87; David M. Kennedy, *Freedom from Fear: The American People in Depression and War, 1929–1945* (New York: Oxford University Press, 1999), 332.

3. Bacon, "Joseph Taylor Robinson," 88–89; Ritchie, "Alben W. Barkley," 132–33; "President's Message: Texts of Roosevelt's Court Message"; Tindall, *America*, 2:A18–A19.

4. Quote from "The Lesson of John Marshall," February 22, 1937, pp. 6–7, box 152, UKSC/Barkley Papers; Tindall, *America*, 2:376–78; Polly [Ann] Davis, "Court Reform and Alben W. Barkley's Election as Majority Leader," *Southern Quarterly* 15 (Spring 1976): 18–19. See also "Barkley Calls Supreme Court 'Stagnant Pool,'" *Louisville Courier-Journal*, May 27, 1937.

5. Quote from "Comment on Address," *New York Times*, March 10, 1937; Ryan, *Franklin D. Roosevelt's Rhetorical Presidency*, 121–24; "The President's Address: Text of the President's 'Fireside Chat' Defending Court Reorganization Program," *New York Times*, March 10, 1937.

6. Bacon, "Joseph Taylor Robinson," 88–89; Davis, "Court Reform and Alben W. Barkley's Election," 21; Burns, *Roosevelt,* 303–6.

7. Burns, *Roosevelt,* 303–7.

8. Bacon, "Joseph Taylor Robinson," 86, 90; Ulric Bell, "Barkley New Senate Leader of Majority," *Louisville Courier-Journal,* June 20, 1937.

9. Burns, *Roosevelt,* 306–8; Arthur Krock, "Court Bill Is Obscured in Senate Bill Haze," *New York Times,* July 11, 1937; 81 Cong. Rec. 6740–41 (1937).

10. Bacon, "Joseph Taylor Robinson," 92–93; Davis, "Court Reform and Alben W. Barkley's Election," 22; "Found Dead Alone: Heart Attack Is Fatal to Majority Leader Who Ignored Symptoms," *New York Times,* July 15, 1937.

11. "The President's Letter: Text of President's Letter Cites Robinson's Views," *New York Times,* July 16, 1937; Barkley, *That Reminds Me,* 154; reel 4, HST/Barkley Papers. Barkley admitted that he lost the original copy of the letter.

12. Arthur Krock, "Roosevelt Embattled to Save His New Deal: Letter to Barkley Makes Court Bill Pivotal in Putting through and Keeping Party Leadership," *New York Times,* July 18, 1937; Bacon, "Joseph Taylor Robinson," 90; Burns, *Roosevelt,* 303–8.

13. Turner Catledge, "Summons Harrison: Roosevelt Assures Him of 'Hands Off' on Robinson Successor," *New York Times,* July 17, 1937; Davis, "Court Reform and Alben W. Barkley's Election," 23–24; "Robinson Funeral Will Be Historic," *New York Times,* July 16, 1937; Margaret Truman, *Harry S. Truman* (New York: William Morrow, 1973), 111.

14. Quote from Barkley, *That Reminds Me,* 156; William E. Leuchtenburg, *The White House Looks South: Franklin D. Roosevelt, Harry S. Truman, Lyndon B. Johnson* (Baton Rouge: Louisiana State University Press, 2005), 79–83; Tully, *Franklin Delano Roosevelt, My Boss,* 225; Burns, *Roosevelt,* 309; Davis, "Court Reform and Alben W. Barkley's Election," 24–28.

15. "Barkley Wins, Court Plan Put Overboard," *Louisville Courier-Journal,* July 22, 1937; "Court Bill Drive Collapses; Foes to 'Write Own Ticket'; Barkley Made Leader 38–37," *New York Times,* July 22, 1937; reels 13, 21, HST/Barkley Papers.

16. Hiram W. Johnson quoted from Turner Catledge, "A Full Surrender: Barkley Declines, and Logan Makes Motion to Bury Measure," *New York Times,* July 23, 1937; Davis, "Court Reform and Alben W. Barkley's Election," 29–30; 81 Cong. Rec. 7381 (1937); Turner Catledge, "Senate in 59 Minutes Votes Changes in Lower Courts: Session End by Aug. 21 Seen," *New York Times,* August 8, 1937.

17. Catledge, "A Full Surrender"; Samuel I. Rosenman, *Working with Roosevelt* (New York: Harper & Bros., 1952), 161; Josh Lee (secretary, US Senate Appropriations Committee) to "My Dear Senator" (form letter), August 2, 1937, PPF 3160, FDR/Roosevelt Papers; Ritchie, "Alben W. Barkley," 133.

18. Barkley quoted from Polly Ann Davis, "Alben W. Barkley: Senate Majority Leader and Vice President" (Ph.D. diss., University of Kentucky, 1963), 44–45; Ritchie, "Alben W. Barkley," 133–34; 81 Cong. Rec. 8694–97 (1937); Freidel, *Franklin D. Roosevelt,* 246–47.

19. Reels 4–5, HST/Barkley Papers; Leuchtenburg, *Franklin D. Roosevelt and the New Deal,* 135–36; "Housing Bill Voted by House . . . Changes in Wagner-Steagall

Proposal, Passed in Senate, Now Force It to Conference," *New York Times,* August 19, 1937.

20. Leuchtenburg, *Franklin D. Roosevelt and the New Deal,* 135; Hal H. Smith, "Review of Principal Legislation Enacted by the 75th Congress First Session," *New York Times,* August 22, 1937. D. M. Kennedy argues that even the housing act was only a "pallid vestige of the New Deal spirit." See Kennedy, *Freedom from Fear,* 340.

21. Ritchie, "Alben W. Barkley," 134; Nancy J. Weiss, *Farewell to the Party of Lincoln: Black Politics in the Age of FDR* (Princeton, NJ: Princeton University Press, 1983), 96–119, 241–49; J. Joseph Huthmacher, *Senator Robert F. Wagner and the Rise of Urban Liberalism* (New York: Atheneum, 1971), 238–43.

22. "President in Doubt on Special Session After Day of Talks," *New York Times,* August 25, 1937; "Barkley Defends Congress Records," *New York Times,* August 26, 1937; "Barkley Asserts U.S. Is Opposed to Force," *New York Times,* September 6, 1937; Herring, *From Colony to Superpower,* 502–17; reel 12, HST/Barkley Papers; "Address Delivered by Senator Alben W. Barkley, President of the American Group of the Inter-Parliamentary Union at the Extraordinary Session Held at Versailles on Sunday, September 5, 1937, President Lebrun of the French Republic Presiding," box 152, UKSC/Barkley Papers.

23. Quote from Robert P. Post, "Roosevelt Urges 'Concerted Action' . . . Would Try 'Quarantine,'" *New York Times,* October 6, 1937; Michael Fullilove, *Rendezvous with Destiny: How Franklin D. Roosevelt and Five Extraordinary Men Took America into the War and into the World* (New York: Penguin, 2013), 18; "Senator Barkley Back," *New York Times,* October 15, 1937; Freidel, *Franklin D. Roosevelt,* 263–64; reel 21, HST/Barkley Papers; Ryan, *Franklin D. Roosevelt's Rhetorical Presidency,* 138–41.

24. "Senator Barkley Back"; Howard Henderson, "Tribute to Barkley Turns into Indorsement for Presidency: Hundreds Welcome Senator to Birthplace as Lowes Celebrates 100th Anniversary," *Louisville Courier-Journal,* October 17, 1937; reel 21, HST/Barkley Papers.

25. Reel 21, HST/Barkley Papers; author interview of David M. Barkley and visit to Angles, May 18, 1977; Bill Powell, "David Barkley, 77 Dies at His Paducah Home," *Louisville Courier-Journal,* June 12, 1983.

26. Ira Katznelson, *Fear Itself: The New Deal and the Origins of Our Time* (New York: Norton, 2013), 179; "'Big Stick' Swung at Filibusters: Barkley Reads 'Riot Act' to Senators on Delays of Anti-Lynching Bill," *New York Times,* January 7, 1938; Leuchtenburg, *The White House Looks South,* 122; reel 16, HST/Barkley Papers; Ritchie, "Alben W. Barkley," 134–35; Davis, "Alben W. Barkley," 46–53; Hal H. Smith, "Summary of Important Legislation Passed in Third Session of 75th Congress," *New York Times,* June 17, 1938; "The President's Address: Text of President Roosevelt's Fireside Chat," *New York Times,* June 25, 1938; Ryan, *Franklin D. Roosevelt's Rhetorical Presidency,* 30.

27. Quote from Ritchie, "Alben W. Barkley," 137 (see also 138–40); Barkley, *That Reminds Me,* 155; Davis, "Alben W. Barkley," 46; Arthur Krock, "In the Nation," *New York Times,* April 12, 1939.

28. Quote from "The President's Address" (June 25, 1938); Katznelson, *Fear Itself,* 171; "Testimonial Dinner Given Senator Alben W. Barkley of Kentucky at [the Brown

Hotel,] Louisville, Ky., January 22, 1938," PPF 3160, FDR/Roosevelt Papers; "Praise Heaped on Barkley by Roosevelt," *Louisville Courier-Journal,* January 23, 1938; Turner Catledge, "New Deal Councils Split over Choice of Foes for 'Purge': Exultation over Roosevelt's 'Fireside' Chat Gives Way to Confusion on 'Blacklist,'" *New York Times,* June 29, 1938; Leuchtenburg, *Franklin D. Roosevelt and the New Deal,* 267–68.

29. Katznelson, *Fear Itself,* 175; "Campaign Tour: Roosevelt Rides West," *New York Times,* July 10, 1938; Tully, *Franklin Delano Roosevelt, My Boss,* 225–26; Harrison, "Chandler, Albert Benjamin"; Robert Damron, "Chandler's Bid to Unseat Barkley" (M.A. thesis, Eastern Kentucky University, 1967), 12–13.

30. Quote from "Barkley Predicts Less Government . . . Chandler Spurns Him . . . Hints He May Run for Senate," *New York Times,* January 23, 1938; Damron, "Chandler's Bid to Unseat Barkley," 29; "Roosevelt Is Sending McIntyre as Emissary to Barkley Dinner," *Louisville Courier-Journal,* January 22, 1938; "Miller Heads Campaign for Barkley," *Louisville Courier-Journal,* January 24, 1938. I follow convention by placing a period after the *S* in Harry S. Truman's name. The *S,* however, is not an initial. Truman had no middle name.

31. Quote from "Complete Text of Opening Address of Senator Alben W. Barkley in Campaign for Renomination," *Lexington Herald-Leader,* June 19, 1938. The speech is also found in box 152, UKSC/Barkley Papers.

32. Barkley quote from reel 17, HST/Barkley Papers; Roosevelt quote from "Campaign Tour: Roosevelt Rides West"; Albert B. Chandler with Vance H. Trimble, *Heroes, Plain Folks, and Skunks* (Chicago: Bonus, 1989), 137; Damron, "Chandler's Bid to Unseat Barkley," 30.

33. Harrison and Klotter, *New History of Kentucky,* 369; reel 17, HST/Barkley Papers; Chandler, *Heroes, Plain Folks, and Skunks,* 135; Davis, "Alben W. Barkley," 61–66; Libbey, *Dear Alben,* 78–79; Kennedy, *Freedom from Fear,* 349; Damron, "Chandler's Bid to Unseat Barkley," 35–42. The campaign can be followed almost on a daily basis by reading the *Louisville Courier-Journal,* which endorsed Barkley. See, e.g., "Barkley Says New Deal Only Issue of Race," *Louisville Courier-Journal,* July 7, 1938.

34. Quote from Tully, *Franklin Delano Roosevelt, My Boss,* 226; Chandler, *Heroes, Plain Folks, and Skunks,* 140; Leuchtenburg, *The White House Looks South,* 102; George Gallup, "Chandler Gaining in Kentucky Race . . . Governor Turning Roosevelt Visit to Aid Opponent into Endorsement of Himself," *New York Times,* July 24, 1938. Chandler's use of the quote from Roosevelt is also cited in Gallup's article.

35. Harrison and Klotter, *New History of Kentucky,* 370; "Chandler Ill, Wife Talks," *New York Times,* July 23, 1938; "Chandler Illness Laid to Poisoning," *New York Times,* July 26, 1938; "New Report Says Chandler Was Poisoned," *New York Times,* July 29, 1938. The last article contains the lab results and short quotes from John Malley and Joseph Stewart. The "new report" was the undocumented belief of Happy's health commissioner that the governor had been poisoned. For other views of the incident, see Chandler, *Heroes, Plain Folks, and Skunks,* 138–40; and Damron, "Chandler's Bid to Unseat Barkley," 59.

36. "Barkley Lead Is 70,785," *New York Times,* August 10, 1938; Robinson, "Barkley and Roosevelt," 267; "Barkley Departs, Defends New Deal," *New York Times,*

August 18, 1938; "Guffey Back, Sees 3d Term Looming," *New York Times,* September 16, 1938. Senator Joseph F. Guffey (PA) had attended the IUP meeting and returned on the same ship as Alben and Dorothy.

37. Herring, *From Colony to Superpower,* 513–15; Robert A. Divine, *The Reluctant Belligerent: American Entry into World War II* (New York: Wiley, 1965), 51–55; Harrison and Klotter, *New History of Kentucky,* 370.

13. The Majority Leader from Neutrality to War

1. Leuchtenburg, *Franklin D. Roosevelt and the New Deal,* 471–74; Freidel, *Franklin D. Roosevelt,* 286–88; Joseph Alsop and Robert Kintner, "Hatch Bill a Trap for President . . . Viewed as Double-Action Blow at Third Term—Veto Would Seem a 'Confession,' Signing It Might Cost Roosevelt 1940 Convention," *New York Times,* July 25, 1939.

2. Turner Catledge, "Senate Sets Lines to Vote on Relief," *New York Times,* January 24, 1939; Charles W. Hurd, "Senate Upholds House Relief Cut by a Vote of 47 to 46: Coalition Triumph," *New York Times,* January 28, 1939; Charles W. Hurd, "150,000,000 More Is Asked for WPA," *New York Times,* February 8, 1938; Charles W. Hurd, "WPA Cut $50,000,000 as Senate, 49 to 28, Rebuffs President: Barkley Defends Compromise on $100,000,000 House Voted as Plain 'Common Sense,'" *New York Times,* April 12, 1939.

3. Quote from "Reorganization, Limited," *New York Times,* March 29, 1939. See also "Conferees Agree on Reorganization," *New York Times,* March 28, 1939; Freidel, *Franklin D. Roosevelt,* 278–80.

4. Leuchtenburg, *Franklin D. Roosevelt and the New Deal,* 278–80; Gilbert, *End of the European Era,* 297–98; Adolf Hitler, *Mein Kampf* (Boston: Houghton Mifflin, 1962), 634; Libbey, *Russian-American Economic Relations,* 112; James K. Libbey, *Alexander P. de Seversky and the Quest for Air Power* (Washington, DC: Potomac, 2013), 137–40.

5. "Big Plane Output Mapped for Army," *New York Times,* November 24, 1938; Libbey, *Alexander P. de Seversky and the Quest for Air Power,* 156; H. H. Arnold, *Global Mission* (New York: Harper & Bros., 1949), 177–78; Irving Brinton Holley, *Buying Aircraft* (Washington, DC: US Department of the Army, 1964), 169–70. Gen. Arnold was head of the US Army Air Corps and its successor, the US Army Air Forces, from 1938 to 1946.

6. All quotes from Harold B. Hinton, "War Referendum Revived in Senate: Isolationists Challenge Air Bill—Nye Demands a Halt in Aid to Democracies," *New York Times,* March 1, 1939; Leuchtenburg, *Franklin D. Roosevelt and the New Deal,* 229–30.

7. Quote from "Barkley Outlines the Foreign Policy of Administration: Aim Is Not Only to Preserve Peace in This Hemisphere, He Tells Senate; Neutrality Revision Seen," *New York Times,* March 8, 1939; John E. Wiltz, *From Isolation to War, 1931–1941* (New York: Thomas Y. Crowell, 1968), 49–54; Herring, *From Colony to Superpower,* 506–11.

8. "Barkley Outlines the Foreign Policy of Administration," *New York Times,* March 8, 1939; "6,000 Army Planes Win in a Test Vote: Senate, 54 to 28, Raises Total

from the 5,500 Limit Set in Bill Passed by House," *New York Times,* March 7, 1939; "Congress Adopts Big Defense Bill," *New York Times,* March 23, 1939; Gilbert, *End of the European Era,* 308–10.

9. Quote from Herring, *From Colony to Superpower,* 516; Divine, *Reluctant Belligerent,* 57–60; Freidel, *Franklin D. Roosevelt,* 315.

10. Harold B. Hinton, "Senate Committee Votes for Delay on Neutrality; Roosevelt Will Fight On," *New York Times,* July 12, 1939; Divine, *Reluctant Belligerent,* 60–62.

11. Hinton, "Senate Committee Votes for Delay on Neutrality"; reel 19, HST/Barkley Papers; "No Neutrality Revision This Session: Roosevelt Told by Leaders of Senate in a Night Conference His Plea Fails," *New York Times,* July 19, 1939.

12. "No Neutrality Revision This Session"; reel 19, HST/Barkley Papers; Neal, "Charles L. McNary," 118; excerpt from Press Conference, Hyde Park, New York, July 22, 1939, http://docs.fdrlibrary.marist.edu/php62239.html.

13. Quote from Turner Catledge, "Roosevelt in Plea: President on Air, Asks the Nation to Observe True Neutrality; Calls All to Unity; Draws Ring around Americas— 'Even a Neutral' May Judge, He Says," *New York Times,* September 4, 1939; Ryan, *Franklin D. Roosevelt's Rhetorical Presidency,* 142; Kort, *The Soviet Colossus,* 230–31.

14. Quote from Turner Catledge, "A Solemn Message: Arms Ban Is a Threat to Peace, Joint Session Is Told by President," *New York Times,* September 22, 1939; Early to Barkley (re: arranging the joint session of Congress), September 18, 1939, PPF 3160, FDR/Roosevelt Papers; Turner Catledge, "Final Vote Swift," *New York Times,* October 28, 1939; Fullilove, *Rendezvous with Destiny,* 19–20; Leuchtenburg, *Franklin D. Roosevelt and the New Deal,* 294–95.

15. Leuchtenburg, *Franklin D. Roosevelt and the New Deal,* 294–95; Freidel, *Franklin D. Roosevelt,* 327–28; Adler, *Isolationist Impulse,* 257–58; Davis, "Alben W. Barkley," 88–89; "Neutrality: Speech of Alben W. Barkley of Kentucky in the Senate of the United States," October 19, 1939, box 153, UKSC/Barkley Papers.

16. Catledge, "Final Vote Swift"; Turner Catledge, "House Vote Today," *New York Times,* November 2, 1939; Harold B. Hinton, "Congress Is Swift," *New York Times,* November 4, 1939; J. E. Kaufmann and H. W. Kaufmann, *Hitler's Blitzkrieg Campaign* (Conshohocken, PA: Combined, 1993), 65–103; Winston S. Churchill, *The Gathering Storm* (New York: Houghton Mifflin, 1948), 393–99.

17. Freidel, *Franklin D. Roosevelt,* 328–29; Walter J. Boyne, *The Influence of Air Power upon History* (Gretna, LA: Pelican, 2003), 150; Divine, *Reluctant Belligerent,* 71–72; Davis, "Alben W. Barkley," 91–92; "Seven Years under Roosevelt: Address of Senator Alben W. Barkley, the Majority Leader, in the United States Senate," March 4th, 1940, Correspondence Folder Barkley, Alben W., 1936–1940, box 1, FDR/Tully Papers.

18. Quotes from "Party Leaders Debate New Deal," *New York Times,* March 4, 1940; "Fish Loses Post: Barkley Becomes U.S. Head [Once Again] of Interparliamentary Union," *New York Times,* January 16, 1940.

19. "Seven Years under Roosevelt"; Felix Belair Jr., "Roosevelt Marks 7 New Deal Years, Silent on 3d Term," *New York Times,* March 5, 1940; Freidel, *Franklin D. Roosevelt,* 327–37; Winston S. Churchill, *Their Finest Hour* (New York: Houghton Mifflin, 1949), 3–191.

20. Freidel, *Franklin D. Roosevelt,* 330–31; "America Girds: Her Peace Menaced," *New York Times,* May 19, 1940; Divine, *Reluctant Belligerent,* 86.

21. Quote from James A. Hagerty, "Choice Left Open . . . Demonstration Quickly Starts—Senator Hits New Deal Critics," *New York Times,* July 17, 1940; "Democratic National Convention: Address by Hon. Alben W. Barkley of Kentucky; As Permanent Chairman of the Democratic National Convention, at Chicago, Ill., on July 16, 1940," box 153, UKSC/Barkley Papers.

22. Quote from Freidel, *Franklin D. Roosevelt,* 344; Barkley, "Democratic National Convention: Address by Hon. Alben W. Barkley of Kentucky"; Hagerty, "Choice Left Open . . . Demonstration Quickly Starts"; Ritchie, "Alben W. Barkley," 139; Roosevelt to Barkley, July 31, 1940, PPF 3160, FDR/Roosevelt Papers.

23. J. Kent Calder, "John Nance Garner (1868–1967)," in Purcell, ed., *The Vice Presidents,* 289–305; Mark L. Kleinman, "Henry Agard Wallace (1888–1965)," in ibid., 289–305; Fullilove, *Rendezvous with Destiny,* 99–100; Jon Meacham, *Franklin and Winston: An Intimate Portrait of an Epic Friendship* (New York: Random House, 2003), 70–73.

24. Floyd M. Riddick, "Third Session of the Seventy-Sixth Congress, January 3, 1940 to January 3, 1941," *American Political Science Review* 35 (1941): 286–87; reel 5, HST/Barkley Papers; David McCulough, *Truman* (New York: Simon & Schuster, 1992), 244–51.

25. McCullough, *Truman,* 252; Freidel, *Franklin D. Roosevelt,* 357; Meacham, *Franklin and Winston,* 78; Herring, *From Colony to Superpower,* 524.

26. Quote from "President's Call for Full Response on Defense," *New York Times,* December 30, 1940; Ryan, *Franklin D. Roosevelt's Rhetorical Presidency,* 144–46; Henry N. Dorris, "Congress Solemn Hearing President," *New York Times,* January 7, 1941; Ryan, *Franklin D. Roosevelt's Rhetorical Presidency,* 146–48; "President's Orders Revamping Defense Set-Up," *New York Times,* January 8, 1941; 87 Cong. Rec. 87–88 (1941).

27. Herring, *From Colony to Superpower,* 524–26; Ryan, *Franklin D. Roosevelt's Rhetorical Presidency,* 148–49; Adler, *Isolationist Impulse,* 262–63, 278–79; A. Scott Berg, *Lindbergh* (New York: Putnam's, 1998), 413–16.

28. Quote from "Speech of Senator Alben W. Barkley, of Kentucky, in the Senate of the United States on February 17th, 1941, on the Bill H.R. 1776, Providing Aid to the Victims of Aggression," box 154, UKSC/Barkley Papers; "The Nation; Lease-Lend Debate," *New York Times,* February 9, 1941; "The Lease-Lend Bill," *New York Times,* February 10, 1941.

29. Quote from "Speech of Senator Alben W. Barkley, of Kentucky, in the Senate of the United States on February 17th, 1941."

30. Quote from Ritchie, "Alben W. Barkley," 140; "The Nation: Lease-Lend Debated," *New York Times,* March 9, 1941; Davis, "Alben W. Barkley," 102–3; Fullilove, *Rendezvous with Destiny,* 104–5; Robinson, "Barkley and Roosevelt," 335–40.

31. Libbey, *Russian-American Economic Relations,* 121; Edward M. Bennett, *Franklin D. Roosevelt and the Search for Victory: American-Soviet Relations, 1939–1945* (Wilmington, DE: Scholarly Resources, 1990), 26–27; George C. Herring Jr., *Aid to Russia, 1941–1946: Strategy, Diplomacy, the Origins of the Cold War* (New York: Columbia University Press, 1973), 6–7.

32. Libbey, *Russian-American Economic Relations*, 122–26; Bennett, *Franklin D. Roosevelt and the Search for Victory*, 28–32; Herring, *Aid to Russia*, 8–21; Roosevelt to Edward R. Stettinius (a Lend-Lease administrator), November 7, 1941, in *Documents of Soviet-American Relations* (5 vols.), ed. Harold J. Goldberg (Gulf Breeze, FL: Academic International, 1993–2006), 4:1.

33. Herring, *From Colony to Superpower*, 533–34; "The President's Speech: President's Address on Freedom of the Seas," *New York Times*, September 12, 1941; Ryan, *Franklin D. Roosevelt's Rhetorical Presidency*, 150–51; James B. Reston, "Ballot Is 50 to 37, All Moves to Restrict Neutrality Act Changes Are Beaten Down After Dramatic Debate," *New York Times*, November 8, 1941; "The Vote in the House on the Neutrality Act," *New York Times*, November 14, 1941; Charles Hurd, "President Signs Ship Ban Repeal," *New York Times*, November 18, 1941.

34. Donald J. Young, *First 24 Hours of War in the Pacific* (Shippensburg, PA: Burd Street, 1998), viii–ix; Kort, *The Soviet Colossus*, 227. For a more thorough understanding of the whole background to the Pearl Harbor attack, see Harry A. Gailey, *The War in the Pacific: From Pearl Harbor to Tokyo Bay* (Novato, CA: Presidio, 1995), 1–70.

35. Quote from Ryan, *Franklin D. Roosevelt's Rhetorical Presidency*, 152 (see also 151, 153–57); Tully, *Franklin Delano Roosevelt, My Boss*, 254–57.

36. Tully, *Franklin Delano Roosevelt, My Boss*, 258–61; Meacham, *Franklin and Winston*, 128–35; Divine, *Reluctant Belligerent*, 157–58.

14. The Senator in a Time of Troubles and Triumphs

1. Frank L. Kluckhohn, "Congress Thrilled: Prime Minister Warns of Dark Days but Holds Victory Is Certain," *New York Times*, December 27, 1941; Arnold, *Global Mission*, 275–83; Libbey, *Alexander P. de Seversky and the Quest for Air Power*, 191, 199; Gailey, *War in the Pacific*, 154–67; Russell Miller, *The Soviet Air Force at War* (Alexandria, VA: Time-Life, 1983), 115–27.

2. Roosevelt to Barkley (re: price control bill), telegram, January 7, 1942, box 75, UKSC/Barkley Papers; Ritchie, "Alben W. Barkley," 141–42; Floyd M. Riddick, "The Second Session of the Seventy-Seventh Congress (January 6–December 16, 1942)," *American Political Science Review* 37 (1943): 290–305; Donald K. Pickens, "World War II," in Northrup, ed., *Encyclopedia of World Trade*, 4:985–92. Katznelson, however, points out that, from the perspective of southern senators, racial issues became worse in wartime. See Katznelson, *Fear Itself*, 186.

3. Quote from William S. White, *The Making of a Journalist* (Lexington: University Press of Kentucky, 1986), 170; Ritchie, "Alben W. Barkley," 143; Barkley, *That Reminds Me*, 71; author interview of Marian Barkley Truitt, June 29, 1980; reel 2, HST/Barkley Papers.

4. Ritchie, "Alben W. Barkley," 153; "John W. Barkley Dies Following Lengthy Illness," *Paducah Sun-Democrat*, July 10, 1932; "Mrs. Electa Barkley, Mother of Senator Barkley, Dies," *Paducah Sun-Democrat*, December 23, 1945; "Mrs. Barkley Buried, Senator Flies Here in Truman's Plane," *Paducah Sun-Democrat*, December 24, 1945; "Mrs. Alben W. Barkley Dies at Washington, Funeral Here," *Paducah Sun-Democrat*, March 10, 1947. See also "Mrs. Barkley, 64, Wife of Senator," *New York Times*, March

11, 1947; reel 22, HST/Barkley Papers; Barkley to Eleanor Roosevelt, March 16, 1947, box 1528, FDR/E. Roosevelt Papers.

5. Quote from 88 Cong. Rec. 4713 (1942); Frederick R. Barkley (no relation), "Weekly Gas Ration Is 2 to 6 Gallons," *New York Times,* May 7, 1942; John MacCormac, "Many in Congress Push X Card Claims," *New York Times,* May 14, 1942; "Senate in Battle over Its Gasoline," *New York Times,* May 15, 1942.

6. Barkley quoted in Frederick R. Barkley, "Poll Tax Upheld as Senate Defeats Closure, 41 to 37, Barkley Shelves Measure as Agreed After Losing Test on Limiting Debate," *New York Times,* November 24, 1942. See also "Anti–Poll Tax Bill Up Today," *New York Times,* November 13, 1942; and John Robert Moore, "The Conservative Coalition in the United States Senate, 1942–1945," *Journal of Southern History* 33 (August 1967): 368–76.

7. Barkley, "Poll Tax Upheld as Senate Defeats Closure, 41 to 37"; Ritchie, "Alben W. Barkley," 143; Davis, "Alben W. Barkley," 120. See also Weiss, *Farewell to the Party of Lincoln;* and Huthmacher, *Senator Robert F. Wagner and the Rise of Urban Liberalism.*

8. Quote from Roosevelt to Barkley, January 8, 1943, box 63, UKSC/Barkley Papers.

9. "Barkley Turns Fire on WPB 'Hobbles': Leader Charges Smaller Plants Corporation Is Restrained," *New York Times,* February 12, 1943; Libbey, *Alexander P. de Seversky and the Quest for Air Power,* 195; Donald R. McCoy, *The Presidency of Harry S. Truman* (Lawrence: University Press of Kansas, 1984), 7; Donald H. Riddle, *The Truman Committee* (New Brunswick, NJ: Rutgers University Press, 1964), 8–9, 28.

10. "A Decade of Achievement: Remarks of Hon. Alben W. Barkley," n.d., box 49, Samuel I. Rosenman Papers, Franklin D. Roosevelt Presidential Library; Ritchie, "Alben W. Barkley," 142.

11. "The President's Veto," *New York Times,* June 12, 1943; "The Anti-Strike Bill," *New York Times,* June 14, 1943.

12. Freidel, *Franklin D. Roosevelt,* 370–71; W. H. Lawrence, "Congress Rebels: President Is Defeated by 56 to 25 in Senate, 244 to 108 in House," *New York Times,* June 26, 1943.

13. Reel 20, HST/Barkley Papers; Gene Teitelbaum, "Brandeis, Louis Dembitz," in Kleber, ed., *Kentucky Encyclopedia,* 113; Gilbert, *End of the European Era,* 248; "Barkley Proposes a Palestine Army: Senator Says Jews Should Be Allowed to Put Strong Forces in the Field, Balfour Pledge Is Cited, Lack of Its Fulfillment Is Deplored on 24th Anniversary of the Declaration," *New York Times,* November 2, 1941.

14. Quote from "Roosevelt Sets Up War Refugee Board," *New York Times,* January 23, 1944; Noah Feldman, "Could FDR Have Done More to Save the Jews," *New York Review of Books* 61 (May 8, 2014): 40, 42, 44; Meacham, *Franklin and Winston,* 191; Libbey, *Alexander P. de Seversky and the Quest for Air Power,* 231; "American Experience: Establishment of the War Refugee Board," n.d., http://www.pbs.org/wgbh/amex/holocaust/peopleevents/pandeAMEX102.html.

15. "Refugee Unit Approved," *New York Times,* September 20, 1943; Hicks, *Republic Ascendancy,* 131–33; "President Roosevelt's Message to Congress [Complete Text]," *New York Times,* January 12, 1944; Gilbert, *End of the European Era,* 331–45.

16. Quote from "President Roosevelt's Message to Congress"; Freidel, *Franklin D. Roosevelt*, 501; "Conferees Agree on Final Tax Bill," *New York Times*, February 1, 1944; "Tax Bill Adopted, Congress Puts It Up to President," *New York Times*, February 8, 1944.

17. Reel 5, HST/Barkley Papers; Ritchie, "Alben W. Barkley," 145; Davis, "Alben W. Barkley," 138–39; Barkley, *That Reminds Me*, 171–72; George W. Robinson, "Alben W. Barkley and the 1944 Tax Veto," *The Register* 67 (July 1969): 197–210.

18. Quotes from "Tax Bill Veto Message," *New York Times*, February 23, 1944; they can also be found in "The War Revenue Bill: Speech of Hon. Alben W. Barkley of Kentucky in the Senate of the United States, February 23, 1944," p. 6, PPF 3160, FDR/Roosevelt Papers; and reel 5, HST/Barkley Papers. See also John N. Criders, "President Vetoes Tax Bill, Calls It Relief for Greedy," *New York Times*, February 23, 1944.

19. Quote from "The War Revenue Bill," 7; Alben W. Barkley, "Congress Should Override Tax Bill Veto," *Vital Speeches* 10 (March 1, 1944): 292–95; "Barkley's Bombshell," *New Republic* 110 (March 6, 1944): 316; "The Barkley Incident," *Time* 43 (March 6, 1944): 17–21; Karl Keyerleber, "Challenge to Roosevelt," *Current History* 6 (April 1944): 311–16.

20. Roosevelt quote from Roosevelt to Barkley, telegram (typed file copy), February 23, 1944, PPF 3160, FDR/Roosevelt Papers; Barkley quotes from Barkley to FDR, February 24, 1944, box 13, UKSC/Barkley Papers; "Revolt in Congress," *New York Times*, February 24, 1944.

21. Barkley, *That Reminds Me*, 170; Davis, "Alben W. Barkley," 154. On FDR's grudges, see Freidel, *Franklin D. Roosevelt*, 221, 223, 310, 502. See also Floyd M. Riddick, "Congress versus the President in 1944," *South Atlantic Quarterly* 44 (July 1945): 308–15.

22. Alben W. Barkley, "Why I Support Roosevelt," *Collier's* 118 (May 20, 1944): 11, 92–93; Harold F. Gosnell, *Truman's Crises: A Political Biography of Harry S. Truman* (Westport, CT: Greenwood, 1980), 190; "Nomination of Franklin Delano Roosevelt for President of the United States by Alben W. Barkley, U.S. Senator from Kentucky at the Democratic National Convention, Chicago, Illinois, July 20, 1944," esp. p. 7, PPF 3160, FDR/Roosevelt Papers; Alben W. Barkley, "A Rendezvous with Destiny," *Vital Speeches* 10 (August 1, 1944): 628–31; Freidel, *Franklin D. Roosevelt*, 530; Tully, *Franklin Delano Roosevelt, My Boss*, 275.

23. Freidel, *Franklin D. Roosevelt*, 529–33; Tully, *Franklin Delano Roosevelt, My Boss*, 275; Davis, "Alben W. Barkley," 158; McCullough, *Truman*, 300; Robinson, "Barkley and Roosevelt," 419.

24. Quote from Roosevelt to Barkley, telegram, July 21, 1944, PPF 3160, FDR/Roosevelt Papers; Freidel, *Franklin D. Roosevelt*, 529–33; McCullough, *Truman*, 299–301; Joseph P. Lash, *Eleanor and Franklin: The Story of Their Relationship* (New York: Norton, 1971), 708.

25. For discussion of the vice presidential nomination process, see McCullough, *Truman*, 299–324; Tully, *Franklin Delano Roosevelt, My Boss*, 276; and "How Barkley Missed Out on the White House," *U.S. News and World Report* 40 (May 11, 1956): 99–101.

26. Lowell H. Harrison, "Willis, Simeon," in Kleber, ed., *Kentucky Encyclopedia,* 958; press release (Barkley's Glasgow speech), September 30, 1944, Democratic Campaign Headquarters, Seelbach Hotel, Louisville, KY, box 156, UKSC/Barkley Papers; Klotter, *Kentucky: Portrait in Paradox,* 325–26.

27. Wallace quote from Henry A. Wallace to Barkley, November 11, 1944, box 4, Henry A. Wallace Papers, Library of Congress; Roosevelt quote from Roosevelt to Barkley, telegram, December 16, 1944, PPF 3160, FDR/Roosevelt Papers; Klotter, *Kentucky: Portrait in Paradox,* 325–26; "Hannegan Issues Victory Statement," *New York Times,* November 8, 1944.

28. "Senator Barkley in Hospital," *New York Times,* January 30, 1945; "Barkley Re-Elected Majority Leader," *New York Times,* January 6, 1945; Freidel, *Franklin D. Roosevelt,* 571, 575.

29. "Text of the Prepared Statement of Henry A. Wallace," *New York Times,* January 26, 1945; "Wallace Rejected by Unit [Commerce Committee]," *New York Times,* January 27, 1945; "Wallace Forces Rely on President," *New York Times,* January 27, 1945; Harry S. Truman, *Memoirs by Harry S. Truman,* 2 vols. (Garden City, NY: Doubleday, 1955–1956), 1:195; Barkley to FDR, draft of message, February 1, 1945, box 64, UKSC/Barkley Papers; 91 Cong. Rec. 694 (1945); "Way Is Cleared for Wallace Vote . . . Roosevelt Signs George Bill," *New York Times,* March 1, 1945; "Senate Confirms Wallace as Secretary by 56 to 32," *New York Times,* March 2, 1945.

30. Quote from "[Roosevelt] Reports on Yalta," *New York Times,* March 2, 1945. See also Freidel, *Franklin D. Roosevelt,* 597–98; and "Report of President in Person to the Congress on the Crimea Conference [Text of Speech]," *New York Times,* March 2, 1945.

31. Reel 5, HST/Barkley Papers; Freidel, *Franklin D. Roosevelt,* 603; Tully, *Franklin Delano Roosevelt, My Boss,* 355–57.

32. McCullough, *Truman,* 340–47; "L. L. Biffle for Senate Secretary," *New York Times,* February 8, 1945; reel 14, HST/Barkley Papers; Truman, *Memoirs by Harry S. Truman,* 1:7; Truman, *Harry S. Truman,* 211.

33. Quote from reel 14, HST/Barkley Papers; Truman, *Memoirs by Harry S. Truman,* 1:64; Barkley, *That Reminds Me,* 206; 91 Cong. Rec. 3596 (1945); McCullough, *Truman,* 356.

34. William S. White, "Congress, Press to View Horrors: Eisenhower Asks Delegates of Both to See German Concentration Camps," *New York Times,* April 22, 1945, and "War Crimes Report Horrifies Capital: Silence Grips Both Houses as German Regime Is Indicted by Congressional Body," *New York Times,* May 16, 1945; reel 2, 12, HST/Barkley Papers; 91 Cong. Rec. 4576–82 (1945).

35. White, "War Crimes Report Horrifies Capital"; Robert A. Divine, *Second Chance: The Triumph of Internationalism in America during World War II* (New York: Atheneum, 1967), 287–98; Truman, *Memoirs by Harry S. Truman,* 1:332–412 (esp. 407–8); Truman to Barkley, July 5, 1945, box PDF 1694, HST/Truman Papers.

36. Paterson et al., *American Foreign Relations,* 2:199; Keith A. Leitich, "Bretton Woods Agreement (1945)," in Northrup, ed., *The American Economy,* 1:32; John H. Crider, "Senate Votes, 52–31, to Act Immediately on World Fund Bill," *New York Times,*

July 19, 1945, and "Senate Votes 61–16 to Adopt Bretton Act," *New York Times,* July 20, 1945; "Three Bills Signed on World Economy," *New York Times,* August 5, 1945.

37. Quote from "United Nations Charter, Speech of Hon. Alben W. Barkley of Kentucky in the Senate of the United States, Tuesday, July 24, 1945," box 156, UKSC/Barkley Papers; Divine, *Second Chance,* 310–14; Truman, *Memoirs by Harry S. Truman,* 1:399–400.

38. Quote from Truman to Barkley, July 27, 1945, box 530, PPF 1694, HST/Truman Papers. See also "Barkley as Leader Praised by Truman," *New York Times,* July 28, 1945.

15. The Iron Man Becomes a Veep

1. Gailey, *War in the Pacific,* 450, 492–94; Libbey, *Alexander P. de Seversky and the Quest for Air Power,* 234–38; William S. White, "Pearl Harbor Inquiry Voted by Senate," *New York Times,* September 7, 1945; Joseph A. Loftus, "House Votes a Full Inquiry on the Pearl Harbor Disaster," *New York Times,* September 12, 1945; reel 22, HST/Barkley Papers.

2. "Pearl Harbor Conclusions," *New York Times,* August 30, 1945; "The Official Pearl Harbor Reports: Army and Navy Boards in Pearl Harbor Inquiry," *New York Times,* August 30, 1945; White, "Pearl Harbor Inquiry Voted by Senate."

3. White, "Pearl Harbor Inquiry Voted by Senate"; reel 20, HST/Barkley Papers; William S. White, "Roosevelt Found Blameless for Pearl Harbor: Eight of Congress Inquiry Group Agree on Conclusions, with Two Dissenting—Military Leaders Are Criticized," *New York Times,* July 21, 1946.

4. Quote from US Congress, *Report of the Joint Committee on the Investigation of the Pearl Harbor Attack* (Washington, DC: US Government Printing Office, 1946), 251; reel 20, HST/Barkley Papers.

5. US Congress, *Report of the Joint Committee on the Investigation of the Pearl Harbor Attack,* 252–66; reel 20, HST/Barkley Papers; Libbey, *Alexander P. de Seversky and the Quest for Air Power,* 195, 244.

6. Quote from Davis, "Alben W. Barkley," 229; James B. Reston, "UNO Delegates Confirmed but Policy Is Challenged," *New York Times,* December 21, 1945; Felix Belair Jr., "Employment Bill Signed by Truman," *New York Times,* February 21, 1946; "Truman Approves School Lunch Bill," *New York Times,* June 5, 1946; "Truman Signed British Loan," *New York Times,* July 6, 1946; Walter H. Waggoner, "Truman Approves Measure for Revisions in Congress," *New York Times,* August 3, 1946; C. P. Trussell, "Major Bills Voted," *New York Times,* August 3, 1946.

7. "Barkley at Party Hailed by Truman: His Colleagues Are Stirred by Tributes After Many Marked Differences," *New York Times,* July 31, 1946. This article was published two days after the event. See also "Barkley Visits Swiss Cemetery," *New York Times,* September 1, 1946; and "Barkley, Back from Europe, Is Optimistic," *New York Times,* September 8, 1946.

8. Libbey, *Dear Alben,* 92; "Mrs. Barkley, 64, Wife of Senator [Discusses Earlier Stroke]," *New York Times,* March 11, 1947; McCullough, *Truman,* 523; McCoy, *The Presidency of Harry S. Truman,* 95.

9. Quotes from Sam Stavisky, "Vice President-Elect Barkley's Mustache Was Prophetic," *Washington Post,* January 10, 1949; Robert W. Merry, "Robert A. Taft: A Study in the Accumulation of Legislative Power," in Baker and Davidson, eds., *First among Equals,* 177; McCullough, *Truman,* 531.

10. Quote from Merry, "Robert A. Taft," 180 (see also 177); John F. Kennedy, *Profiles in Courage* (New York: Harper & Row, 1956), 241–44; reel 6, HST/Barkley Papers; McCullough, *Truman,* 529–30; Michael J. Hogan, *A Cross of Iron: Harry S. Truman and the Origins of the National Security State, 1945–1954* (Cambridge: Cambridge University Press, 1998), 11–12.

11. Quote from Truman, *Memoirs by Harry S. Truman,* 2:106 (see also 105, 107–9); Felix Belair Jr., "New Policy Set Up: President Blunt in Plea to Combat 'Coercion' as World Peril," *New York Times,* March 13, 1947; Hogan, *Cross of Iron,* 11–16.

12. "Bad Weather Delays Congressional Party," *New York Times,* April 5, 1947; "Tolerance on U.S. Urged by Barkley," *New York Times,* April 9, 1947; "Congressmen to Visit Greece," *New York Times,* April 11, 1947; "Congressmen Reach Istanbul on Voyage," *New York Times,* April 14, 1947; "Delegation from Congress Is on Way Home from Cairo," *New York Times,* April 16, 1947; C. P. Trussell, "Party Lines Merge: Both Sides Back Bill to Bulwark Countries Pressed by Reds," *New York Times,* April 23, 1947.

13. Trussell, "Party Lines Merge"; William S. White, "Opposition Is Weak: Majorities for Measure [Taft-Hartley] Given by Both Parties," *New York Times,* June 7, 1947; Merry, "Robert A. Taft," 184–86.

14. White quote from White, "Opposition Is Weak: Majorities for Measure Given by Both Parties"; Truman quote from Truman to Barkley, June 23, 1947, box 530, PPF 1694, HST/Truman Papers; Truman, *Memoirs by Harry S. Truman,* 2:30.

15. Quote from US Congress, *Report of the Joint Committee on the Investigation of the Pearl Harbor Attack,* 254; Truman, *Memoirs by Harry S. Truman,* 2:51–53; Hogan, *Cross of Iron,* 89–104; Libbey, *Russian-American Economic Relations,* 141–43.

16. James C. Derieux, "For Distinguished Congressional Service," *Collier's* 121 (May 15, 1948): 22–23; Ritchie, "Alben W. Barkley," 153; "Collier Awards Go to Barkley, [Representative Christian A.] Herter [MA]," *New York Times,* May 9, 1948. Future secretary of state (1959–1961) Herter was recognized for his contribution to bipartisan foreign policy in the House. Truman's actual birthday party took place later among forty guests at the F Street Club. More than likely, Barkley was one of the guests. See McCullough, *Truman,* 614.

17. Quote from Barkley, *That Reminds Me,* 200; W. H. Lawrence, "Two Conventions in Sharp Contrast," *New York Times,* July 11, 1948; Gosnell, *Truman's Crises,* 377; McCullough, *Truman,* 632–35; Truman, *Memoirs by Harry S. Truman,* 2:180–87.

18. Quote from Truman, *Memoirs by Harry S. Truman,* 2:190; Felix Belair Jr., "Barkley Is Put Foremost in Field for Second Place," *New York Times,* July 11, 1948; Alben W. Barkley, "Record of Democratic Party: Keynote Address," *Vital Speeches* 14 (August 1, 1948): 612–19. The latter can also be found in box 157, UKSC/Barkley Papers.

19. Quote from Barkley, "Record of Democratic Party," 617.

20. "Convention Gives Barkley Big Hand: His Speech Attacking GOP Stirs Crowd," *New York Times,* July 13, 1948; Truman, *Memoirs by Harry S. Truman,* 2:204–5; Alonzo

L. Hamby, *Man of the People: A Life of Harry S. Truman* (New York: Oxford University Press, 1995), 450–51; "The Acceptance Speech of President Harry S. Truman with the Acceptance Speech of Senator Alben W. Barkley of Kentucky," July 15, 1948, box 157, UKSC/Barkley Papers.

21. McCullough, *Truman,* 638–41; John N. Popham, "Southerners Name Thurmond to Lead Anti-Truman Fight," *New York Times,* July 18, 1948; W. H. Lawrence, "'Wallace or War' Keynotes Progressive Party Conclave," *New York Times,* July 24, 1948.

22. Quote from "The Acceptance Speech of President Harry S. Truman with the Acceptance Speech of Senator Alben W. Barkley of Kentucky," p. 4 (see also p. 5); "The Text of President Truman's Executive Orders Governing Fair Employment Practices," *New York Times,* July 27, 1948.

23. Quote from C. P. Trussell, "Program Is Doomed: Republicans, Declaring Truman Call Political, Bar Most of Agenda, Swift Senate Tie-Up Due," *New York Times,* July 28, 1948. See also William S. White, "Senate Bloc Plans Rigid 'Rights' Fight," *New York Times,* July 27, 1948.

24. McCullough, *Truman,* 653–57; Truman, *Memoirs by Harry S. Truman,* 2:210–12; Gosnell, *Truman's Crises,* 396–406; McCoy, *The Presidency of Harry S. Truman,* 159–62.

25. Reels 10, 14, HST/Barkley Papers; author interview of David M. Barkley, May 18, 1977; William F. Mellberg, *Famous Airliners: Seventy Years of Aviation and Transport Progress* (Plymouth, MI: Plymouth, 1995), 28–31; Tom D. Crouch, *Wings: A History of Aviation from Kites to the Space Age* (Washington, DC: Smithsonian National Air and Space Museum, 2003), 608.

26. Louisville quote from "Speech by the Honorable Alben W. Barkley at Memorial Auditorium, Louisville, Kentucky, 8:30 P.M. October 23, 1948," p. 1, Special Collections, Murray State University Library; Pittsburgh quote from "Speech by the Honorable Alben W. Barkley at Pittsburgh, Pennsylvania, October 1, 1948, to Be Broadcast over the Columbia Broadcasting Company at 10:00 to 10:30 P.M. Eastern Standard Time," p. 1, box 158, UKSC/Barkley Papers; Davis, "Alben W. Barkley," 267 (second to last quote); reel 14, HST/Barkley Papers (last quote). For a thorough discussion of the complete Barkley campaign, see Mofield, "The Speaking Role of Alben Barkley," 170–296.

27. Quote from "Text of Truman's Final Words to the Voters," *New York Times,* November 2, 1948; McCullough, *Truman,* 697; Mofield, "The Speaking Role of Alben Barkley," 276–98.

28. Sam Stavisky, "People in the News: Vice President-Elect Alben William Barkley," *Washington Post,* November 5, 1948; Barkley to Eleanor Roosevelt, November 9, 1948, box 1528, FDR/E. Roosevelt Papers; Klotter, *Kentucky: Portrait in Paradox,* 333; McCullough, *Truman,* 723–34; Harrison and Klotter, *New History of Kentucky,* 401; Hedlund, "Vinson, Frederick Moore"; John Klee, "Reed, Stanley Forman," in Kleber, ed., *Kentucky Encyclopedia,* 760–61.

29. Quote from Libbey, "Alben W. Barkley" (in Purcell, ed.), 319; Hamby, *Man of the People,* 492, 497; McCullough, *Truman,* 808–13; Anthony Leviero, "President Resting: Awakened by Shots, He Sees Battle in Which Three Are Wounded [and Two

Are Killed], He Keeps Appointments, Documents Link 2 Assassins, Who Lived Here, to Puerto Rican Extremist Leader," *New York Times,* November 2, 1950. For the vice presidents mentioned, see Purcell, ed., *The Vice Presidents,* 90–101, 113–21, 147–53, 178–85, 226–36, 262–71, 306–13.

30. Ritchie, "Alben W. Barkley," 154; Truman, *Memoirs by Harry S. Truman,* 2:59; Leistner, "Political Campaign Speaking of Alben W. Barkley," 315; William S. White, "Dignitary Greeter and Politician—the 'Veep,'" *New York Times Magazine,* September 4, 1949, 12–13; reel 6, HST/Barkley Papers.

31. Quote from Clark, *Kentucky: Land of Contrast,* 159; Ritchie, "Alben W. Barkley," 154, 298. For a sample of the many messages that Truman sent to Barkley, see, e.g., Truman to Barkley, March 7, 1950, September 20, 1951, and June 9, 1952, box 530, PPF 1694, HST/Truman Papers.

32. Vandenberg quotes from 95 Cong. Rec. 3 (1949); Barkley quote from 95 Cong. Rec. 2172 (1949); William S. White, "Defeat Conceded by Truman Forces in Gag-Rule Fight: Senate Chiefs Agree to Meet Today for Compromise Talk with Coalition Forces," *New York Times,* March 13, 1949.

33. Brown and White quotes from White, "Defeat by Truman Forces in Gag-Rule Fight."

34. Quote from Truman to Ferdinand Pecora, May 10, 1949, box 530, PPF 1694, HST/Truman Papers; "Barkley Receives 4-Freedom Award," *New York Times,* May 14, 1949; McCullough, *Truman,* 876–78; reel 17, HST/Barkley Papers.

35. Barkley, *That Reminds Me,* 210; author interview of Marian Barkley Truitt, June 29, 1980; Libbey, "Alben W. Barkley" (in Purcell, ed.), 320; "Barkleys Find a Shangri-La at Georgia Coastal Resort," *Washington Post,* November 22, 1949.

16. The Iron Man Keeps His Mettle

1. McCullough, *Truman,* 506; Ritchie, "Alben W. Barkley," 154; Barkley, *I Married the Veep,* 13–22; Mary Van Rensselaer Thayer, "It Was Love at First Sight When Veep and Jane Hadley Met at Cliffords' Party," *Washington Post,* November 1, 1949.

2. Quotes from "The Veep Gets His Girl Friend and the Capital Is 'Tickled Pink,'" *Washington Daily News,* October 31, 1949; reel 9, HST/Barkley Papers; Barkley, *I Married the Veep,* 154–66.

3. Quotes from Victor Lasky, "Democratic Smiles: Mrs. Veep Beams as Barkley Quips," *New York World-Telegram,* December 3, 1949; reel 10, HST/Barkley Papers; Barkley, *I Married the Veep,* 172–82.

4. Barkley, *I Married the Veep,* 165; Libbey, *Alexander P. de Seversky and the Quest for Air Power,* 249–50; Herring, *From Colony to Superpower,* 625–26.

5. Stephen G. Craft, *V. K. Wellington Koo and the Emergence of Modern China* (Lexington: University Press of Kentucky, 2004), 226–28; Dean Acheson, *Present at the Creation: My Years in the State Department* (New York: Norton, 1969), 354–57; David Halberstam, *The Coldest Winter: America and the Korean War* (New York: Hyperion, 2007), 48.

6. Acheson, *Present at the Creation,* 357; David Rees, *Korea: The Limited War* (Baltimore: Penguin, 1970), 10–20; Arthur H. Mitchell, *Understanding the Korean War: The*

Participants, the Tactics, and the Course of Conflict (Jefferson, NC: McFarland, 2013), 16–25.

7. Reel 6, HST/Barkley Papers; John Lewis Gaddis, *We Now Know: Rethinking Cold War History* (New York: Oxford University Press, 1997), 71; Rees, *Korea,* 21–28; Truman, *Memoirs by Harry S. Truman,* 2:338; Wada Haruki, *The Korean War: An International History* (Lanham, MD: Rowman & Littlefield, 2004), 82–89; Truman, *Harry S. Truman,* 470–71.

8. UN resolution quote from Rees, *Korea,* 108; McCoy, *The Presidency of Harry S. Truman,* 217–20; Burton I. Kaufman, *The Korean Conflict* (Westport, CT: Greenwood, 1999), 7–11; Gaddis, *We Now Know,* 79; Halberstam, *Coldest Winter,* 293–315.

9. Quote from MacArthur's communiqué of November 24, 1950, in Lynn Montross, Nicholas Canzona, et al., *US Marine Corps Operations in Korea,* 5 vols. (Washington, DC: US Marine Corps Historical Branch, 1954–72), 3:144; McCullough, *Truman,* 817; Rees, *Korea,* 148–57; Kaufman, *Korean Conflict,* 11; Haruki, *Korean War,* 143–47.

10. MacArthur quote in Rees, *Korea,* 150; Barkley quote in Truman, *Memoirs by Harry S. Truman,* 2:386–87; McCullough, *Truman,* 817; Matthew B. Ridgeway, *The Korean War* (New York: Doubleday, 1967), 150. Three days after the NSC meeting, Truman requested that Congress approve $16.8 billion in supplemental funds for the US military. See Hogan, *Cross of Iron,* 311.

11. McCullough, *Truman,* 817; Truman, *Memoirs by Harry S. Truman,* 2:387; Kaufman, *Korean Conflict,* 12; Rees, *Korea,* 160–95; Ridgeway, *Korean War,* 108–11.

12. Truman, *Memoirs by Harry S. Truman,* 2:440–48; Hamby, *Man of the People,* 555; Rees, *Korea,* 214–17; reel 6, HST/Barkley Papers; Barkley, *That Reminds Me,* 213–14.

13. Quote from "General Douglas MacArthur's Speech to a Joint Session of Congress, Peroration, April 19, 1951," in Kaufman, *Korean Conflict,* "Primary Documents of the Korean Conflict," 153–54; "President Harry Truman's Speech to the Nation Explaining His Decision to Relieve MacArthur of His Commands, April 11, 1951," in ibid., 150–53; reel 12, HST/Barkley Papers; Ridgeway, *Korean War,* 141–57.

14. Tindall, *America,* 2:A27–A28; McCullough, *Truman,* 837, 891; Truman, *Memoirs by Harry S. Truman,* 2:491–92.

15. Quote from *Memoirs by Harry S. Truman,* 2:492 (see also 489–91); "Text of Truman Speech at Jefferson-Jackson Dinner," *New York Times,* March 30, 1952; John H. Fenton, "Eisenhower Defeats Taft, Kefauver Wins over Truman in New Hampshire's Primary," *New York Times,* March 12, 1952; McCoy, *The Presidency of Harry S. Truman,* 300–302; Arthur Krock, "Race Is Wide Open," *New York Times,* March 30, 1952.

16. McCullough, *Truman,* 887–92; Ritchie, "Alben W. Barkley," 155; Hedlund, "Vinson, Frederick Moore." For samples of the large-print materials that Barkley had to use, see box 165, UKSC/Barkley Papers.

17. Barkley, "Accustomed as I Am to Public Speaking"; Barkley, *I Married the Veep,* 242–44; "Statement of Vice President Alben W. Barkley: For Release Monday Morning Papers—July 7, 1952," box 164, UKSC/Barkley Papers.

18. Truman, *Memoirs by Harry S. Truman,* 2:495; Barkley, *I Married the Veep,* 243;

Truman to Tom Gavin, memorandum, July 16, 1952, no. 494, Miscellaneous Historical Documents Collection, HST/Truman Papers.

19. Quote from *Memoirs by Harry S. Truman,* 2:495; "The Tie That Binds," *Time* 60 (July 28, 1952): 10 (see also 11–12); Barkley, *I Married the Veep,* 245; McCullough, *Truman,* 904.

20. William S. White, "Gains for Barkley Reported; At 74, He Looks to Future," *New York Times,* July 19, 1952 (see also the picture on p. 6, a continuation of the front-page story); Barkley, *I Married the Veep,* 245–47; Lowell H. Harrison, "Wetherby, Lawrence Winchester," in Kleber, ed., *Kentucky Encyclopedia,* 945–46.

21. Quote from White, "Gains for Barkley Reported"; Truman, *Memoirs by Harry S. Truman,* 2:495.

22. Harrison quote from Joseph A. Loftus, "Labor Turns Down Barkley as Too Old," *New York Times,* July 21, 1952; Barkley quote from "Statement by Vice President Alben W. Barkley: Issued 11 p.m., July 21, 1952," box 164, UKSC/Barkley Papers; Les Egan, "Barkley Lashes Out at Labor for Refusal to Support Him," *New York Times,* July 22, 1952; Gosnell, *Truman's Crises,* 511; Hamby, *Man of the People,* 608–9; Truman, *Memoirs by Harry S. Truman,* 2:495; Barkley, *I Married the Veep,* 248–51; reel 20, HST/Barkley Papers.

23. Truman quote from Truman, *Memoirs by Harry S. Truman,* 2:496; Barkley quote from "Address by the Honorable Alben W. Barkley, Democratic National Convention—Chicago, Ill., Wednesday Evening, July 23, 1952," transcript, box 164, UKSC/Barkley Papers; Truman, *Harry S. Truman,* 542; reel 21, HST/Barkley Papers.

24. Barkley quote from Barkley, *That Reminds Me,* 247–48; Belair quote from Felix Belair Jr., "Barkley Cheered in Two Ovations," *New York Times,* July 24, 1952; reel 6, HST/Barkley Papers; Stephen E. Ambrose, *Eisenhower: Soldier and President* (New York: Simon & Schuster, 1991), 286.

25. Ambrose, *Eisenhower,* 285, 294, 303; Rees, *Korea,* 421–34; Libbey, *Alexander P. de Seversky and the Quest for Air Power,* 259; Gaddis, *We Now Know,* 108–10. In terms of Stalin, an opposing view against Gaddis is found in Haruki, *Korean War,* 251–59.

26. Barkley, *I Married the Veep,* 267–74. For a sample transcribed transcript, see "Meet the Veep, Friday, May 8, 1953, NBC Television, Alben W. Barkley, Earle Godwin," box 164, UKSC/Barkley Papers.

27. Barkley, *I Married the Veep,* 274; Alfred A. Knopf to Barkley, January 21, 1947, box 101, UKSC/Barkley Papers; Smith, "Washington's Greatest Storyteller"; Elizabeth Bragdon (Bobbs-Merrill) to Barkley, March 12, 1951, and Ken McCormick (Doubleday) to Barkley, March 15, 1951, both in box 101, UKSC/Barkley Papers.

28. McCormick to Barkley, March 15, 1951, and Ralph A. Beebe (a Doubleday editor) to Barkley, January 10, 1952, both in box 101, UKSC/Barkley Papers.

29. Beebe to Barkley, January 10, 1952, April 24, 1953, and Barkley to Bragdon (Bobbs-Merrill) (requesting return of chapters), March 2, 1955, all in box 101, UKSC/Barkley Papers.

30. Beebe to Barkley, September 3, 1953, Beebe and McCormick to Barkley, September 24, 1953, McCormick to Barkley, January 14, 1954, contract between Curtis Publishing Co. and Barkley, February 5, 1954, and Beebe to Barkley, April 15, June 2,

October 13, 1954, all in box 101, UKSC/Barkley Papers. See also Alben William Barkley, "That Reminds Me," *Saturday Evening Post* 226 (April 17, 1954): 19; review of *That Reminds Me*, by Alben W. Barkley, *New Yorker* 30 (November 20, 1954): 222; and "The Veep Looks Back," *New York Times*, November 7, 1954.

31. Lowell H. Harrison, "Clements, Earle Chester," in Kleber, ed., *Kentucky Encyclopedia*, 206–7; William Cooper, "Cooper, John Sherman," in ibid., 227–28; Harrison, "Wetherby, Lawrence Winchester"; "Statement by Alben W. Barkley, March 27, 1954," box 165, UKSC/Barkley Papers; Foster Hailey, "Barkley to Run for Senate at Behest of Party Chiefs," *New York Times*, March 28, 1954; "Barkley, Cooper Win in Kentucky [Primary]," *New York Times*, August 8, 1954; John N. Popham, "Barkley Is Victor in Kentucky Vote," *New York Times*, November 3, 1954. See also Barkley, *I Married the Veep*, 290; "Address of Alben W. Barkley . . . Shelbyville, September 30, 1954," box 165, UKSC/Barkley Papers; Harrison and Klotter, *New History of Kentucky*, 402; Robert Schulman, *John Sherman Cooper: The Global Kentuckian* (Lexington: University Press of Kentucky, 1976), 65–66; Paul F. Healy, "Battle of Giants in Kentucky," *Saturday Evening Post* 227 (September 18, 1954): 32–33, 117.

32. Barkley, *I Married the Veep*, 292–93; Ritchie, "Alben W. Barkley," 155; Howard E. Shuman, "Lyndon B. Johnson: The Senate's Powerful Persuader," in Baker and Davidson, eds., *First among Equals*, 217–20.

33. Schulman, *John Sherman Cooper*, 69; Cooper, "Cooper, John Sherman," 227. "Address of Alben W. Barkley . . . Shelbyville, September 30th, 1954" is an example of a prepared scripted speech with standard type accompanied by a version in ultralarge print that Barkley could read.

34. Barkley, *I Married the Veep*, 295–98.

35. Quote from "President Mourns at Barkley Rites," *New York Times*, May 3, 1956; "Barkley, 78, Dies of Heart Attack during a Speech," *New York Times*, May 1, 1956.

36. Anthony Lewis, "Barkley Buried with Simple Rite: Senate Delegation, Truman, Stevenson and Kefauver Join Paducah Throngs," *New York Times*, May 4, 1956.

37. Chandler quoted from "Eisenhower Leads Barkley Tribute," *New York Times*, May 1, 1956.

Selected Bibliography

Interviews

Richard A. Baker, June 28, 1980, Washington, DC
David M. Barkley, May 18, 1977, Paducah, KY
Virginia J. H. Cain, April 29, 1980, Atlanta, GA
Jackie Caraway, March 13, 1979, Clinton, KY
Berry Craig, March 13, 1979, Paducah, KY
Thomas Harper, March 13, 1979, Clinton, KY
Virginia Jewell, March 13, 1979, Clinton, KY
Joe La Gore, July 7, 1980, Paducah, KY
Lucille B. Owings, March 13, 1979, Columbus, KY
Ginny Raymond, March 13, 1979, Paducah, KY
Donald A. Ritchie, June 28, 1980, Washington, DC
Marian Barkley Truitt, June 29, 1980, Washington, DC
Earl Warren, March 13, 1979, Clinton, KY

Books and Articles

Adams, Samuel Hopkins. *Incredible Era: The Life and Times of Warren Gamaliel Harding.* Boston: Houghton Mifflin, 1939.

Adler, Selig. *The Isolationist Impulse: Its Twentieth Century Reaction.* New York: Collier, 1961.

Ambrose, Stephen E. *Eisenhower: Soldier and President.* New York: Simon & Schuster, 1991.

Ashby, Le Roy. *William Jennings Bryan: Champion of Democracy.* Boston: Twayne, 1987.

Axton, W. F. *Tobacco and Kentucky.* Lexington: University Press of Kentucky, 1975.

Bacon, Donald C. "Joseph Taylor Robinson: The Good Soldier." In *First among Equals: Outstanding Senate Leaders of the Twentieth Century,* ed. Richard A. Baker and Roger H. Davidson, 63–97. Washington, DC: Congressional Quarterly, 1991.

Bailey, Thomas A. *Woodrow Wilson and the Great Betrayal.* Chicago: Quadrangle, 1963.

Baker, Ray Stannard. *Woodrow Wilson: Life and Letters.* 8 vols. New York: Scribner's, 1946.

Baker, Richard A., and Roger H. Davidson, eds. *First among Equals: Outstanding Senate Leaders of the Twentieth Century.* Washington, DC: Congressional Quarterly, 1991.

Barkley, Alben W. "Speech of A. W. Barkley." *Railroad Telegrapher* 43 (June 1926): 594–620.

———. "Congress Should Override Tax Bill Veto." *Vital Speeches* 10 (March 1, 1944): 292–94.

———. "A Rendezvous with Destiny." *Vital Speeches* 10 (April 1, 1944): 628–31.

———. "Why I Support Roosevelt." *Collier's* 118 (May 20, 1944): 11, 92–93.

———. "Record of Democratic Party: Keynote Address." *Vital Speeches* 14 (August 1, 1948): 612–19.

———. "Accustomed as I Am to Public Speaking." *Collier's* 127 (June 19, 1951): 20–21, 66–67.

———. "Keeping Posted." *Saturday Evening Post* 228 (May 29, 1954): 116.

———. "That Reminds Me." *Saturday Evening Post* 226 (April 17, 1954): 19.

———. "That Reminds Me." *Saturday Evening Post* 226 (May 8, 1954): 38.

———. "That Reminds Me." *Saturday Evening Post* 226 (May 22, 1954): 36.

———. "That Reminds Me." *Saturday Evening Post* 226 (May 29, 1954): 30.

———. *That Reminds Me.* Garden City, NY: Doubleday, 1954.

Barkley, Jane R. *I Married the Veep.* New York: Vanguard, 1958.

"Barkley's Bombshell." *New Republic* 110 (March 6, 1944): 316.

Baylor, Orval W. *J. Dan Talbott, Champion of Good Government: A Saga of Kentucky Politics from 1900 to 1942.* Louisville: Kentucky Printing Corp., 1942.

Berg, A. Scott. *Wilson.* New York: Putnam's, 2013.

Brands, H. W. *T.R.: The Last Romantic.* New York: Basic, 1997.

Burner, David. *Herbert Hoover: A Public Life.* New York: Knopf, 1979.

Burns, James MacGregor. *Roosevelt: The Lion and the Fox.* New York: Harcourt, Brace & World, 1956.

Calder, J. Kent. "John Nance Garner (1868–1967)." In *The Vice Presidents: A Biographical Dictionary,* ed. L. Edward Purcell, 289–96. New York: Facts on File, 1998.

Callahan, Patrick H. "Religious Prejudice and the Election." *Current History* 29 (December 1928): 381–83.

Chace, James. *1912: Wilson, Roosevelt, Taft and Debs—the Election That Changed the Country.* New York: Simon & Schuster, 2004.

Chandler, Albert B., with Vance H. Trimble. *Heroes, Plain Folks, and Skunks.* Chicago: Bonus, 1989.

Channing, Steven A. *Kentucky: A Bicentennial History.* New York: Norton, 1977.

Clark, Norman H. *Deliver Us from Evil: An Interpretation of American Prohibition.* New York: Norton, 1976.

Clark, Thomas D. *Pills, Petticoats and Plows: The Southern Country Store.* New York: Bobbs-Merrill, 1944.

———. *A History of Kentucky.* Lexington, KY: John Bradford, 1960.

———. *Kentucky: Land of Contrast.* New York: Harper & Row, 1968.

———. *Agrarian Kentucky.* Lexington: University Press of Kentucky, 1977.

Clements, Kendrick A. *The Presidency of Woodrow Wilson.* Lawrence: University Press of Kansas, 1992.

Cobb, Irvin S. *Exit Laughing.* New York: Bobbs-Merrill, 1941.

Coolidge, Calvin. *The Autobiography of Calvin Coolidge.* New York: Cosmopolitan, 1929.

Cooper, John Milton, Jr. *Woodrow Wilson: A Biography.* New York: Knopf, 2009.

Damron, Robert. "Chandler's Bid to Unseat Barkley." M.A. thesis, Eastern Kentucky University, 1967.

Daniels, Josephus. *The Wilson Era: Years of Peace, 1910–1917.* Chapel Hill: University of North Carolina Press, 1946.

Davis, Polly Ann. "Alben W. Barkley: Majority Leader and Vice President." Ph.D. diss., University of Kentucky, 1963.

———. "Court Reform and Alben W. Barkley's Election as Majority Leader." *Southern Quarterly* 15 (Spring 1976): 15–31.

Derieux, James C. "For Distinguished Congressional Service." *Collier's* 121 (May 15, 1948): 22–23.

Divine, Robert A. *The Reluctant Belligerent: American Entry into World War II.* New York: Wiley, 1965.

Douglas, James. *Parliaments across Frontiers: A Short History of the Inter-Parliamentary Union.* London: H.M. Stationery Office, 1975.

Farwell, Byron. *Over There: The United States in the Great War, 1917–1918.* New York: Norton, 1999.

Fausold, Martin L. *The Presidency of Herbert C. Hoover.* Lawrence: University Press of Kansas, 1985.

Ferrell, Robert H. *The Presidency of Calvin Coolidge.* Lawrence: University Press of Kansas, 1998.

Freidel, Frank. "The Sick Chicken Case." In *Quarrels That Have Shaped the Constitution,* ed. John A. Garraty, 233–52. New York: Harper & Row, 1988.

———. *Franklin D. Roosevelt: A Rendezvous with Destiny.* New York: Little, Brown, 1990.

Fullilove, Michael. *Rendezvous with Destiny: How Franklin D. Roosevelt and Five Extraordinary Men Took America into the War and into the World.* New York: Penguin, 2013.

Gailey, Harry A. *The War in the Pacific: From Pearl Harbor to Tokyo Bay.* Novato, CA: Presidio, 1995.

Gilbert, Felix, with David Clay Large. *The End of the European Era, 1890 to the Present.* New York: Norton, 1991.

Gilbert, Robert E. *The Tormented President: Calvin Coolidge, Death, and Clinical Depression.* Westport, CT: Praeger, 2003.

Glad, Paul W. *The Trumpet Soundeth: William Jennings Bryan and His Democracy, 1896–1912.* Lincoln: University of Nebraska Press, 1960.

Goldberg, David J. *Discontented America: The United States in the 1920s.* Baltimore: Johns Hopkins University Press, 1999.

Gosnell, Harold F. *Truman's Crises: A Political Biography of Harry S. Truman.* Westport, CT: Greenwood, 1980.

Grinde, Gerald S. "The Early Political Career of Alben W. Barkley, 1877–1937." Ph.D. diss., University of Illinois, 1976.

———. "Politics and Scandal in the Progressive Era: Alben W. Barkley and the

McCracken County Campaign of 1909." *Filson Club History Quarterly* 50 (April 1976): 36–51.

Halberstam, David. *The Coldest Winter: America and the Korean War.* New York: Hyperion, 2007.

Hamby, Alonzo L. *Man of the People: A Life of Harry S. Truman.* New York: Oxford University Press, 1995.

Harrison, Lowell H., and James C. Klotter. *A New History of Kentucky.* Lexington: University Press of Kentucky, 1997.

Haruki, Wada. *The Korean War: An International History.* Lanham, MD: Rowman & Littlefield, 2014.

Healy, Paul F. "Battle of Giants in Kentucky." *Saturday Evening Post* 227 (September 18, 1954): 32–33, 117.

Heckscher, August. *Woodrow Wilson.* New York: Scribner's, 1991.

Herring, George C. *From Colony to Superpower: U.S. Foreign Relations since 1776.* New York: Oxford University Press, 2008.

Hicks, John D. *Republican Ascendancy, 1921–1933.* New York: Harper & Bros., 1960.

Hofstadter, Richard. *The Age of Reform.* New York: Vintage, 1955.

Hogan, Michael J. *A Cross of Iron: Harry S. Truman and the Origins of the National Security State, 1945–1954.* Cambridge: Cambridge University Press, 1998.

"How Barkley Missed Out on the White House." *U.S. News and World Report* 40 (May 11, 1956): 99–101.

Ireland, Robert M. *The County in Kentucky History.* Lexington: University Press of Kentucky, 1976.

Jewell, Malcolm E., and Everett W. Cunningham. *Kentucky Politics.* Lexington: University of Kentucky Press, 1968.

Karan, P. P., and Cotton Mather, eds. *Atlas of Kentucky.* Lexington: University Press of Kentucky, 1977.

Katznelson, Ira. *Fear Itself: The New Deal and the Origins of Our Time.* New York: Norton, 2013.

Kaufman, Burton I. *The Korean Conflict.* Westport, CT: Greenwood, 1999.

Kennedy, David M. *Freedom from Fear: The American People in Depression and War, 1929–1945.* New York: Oxford University Press, 1999.

Keyerleber, Karl. "Challenge to Roosevelt." *Current History* 6 (April 1944): 311–16.

Kleber, John E., ed. *The Kentucky Encyclopedia.* Lexington: University Press of Kentucky, 1992.

Kleinman, Mark L. "Henry Agard Wallace (1888–1965)." In *The Vice Presidents: A Biographical Dictionary,* ed. L. Edward Purcell, 297–305. New York: Facts on File, 1998.

Klotter, James C. *Kentucky: Portrait in Paradox, 1900–1950.* Frankfort: Kentucky Historical Society, 1996.

Klotter, James C., and Freda C. Klotter. *A Concise History of Kentucky.* Lexington: University Press of Kentucky, 2008.

Kornitzer, Bela. *American Fathers and Sons.* N.p.: Hermitage, 1952.

Kort, Michael. *The Soviet Colossus: History and Aftermath.* Armonk, NY: M. E. Sharpe, 2001.

Lawson, Alan. *A Commonwealth of Hope: The New Deal Response to Crisis.* Baltimore: Johns Hopkins University Press, 2006.

Leistner, Charley A. "The Political Campaign Speaking of Alben W. Barkley." Ph.D. diss., University of Missouri, 1958.

Leuchtenburg, William E. *Franklin D. Roosevelt and the New Deal, 1933–1940.* New York: Harper & Row, 1963.

———. *The White House Looks South: Franklin D. Roosevelt, Harry S. Truman, Lyndon B. Johnson.* Baton Rouge: Louisiana State University Press, 2005.

Libbey, James K. *Dear Alben: Mr. Barkley of Kentucky.* Lexington: University Press of Kentucky, 1979.

———. "Alben W. Barkley (1877–1956)." In *The Vice Presidents: A Biographical Dictionary,* ed. L. Edward Purcell, 314–21. New York: Facts on File, 1998.

Link, Arthur S. *Woodrow Wilson and the Progressive Era, 1910–1917.* New York: Harper & Row, 1954.

Lisio, Donald J. *The President and Protest: Hoover, Conspiracy, and the Bonus Riot.* Columbia: University of Missouri Press, 1974.

Livermore, Seward W. *Politics Is Adjourned: Woodrow Wilson and the War Congress, 1916–1918.* Middletown, CT: Wesleyan University Press, 1966.

Lott, David Newton. *The Presidents Speak: The Inaugural Addresses of the American Presidents from Washington to Clinton.* New York: Henry Holt, 1994.

Merry, Robert W. "Robert A. Taft: A Study in the Accumulation of Power." In *First among Equals: Outstanding Senate Leaders of the Twentieth Century,* ed. Richard A. Baker and Roger H. Davidson, 163–98. Washington, DC: Congressional Quarterly, 1991.

Mitchell, Arthur H. *Understanding the Korean War: The Participants, the Tactics, and the Course of Conflict.* Jefferson, NC: McFarland, 2013.

Mofield, William R. "The Speaking Role of Alben Barkley in the Campaign of 1948." Ph.D. diss., Southern Illinois University, 1964.

Moley, Raymond. *After Seven Years.* New York: Harper & Bros., 1939.

Moore, John Robert. "The Conservative Coalition in the United States Senate, 1942–1945." *Journal of Southern History* 33 (August 1967): 368–76.

Morris, Edmund. *Colonel Roosevelt.* New York: Random House, 2010.

Mowry, George E. *The Era of Theodore Roosevelt and the Birth of Modern America, 1900–1912.* New York: Harper & Row, 1958.

Murray, Robert K. *Red Scare: A Study of National Hysteria, 1919–1920.* New York: McGraw-Hill, 1964.

———. *The Harding Era: Warren G. Harding and His Administration.* Minneapolis: University of Minnesota Press, 1969.

McCoy, Donald R. *The Presidency of Harry S. Truman.* Lawrence: University Press of Kansas, 1984.

McCullough, David. *Truman.* New York: Simon & Schuster, 1992.

Neal, Steve. "Charles L. McNary: The Quiet Man." In *First among Equals: Outstanding Senate Leaders of the Twentieth Century,* ed. Richard A. Baker and Roger H. Davidson, 98–126. Washington, DC: Congressional Quarterly, 1991.

Neuman, Fred G. *Paducahans in History.* Paducah, KY: Young Printing Co., 1922.

―――. *The Story of Paducah.* Paducah, KY: Young Printing Co., 1927.

Pegram, Thomas R. *Battling Demon Rum: The Struggle for a Dry America, 1800–1933.* Chicago: Ivan R. Dee, 1998.

Plummer, Marguerite R. "Louis D. Brandeis: Pioneer Progressive." In *Great Justices of the U.S. Supreme Court: Ratings and Case Studies,* ed. William D. Pederson and Norman W. Provizer. New York: Peter Lang, 1993.

Pogue, Forrest Carlisle, Jr. "The Life and Work of Senator Ollie Murray James." M.A. thesis, University of Kentucky, 1932.

Purcell, L. Edward, ed. *The Vice Presidents: A Biographical Dictionary.* New York: Facts on File, 1998.

Rees, David. *Korea: The Limited War.* Baltimore: Penguin, 1970.

Reisser, Wesley J. *The Black Book: Woodrow Wilson's Secret Plan for Peace.* Lanham, MD: Lexington, 2012.

Riddick, Floyd M. "Congress versus the President in 1944." *South Atlantic Quarterly* 44 (July 1945): 308–15.

Riddle, Donald H. *The Truman Committee.* New Brunswick, NJ: Rutgers University Press, 1964.

Ridgeway, Matthew B. *The Korean War.* New York: Doubleday, 1967.

Ripley, Randall B. *Majority Party Leadership in Congress.* Boston: Little, Brown, 1969.

Ritchie, Donald A. "Alben W. Barkley: The President's Man." In *First among Equals: Outstanding Senate Leaders of the Twentieth Century,* ed. Richard A. Baker and Roger H. Davidson, 127–62. Washington, DC: Congressional Quarterly, 1991.

Robinson, George W. "The Making of a Kentucky Senator: Alben W. Barkley and the Gubernatorial Primary of 1923." *Filson Club History Quarterly* 40 (April 1966): 123–35.

―――. "Alben W. Barkley and the 1944 Tax Veto." *The Register* 67 (July 1969): 197–210.

―――. "Barkley and Roosevelt: A Political Relationship." N.d. Crabbe Library, Eastern Kentucky University, typescript.

Rosenman, Samuel I. *Working with Roosevelt.* New York: Harper & Bros., 1952.

Ryan, Halford R. *Franklin D. Roosevelt's Rhetorical Presidency.* New York: Greenwood, 1988.

Salter, J. T., ed. *Public Men: In and Out of Office.* Chapel Hill: University of North Carolina Press, 1946.

Sanders, Elizabeth. *Roots of Reform: Farmers, Workers, and the American State, 1877–1917.* Chicago: University of Chicago Press, 1999.

Schulman, Robert. *John Sherman Cooper: The Global Kentuckian.* Lexington: University Press of Kentucky, 1976.

Sexton, Robert F. "The Crusade against Pari-Mutuel Gambling in Kentucky: A Study of Southern Progressivism in the 1920s." *Filson Club History Quarterly* 50 (January 1976): 47–57.

Shuman, Howard E. "Lyndon B. Johnson: The Senate's Powerful Persuader." In *First among Equals: Outstanding Senate Leaders of the Twentieth Century,* ed. Richard A. Baker and Roger H. Davidson, 199–235. Washington, DC: Congressional Quarterly, 1991.

Smith, Beverly. "Washington's Greatest Storyteller." *Saturday Evening Post* 222 (July 2, 1949): 17–19, 66–68.

Smith, Gene. *When the Cheering Stopped: The Last Years of Woodrow Wilson*. New York: William Morrow, 1964.

Springen, Donald K. *William Jennings Bryan: Orator of Small-Town America*. New York: Greenwood Press, 1991.

Tapp, Hambleton, and James C. Klotter. *Decades of Discord*. Frankfort: Kentucky Historical Society, 1977.

Taussig, F. W. *The Tariff History of the United States*. New York: Capricorn, 1964.

"The Tie That Binds." *Time* 60 (July 28, 1952): 10–12.

Tobin, James. *The Man He Became: How FDR Defied Polio to Win the Presidency*. New York: Simon & Schuster, 2013.

Trani, Eugene P., and David L. Wilson. *The Presidency of Warren G. Harding*. Lawrence: University Press of Kansas, 1977.

Truman, Harry S. *Memoirs by Harry S. Truman*. Vol. 1, *Year of Decisions*. Vol. 2, *Years of Trial and Hope*. Garden City, NY: Doubleday, 1955–1956.

Truman, Margaret. *Harry S. Truman*. New York: William Morrow, 1973.

Tully, Grace. *Franklin Delano Roosevelt, My Boss*. New York: Scribner's, 1949.

Urofsky, Melvin I. *Louis Brandeis and the Progressive Tradition*. Boston: Little, Brown, 1981.

US Congress. *Congressional Record: Proceedings and Debates of the United States Congress*. Vols. 50–95. Washington, DC: US Government Printing Office, 1913–1949.

———. *Tariff Act of 1929: Hearings before a Subcommittee of the Senate Finance Committee on H.R. 2667*. 2 vols. Washington, DC: US Government Printing Office, 1929.

———. Senate Banking and Currency Committee. *A Bill to Improve Nation-Wide Housing Standards, Provide Employment and Stimulate Industry: Hearings on S. 3603*. Washington, DC: US Government Printing Office, 1934.

———. Senate Select Committee. *Investigation of Presidential Campaign Expenditures*. Washington, DC: US Government Printing Office, 1928.

Warren, Harris Gaylord. *Herbert Hoover and the Great Depression*. Oxford: Oxford University Press, 1959.

Weeks, Philip. *Buckeye Presidents: Ohioans in the White House*. Kent, OH: Kent State University Press, 2003.

Weinstein, Edwin. *Woodrow Wilson: A Medical and Psychological Biography*. Princeton, NJ: Princeton University Press, 1981.

Weisman, Steven R. *The Great Tax Wars, Lincoln to Wilson: The Fierce Battles over Money and Power That Transformed the Nation*. New York: Simon & Schuster, 2002.

White, William Allen. *A Puritan in Babylon: The Story of Calvin Coolidge*. New York: Macmillan, 1938.

Wilson, Joan Hoff. *Herbert Hoover: Forgotten Progressive*. Boston: Little, Brown, 1975.

Wilson, Woodrow. *Congressional Government: A Study in American Politics*. Boston: Houghton, Mifflin, 1885.

Wiltz, John E. *From Isolation to War, 1931–1941*. New York: Thomas Y. Crowell, 1968.

Woodward, C. Van. *The Strange Career of Jim Crow*. New York: Oxford University Press, 1955.

Index

Barkley, Alben W. *(cont.)* 245–48; and Nazi death camps, 237–38; 1932 keynote speaker, 160–62; 1936 keynote speaker, 178–80; 1948 keynote speaker, 248–50; nominates Roosevelt, 232; opposes Roosevelt's tax bill, 229–32; Pearl Harbor investigation, 241–44; permanent convention chairman, 211; philosophy of, 111, 116, 138, 141, 168; as Presbyterian, 12, 16, 80; as presidential candidate, 266–69; prop-stop campaign, 253; on radio, 170, 174–75, 177, 209; as senator, 130–67; siblings of, 8, 10, 51; and Soviet Russia trip, 145–47; Supreme Court candidate, 225; Truman's senatorial reelection, 212–13; as TV personality, 271–72; United Nations supporter, 238–39; as vice president, 254–70; wartime bills (WWII), 221–22; Western Front visit (WWI), 92–95; woos and weds Jane Rucker Hadley, 259–60; as working vice president, 255. *See also* Barkley elections; Inter-Parliamentary Union

Barkley, Amanda Louise, 7, 9

Barkley, David Murrell, 40, 58–59, 92, 94, 121, 131, 170; managed Angles farm, 195, 223, 274

Barkley, Dorothy, 121, 124, 131, 135, 152, 170, 180, 193–94, 200; cultured, 40–41; death of, 223; description, 37, 39, 58–59; heart attack, 222; marries Alben, 40

Barkley, Electa Eliza, 31; characteristics of, 7–8; death of, 222–23

Barkley, Jane Rucker, 1, 60, 271, 277; meets and marries Barkley, 259–60

Barkley, John Wilson, 1, 31, 80, 98; dark tobacco, 10; farm owner, 13; juvenile probation officer, 51; populist, 8, 33; tenant farmer, 7; US House of Representatives doorkeeper, 58; worker, 29

Barkley, Laura Louise, 40, 58–59, 121, 131, 135, 152, 170–71, 174, 223, 256

Barkley, Marian Frances, 40, 58–59, 108, 121, 131, 135, 152, 170, 223, 260; as Barkley's official hostess, 258

Barkley elections: 1905, 41–44; 1909, 48–49; 1912, 52–54; 1914, 67; 1916, 82; 1918, 95; 1920, 107; 1922, 115; 1923, 115–20; 1926, 121–24; 1932, 165–66; 1938, 196–200; 1944, 234; 1954, 274. *See also* presidential elections

Barkley-Sheppard Act, 78–79

Battling Demon Rum (Pegram), 76

Beckham, John C. W., 100, 109, 117, 132

Belgium, 85, 110, 172, 210, 261

Biffle, Leslie L., 173–74, 186–87, 195, 204, 217, 237, 249, 267

Bingham, Robert Worth, 117–18

Bishop, William S., 34–35

blitzkrieg, 209, 210

Borah, William E., 77, 109, 142, 206

Brain Trust, 167–68

Brandeis, Louis D., 57, 78

Breathitt, James, Jr., 132–33

Bretton Woods, 238–39

Brower, Dorothy. *See* Barkley, Dorothy

Bryan, William Jennings, 33, 53, 56–57; and brother Charles, 128; as US secretary of state, 71, 87

Bulgaria, 91, 94, 202, 228

Bull Moose. *See* progressivism

Byrd, Harry F., 276–77

Byrnes, James F. "Jimmy," 177, 186, 230

Cantrill, J. Campbell, 82, 116–17, 120

Capitol Building, 56, 60, 61, 81, 99, 108, 152, 157, 175, 183, 187, 210, 236–37; and US Senate president's room, 257–58

Central Intelligence Agency. *See* National Security Act

West, Charlie, 23–25
Wheeler, Burton K., 145–46, 190, 211, 214–15
Wheeler, Charles K., 32–35
White, William Allen, 105, 112, 125
Wilson, T. Woodrow, 2, 74–76, 78, 80–83, 85–86, 89–91, 101, 106, 190; and Mexico, 69–70; New Freedom ends, 67–68; New Freedom program, 57, 60–68, 78, 168; pleads for votes, 95–96; as president, 55–103; as progressive, 54; suffers stroke, 98–99; and war declaration, 84, 87; and Edith B. Wilson, 68, 106, 108, 134

Women's Christian Temperance Union, 77
Woodmen of the World, 37, 54
Woolley, Robert W., 158, 178
Works Progress Administration Act, 169–70, 186–87, 201
World Bank. *See* Bretton Woods

Yale University, 174
Yalta Conference. *See* Roosevelt, Franklin D.

Zedong, Mao, 261, 263
Zimmermann, Arthur: infamous telegram, 86

www.ingramcontent.com/pod-product-compliance
Lightning Source LLC
Chambersburg PA
CBHW021152160426
42812CB00078B/672